Works by the Author

The Federal Writers' Project: A Study in Government Patronage of the Arts

The Jews Were Expendable: Free World Diplomacy and the Holocaust

The Emergence of Zionist Thought

The Holocaust and Israel Reborn: From Catastrophe to Sovereignty

Twentieth Century Jews: Forging Identity in the Land of Promise and in the Promised Land

The Swastika's Darkening Shadow: Voices before the Holocaust

Palestine in Turmoil: The Struggle for Sovereignty, 1933-1939, vol. 1 - Prelude to Revolt, 1933-1936

Palestine in Turmoil: The Struggle for Sovereignty, 1933-1939, vol. 2 - Retreat from the Mandate, 1937-1939

Decision on Palestine Deferred: America, Britain and Wartime Diplomacy, 1939-1945

Palestine to Israel: Mandate to State, 1945-1948, vol. 1 - Rebellion Launched, 1945-1946

Palestine to Israel: Mandate to State, 1945-1948, vol. 2 – Into the International Arena, 1947-1948

Israel: As A Phoenix Ascending

After the Holocaust

The Holocaust and Israel Restored: From Rupture to Revival

Awakening to Radical Islamist Evil: The Hamas War Against Israel and the Jews – I

Awakening to Radical Islamist Evil: The Hamas War Against Israel and the Jews – II

THE HOLOCAUST AND ISRAEL RESTORED
FROM RUPTURE TO REVIVAL

THE HOLOCAUST AND ISRAEL RESTORED
FROM RUPTURE TO REVIVAL

Monty Noam Penkower

NEW YORK
2025

Library of Congress Cataloging-in-Publication Data

Names: Penkower, Monty Noam, 1942- author.

Title: The Holocaust and Israel restored : from rupture to revival / Monty Noam Penkower.

Description: Boston : Touro University Press, 2025. | Includes bibliographical references and index.

Identifiers: LCCN 2024048056 (print) | LCCN 2024048057 (ebook) | ISBN 9798887197746 (hardback) | ISBN 9798887197784 (paperback) | ISBN 9798887197753 (adobe pdf) | ISBN 9798887197760 (epub)

Subjects: LCSH: Zionism--History. | Jews--Restoration. | Holocaust, Jewish (1939-1945) | Jews--History--20th century. | Israel--History--20th century.

Classification: LCC DS149 .P42354 2025 (print) | LCC DS149 (ebook) | DDC 940.53/18--dc23/eng/20241231

LC record available at https://lccn.loc.gov/2024048056
LC ebook record available at https://lccn.loc.gov/2024048057

Copyright © Touro University Press, 2025
Published by Touro University Press and Academic Studies Press

Touro University Press
Michael A. Shmidman and Simcha Fishbane, Editors
3 Times Square, Room 654,
New York, NY 10036, USA
press@touro.edu

Book design by Kryon Publishing Services
Cover design by Ivan Grave
On the cover: photograph by Anat Morderer, Shutterstock

Typeset, printed, and distributed by Academic Studies Press
1007 Chestnut St.
Newton, MA 02464, USA
press@academicstudiespress.com
www.academicstudiespress.com

To

My Fourth Generation

"A generation of righteous people will be blessed" (*Psalms* 112:2)

Contents

Preface	ix
1. Theodor Herzl: Zionism's Driven Prophet	1
2. Honorable Failures against Nazi Germany: McDonald's Letter of Resignation and the Petition in Its Support	27
3. The Swastika's Darkening Shadow	69
4. Vladimir (Ze'ev) Jabotinsky, Hillel Kook-Peter Bergson, and the Campaign for a Jewish Army	95
5. The Steinberg-Lazaron-Frank Debate on Zionism and Jewish Survival	129
6. *The Basic Equities of the Palestine Problem*	153
7. Poland's Distortion of the Holocaust	181
8. *The Jews Were Expendable: Free World Diplomacy and the Holocaust –* Forty Years Later	205
Endnotes	231
Index	269

Preface

Shevah Weiss was born on July 5, 1935, in Borysław, Poland (today Boryslav in Ukraine), to Gienia and Meir Wolf Weiss. During the Holocaust, his father fashioned a hiding place measuring sixty centimeters wide for the family behind the wall of their store. He built bunk beds, one on top of the other, up to the ceiling. Weiss lived there with his parents, sister, brother, aunt, uncle, cousin and a neighbor, who lay down all day in that tiny space. Later they stayed in the basement of a children's orphanage. A few neighbors, subsequently to be recognized as Righteous among the Nations by Yad Vashem, Israel's World Holocaust Remembrance Center, provided them with food and water. "There we ate a slice of black and shriveled bread, one slice for the day, a slice seasoned with unsanitary water," Weiss recalled: "My father cooked a soup consisting of one potato and water for our whole group. But in the end, we were reduced to chewing book covers made of genuine leather."

Through the crack in the northern wall, he looked at the road leading from the forest. Ukrainians would pass this way on holidays and feast days on their way to church. "Along this route," Weiss remembered, "the soldiers led the Jewish men and women into the woods and then we heard the sound of gunshots. Once I looked through this crack at the daily death march and, among the marchers, I saw my aunt and her children, my cousins."

In 1947, Weiss emigrated to British Mandate Palestine as part of Youth Aliya, the Zionist movement's program to rescue Jewish youth from Europe. The teenager became known for a phenomenal memory, and wrote a number of puzzle books as well as presenting a radio show. Weiss went on to study at the Hebrew University in Jerusalem, served in the IDF military forces as a sergeant in the Engineering Corps and assistant to the command education officer, then in 1975 became a professor of political science at Haifa University. He entered political life in 1969 with his election to the Haifa municipal council. In 1981, he was elected to the Knesset on the Labor Party slate, served as a Deputy Speaker between 1988 and 1992, and was elected Knesset Speaker during Prime Minister Yitzhak Rabin's second government from 1992 until 1996.

On November 4, 1995, Weiss stood on stage with Rabin and Foreign Minister Shimon Peres for a rendition of the *Song for Peace* at the end of a rally in Tel Aviv. At the song's conclusion, Rabin came off the stage and was assassinated by Yigal Amir.

Losing his Knesset seat, in 2000 Weiss was appointed Israel's ambassador to Poland, a post he would occupy until 2004. He also served as chairman of the Yad Vashem Council from 2000 until 2006. In January 2004, for his contribution to the growing cooperation between Poland and Israel, President Aleksander Kwaśniewski bestowed upon him the Grand Cross (1st class) of the Order of Merit of the Republic of Poland. Thirteen years later, while awarding Weiss with Poland's highest honor, the Order of the White Eagle, at a ceremony in Jerusalem, President Andrzej Duda called Weiss "a son of the Jewish nation and Polish soil," and hailed his role in promoting closer ties between Israel and Poland.

In his special way, this Holocaust survivor with numerous achievements and a mastery of five languages reached many hearts, always with a pipe in his hand and a good story to tell. In 2001, while Poland was astir, shaken over Jan T. Gross's slim volume *Neighbors* for its explosive charge of how on July 10, 1941, ethnic Poles of Nazi-occupied Jedwabne and a few from the surrounding area massacred close to 1,600 of their fellow Jewish citizens, Weiss visited that village incognito with only his security guard and a driver. He cried uncontrollably for some time at the scene of premeditated murder, rare indeed for him. Five years later, on the way to a course at the Israeli president's invitation for guides to Poland, Weiss related that during the Second Lebanon War in 2006, as he was being interviewed by a Polish TV broadcaster, a large sound could clearly be heard not far from the Haifa station. Told that this had come from a rocket hitting the city, the frightened woman asked: "Perhaps you are not so suited for the Middle East?" Weiss answered in his native Polish: "*Być może. Ale już próbowaliśmy z tobą*"—"Perhaps. But we already tried with you." On February 3, 2023, the accomplished, proud Israeli died in Tel-Aviv, his final resting place Jerusalem's Har Herzl.[1]

For more than five decades, I have devoted my scholarly pursuits to these same two intertwined subjects—the Holocaust and Israel's sovereign rebirth. Undoubtedly the most significant events in modern Jewish history, if not in all of Jewry's bimillennial experience since the destruction by Roman Legions of the Second Holy Temple in Jerusalem, they continue to claim my primary attention. As to the *Shoah*, the Hebrew term for the Holocaust, a fundamental query arises: When Europe's Jews lived in the half-life between rescue and death, with the darkness of the latter claiming most in Adolf Hitler's uncompromising "Final

Solution of the Jewish Question," what explains the moral collapse of the free world which stood by when confronted by the ongoing systematic slaughter? As to the emergence of the renewed State of Israel, what factors made the arc of history bend to that momentous denouement? As in my past writing, the essays that follow seek to shed further light on these critical questions.

Chapter one, an examination of the career of Theodor Herzl, serves as the prelude to this volume. The father of political Zionism, an assimilated, liberal author who sought to join the best of Western culture to a traditional Jewish hope for "the return to Jerusalem," had an almost prophetic sense that apocalyptic catastrophe loomed for his people unless a mass exodus from Europe occurred soon. Creating the ideology and instruments to enable Jews, for millennia viewed as the eternally persecuted "other," to reenter history as actors in their own fate, his dream would be turned into Jewish destiny. Yet the desacralized, progressive "Jews' state" that this Zionist zealot envisioned cannot be a nation "like all other nations" (*KeKhol Am V'Am*), the phrase even entered in Israel's Declaration of Independence. It cannot be divorced from the spiritual, moral essence which has always made Judaism unique. The content of the specific Jewish experience, its quality both in the State of Israel—where the totality of Judaism can be lived – and in the Diaspora, is fundamental. It still remains to be realized.

Chapter two examines the valiant but fruitless efforts in the years 1933–1935 by James G. McDonald, then serving as the League of Nations' High Commissioner for Refugees (Jewish and Other) Coming from Germany, which culminated in his much publicized, lengthy letter of resignation. Presciently, but to no avail, the tall American warned that the Nazi concepts of "blood, race, and soil," propagated with "fanatical enthusiasm," menaced not only Jews, but "all those who remain definitely loyal to the old ideals of religious and individual freedom." That historic document and the subsequent Petition to the League in its support reflected honorable failures at a time when Hitler's Third Reich and others in the international arena insisted on the absolute supremacy of states, leaving the Jews, not masters of their own destiny, vulnerable to unimaginable, brutal tragedy.[2]

The tumultuous 1930s found that defenseless people hounded across the European Continent. Chapter three reviews how the shadow of the Nazi swastika darkened Poland, Rumania, and many other countries, where virulent Jew-hatred assaults were common knowledge. Throughout that perilous decade, statesmen who grappled with unemployment, rearmament, chauvinism, xenophobia, and pervasive antisemitism shut their hearts and their doors to trapped Jews. Aside from appeasing Germany, these powers regularly masked the communal identity of world Jewry behind the term "refugees" (such as in the very title of the July 1938 Evian Conference on Refugees) or denied it outright. None could have foreseen the Holocaust, when Jewish hopes would be literally reduced to ashes, but all sensed the screw press of history inexorably tightening around Europe's Jews.³

The young Palestinian Hillel Kook (alias Peter Bergson), echoing the call of Revisionist-Zionist leader Vladimir (Ze'ev) Jabotinsky, sought to gain American non-partisan backing for a Jewish army to fight alongside the Allied forces against Hitler. Chapter four relates how, with a few right-wing Irgun Tzva'i Le'umi emissaries in the United States under his command and the spirited pen of famed Hollywood writer Ben Hecht, Kook garnered widespread support. When news of the Nazi annihilation campaign became public, the group immediately shifted its efforts towards the imperative of rescue. Their ceaseless campaign played a decisive role in the creation of the US War Refugee Board in January 1944. Yet fundamental decisions rested with Washington and London (Moscow ignored the entire matter), whose leaders chose not to try to save an innocent people uniquely targeted for death in World War II, an independent entity desperate for, and surely deserving of, help in its darkest hour.⁴

The debate over Zionism and the Jewish future as conducted between Milton Steinberg, Morris S. Lazaron, and Jerome Frank is the subject of chapter five. Steinberg's *A Partisan Guide to the Jewish Problem*, published in the autumn of 1945, well reflected its author's embrace of Zionist aspirations. Frank, once associated with the anti-Zionist American Council for Judaism, would eventually join in a legal brief to the UN General Assembly in September 1947 advocating for a Jewish State despite harboring some personal ideological reservations. The Council's Lazaron remained obdurate in opposition. American Jewry, however, seared by the fires of the Holocaust, overwhelmingly rallied to the political Zionist banner after World War II, understanding the indissoluble link that existed between catastrophe and sovereignty.

Chapter six brings to light for the first time the best juridical defense for the Zionist objective before the UN General Assembly's seminal vote of November 29, 1947, to partition Palestine into a Jewish and an Arab state. The genesis of *The Basic Equities of the Palestine Problem*, a memorandum composed by eight distinguished American Jewish practitioners of the law, emerged from London's requesting the UN for its recommendation as regards a settlement for the highly contested country. A detailed analysis of that legal brief reveals that its authors focused on the official Allied promises regarding Palestine that had been made to the Jewish people worldwide for over a quarter of a century; the tragic situation of the Holocaust survivors in Europe; and Palestinian Jewry's impressive achievements in reclaiming the land while much benefiting the Arab population there—this despite Great Britain's subverting its obligations under the League of Nations Mandate. The document had "great—perhaps decisive—influence on the thinking of most members of the United Nations Assembly," wrote James G. McDonald, soon to become the first US ambassador to the new State of Israel.

Poland's consistent refusal to acknowledge the violence and killings committed by Poles against their Jewish neighbors while under the German occupation, the subject of chapter seven, reflects that government's use and abuse of history. A vigorous challenge by Polish historians to the official narrative, stretching from the year 2000 to the present, continues to meet with strong recrimination from right-wing Polish nationalist groups. The latter majority in parliament passed a Holocaust Law making suggestions that Poland bore responsibility for alleged Nazi crimes in the country a criminal offense (amended under international pressure to a civil offense), in turn triggering a new wave of agitation against Jews in the media and the internet. Another law effectively prevents Jews from receiving restitution for property stolen from their families during the Holocaust. Strained relations with the State of Israel are only slowly being mended. Antisemitism in Poland has not disappeared, while prevalent universalizing of the Holocaust refuses to acknowledge that Jews, not the ethnic Poles, faced annihilation. A full, honest healing has yet to begin.

The final chapter begins with a description of how I came to write *The Jews Were Expendable: Free World Diplomacy and the Holocaust*, the first overview of how and why those governments and organizations outside of Hitler's *Festung Europa* responded in the years of Jewry's bleakest travail. *The Jews Were Expendable* also details how a few courageous souls attempted to shatter the Allied conspiracy of silence, as well as the prevailing illusion that nothing could be done. Yet their valiant race against calculated mass-production murder wrested only limited successes. Zealous killers and indifferent bystanders, by depersonalizing the Jews of Europe, marked these innocents for doom. The chapter then reviews my subsequent publications and additional scholarship on the world of the bystanders which appeared during the forty years since that volume's appearance in 1983, including those studies which sought to exonerate the scant record of U.S. President Franklin D. Roosevelt, in whom Jews placed their greatest trust, and the inaction of other Allied leaders in World War II.[5]

As the Holocaust continues to be universalized, trivialized, even brazenly denied outright, it is essential to understand that the Nazi regime's firm conviction of the Jew as the incarnation of evil threatening world survival, shared by collaborator nations and driven by a pathological, Manichean view, was not countered by an Allied will to save. Already evident ever since Hitler's ascension to the German chancellorship on January 30, 1933, the kingdom of barbed wire and death would consequently enjoy an unbridled reign, human beings reduced to ash and anonymity. Two out of every three of Europe's Jews (ninety percent and more in Eastern Europe) and 5,000 of their communities were obliterated forever. Further, as John Updike, recipient of the Medal for Distinguished Contribution to American Letters, put it years later, Auschwitz-Birkenau and the other death camps "ended forever Europe's concept of itself as civilized and of the Western world as proceeding under a benign special Providence."[6]

Most Holocaust survivors had few doubts about Jewish independence in Palestine. A few days after Bergen-Belsen's liberation on April 15, 1945, by British troops, a few hundred Jewish prisoners, knowing that they were being recorded by the BBC radio service, sang the Zionist anthem *HaTikva* ("The Hope"). The first large boatload to reach Haifa harbor after V-E Day, including 242 traumatized orphans from Auschwitz, Buchenwald, Dachau, and Bergen-Belsen, hoisted a Zionist flag when arriving aboard the *Mataroa* on July 15, 1945. The first conference of the "surviving remnant" (*Sh'eirit HaPleita*), convening on July 25 in St. Ottilien, Germany, demanded "the immediate establishment of a Jewish State in Palestine, the recognition of the Jewish people as an equal with all the Allied nations, and its inclusion in the peace conference." They would return to their ancestral patrimony, united in the firm belief that Jews possessed the inalienable right to self-determination in the one country that had seen their emergence as an autonomous people and that beckoned now as the end to their anguished wanderings in exile.

This remnant came to the identical conclusion drawn by Dr. Elchanan Elkes, heroic chairman of the Kovno (Kaunas) *Judenrat*, who had written a last testament to his son Joel in London on October 19, 1943: "Try to settle in the Land of Israel. Tie your destiny to the land of our future. Even if life there may be hard, it is a life full of content and meaning."[7] With no state of their own—the Zionists had always grasped this—Jews under the swastika could conveniently be considered by the free world powers expendable in the World War II years. Thereafter, Jews everywhere, bolstered by impressive non-Jewish support and now converts to political supremacy in the biblically covenanted Promised Land, hailed the tangible Jewish community (*Yishuv*) of 600,000 strong in

Eretz Israel that was ready to fight for self-government and the only collective entity prepared to receive the survivors.

Jewish intellectuals Hannah Arendt, George Steiner, and their like might still champion the alienation of "the exiled Jew," calling for a common human consciousness that dissolves barriers of language, ethnicity, and territory, but, as we are reminded by literary master and critic Cynthia Ozick, herself taunted in childhood as a "Christ-killer," "universalism is the ultimate Jewish parochialism."[8] Abstractions, though alluring, must yield to reality. That actually insular view overlooks the need, then as now, of the centuries-old "pariah people"[9] leading a sovereign existence freed of the indignities of persecution, marginality, and assimilation. From Israel's Declaration of Independence on May 14, 1948, and beyond, the Jewish people re-entered the arena of world history, actors in their own fate[10] at last afforded a place in the family of nations. Its restoration after 2,000 years gave official stamp to the audacity of vision and the depth of the revolution that is Zionism.

A loving family has eased my professional dedication to exploring these two complex themes. My sisters and their spouses, my brother, my children and their spouses, and my grandchildren, with keen understanding and unflagging encouragement, have each played their individual part in the loom on which my narratives have been woven over the years. My dear wife Phyllis has provided incomparable gifts of warmth and grace. Professor Michael Popkin, former colleague at Touro College and head of its Humanities-Literature department, again merits my great appreciation for reviewing the text for clarity. He is a cherished friend. Thanks are also due to the collaborative effort, as in the past, of Touro University Press and Academic Studies Press in bringing the manuscript to ultimate publication, and to Dr. Alan Kadish, President of Touro University, for his support.

I have been privileged, like the biblical Joseph (Genesis 50:23), to see the first births of my fourth generation. This volume is dedicated with much affection to Shachar Ayelet Simon, Ofri Yael Simon, Matan Binyamin Mayer, Yakira Nili Mayer, Gilad Daniel Haik, Eyal Oren Haik, Sophie Leora Mayer, Avery Micah Mayer, and all my great-grandchildren to follow. Despite the Holocaust, the triumph of radical evil against powerless European Jewry, our planet is plagued by on-going genocides, terrorism, antisemitism, and baseless hatreds that continue to stigmatize and target certain human beings as "the other." To wage resolute battle against these, to forge a better tomorrow, the clarion call of truth and human decency must be answered forthrightly. I wish them to appreciate in time that complacency must give way to personal commitment, and that active compassion which flows from mutual need must replace the crime of indifference.

As for the State of Israel, I hope that they will become conscious of the fact that the victorious Principal Allied Powers at the 1920 San Remo Conference recognized, with the wording of a solemn pledge that was to be repeated by the League of Nations when according the Mandate for Palestine to Great Britain two years later, "the historical connection of the Jewish people with Palestine and to the grounds for reconstituting their national home in that country." Iran, Hamas, and Hezbollah have unabashedly committed themselves to Israel's destruction, while the Fatah-controlled Palestinian Authority's "pay for slay" bounties award monthly salaries and benefits to terrorists and the families of "martyrs."[11] Moreover, the Third Jewish Commonwealth is regularly and singularly vilified by the very international organization that had bestowed upon it a certificate of national legitimacy. A global delegitimization, even a demonizing campaign, denies the one Jewish state the right to be.

Yet *Medinat Yisrael*, despite the precariousness of survival in several Arab wars against its very existence, stands steadfast. Echoing Judaism as the voice of hope, it proudly and deservedly celebrates a seventy-sixth birthday. There is much remarkable achievement to salute, a community with continuity of heritage and language intact that defies historical parallel. There is more yet to be done to preserve its robust Jewish and democratic character. The transformation from unimaginable rupture to extraordinary revival, against all odds, continues apace.

Jerusalem
Pesach 5784

CHAPTER 1

Theodor Herzl: Zionism's Driven Prophet

On February 14, 1896, the Viennese publisher Max Breitenstein issued an eighty-six-page brochure by Theodor Herzl, Doctor of Law, under the title *Der Judenstaat. Versuch einer Modernen Lösung der Judenfrage* ("The Jews' State. An Attempt at a Modern Solution of the Jewish Question"). Receiving his 500 copies the same evening at his home in the city's respectable Jewish middle-class Alsergrund district, the author of the 6x9-inch pamphlet confided to a diary that he trembled violently. "The great decision stands wrapped up in this bundle," penned he on Türkenstrasse that night. "From here on, my life will perhaps take a new turn."

The career up to this point of the young Paris correspondent to the *Neue Freie Presse*, one of Europe's greatest and most influential journals, scarcely hinted at the dramatic change to follow. Born to a comfortable Budapest couple on May 2, 1860, Herzl had an early education that fused the spirit of the liberal German Jewish enlightenment with intense Magyar patriotism. Aside from messianic thoughts sometime before his thirteenth birthday, Herzl exhibited scant interest in the Jewish world. He could not have been oblivious, at the same time, to initial speeches in the Hungarian Diet against Jewish emancipation, one expressly in favor of "the restoration of the ancient Jewish state" for those refusing to embrace the Christian fold body and soul.

At eighteen years of age, the "Pest Jew," as he later called himself, entered the University of Vienna as a law student. In the course of his studies, a reading of German philosopher Eugen Dühring's open call for a racist war against the Jews in *Die Judenfrage als Rassen-Sitten- und Kultur-Frage* ("The Jewish Problem as a Problem of Race, Morals, and Culture") had a profound effect on Herzl. This practically coincided with the notorious Tiszaeszlár blood libel trial, which antisemitic politicians would exploit in Hungary and throughout Europe. One year later, he resigned from a German student dueling fraternity in protest against its anti-Jewish attitude. Yet Herzl shrank from the logical consequences of his reactions. This remained the case even when he abandoned the legal profession, one year after receiving a doctorate in law from the university, upon realizing that the highest levels of the civil service hierarchy would be closed to him because of his Jewish origin.

Herzl's decision to enter the literary world brought him considerable success during the next decade. Traveling throughout Western Europe, he contributed regularly to several important newspapers, wrote several plays which were successfully performed in Europe and even in New York City, mastered the style of the feuilleton, and published a number of articles and philosophical short stories in book form. Two years after his marriage to Julia Naschauer, this record was capped with his appointment in October 1891 as Paris correspondent to Vienna's leading daily. The *Neue Freie Presse* was distinguished for its middle-of-the-road voice of reasonable compromise under the expert guidance of like-minded Jews Eduard Bacher and Moritz Benedikt.

In "the city of light" this aristocrat of the spirit began his deepest search for an explanation for the universal enmity directed against the Jewish people. Edouard-Adolphe Drumont's *La France Juive* and his influential newspaper *La Libre Parole*, which depicted a historical clash between "capitalist" Jews and "Aryan" Christian France, deeply moved the Francophile Herzl. The suicide of a Jewish comrade brought an end to his unchecked optimism. He remained an integrationist, however, did not bother to have his son circumcised according to Jewish tradition, and even set up a Christmas tree in his home.

Responding to the evasive debates in the Austrian Reichstag in 1892–1893 over the status of Jews in that country, Herzl declared that the "Jewish question is neither nationalistic nor religious. It is a social question." He seriously thought of solving it at one point by a mass baptism ceremony of the younger generation in Vienna's Cathedral of St. Stephen, or by having its members join the socialist government. Either scheme would conform to Herzl's quest for Gentile acceptance and his fantasies of personal grandeur and the heroic gesture. But the troubled Viennese aesthete, vacillating between Jewish pride and Jewish self-contempt, soon rejected these, as he did the Zionist solution. Discussing the novel *La Femme de Claude* by Alexandre Dumas Fils, Herzl asserts: "The historic homeland of the Jews no longer has any value for them." And if the Jews really "returned home" one day, they would "discover on the next day that they do not belong together," rooted as they were in diverse nationalities.

His continued groping, intensified by antisemitic agitation over the Panama Scandal's link to leading French Third Republic politicians, came to a sudden denouement during a session in the fall of 1894 with the sculptor

Samuel Beer. In the midst of their conversation about the rapid growth of antisemitism in Vienna under the demagogic Christian Social Party leader Karl Lueger, Herzl described how it was useless for the Jew to turn artist and dissociate himself from money: "The blot sticks. We can't break away from the ghetto." He left the studio in great excitement, and on the way home the complete outline of a play struck him. In only three weeks the full script was ready.

The play, *The New Ghetto*, marks Herzl's inner return, as Alex Bein has put it, to his people. The transformation which unfolds in his main character, the idealist Reform lawyer Jacob Samuel, is that which was currently unfolding in Herzl himself. Samuel, having criticized a bankrupt Christian aristocrat for the appalling conditions in his mine, is grossly insulted by the latter. Determined to show that Jews cannot be treated with such impunity, he fights a duel of honor with this Gentile opponent. (Two years earlier, Herzl had informed the Society for Defense against Antisemitism that "a half dozen duels," rather than reliance on rational persuasion, "would very much raise the social position of the Jews.") Mortally wounded in the encounter, Samuel utters last words that are a cry to his people: "Jews, my brothers, there will come a time when they will let you live again—when you know how to die." And, turning to his friends who are holding the stricken man down, he murmurs, "Why do you hold me fast? . . . I want to get out! . . . Out! Out-of-the-Ghetto!" Thus, Herzl had begun to realize that assimilation and conversion were both ruled out as a solution for the Jews. Yet what better future the despairing bourgeois liberal foresaw still remained unclear. He visited the central synagogue in Paris on Rue de la Victoire a while later, wanting to do something for the Jews.

Obsessed by then with the Jewish question, Herzl covered the Dreyfus trial for his newspaper the following month. Having taken the ultimate decision in *The New Ghetto* to stand proudly by his Jewishness while still preaching the ideal of human reconciliation, Herzl now witnessed a humiliating ceremony on the bitter cold morning of January, 5, 1895, in which the Jewish captain Alfred Dreyfus, accused of high treason for selling military secrets to Germany, was drummed out of the French Army at the gates of the École Militaire to the shouts of a mob howling, "Death to the Jews!" Herzl wrote in 1899 that the scene had made him a Zionist, yet his dispatches at the time do not suggest that he accorded the trial historic significance. No word of the case's effect appeared in his diaries a few months later when he sought to explain how he came to Zionism, and its antisemitic implications would only begin to unfold in 1897. A few days after Dreyfus's public degradation, the French parliament rang with calls against Jewish "infiltration."

Most ominously, in April 1895, the municipal elections in Vienna saw an enormous increase in the number of antisemitic aldermen. The following month, Lueger was elected mayor, although he resigned in the face of Emperor Franz Joseph I's opposition. (Lueger would enter that office in 1897 and hold the post until his death in 1910.) The crisis, which saw the Christian Social Party capture the city council by a wide majority that September—thus bringing the first major city in the Western world under control of a party openly committed to antisemitism, preoccupied Herzl.

In response, he thought of writing a novel that went beyond Jacob Samuel's honorable death by envisaging a mass Jewish emigration to Palestine, with the proper political negotiations, so that the upright human type of a Samuel could be given its chance to emerge. Remarkably, he was then ignorant of George Eliot's *Daniel Deronda* (1876), whose hero departs for Palestine after discovering his Jewish identity in order to help "revive the organic center" of his people's existence.

Herzl imparted these ideas during a meeting on June 2, 1895, with financier Baron Maurice de Hirsch, founder of an association to settle Jews in agricultural colonies, mainly in Argentina. The half-hour interview, for which Herzl had prepared extensive notes, and subsequent correspondence between the two men went badly. His ideas for a "general uplift" of the demoralized Jewish people, followed by emigration thanks to a Jewish national loan of ten billion marks, "prodigious propaganda," a flag, and the approval of the German Kaiser and other western leaders, Hirsch dismissed as chimerical. In a final letter, the young journalist captured the essence of the gulf between them: "You believe that you can, as you do, export poor Jews. I saw that you are only creating new markets for antisemitism."

Not discouraged, Herzl saw his wife and family off to Vienna, returned to his desk in the Castille Hotel on Paris's Rue Cambon, and began a diary under the title "The Jewish Question." "For some time now," the notebook opens, "I have been engaged upon a work of indescribable greatness. I do not know yet whether I shall carry it through." A mighty vision had seized him: "The Jewish state is a world necessity." For weeks, he committed to slips of paper a torrent of ideas, ultimately running to some 50,000 words, which had poured out in a deluge at all hours of the day and the dead of night. "I have the solution to the Jewish question," Herzl wrote while working on his manifesto. "I know it sounds mad; and at the beginning I shall be called mad more than once—until the truth of what I am saying is recognized in all its shattering force." Regarding his thoughts and feelings at the time of the writing, Herzl later remarked: "I do not recollect ever having written anything in such an elevated frame of mind as that book. [Heinrich] Heine says that he heard the wings of an eagle beating over his head while writing certain verses. I do believe that something also beat its wings above my head while I was writing that book."

The final goal of his enterprise, to be found amidst the random jottings of his feverish thoughts about a welter of topics, is enunciated early on. Thus, an entry of June 14, 1895:

> The Promised Land, where we can have hooked noses, black or red beards, and bandy legs, without being despised for it. Where at last we can live as free men on our own soil, and where we can die tranquilly in our own homeland. Where we can expect the reward of honor for great deeds; where we shall live at peace with all the world, which we have freed through our own freedom, enriched by our wealth, and made greater by our greatness. So that the decisive cry of "Jew!" may become an honorable appellation, like German, Englishman, Frenchman—in short, like that of all civilized peoples. So that by means of our State we can educate our people for the tasks which still lie beyond our ken. For God would not have kept us alive so long if there were not left for us a role to play in the history of mankind.

Three days later, he showed the evolving manuscript for the first time to a friend, Dr. Friedrich Schiff. "In the middle of the reading," Herzl subsequently wrote in an autobiographical sketch, the Paris correspondent of the Wolff Telegraphic Agency "suddenly burst into tears . . . he thought that I had lost my mind." Someone had tried to accomplish this in the seventeenth century, Schiff pointed out: the false messiah Shabbatai Zvi. In past centuries it was impossible, Herzl concurred, but now "we have machines." Seeking an escape from the "mental torment" into which Schiff's anguished opposition had plunged him, the depressed Herzl wrote a long letter to Otto von Bismarck, asking whether his plan for a Jewish state was feasible or fantastic. Germany's first and former chancellor did not reply.

As Herzl initially conceived it, these notes had several end purposes. The major themes contained in them were put down in "An Address to the Rothschilds," whose 20,000 words were dashed off in five days with the intention of reading them before the illustrious banking family in council assembled. Aside from the eventual book—whether a political treatise or novel remained to be decided—a part also served for a memorandum which he read to Vienna

Chief Rabbi Moritz Güdemann and to an experienced businessman, who were to tell him how to gather the Rothschilds together.

Herzl's tempestuous ideas at this gestation state actually proposed nothing unknown or impossible. Rather than a utopian extravagance, the notes reflect, in Marvin Lowenthal's apt characterization, "a liberal-spirited Viennese version of a decent righteous order of things, with time out for light opera, *Schlagsahne*, and pretty women in stylish gowns." Sundry entries on a labor department, a professional army, high priests, political negotiations, decorations, and a clearance office for capital jostle with an evening performance of Richard Wagner's opera *Tannhäuser* and walks in the Palais Royal gardens and the Tuileries. Thoughts also surface of a future Jewish commonwealth with bright airy halls borne on columns and breathing space between towns, a seven-hour working day, English sports, and the lingual dominance of German.

Antisemitism plays a minor role here, the dominant mood one of exhilaration in planning a new world witness to finer and truer lives. "Perhaps I am solving more than the Jewish question," Herzl writes at one point, proposing "a virginal soil" where new conditions could be created for men everywhere "hamstrung by ancient abuses, habitual inertia, and inherited or acquired wrongs." But if it turns out to be true, he adds, "what a gift of God to the Jews!"

Throughout that summer and autumn, Herzl sought converts to what he termed "a simple idea, a skillful and rational combination that operates, to be sure, with large masses." Max Nordau, a Paris-based doctor and internationally acclaimed author of such provocative works as *Paradoxes* and *Degeneration*, proved to be the easiest and most valuable conquest. After a professional examination of the agitated Herzl, he explained: "If you are insane, we are insane together!" In Nordau's view, "the Jewish people can be freed from its bitter poverty only when it leads a normal economic existence on its own soil." Subsequently, he would describe the broken Jew's purgatory: "He has lost his home in the ghetto, and he is denied a home in his native land."

Güdemann, however, breathed hot and cold to Herzl's appeal that the tragic homelessness of their people was now a strong and vital enough force to "drive a great machine and set a people in motion." Rather than accept the offer of editing a journal as the organ of the new Austro-Hungarian Habsburg government, Herzl agreed to a suggestion from his employers Bacher and Benedikt that he create a study commission in Paris or London which would evaluate the whole Zionist plan; if nothing came of this, he would commit the proposal to a pamphlet, which would then be discussed in the *Neue Freie Presse*.

His trips abroad yielded scant practical support. The Chief Rabbi of France, Zadoc Kahn, listened sympathetically to his "Address" (all reference to the

Rothschilds had been eliminated), but rebuff followed. That November, a group of Anglo-Jewish professionals styled "The Maccabeans" applauded his presentation, arranged by the popular British author Israel Zangwill following a letter of introduction from Nordau, yet Herzl's plan for a central committee to direct the project also came to nothing. At most, his summary "The Solution of the Jewish Question" appeared as an article in the London *Jewish Chronicle* in January 1896.

This first step in publicity coincided with final arrangements for printing *Der Judenstaat* (the cost to be covered by Herzl), the treatise he completed after much effort by mid-January. After a few firms turned Herzl down, including Berlin-based publisher Siegfried Cronbach, who insisted that antisemitism was a waning force throughout the world, Breitenstein agreed to a first edition of only 3,000 copies because the latter remained uncertain of its selling power. The preliminary article in the *Jewish Chronicle* had already triggered sharp opposition from Herzl's editors, Bacher chiefly fearing that antisemites would exploit his anti-assimilationist thesis, with Benedikt urging that Herzl desist from publication rather than set "this avalanche" in motion: "Your idea is a powerful machine gun and it may go off backwards." England's chief Ashkenazic rabbi, Hermann Adler, wrote Güdemann in like vein that he deemed the matter both impractical and dangerous. Already in 1878, in the noted British monthly journal *Nineteenth Century*, he had asserted that Jews "have ceased to be a body politic; we are citizens of the country in which we dwell. . . . Judaism has no political bearing whatsoever . . . religion is the main bond."

The article across the Channel having pledged his honor, Herzl decided to stand firm. Some encouragement came from Güdemann (who hoped, mistakenly, to use Herzl to mobilize the *Neue Freie Presse* for the struggle against Austrian antisemitism), the Austrian bank director Adolf Dessauer, the London rabbi Simon Singer, and an enthusiastic group of students who crowded round Herzl at Vienna's *Jüdische Akademische Lesehall*. Yet heart palpitations and labored breathing, following a bout of malaria, also began to plague the obsessed visionary. He abruptly found "dumbfounding agreement on the critical side, great similarity on the constructive" in his first reading of Leo Pinsker's 1882 tract *Auto-Emancipation*. "A pity that I had not read it before my own pamphlet was printed," confessed Herzl in his diary. "Still, it is a good thing I knew nothing of it—or perhaps I might have abandoned my own undertaking," he wrote of the treatise arguing for that homeland. Four days later, on February 14, 1896, *Der Judenstaat* saw the light of day.

Although its title is usually translated as "The Jewish State," this pamphlet of some 30,000 words should more properly be called *The Jews' State*, a title aimed both at antisemites and acculturated Jews who preferred the term "Hebrew" or "Israelite." "An Attempt at a Modern Solution of the Jewish Question," its subtitle, is equally unambiguous. So, too, is the rest of the work, beginning with the words: "The idea which I have developed in this pamphlet is a very old one: It is the restoration of the Jews' State."

Presenting his practical ideas as "an inescapable conclusion," Herzl early on asserts that antisemitism (defined here in economic terms) cannot be checked without openly bringing the still-existing Jewish *national* question into the world arena. "We are a people—one people"; only a mass exodus into their own commonwealth, with supremacy to be assured by international law, would end the bimillennial Jewish tragedy. European nations would be keenly interested in encouraging this endeavor, with Christian citizens moving gradually into the positions relinquished by departing proletarian Jews. Assimilated Jews could be accepted fully at last if they maintained their current residence after the creation of the new commonwealth.

This idea can be converted into a living reality, Herzl quickly points out to the reader, by means of a corporate body known as "The Society of Jews" and a "Jewish company." The company stock venture should be established in London with a share capital of $200 million, to be provided either by the "big Jewish financiers" in the first instance, or by popular subscription. Argentina and Palestine come under consideration, although Palestine, "our ever-memorable historic home," would be the logical first choice.

Yet Herzl is not content with merely the establishment of a state. He wants to see it become a model commonwealth, created on clearly formulated principles of social justice. The public interest must supersede all, with private initiative encouraged. Equality of the sexes and freedom in religious practice are required in this neutral, "aristocratic republic"; the seven-hour day will be introduced as an experiment for humanity's good. A white flag, symbolizing Jewry's "pure, new life," would carry seven gold stars reflecting seven "golden hours" of work.

A common language is an impossibility ("Who amongst us has a sufficient acquaintance with Hebrew to ask for a railway ticket in that language?"), but a federation of tongues along the Swiss example will replace the "miserable stunted jargon" of the ghetto. The accustomed ways need not be discarded all at once, the author declares. The various local groups may continue older customs: "When we journey out of Egypt again we shall not leave the fleshpots behind." Propaganda throughout the Jewish Diaspora is the immediate task ahead. No one was powerful or wealthy enough to transplant a nation from one home to another. "Only an idea can achieve that. . . . All through the night of their history, the Jews have not ceased to dream this royal dream: 'Next year in Jerusalem!'" If these concepts capture minds, Herzl ends, "the Maccabeans shall rise again." "The Jews who wish for a state will have it."

Certain assumptions inform this striking thesis, now pruned and organized from Herzl's voluminous pastiche of notes into a tempered, persuasive whole. The assimilated, agnostic author had no appreciation of the arguments raised by nineteenth-century Orthodox proto-Zionists like Rabbis Judah Alkalai and Zvi Hirsch Kalischer, or of Moses Hess's socialist linking of Jewish nationalism and tradition in *Rome and Jerusalem* (1862). Since Hess's time, moreover, the procession of historical developments indicated that racism and antisemitism were not limited to Germany, and that liberal humanitarianism would not guarantee Jewish restoration. Yet, as an heir of the European Enlightenment, with its faith in inexorable progress, Herzl is far more optimistic than such outsiders as the Russians Pinsker and Moses Lilienblum of Hibbat Zion, a movement begun in 1882 advocating revival of Jewish life in the biblically covenanted Promised Land, about the inevitability of his new-found progressive cause.

Therein, as Arthur Hertzberg pointed out, lies Herzl's most profound and original thesis: Jew-hatred, like all else, can be understood and then treated in a rational manner. (Herzl simultaneously espoused the counter-emphasis on bestirring the masses' innermost desire with symbols, rituals, and appeals to archaic aspirations, but these he viewed as instruments to an end far different from embracing, as Carl Schorske has suggested, contemporary radical German *völkisch* doctrines.) Nations, just like individuals, operate out of self-interest. They can be persuaded to help the Zionists, since the latter can serve as "peacemakers," in Herzl's later phrase. Departure of the indigestible Jewish masses from Europe to their own social-reformist state, according to the author's argument, would be pleasing to the Gentile masses and preclude the entry of dissatisfied Jews into revolutionary causes. Hence Herzl's bold projection of Zionism into modern international statecraft as an integral part of the continuing evolution of a liberal, Western world order.

The exalted call for secular sovereignty as an immediate goal could gain for the self-deprecating Jew the traits of physical courage, idealism, and especially honor, virtues which Herzl had previously believed could be realized only through outright assimilation. His rejection of the latter course, begun in reaction to the meteoric success of Austrian political antisemitism in the 1890s and first articulated in *The New Ghetto*, comes to full definition in *Der Judenstaat*. Zionism, explains Jacques Kornberg, resolved Herzl's long-time conflict between what he saw as Jewish cowardice and capitalistic materialism on the one hand, and his concurrent feelings of personal loyalty and admiration for Jewish steadfastness in the face of victimization on the other. Together with Nordau, the herald of political Zionism insisted that Jews first transform themselves, recalling the glorious past of heroic Jewish statehood while seeking diplomatic acceptance in Europe's capitals to achieve a normal existence after 2,000 years. The new nationalist reality, leading to the disappearance of antisemitism, would thus reflect the fulfillment of European emancipation and assimilation in a joint Jewish-Gentile effort.

The majority of Western Jewry rejected the basic premise and prognosis formulated in Herzl's *Der Judenstaat*. Some of the Russian *Hovevei Zion* leaders, like Ahad Ha'am (Asher Ginzberg) and Menachem Ussishkin, reacted with skepticism. Yet Nathan Birnbaum's Kadimah student society in Vienna and businessman David Wolffsohn of Cologne greeted him warmly. They also made Herzl subsequently aware of the writings of Hess and Pinsker, and of the tremendous Zionist renaissance in Eastern Europe. In addition, they impressed upon him the fact that only Palestine carried the power of attraction necessary for the Jewish people, which would favor the establishment in the ancient Promised Land of the Jewish commonwealth.

Jews of both conservative and leftist bent in Western Europe hurled their critical shafts against the liberal commonwealth advanced in *Der Judenstaat*. While the *Neue Freie Presse* responded with total silence, the *Allgemeine Zeitung* of Vienna characterized Zionism as "the madness of despair," and its Munich counterpart of the same name described Herzl's pamphlet as the fantastic dream of a feuilletonist whose mind had been unhinged by Jewish enthusiasm. In 1897, Güdemann would attack the work in *National Judentum*, seeking to prove (close to the notion of a Jewish messianic mission as propagated by German Reform Judaism) that the main task of the Jews, a "community of faith" ever since the Babylonian exile, was to work towards the unification of all humankind into a single comprehensive family. In his opinion, the "profane" political Zionism preached by Herzl and Nordau, was also liable to prejudice the civil rights of Jews in their European fatherlands.

On the other hand, Nathan Birnbaum, a founder of Vienna's Kadimah Society (1883) and coiner of the term "Zionism" in his journal *Selbst-Emancipation!* (1885), came to look upon the newcomer Herzl as "a real bourgeois and opportunist" who possessed "a very hard, un-Jewish heart." The French socialist writer Bernard Lazare, one of the first to raise a voice at the injustice done to Dreyfus, would leave the Zionist movement because he disapproved of Herzl's efforts to befriend the Turks, and thought the character of what became the Jewish Colonial Trust repugnant to his socialist principles. Nachman Syrkin, the first theoretician of Socialist Zionism, sharply critiqued Herzl on related grounds.

The young Marxist Leon Trotsky (né Lev Davidovich Bronstein), who would observe the Sixth World Zionist Congress, branded Herzl a "shameless adventurer" who had the impudence and "devilish perfidy" to seek a fatherland for the Jews; that political movement, he predicted, was destined to collapse. The anti-Zionist members of the Jewish Socialist Bund, founded in Vilna in October 1897 and also vigorously opposed by Trotsky for their national particularism, focused on libertarian socialism and support for secular Jewish culture and the Yiddish language. Its central principle of *doikayt* ("hereness") took a local approach to Jewish struggle, the new organization calling for labor rights inside the community while defending Jewish workers from pogroms. Zionism's emphasis on emigration to Palestine was, in the Bund's view, a form of escapism. "One thing is clear to us," wrote prominent Bundist ideologue Vladimir Medem (né Grinberg) after attending the 1903 World Zionist Congress: "political Zionism is bankrupt . . . the liquidation of Zionism has begun."

The Jewish intellectuals of *fin-de-siècle* Vienna, commanding an importance in that cosmopolitan metropolis's cultural life out of all proportion to their number, could not ignore *Der Judenstaat*: one of their own had thrown down the gauntlet. Affirming Jewish identity as cultural (rather than embracing Zionist politics), the poet Richard Beer-Hoffman sent a disappointed Herzl his approval of what was behind the pamphlet: "At last someone who does not carry his Jewishness with resignation, like a burden or a misfortune, but shows pride at being the legitimate heir to an ancestral culture." Sigmund Freud, who only met Herzl via correspondence, had a dream provoked by seeing *The New Ghetto*, and subsequently asked the Zionist crusader to keep a copy of his own *Die Traumdeutung* (1899) as "a sign of the high esteem with which I—like so many others—have for many years regarded the poet and fighter for the human rights [sic] of our people," would eventually opt for a home in liberal London when Nazi Germany took over Austria in 1938.

In Germany, Jewish industrialist Walter Rathenau, responding in *Höre Israel* (1897) to a new wave of antisemitism that arose during the economic hard times of the decade, denounced "primitive" Jews—"an isolated, strange human tribe"—for being "loud and self-conscious in their dress, hot-blooded and restless in their manner." His solution was to endorse the active assimilation by co-religionists into society, "Jews who are German by nature and education." Publisher Salman Schocken judged Herzl's dream of a Jewish republic in the desert to be little more than a joke. He told brother Simon that *Der Judenstaat* was bad theater: the product of a "cheap playwright" who could only write "sweet and worthless feuilletons and light comedies," offering Herzl's play

Prinzen aus Genieland ("Prince from a Land of Genius") as proof. Max Nordau, Schocken added, was a charlatan and half-baked social critic.

Two others reacted far more violently. Karl Kraus's *Eine Krone für Zion* (1898) and his journal *Die Fackel* restated the virtues of unbridled assimilation (he personally embraced Catholicism). Kraus viciously scoffed at the attempt of "King Herzl I" to refashion "hooked noses into badges of merit," and drifted into a racist Jewish self-hatred. Another convert to Christianity, the Austrian psychologist Otto Weininger, whose anti-feminist and antisemitic *Geschlecht und Charakter* (1906) had profoundly affected Kraus, would go to the extreme: he committed suicide after concluding that the Jew was a force—located within people—that believed in nothing.

Herzl's principal intellectual protagonist within Zionist ranks, Ahad Ha'am, leveled a very different charge. He judged "political Zionism" to be an artificial creation by Western Jews, always having "their eyes fixed on the non-Jewish world," who had little appreciation of things actually Jewish. Whereas the problem of the Jews that Herzl addressed was dependent on antisemitism, the problem of Judaism, which Ahad Ha'Am sought to answer, arose because a national culture of millennia faced the danger of losing its essential being upon leaving the ghetto walls. This, the brilliant Hebrew stylist maintained, necessitated a return to Jewry's historic roots—Eretz Israel. To live there unhampered, according to its own spiritual values, Judaism needed not an independent state *à la* Herzl. It required, rather, a good-sized, gradually developed, settlement of Jews working without hindrance, creating and maintaining a unique lifestyle which would radiate the special values of Judaism throughout the Diaspora. And when the opportunity offered itself, what Ahad Ha'am termed the "spiritual center" in Palestine would establish a Jewish state there, not merely a state.

Natural skepticism, an elitist strain, and a lack of confidence led to his questioning the efficacy of Herzl's reliance on diplomacy and its ability to protect the Jewish people against the long-term ravages of cultural sterility and assimilation. Only a cautious, systematic approach to settlement might overcome the facts of limited cultivable land in Palestine, inevitable Arab opposition, and Turkish intransigence, noted Ahad Ha'am in his essays. *Der Judenstaat*, the mentor of "spiritual Zionism" (or "cultural Zionism") observed, like the rejuvenated Promised Land subsequently depicted in Herzl's utopian novel *Altneuland*, had little to mark it as specifically Jewish. This regrettable omission, hardly surprising in light of Herzl's very limited knowledge of his people's rich history and tradition, would weaken a Zionism removed from the root experiences of the Jewish people. Equally worrisome, acutely warned this pessimist, the thrust of *Der Judenstaat* might also lead to an apotheosis of statism, losing sight of Jewish ethics and the fundamental limitations of power.

These various strictures did not prevent a driven Herzl from plunging headlong into the world of *realpolitik* and high finance, beginning with the Grand Duke Frederick of Baden via British Embassy chaplain William Henry Hechler, who had helped Jews immigrate to Palestine after the Russian pogroms of 1881. Thanks to Hechler, former tutor to the son of the Grand Duke (uncle to German Kaiser Wilhelm II) and inspired by *Der Judenstaat*, he found a sympathetic ear in the Grand Duke. The latter, a committed Christian interested in biblical prophecy who also opposed antisemitism, would pave the way eventually to Herzl's speaking directly to the Kaiser. A foray in Constantinople's murky diplomatic waters yielded little, however, and an audience with Sultan Abdul Hamid II could not be obtained. Herzl offered Baron Edmond de Rothschild political leadership of the cause in July, but the philanthropic supporter of Hibbat Zion settlements in Palestine concluded that even if he believed in Turkish promises, he did not feel equal to feed "the 150,000 *schnorrers* who would pour in" as the first wave of the Jewish masses toward Palestine.

The sharp-toned interview of two hours' duration convinced Herzl that the answer to Rothschild's argument was the organization without delay of these very Jews. The latter had already demonstrated their fervent Zionist enthusiasm in meetings which he addressed in Sofia and in London's East End. The time had come, the second decisive turn in Herzl's life after his beginning the diary, to organize them for political action. Nordau, who thought *Der Judenstaat* "a great deed . . . a revelation," declared himself in complete agreement with this revolutionary step.

Over the course of the next thirteen months, Herzl pressed forward on the long and arduous journey of what would eventually result in the first World Zionist Congress. At his expense, an English translation of *Der Judenstaat*, by Sylvie d'Avigdor, was soon published in 500 copies by David Nutt of London; the same year, Michael Berkowicz presented a Hebrew translation in Warsaw. Editions in French, Russian, and Romanian also appeared in 1896, with the book ultimately published in eighty separate editions in eighteen languages. Diplomatic efforts gained nothing, but an exhausted Herzl was heartened by a few enthusiastic Gentiles and early Jewish disciples like Wolffsohn and London's Jacob de Haas (also editor of the first American publication of *Der Judenstaat* in 1904.)

Hibbat Zion representatives from Germany, Austria, and Galicia endorsed Herzl's call in March 1897 for a Zionist congress to be convened in Munich that

August. *Die Welt*, a weekly which began appearing in June under Herzl's chief editorship and financial backing, spread the congress idea. German-Jewish protest, expressed in editorials and Reform declarations (Herzl dubbed them the *Protestrabbiner*), led Herzl finally to shift the site to Basle, Switzerland.

The first national assembly of Jews striving for the renaissance of their people, held on August 29–31, 1897, at Basle's elegant Stadtcasino, gave *Der Judenstaat*'s clarion call an international focus. It was here that 203 delegates, assembled from fifteen countries (including the United States) and reflecting every stratum of Jewish society and thought, presented a dignified, unified picture of purpose. As he approached the podium, shouts of "Long live the king!" resounded. His charismatic person and aristocratic demeanor, buttressed by top hat and tails, enhanced the theme of Herzl's unequivocal, if restrained, opening address: "We want to lay the cornerstone of the edifice which is one day to house the Jewish nation."

He skillfully presided over the discussions, while Nordau stirred the assembled with brilliant oratory. The program of the congress, largely Nordau's draft, became the movement's official platform: "Zionism seeks to establish a home for the Jewish people in Palestine secured by public law." (Herzl had proposed the compromise to a preliminary group which feared that "state" would antagonize Turkey and frighten certain Jewish circles.) To achieve the Basle Program, the World Zionist Organization—Herzl elected its president—was established as the political instrument of Jewry, with plans approved for agricultural colonization, a Jewish National Fund to purchase Palestinian territory, and subsidization of Hebrew culture. Thunderous applause greeted Herzl at the close.

Simultaneously, Herzl's Zionism began to develop a transcendent quality. In a speech one year before the First Zionist Congress, he had referred to Jews gaining "not a Marrano-like, borrowed, untruthful character, but our own." Three months after the historic meeting in Basle, his short story *"Die Menorah"* (*"The Menorah"*) has his Jewish artist protagonist combat the darkness of antisemitism by reclaiming a traditional Hanukkah observance, the lighting of a Menorah which filled the house with light and glory. "If there is such a thing as a legitimate claim to a portion of the earth's surface," he declared at the Second Zionist Congress, "all peoples who believe in the Bible must recognize the rights of the Jews." And at the tumultuous Sixth Zionist Congress, which debated the proposed creation of a temporary Jewish state in Uganda after the Kishinev pogrom of April 1903, Herzl (who supported the plan) would stand to his feet and affirm the ancient Jewish oath (Psalms 137:5), "If I forget thee, O Jerusalem, let my right hand forget its cunning."

A different atmosphere prevailed in the Zionist movement from August 1897 onwards. The concept of world Jewry's *Risorgimento* acquired what the historian Joseph Klausner characterized as "something regal," owing largely to Herzl, the lofty theoretician of *Der Judenstaat* turned activist. Certainly, in the eyes of East European Jewry, on whom depended the exodus to Palestine and statehood, this tall, handsome individual with a princely Assyrian beard became a legendary modern Moses already in his own lifetime. Even the urbane Zangwill, who would break with the movement in favor of territorialism, seeking an alternative haven to that of Palestine, observed of Herzl's moderate, mostly subdued bearing at the congress: "And yet beneath all this statesmanlike prose, touched with the special dryness of a jurist, lurk the romance of the poet and the purposeful vagueness of the modern evolutionist, the fantasy of the Hungarian, the dramatic self-consciousness of the literary artist, the heart of the Jew." Herzl had fulfilled his innermost hopes for a bold, public display of Jewish aspirations and for giving fellow Jews renewed pride and political discipline. Deeply inspired by this watershed event in Jewish history, hundreds of societies sprang up in affiliation with the newly established World Zionist Organization.

A whole generation of youth in Russia and Eastern Europe was ripe for Herzl's message. David Ben-Gurion (né Gruen), first Prime Minister of the State of Israel, recalled that when the charismatic Zionist leader with striking black beard appeared in his hometown of Plonsk in Russian Poland, everyone went around saying "The Messiah has come." "One glimpse of him and I was ready to follow him then and there to the land of my ancestors." He "galvanized" the feeling of the youth that Eretz Israel was achievable, and that "it could only come to pass with our own hands." Even the German philosopher Martin Buber, especially critical that Herzl had no inward relationship to Judaism or to his own Jewishness, realized (in Robert Wistrich's summary) that he was "a master myth maker, whose overwhelming sense of 'Jewish fate' (that is, Jewish suffering) enabled him to rise above petty politics, to give meaning and a world-historical dimension to Zionism."

In an autobiographical account for the *Jewish Chronicle* in January 1898, the Zionist leader recalled, not without humor, his four-year attendance in the primary school of the Budapest Jewish community. "My earliest recollection of that school consists of the caning which I received from the master because I did not know the details of the Exodus of the Jews from Egypt." He then quipped: "At the present time a great many school masters want to give me a caning because I recollect too much of the Exodus from Egypt."

Yet Herzl's personal achievements thereafter were, in fact, disappointing. His scheme for a substantial fund of two million pounds to negotiate with the

Turkish government eventually secured only 250 thousand. Kaiser Wilhelm II, the fundamentalist Lutheran who thought the centuries-old persecution of the Jews was due to their having "killed Our Saviour," at first expressed to Herzl a willingness to commend the cause to the sultan. In their first encounter on October 18, 1898, in Istanbul, he even proposed to assume patronage of the Settlement Company for Palestine and Syria which Herzl planned to establish. The Kaiser drew back, however, and made no promises of support when meeting Herzl on October 28 at the gate of the Mikveh Israel agricultural school near Jaffa and then in Jerusalem on November 2.

Although some 100,000 Jews would serve in the German Army during World War I—of whom 12,000 were killed in action, the Kaiser blamed "the tribe of Juda" for his country's defeat. He added this to Field Marshal August von Mackensen on December 2, 1919: "Let no German ever forget this, nor rest until these parasites have been destroyed and exterminated [*vertilgt und ausgerottet*] from German soil"—gas (*sic*!) "the best cure" for humanity to rid itself of "Jews and Mosquitoes." For their part, Jewish financiers were not persuaded to give Zionism's spokesman the necessary funds, requested by Abdul Hamid II during a private audience with Herzl, to end the Ottoman debt. Furious, Herzl privately condemned them as despicable "Yids."

The apparent failure of his years of selfless activity in the world of foreign affairs converged with a number of other factors to bring the possessed author of *Der Judenstaat* to a state of melancholia. The rapid depletion of his personal fortunes for the movement's sake coincided with the mounting animus of anti-Zionists, ranging from Western integrationists Hermann Cohen and Lucien Wolf to Lithuania's Rabbi Haim Soloveitchik of Brisk and the hassidic rebbes of Lubavitch (Shalom Dov Ber Schneersohn) and Ger (Yehuda Leib Aryeh Alter), who viewed Herzl *et al.* as freethinkers profanely challenging divinely ordained exile. The rabbinic and lay organizations of the American Reform movement stood firmly by the 1885 Pittsburg Platform's abandonment of Jewish nationhood. The *Hovevei Zion* of Eastern Europe, particularly from Russia, remained skeptical of his fixation with diplomacy and quick solutions, and expressed anxiety over the palpable lack of Judaic "spirit" in the activities of Herzl and his closest associates. These opponents formed a "Democratic Fraction" in December 1901, which would press at subsequent Zionist congresses for incremental, methodic colonization in Palestine and (following Ahad Ha'am) for a Jewish cultural renaissance.

Earlier that same year, Herzl drew up a draft charter with the Hungarian Jewish Orientalist Arminius Vambéry to create a Jewish-Ottoman Company, empowered by the Ottoman Sultan to purchase and develop lands in Palestine and Syria. This markedly differs from his diary entry of June 12, 1895, which considers a total separation between the Jewish polity and neighboring states and an attempt to "spirit the penniless population across the border by procuring employment for it in the transit countries, while denying it employment in our own country." Here, the earlier total expropriation is replaced by a highly limited transfer and under the most humane of conditions. The Palestinian Arab owners "are to receive plots of equal size and quality procured by it in other provinces and territories of the Ottoman Empire. It will not only compensate these owners for the costs of resettlement from its own funds, but it will also grant modest loans for the building of necessary housing and the acquisition of the necessary equipment. These loans are to be repaid in equal installments over several years, and the new plots can be used as collateral" [for the loan]. The draft, connected to his failed efforts to establish a Jewish-Ottoman colonization company, termed by David Vital "the insurmountable obstacle," reflects Herzl's characteristic audacity joined to political maturity.

Given growing fissures within the World Zionist Organization and being an eyewitness to the pressing misery of Galician Jewry in the Habsburg Empire, Herzl approached the British government seeking some progress towards the realization of Zionist aims. Jewish settlement in Cyprus and the Sinai Peninsula could obviate official worry over an influx of Russian Jews into Great Britain, he suggested to a royal commission on July 7, 1902. "Misery and Exile have ever been synonymous for the Jew," he averred, "a life sentence." Assimilation he deemed impossible; the Jew "lives in a perpetual fear of the madness of persecution." Colonial Secretary Joseph Chamberlain supported Herzl's proposal regarding el-Arish, yet this also came to naught. In the meantime, Herzl's heart condition, an ailment of which he became aware soon after publishing *Der Judenstaat*, steadily deteriorated.

Simultaneously, publication of his novel *Altneuland* ("Old-New Land"), a fantasy about the Zionist state which Herzl envisaged, widened the gap between the "politicals" favoring a diplomatic solution and the "practicals"— advocates of steady consolidation of a Palestinian *Yishuv* (community) thoroughly grounded in the Jewish heritage. Herzl's vision of the model Zionist commonwealth in Palestine, projected in his new book, was set in 1923. It portrayed a modern system of communications, economic advancement within a cooperative system, a "Zion" university, and a rebuilt Temple in Jerusalem. Equality reigned between man and woman and between Jew and Arab, together with the concomitant disappearance of antisemitism in Europe following the decline of Jewish economic competition there. "If you will it, it is no fable," asserted the epilogue to this utopia. Critics quickly pointed out that, like

Der Judenstaat, this rejuvenated, progressive Promised Land could qualify at best as the state of the Jews, not the *Jewish* state.

Herzl's final diplomatic endeavor aggravated the internecine struggle within the Zionist movement. Under the impact of the Kishinev pogrom, despite which he had met with antisemitic Russian Minister of Interior Vyacheslav von Plehve in the hope of spurring Jewish emigration, he welcomed a British proposal of territory in East Africa for large Jewish colonization. Nordau defended the concept behind "the Uganda project" at the Sixth Zionist Congress that August as representing, at most, a temporary *Nachtasyl* ("an asylum for the night") which promised further commitments from the British; Herzl pledged that Palestine remained Zionism's ultimate aim. He gained a Pyrrhic victory, however, when a majority of the 600 delegates voted to send a study commission to the area; a large number of delegates, mainly from Eastern Europe and including the Kishinev delegation, vehemently opposed.

The rift, spearheaded by Ussishkin, continued to April 1904. By then, the British (hearing of the opposition of British colonialists who lived in the proposed Uganda area) backed down. Pope Pius X gave the driven Zionist prophet no encouragement, informing him in a private audience on January 25 that "if you come to Palestine and settle your people there, we shall have churches and priests ready to baptize all of you." Herzl promised at a meeting of the Zionist Actions Committee that, henceforth, Palestine would be the focus of his efforts. But the incessant activity and strain since 1896 had taken their toll, "making me old, tired, and poor." "My mistake, I started too late," he confided to a friend. Herzl suffered a heart attack, did not fully recover, and died in Edlach, a village in Lower Austria, on July 3, 1904. One day before his death, he told his Zionist colleague and trusted friend Reverend Hechler: "Greet Palestine for me. I gave my heart's blood for my people."

Herzl's sudden passing at the age of 44 left Zionism further than ever from its goal. The *Neue Freie Presse*'s glowing obituary listing his achievements as journalist and editor contained a solitary reference, buried deep in the middle of the newspaper, to the movement for which he had given up his life: "The deceased devoted much time and energy to the Zionist cause." Herzl's theoretical expositions did not go beyond those of Pinsker and were most often devoid of Jewish content, while his sedulous activity failed to sway the world's rulers or to enlist the Jewish notables of Western and Central Europe to this revolutionary cause. One may take issue with his autocratic methods, over-simplification of the power of personal diplomacy, inability to foresee the clash with an Arab nationalist movement (then practically non-existent), and optimistic prognosis on the disappearance of antisemitism. Personal strengths and flaws mixed in truly heroic proportion: Herzl was a realist; a dreamer; given to outbursts of egoism and childish naivete. Yet he never negotiated from actual strength, a situation which, although filling him with despair, he secreted within the pages of his remarkable diaries.

When viewed from the perspective of more than a century since its publication, *Der Judenstaat* is most significant in marking the first decisive step in Jewry's re-entry as actors on the stage of history. Long ambivalent over his Jewish origins, Herzl arrived on his own at a solution to the dangerous, rapidly spreading brew of political and racist antisemitism in Austria and elsewhere across Europe. This acclaimed journalist's tract, unlike Pinsker's anonymously published "admonition to his brethren by a Russian Jew" following the pogroms that swept across south-western Imperial Russia after the assassination of Czar Alexander II in 1881, aimed broadly at political leaders, Jewish financiers, molders of public opinion, and the Jewish masses. Now, he candidly declared with dignity and clarity, Jews wished to rule themselves on their own soil, negotiating with Gentiles as equals.

With his publication of *Der Judenstaat*, the second, vital step could next be taken: elevating the singular Jewish plight into a challenging international issue via action on a grand scale. Even as East European Jewry was moved by the sight of this majestic-looking, successful Western champion of Jewish restoration in their ancestral homeland, he and his supporters created the first instruments for the resettlement of masses of Jews in their future commonwealth—the Zionist Congress in the likeness of a Jewish parliament, the Jewish National Fund to develop the future commonwealth, and the Jewish Colonial Trust to mobilize funds. In so doing, Herzl made "Zionism" a commonplace in the salons and capitals of Europe.

Unlike Pinsker, Herzl gave a comatose movement dynamic leadership, removing it from the narrow confines of Hibbat Zion's philanthropic, cautious approach and bringing it to the international corridors of power. The World Zionist Organization became the address of the Jewish people henceforth, and the England which first negotiated with Herzl would soon resume the political connection, thanks to future leaders like Chaim Weizmann. This would culminate in the Balfour Declaration of November 2, 1917, wherein His Majesty's Government stated that it "view with favor the establishment in Palestine of a national home for the Jewish people, and will use their best endeavours to facilitate the achievement of this object, it being clearly understood that nothing shall be done which may prejudice the civil and religious rights of existing non-Jewish communities in Palestine, or the rights and political status enjoyed by Jews in any other country."

Herzl contributed immeasurably to the Zionist movement—both in thought and in deed. His ideological postulates were clear: the Jews are a people, one people; this people needs a state for its own sake and to relieve humankind of "the Jewish question"; the establishment of the Jewish commonwealth requires international sanction and aid; the creation of Jewish sovereignty depends, at the same time, on the skill of the Jewish people itself ("if you will it, it is no fable"); and the Jewish state must be a model of social justice and of a cooperative society. This was to signal, in the phrase of his address to the First Zionist Congress, "the rebirth of a nation."

In the realm of concrete action, Herzl's contribution is no less seminal. He gave Jewry an organized form through the World Zionist Congress; he placed the Jewish question on the agency of international diplomacy; he, together with his supporters, created the first instruments for the resettlement of masses of Jews in Eretz Israel. His Zionist career lasted only nine years before he burned himself out physically. But it can indeed be said that this unique personality rallied a people, marshaled non-Jewish support, and laid the foundations of the Jewish commonwealth in the Promised Land.

"If I were to sum up the Basle Congress in a word," Herzl confided to his diary immediately after the First Zionist Congress, "it would be this. At Basle I founded the Jewish State. Were I to say this today I would be greeted by universal laughter. In five years perhaps, and certainly in fifty years, everyone will perceive it." Precisely fifty years later, on September 1, 1947, the majority of the United Nations Special Committee on Palestine recommended Jewish sovereignty in a partitioned Palestine. Fittingly, when David Ben-Gurion, on behalf of the Jewish *Yishuv* in Palestine, declared the independence of *Medinat Yisrael* on May 14, 1948, the solitary portrait of Herzl hung near a blue and white flag such as had graced the First Zionist Congress. On August 16, 1949, Herzl's remains were flown from Vienna's Döbling Cemetery to the State of Israel, as requested in his last will, and interred the following day on a Jerusalem ridge—Har Herzl.

In hindsight, the classical Zionist thesis enunciated in *Der Judenstaat* that statehood would normalize the Jewish people, a premise reflective of liberal nineteenth-century Western rationalism, correctly understood the first priority: the rescue of a downtrodden Jewry from the external danger of strident, murderous antisemitism. While unable, understandably, to imagine the Holocaust, a diary entry foresaw the consequences of spreading Jew-hatred across the European Continent: "Will it be expropriation by some revolutionary force from below? Will it be proscription by some reactionary force from above? Will they banish us? Will they kill us? I expect all these forms and others." He foresaw the crumbling of the Hapsburg Empire with its two million Jews into nation-states and concluded that his people would not have a motherland like all the other nations.

The anxious reality pressing upon the Jews of Europe, reflected in the urgency of his tone, made Herzl appeal greatly to the masses' immediate need. And like Pinsker, Nordau, and then Vladimir (Ze'ev) Jabotinsky, Herzl also understood that an internationally sanctioned state was imperative under these circumstances. Fusing thought and action, he became, in Stefan Zweig's later panegyrical phrase, a man of "world-historical presence." Thus he, in contradistinction to contemporary opponents within and without the Zionist camp, stirred the will of Jewry to remake history forthrightly as a political force.

Herzl, more than any other individual, wrought the beginning of that radical transformation in Jewish life. Recalling Victor Hugo's pithy remark, "there is nothing like a dream to create the future," one can better appreciate that the practical vision of *Der Judenstaat,* coupled with the persistent, single-minded vigor subsequently displayed by its creator, effectively moved a people's dream of national restoration in Eretz Israel towards fulfillment. "We are organizing Jewry for its coming destiny," Herzl averred at the Fourth Zionist Congress. In the process, to use Ernst Pawel's phrase, this ambassador of his people led the Jews out of their labyrinth of exile.

The tireless, brooding paladin of Zionism made a deep impression upon prominent non-Jews as well. French prime minister Georges Clemenceau later declared that there was "a breath of eternity" in this "rare man of genius," the biblical "Burning Bush and the Revolutionary Sinai" taking shape in his appearance. The king of Italy, Victor Emmanuel III, kept a picture of Herzl on his desk for years, saying that he had scarcely met a man of such "magnetic charm"; his Bulgarian counterpart, Ferdinand I, reminisced about one "half glowing with inner fire." They and others appreciated the dynamic force of this individual, realizing that fate had visited upon, rather than been achieved by, the Jew prior to Herzl's advent. He now offered a revolutionary cure to what the baptized poet Heinrich Heine had earlier dubbed Judaism as "the millennial family affliction"—homecoming to the source of a people's life.

To be so extraordinarily committed for nine years to the point that he sacrificed his wife and three children, his finances (substantial sums also came from his devoted father, Jacob), and, before long, his very health, Herzl first had to come to terms with his own Jewish identity and his pain at the anguish of the East European Jewish masses. Personal experience instructed, as he told the First Zionist Congress, that the movement "is a home-coming to the Jewish fold even before it is a home-coming to the Jewish land." Great is the divide, indeed, between the earlier wish to be a member of the old Prussian nobility, a diary entry as late as July 5, 1895, and Herzl's using the *nom de plume* Benjamin Seff—based on his Hebrew name (Binyamin Ze'ev)—for subsequent articles in *Die Welt* on what developed into the Dreyfus Affair.

His remarkable conversion from assimilated aesthete to Zionist zealot provides another telling example of the truism that the Jewish experience has never conformed to reasonable expectation. Upon witnessing Dreyfus's public humiliation in January 1895, Herzl had written about "the Jew who tried to adapt himself to his environment, to speak its languages, to think its thoughts, to sew its insignia on his sleeve—only to see them ruthlessly ripped away." The discomforting truth did not apply to him then, Herzl announcing in his speech to the Rothschilds that "I am a German Jew from Hungary, and I can never be anything but a German." Within a short time, however, he underwent a process of existential self-liberation, one that inspired the Jews of Eastern Europe with the hope for a sovereign future in their Promised Land.

Herzl symbolized the vitality that had been stunted by centuries of timorous ghetto life, his chivalrous new Jew harkening back to the glory and honor of the sovereign Maccabees while embracing the best of Western European culture. This man of high culture and of the wider world, impelled by a quasi-messianic sense of personal mission and radiating authority, impressed Jew and non-Jew alike. His nobility of bearing, as if born to the purple, struck many; while the face of this towering figure had become over time that of "a man of sorrows," in the judgment of the artist Hermann Struck, "his eyes had become the eyes of a seer." Eulogizing "the leader of the movement" without once mentioning Herzl by name, the newly chosen rabbi of Jaffa and its surrounding agricultural settlements, Rav Avraham Yitzhak Kook, lamented him as a precursor of the Mashiach (Messiah) ben Yosef, standing in the Jewish eschatological tradition for the material redemption of Jews and their physical development as a nation. The final redemption, he emphasized, the harmonizing of Jewry's body and soul, would come with the Mashiach ben David, representing the Torah-inspired values of Judaism.

The dispersed, fragmented Jewish masses viewed Herzl as a mythical hero who, personally giving up all for a greater cause, could mobilize them to work toward a common end. How else to explain the arrival of some 6,000 Jews, hailing from every corner of the world, who converged upon Vienna on July 7, 1904, to pay their last respects at his funeral? Herein lay his cardinal significance for a long-suffering Jewry. On the twenty-fifth anniversary of Herzl's passing, Chaim Weizmann's tribute aptly concluded that he "will for all time be justly regarded as one of those fortunate men of destiny who, in their very hour of death, have wrested from seeming failure the laurels of immortality."

In that same memorial volume, Israel Zangwill's poem "Theodor Herzl" captured well a people's joined grief and veneration.

> Farewell, O Prince, farewell, O sorely tried;
> You dreamed a dream and you have paid the cost:
> To save a people, leaders must be lost
> By foes and followers be crucified;
> Yet 'tis your body only that has died.
> The noblest soul in Judah is not dust
> But fire that works in every vein and must
> Reshape our life, rekindling Israel's pride.
>
> So we behold the captain of our strife
> Triumphant in this moment of eclipse;
> Death has but fixed him to immortal life,
> His flag upheld, the trumpet at his lips.
> And while we, weeping, rend our garment's hem,
> "Next year," we cry, "next year, Jerusalem."

Yet even once Herzl and succeeding avatars of political Zionism were proven correct in their contention that group survival mandated full engagement in power politics, achieving its ultimate realization in the establishment of the State of Israel, the sober strictures of those who focused upon the problem of Judaism would remain. In their separate ways, A. D. Gordon, Martin Buber (far more than in the thinly veiled skepticism of his mentor, Ahad Ha'am), Rabbis Kook and Mizrachi religious Zionist party founder Yitzhak Ya'akov Reines provided the essential reminder that even a desacralized state of the Jews as enunciated in *Der Judenstaat* could never be "like any other nation." Zionism, although conditioned by modern European nationalism, cannot be divorced from the moral essence which has always made Judaism unique. The content of the specific Jewish experience, its quality both in Israel—where the totality of Judaism can be lived—and in the Diaspora, is fundamental. And it still remains to be realized.

Herzl's progressive commonwealth cannot alone sustain a people—particularly when Jewish existence has become a voluntary proposition. In light of the Holocaust, that realized state vindicates for the vast majority of

Jews today their faith in the continuity of the Jewish people. For many, as he predicted in *Der Judenstaat*, it gives them "self-respect and the joy of freedom of soul." Yet memory of the *Shoah* and the aura which long surrounded Jewry's heroic national rebirth is fading. The ongoing interaction between Israel and the Diaspora will only be secured by their common awareness of identity, of spiritual connection, and of a singular history. Finding a basis for a shared past, they can thereby create a shared future.

Bibliography

Bein, Alex. *Theodor Herzl: A Biography*. Translated by Maurice Samuel. New York: Jewish Publication Society of America, 1970.

Brenner, Michael. *In Search of Israel: The History of an Idea*. Princeton: Princeton University Press, 2018.

David, Anthony. *The Patron: A Life of Salman Schocken, 1877–1959*. New York: Metropolitan Books, 2003.

Elon, Amos. *Herzl*. New York: Holt, Rinehart and Winston, 1975.

Halpern, Ben. *The Idea of the Jewish State*. Cambridge, MA: Harvard University Press, 1969.

Hertzberg, Arthur. *The Zionist Idea. A Historical Analysis and Reader*. New York: Herzl Press, 1964.

Herzl, Theodor. *The Complete Diaries of Theodor Herzl*, 5 vols. Edited by Raphael Patai, translated by Harry Zohn. New York: Herzl Press, 1960.

———. *The Diaries of Theodor Herzl*. Edited and translated by Marvin Lowenthal. New York: Grosset & Dunlap, 1962.

———. *The Jewish State*. Translated by Harry Zohn. New York: Herzl Press, 1970.

———. *The New Ghetto*. Translated by Heinz Norden. New York: Theodor Herzl Foundation, 1955.

———. *Old-New Land*. Translated by Paula Arnold. Haifa: Bloch, 1960.

Kornberg, Jacques. *Theodor Herzl: From Assimilation to Zionism*. Bloomington: Indiana University Press, 1993.

Le Rider, Jacques. *Modernity and Crises of Identity: Culture and Society in Fin-de-Siecle Vienna*. Translated by Rosemary Morris. New York: Continuum, 1993.

Lewisohn, Ludwig, ed. *Theodor Herzl: A Portrait for This Age*. Cleveland: World Publishing Company, 1955.

Pawel, Ernst. *The Labyrinth of Exile: A Life of Theodor Herzl*. New York: Farrar, Straus and Giroux, 1989.

Penkower, Monty. *The Emergence of Zionist Thought*. Millwood, WA: Associated Faculty Press, 1986.

Penslar, Derek J. "Herzl and the Palestinian Arabs: Myth and Counter-Myth." *The Journal of Israeli History* 24:1 (March 2005): 65–77.

Pulzer, Peter. *The Rise of Political Anti-Semitism in Germany and Austria*, 2nd ed. Cambridge, MA: Harvard University Press, 1988.

Rohl, John C. G. *The Kaiser and His Court: Wilhelm II and the Government of Germany*. Translated by T. F. Cole. Cambridge: Cambridge University Press, 2015.

Rozenblit, Marsha L. *The Jews of Vienna, 1967–1914: Assimilation and Identity*. Albany: State University of New York Press, 1983.

Schorske, Carl L. *Fin-de-Siecle Vienna, Politics and Culture*. Cambridge: Cambridge University Press, 1981.

Shimoni, Gideon and Robert S. Wistrich, eds. *Theodor Herzl, Visionary of the Jewish State*. Jerusalem: Herzl Press, 1999.

Troy, Gil, ed., and Harry Zohn and Uri Bollag, trans. *Theodor Herzl, The Collected Zionist Writings and Addresses of Israel's Founder*, 3 vols. Jerusalem: The Library of the Jewish People, 2022.

Vital, David. *The Origins of Zionism*. Oxford: Oxford University Press, 1975.

———. *Zionism. The Formative Years*. Oxford: Oxford University Press, 1982.

Weisgal, M., ed. *Theodor Herzl, A Memorial*. New York: New Palestine, 1929.

Wistrich, Robert S. *The Jews of Vienna in the Age of Franz Joseph*. Oxford: Oxford University Press, 1989.

Zangwill, Israel. "Dreamers in Congress." In *Works of Israel Zangwill: Dreamers of the Ghetto*, New York: Bloch, 1921, 430–440.

Zipperstein, Steven, *Elusive Prophet: Ahad Ha'am and the Origins of Zionism*. Berkeley: University of California Press, 1993.

Zweig, Stefan. *The World of Yesterday: An Autobiography*. Lincoln: University of Nebraska Press, 1964.

CHAPTER 2

Honorable Failures against Nazi Germany: McDonald's Letter of Resignation and the Petition in Its Support

I

During supper and a long talk on June 11, 1935, that lasted until almost midnight, James G. McDonald informed James N. Rosenberg that he would definitely resign the office of League of Nations High Commissioner for Refugees (Jewish and Other) Coming from Germany. For the past year and a half since his appointment, the former chairman of the Foreign Policy Association (FPA) had sought aid from the international community to resettle Jews and others persecuted in Adolf Hitler's Third Reich. Neither the League nor the world's nations gave him anything better than "empty lip service," however. McDonald's thatch of yellow hair, his host that Tuesday evening would later recall, had turned by then to silver. His most recent search for havens, a three-month trip to South America, had yielded nothing but more frustration. The only course open to him, McDonald concluded, was to resign in protest at the lack of support for his efforts.

Rosenberg, a lawyer who served on the executive boards of the American Jewish Joint Distribution Committee (JDC) and the American Jewish Committee (AJC), had suggested McDonald for the post in August 1933. He now argued at length that his "tried friend and true" should take the occasion to present the League with a dramatic letter. The statement, its form to be agreed upon, would address the rights of religious and racial minorities, a sort of "bill of rights." It would focus the reader's attention not only on the persecution of Jews, but on the Nazi threat of world war. While accepting in principle the desirability of making this final gesture, McDonald in turn doubted that a sufficient basis could be found for formally requesting an Advisory Opinion from the World Court. He was unwilling at this stage to commit himself; Rosenberg found these reservations commendable.

The pair next discussed Rosenberg's further program of making available to McDonald two individuals for this purpose, Oscar I. Janowsky and Melvin M. Fagen. Janowsky had written a fine book on the origin and meaning of the minority treaties that resulted from the Versailles Peace Conference after World War I, and was planning a year in Geneva to continue these studies. Rosenberg thought that Fagen, whose recent memorandum to Rosenberg on the subject had impressed McDonald most favorably, could be released from his work at the AJC. McDonald proposed that Fagen, Janowsky, and Morris R. Cohen, with whom Janowsky was associated, meet with him and Rosenberg for lunch in the near future. After that, he would give a definite answer as to the two men suggested.[1]

Technically, the League Covenant made no express provision for international help to refugees. Sanction for League action rested on the broad objective of the Preamble to the Covenant—"to promote international cooperation by the maintenance of justice," as well as on Article XXIII(a) prescribing that members seek to "establish and maintain the necessary international institutions," which would "secure and maintain fair and humane conditions of labor" in all countries within their economic purview. In 1921, the Arctic explorer Fridtjof Nansen was appointed High Commissioner for Refugees to deal with the problem of the million or more émigrés who had departed Russia at the time of the Bolshevik Revolution. Soon were added the 1,500,000 Greeks who were forced to leave their homes in Anatolia and in the Turkish provinces, and the 350,000 Armenians who fled from Asia Minor because of Turkish persecution. "Nansen passports," their issue left to the discretion of the state sheltering the refugee and valid for only one year, offered little protection to these stateless persons. After Nansen's death in 1930, the League Assembly set up the Nansen International Office as successor to the High Commissioner, to be funded mainly from philanthropic sources and liquidated by 1939. Confronted by worldwide economic depression and the habitual disregard by governments of Assembly recommendations not to expel refugees, the new office languished.[2]

Hitler's seizure of power in 1933, with antisemitism immediately becoming official German policy, brought a new refugee problem into sharp focus. The country's more than a half million Jews (then half of one percent of the population) became prey to physical assault, coupled with legislation removing them from government service, industry, the professions, and higher education. Political "undesirables" suffered similar treatment. Some 60,000 people (eighty-five percent of them Jews) left the country by that summer as a consequence, catching the world's leaders off guard. Already shaken by Japan's withdrawal in March after the Assembly refused to recognize its conquest of Manchuria, the League was undergoing key personnel changes that further weakened the cause of minority protection. Wary of antagonizing its eastern neighbor, France expected Great Britain to take the lead; the British, facing Arab unrest in mandatory Palestine, contemplated no major step against the Third Reich. With the United States, not a League member, mired in massive economic unemployment, the newly elected administration of President Franklin D. Roosevelt maintained diplomatic silence. "We all suffer at present from a feeling of powerlessness," observed the young lawyer Nathan Feinberg in Geneva to colleague Jacob Robinson of the Comité des Delegations Juives.[3]

The Comité, initially created to advocate Jewish minority rights at the Versailles Peace Conference, mounted the first international opposition to Nazi rule. Notwithstanding the skepticism of Norman Bentwich, former Attorney General in the mandatory Palestine government and now legal advisor to the Anglo-Jewish establishment's Joint Foreign Committee (JFC), it succeeded in organizing the petition to the League of Franz Bernheim and five other claimants against the application of the anti-Jewish "Aryan" laws in Upper Silesia. Having just chastised Nazi persecution publicly in the *Journal de Geneve*, Viscount Robert Cecil, one of the League's founders and a pro-Zionist, lent valuable support. Against German objections, a League report concluded that the 1922 German-Polish treaty continued until its expiration in July 1937 to protect the Jews of Upper Silesia as a racial minority. After career diplomat Friedrich von Keller announced on May 30 that Berlin would honor its treaty obligations, several League Council members proceeded to decry the treatment of Jews throughout the Third Reich. Three eminent jurists concluded that the Bernheim petition could be lodged according to Article 147 of the Geneva convention, and the Council, with Germany and Italy abstaining, adopted the report on June 6, 1933.[4]

That same week, at the seventeenth plenary congress of the International Federation of League of Nations Societies, Cecil kept up the drumbeat of condemnation. As Federation president, he saw to it that the Germans did not leave when a strong protest from the Palestine League of Nations Union delegation was debated in the policy committee. He also arranged that the committee hear the Palestine delegation's Leo Motzkin, long-time head of the Comité, charge that "the entire Jewish population in Germany is doomed to a swift and sure destruction" and Ben-Zion Mossinsohn call for Zionism to solve the plight of suffering Jewry. On June 6, Cecil conveyed to the German chief representative the Federation's conviction that Reich anti-Jewish discrimination "seems impossible to reconcile" with the spirit of the League Covenant and the progress of western civilization, reflecting as it did "a recrudescence of a belief in mere force independent of justice as an instrument of Government," which has caused profound anxiety in very many countries."[5]

Cecil's last observation suggested that the League Council and Assembly could consider the broad issue of antisemitic persecution under Article II of the Covenant, which allowed a member to raise any circumstance which threatened "to disturb international peace." The *Manchester Guardian* and the University of London's Hersh Lauterpacht, among other British jurists, advocated this approach, but Bentwich and Board of Deputies of British Jews president Judge Neville Laski found London and other governments unwilling to pick up the gauntlet. The British Foreign Office supported a resolution passed by the Leagues International Labor Organization, whose annual conference advocated that it study the means of settling refugees from Germany in other countries. Yet Undersecretary of State Robert Vansittart saw no possibility of a successful political approach to the Germans, since Hitler was "quite mad" on two subjects: Jews and Austria. All the JFC could do, he told Laski, was to "peg away and retain and arouse public opinion." Accordingly, much to Lauterpacht's dissatisfaction, the JFC shifted to finding ways whereby the League could help resettle German Jews in an orderly and humane manner.[6]

Across the Atlantic, Ernst H. Feilchenfeld had already concluded that action based on Article II or alleged minority rights other than in Upper Silesia appeared legally impossible. The League only had clear jurisdiction with regard to relief measures, argued the Harvard University instructor of international law, who presented his thoughts to Samuel Untermyer and to AJC Secretary Morris D. Waldman. At the request of Untermyer, a corporate lawyer then leading the American Jewish boycott of German goods, Feilchenfeld submitted a sixty-page memorandum on July 4, which called for reestablishing the League office of High Commissioner for Refugees. Untermyer shared the memorandum with James N. Rosenberg. An enthusiastic Rosenberg asked Feilchenfeld to draft a petition to the League endorsing such an office, which he proceeded to draw up in consultation with Professor Joseph P. Chamberlain of Columbia University's law school. On July 27 it was decided that Feilchenfeld would cooperate with Max J. Kohler, head of a special Joint Council formed by the

AJC, the B'nai Brith, and the American Jewish Congress in order to aid German Jewish refugees. In the first week of August, Chamberlain chose to inform his fellow FPA board members McDonald and lawyer Herbert L. May, then on a ship bound for Hamburg, about this endeavor.[7]

McDonald had long maintained contact with some men in the German chancellor's inner circle, who knew of his expressed sympathy for Germany during World War I. On April 8, Hitler told the visiting FPA chairman that "I will do the thing that the rest of the world would like to do. It doesn't know how to get rid of the Jews. I will show them." McDonald entertained few illusions thereafter about the future of Jewry under the swastika, and so informed American Jewish leaders upon his return home. At the same time, his dispassionate evaluation of Nazism as a "fascinating revolutionary phenomenon" and of Hitler's unifying Germany as never before in its history led American Jewish Congress president Stephen Wise to assert that it would be "calamitous" if McDonald attained his desire of becoming the new US ambassador to Berlin. Once William E. Dodd received that post in June, McDonald spoke more freely in public about the regular insecurity faced by German Jews and of the need for Christians to respond, because the Nazi regime was "violating every principle of Christianity" and posed "a challenge to civilized men."[8]

Convinced that reestablishing a High Commissioner for Refugees would bring the matter before the public as a world problem, Rosenberg also lobbied JDC colleagues Paul Baerwald and Felix Warburg, a long-time FPA supporter and personal friend of McDonald's, to provide quiet financial backing. Once Kohler's committee endorsed the idea, the skeptical JFC followed suit. In August, Rosenberg proposed McDonald for the new office, but the tall Midwestern American of Scotch and German ancestry asked not to be considered. Then visiting Europe on the FPA's behalf, McDonald thought it would appear that he was being self-serving in working towards this objective. During the trip he found no change in Hitler's "unqualified intransigency" regarding Jews, while the German authorities claimed that no refugee problem existed because those who left the country could return and get protection. All the members of the League Secretariat expressed to McDonald their conviction that efforts to pressure Germany to alter its domestic policy would almost certainly fail and probably endanger any League program for refugees; Secretary General Joseph Avenol particularly feared that Germany might "embarrass" the League by asking it to "take care of all the Jews." Eugenio Cardinal Pacelli, the papal secretary of state, defended the 1933 Concordat of understanding with the Nazi government, and indicated to McDonald that the Vatican would not do anything in the matter.[9]

By the end of September, success for setting up a new High Commissioner for Refugees appeared within grasp. The JFC approved the petition draft and approached Great Britain, France, Spain, and Holland to move the draft resolution—both documents speaking of "refugees," *not* "Jews". The British, Laski advised the JFC, could not initiate the scheme but would support it. On the 23rd, McDonald confidentially relayed that the Dutch government would advocate the cause in the League Assembly, and was about to inform Berlin of its contemplated action. The FPA and AJC briefed the US State Department in hopes of aid from the Roosevelt Administration, but European Affairs Division Chief J. P. Moffat thought it "seemed extremely difficult to know how we could help in any way." On the 29th, Jonkheer de Graeff of the Netherlands presented to the Assembly's fourth Plenary Meeting his country's resolution. To make acceptance as easy as possible for Germany, it referred to the fact that "a great number of German nationals" having "taken refuge in recent months in several countries" created "an economical, financial, and social problem"—not a humanitarian one, which could "only be solved by international collaboration." He then requested that the Council consider "as soon as possible methods for bringing about a practical arrangement for this purpose," and to take the "necessary measures" for its execution. The Agenda Committee referred this to the Second Committee, which dealt with technical matters, a few days later.[10]

That choice, rather than discussion in the Sixth Committee, which focused on political matters, was calculated to render the acquiescence of the German delegation more likely. Indeed, when Keller asserted in the Sixth Committee that a nation must be racially or ethnically homogeneous, and that the Jewish question was a unique "demographical, social and moral problem," the British, Czech, and numerous other representatives vigorously attacked his stance and reaffirmed the Assembly's 1922 resolution to protect Jews and other minorities. On October 7, a sub-committee appointed by the Second Committee proposed the nomination of a High Commissioner for Refugees, promptly leading the German delegate to announce his opposition. To overcome this, the Second Committee agreed that the commissioner would report to an entirely autonomous Governing Body of twelve government representatives interested in the German refugee problem, which would forward this information to their respective states. With Keller abstaining, the Assembly adopted the resolution on October 11. The newly designated High Commissioner for Refugees (Jewish and Other) Coming from Germany would be headquartered in Lausanne, thus emphasizing his separation from the League, and his expenses defrayed by voluntary funding from private and other sources. The Governing Body could include, if the League Council thought advisable, private organizations best able to assist these refugees.[11]

Warburg and Rosenberg, assuring that the JDC would supply most of the American funds, lost little time in championing the forty-seven-year-old McDonald for the new post. They praised his vigorous efforts in Europe on its behalf, noted that large funding would be coming from the United States, and pointed to his being independent of pressure from a government which had the Palestine mandate. McDonald himself spent the next week talking with the State Department and a few influential people about his candidacy. US Supreme Court Justice Louis D. Brandeis was strongly opposed, arguing that an American would be disadvantaged because Washington had done "so little to help." AJC president Cyrus Adler and others favored a former undersecretary general of the League, the American lawyer Raymond Fosdick, but the Rockefeller Foundation officer was not willing and backed McDonald. The JFC and World Zionist Organization leader Chaim Weizmann, thinking McDonald a Germanophile and not a world figure capable of commanding authority, preferred Cecil. The greatly respected statesman begged off because of advanced age, however, while finally agreeing to serve on the Governing Body. The French, for their part, objected to any British appointee. On the 26th Avenol offered the position to McDonald, who, "deeply sensible of the honor conferred upon me and of the opportunity of service," cabled his acceptance soon thereafter.[12]

The American press enthusiastically lauded McDonald's appointment, but international realities augured poorly for his success. The cautious Avenol, a Frenchman who sought not to antagonize Germany any further after its withdrawal from the League two weeks earlier, made it clear that McDonald was not a League official. The British insisted that the High Commissioner's jurisdiction did not include Palestine. Although having temporarily admitted some 25,000 German refugees to date, France announced at the first meeting of the Governing Body, when Cecil reluctantly agreed to serve as chairman, that its generous policy had ended. In Senator Henri Bérenger's regularly repeated phrase, "*La France c'est un passage, pas un garage.*" It was hoped that room could be found for a substantial number in Spain, Argentina, and Brazil, but these countries did not even answer an invitation to join the advisory group. Washington agreed to send Chamberlain, who promptly declared that his country's restrictive quota system "allowed for no elasticity" except for an important but small group of scientists. Several delegates stressed, as well, that no money or responsibility could be expected from their governments. A memorandum by Bentwich, whom McDonald chose as his deputy, in favor of protective documents for the new refugees was referred back to the High Commissioner for further study. As for McDonald's personal telegram to the Reichsbank president suggesting that he arrange for an interview with Hitler, during which the High Commissioner would outline the office's future activity, Hjalmar Schacht thought the suggestion "not appropriate at present."[13]

Politically and financially divorced from the League, McDonald understood that very large funds would be needed to effectuate a comprehensive program for refugee relief, retraining, and placement. To this end, he set up an Advisory Council of Jewish and non-Jewish organizations, only to discover that the non-Jewish groups and the Rockefeller Foundation manifested scant interest. The JDC and other conservative Jewish groups objected to the Comité's involvement, but an irritable McDonald carried the day when he obtained Warburg's telegram calling for unity. Weizmann thought that McDonald, "while an energetic man with a high-pressure American outlook," had little idea how to proceed. Warburg again came to the High Commissioner's rescue, having JDC associate Charles Liebman present a brief memorandum at McDonald's home in Bronxville, New York, for setting up a $50–100 million corporation to invest anywhere in the world and utilize a part of the funds for philanthropic ends. At that meeting on Christmas Day, Rosenberg urged very strongly that the project be put forward as McDonald's own. Warburg, Rosenberg, Baerwald, and Liebman assured him of their full support. After hearing the High Commissioner's presentation to American Jewish leaders two days later, at which Rosenberg presided, Stephen Wise wrote to Brandeis: "I think that McD is going to try to do a good job. I never quite get the feeling that he is perfectly trustworthy. Still one hopes that he will do his best."[14]

McDonald's actual accomplishments in the first six months of 1934, aptly concluded the State Department's Moffat, were "perilously close to nil." His report to Roosevelt about worsening conditions in Germany elicited a frank response: "I did not see that there was anything that I could do." London refused to consider refugee settlement in Transjordan, which Rosenberg touted as a first specific objective. Paris and Ottawa offered no encouragement. The German Foreign Office, with which McDonald and his office Secretary General Andre Wurfbain negotiated over refugee passports, money transfers, and property taxes, persisted in its immobility. The task of locating funds, made much more difficult by what McDonald termed "civil war within the Jewish ranks," took up much of his time. Jewish experts in Europe disagreed about emigration possibilities. Furthermore, the Jews were "a drag on the market," McDonald pointed out to Baron Robert de Rothschild, antisemitism rising everywhere. Palestine presented almost the only immediate opportunity for refugee colonization on an appreciable scale, he reported in May to the Governing Body's second session; all other schemes offered to the High Commissioner were still in the realm of suggestion without any financial instrument to enable them to be carried out.[15]

The latter half of the year proved even more disappointing, McDonald's labors taking on the nature of a Sisyphean task. The refugee corporation had yet to emerge. In September, Poland's foreign minister denounced the League's continued protection of minorities within his country (which included 3.3 million Jews). The French, British, and Italians, among others, refused to make a financial contribution to the High Commissioner's office. All of Germany, McDonald wrote to a friend, was being mobilized "for the economic struggle and ultimately for a struggle of a different order." In addition, the restrictions on withdrawal of property from the Reich had become steadily intensified, he reported to the Governing Body in November, destitution increasing among the emigrants because their resources were exhausted. A new wave from Germany of stateless Jews of Polish and Russian origin, in "a state of indescribable misery," began arriving in Czechoslovakia. The very likely return of the Saar Basin to Germany in early 1935, based upon a plebiscite to be conducted by the League in accordance with the Treaty of Versailles, suggested that some 50,000 people would have to seek haven elsewhere. The Soviet Union refused to join the Governing Body, while Avenol left little doubt that he would not risk the "slightest jeopardy" to the League's relations with Germany in order to help McDonald's efforts.[16]

Given the obstruction of governments, the lack of independent funds, and the absence of any organizations either dependent on the High Commission or which were wholly devoted to the refugee cause, a greatly discouraged McDonald suggested to Warburg in mid-August that he might announce at the Governing Body's meeting in London two months hence the office's liquidation by January 1935. His prime financial supporter soon replied at length that McDonald had done "remarkably well," represented an "outstanding figure in illustrating that Christian idealism is not dead," and had united many Jewish groups hitherto not interested in the suffering of their coreligionists. McDonald's resignation, Warburg then cabled to some prominent European Jewish leaders, would probably result in the collapse of the entire Governing Body and would be "a serious blow to the Jewish Cause throughout the world." Rosenberg added to McDonald that, from a personal point of view, it would be a serious mistake to discontinue the work at the end of 1934. Even if large funds were not available, Rosenberg also insisted, the High Commissioner should not consider himself a relief agent, but conduct himself proudly as an equal dealing with government officialdom over worthwhile matters. Perhaps, he wondered, McDonald had not always made as much of the position as he might have done in this regard.[17]

"You cannot continue an emergency organization indefinitely," Cecil put it to McDonald on October 10, when the High Commissioner confided his feeling that there should be a definite terminus for the office. The Governing Body president recognized that there might be a need for a similar organization to deal with Jewish immigration or related matters, but he was certain that this should be another organization directly under the League auspices. Sir Osmond E. D'Avigdor-Goldsmid, President of the Jewish Colonization Association (known by its Yiddish acronym ICA), doubted that the office should be so perpetuated, however, chiefly because it would tend to indicate that there should be "a sort of extraterritoriality" for Jews, "which he, as an ardent Englishman, could never admit." The British ambassador to Rome thought a direct connection of the High Commission to the League highly unlikely, and saw difficulties in McDonald's being present occasionally in Europe with authority delegated to another individual within a modified organization. Throughout, Warburg remained a firm ally, prepared to assume responsibility that the different Jewish groups would take care of three-quarters of the office's budget in the next year, and expressing his view that as much had been done as could be expected. The High Commission could continue to carry on effectively, Warburg declared while indicating to McDonald his great appreciation when they met on Thanksgiving Day, 1934.[18]

Within the next six months, McDonald had decided on leaving his post. In early February 1935, he explained to Cecil why it appeared necessary to envisage a procedure whereby the office would be closed by the year's end, and some of its remaining duties transferred to another organization, preferably with the League. Acknowledging that the Governing Body was "useless" at present, Cecil in turn revealed that some months ago the Foreign Office had rejected his own request to move the High Commission nearer the League on the grounds that it would irritate Germany and might imply that London was prepared to assume a financial obligation. Washington also decided not to make a $10,000 contribution to the High Commission, McDonald's direct intervention with Roosevelt and Chamberlain's press of the State Department notwithstanding. The newly created US Refugee Economic Corporation had raised only a bit more than $1,000,000, none of which had yet been made available. McDonald's travels that spring in Brazil, Argentina, and Uruguay, together with the extensive trips of his friend Samuel Guy Inman across South America, revealed growing antisemitism and little promise for any large refugee settlements. Returning home in early June, McDonald discussed with *New York Times* publisher Arthur

Hays Sulzberger the possibility of becoming a foreign affairs columnist and that newspaper's spokesman, then met with Rosenberg the following day to talk about his resignation.[19]

By then, Rosenberg and some AJC associates had considered presenting a legal brief to the League of Nations on the German situation as it affected Jews. The idea had been suggested by a Catholic initiative to have the World Court intervene in the dispute between Mexico and the Catholic Church, with two Catholic countries pursuing this at Geneva on the ground that the issue endangered the good relations between Mexico and other nations, and therefore violated Article XII of the Covenant. Very difficult questions of international law, as well as political aspects of the proposal, suggested that active opposition could be expected from the Secretariat and many of the major countries. Roosevelt had hailed the World Court as "the movement to make international justice practicable and serviceable." He could hardly be expected to lend support, however, having just suffered a striking defeat when isolationist sentiment prevented the securing of a majority vote in the Senate to have the United States join that body. Nonetheless, Rosenberg and Judge Julian M. Mack, a Zionist member of the AJC, thought that an intensive, far-reaching study of the whole subject could be undertaken.[20]

The issue also demanded a thorough investigation of minorities and minority rights, as Mack and AJC President Adler readily understood. Having both advocated rights for Jews and other minorities at the Versailles Peace Conference, the two men now formulated a letter to Geneva inquiring whether the League had such records, and if related documents would be open to private research with a view to possible publication. Mack and Professor Morris R. Cohen of City College's Department of Philosophy, who had also been the founding president of the Conference on Jewish Relations, recommended Oscar I. Janowsky to undertake the work. The thirty-five-year-old City College Assistant Professor had published a book on the Jews and minority rights from 1898 to 1919, based upon his doctoral thesis in History at Columbia University. Adler advised Rosenberg against this particular choice, however, claiming that Janowsky "could only deal with it at arm's length and did not seem to me to be an objective person." Instead, he suggested that either the League, someone connected to it in Geneva, or Feinberg of the Comité undertake the task.[21]

Janowsky's study, the first on a Jewish subject that had been approved by Professor Salo W. Baron, had roiled some waters. Adler was a non-Zionist who, like his fellow AJC mandarins, viewed Jews exclusively as a religious community. He disagreed sharply with Janowsky's use of the term "national rights" (as the East European and some "Western" Jews had advocated at the time) for the group rights incorporated in the post-World War I minority treaties. Accordingly, he refused the PhD candidate access to his diaries of that period, but the AJC's Waldman and Baron, the first Jew to be installed in Columbia's History department, persuaded Adler to relent; the lengthy manuscript was completed in 1932. Yet Professor Carlton Hayes, highly critical of Zionism and (according to the History chairman at City College) wanting to have Baron "remember who was master" in the History department at Columbia, withheld his approval of the degree for a year. Having intimate knowledge of the subject as the first elected chairman of the Comité des Delegations Juives at the Peace Conference, Mack fully endorsed the Zionist Janowsky's interpretation regarding "national rights." In a preface to the book, which was published in April 1933 by Columbia University Press, Mack hailed the "profound study" and its "acute interpretation" of the individuals involved, and expressed the hope that Janowsky would soon write the story of how and to what extent the Minority Treaties had been enforced since.[22]

The promise of a grant-in-aid through the agency of Professor Cohen and the Conference on Jewish Relations, an idea which initiated with Justice Brandeis, enabled Janowsky to consider pursuing this study abroad. Although a firm anti-Zionist, Cohen appreciated Janowsky's book and would invite him to join the editorial board of the Conference's *Jewish Social Studies* journal. Cohen, Mack, Bernard Flexner, and Lucius Littauer finally agreed in January 1935 to raise $2,500 for the study, so that Janowsky could spend the following year in Europe, with his wife and children to live in Palestine. On March 17, Janowsky presented a lecture on "The Problem of Minorities: Meaning and Significance" to the Conference, which published his paper the next month in its newsletter along with Harvard University Law Professor Felix Frankfurter's endorsement that "no one has given more thoughtful consideration to these problems than Dr. Janowsky." He obtained a *New York Post* press card and valuable letters of introduction, even one from US Secretary of State Cordell Hull thanks to school chum Simon H. Rifkind (legislative secretary to New York Senator Robert F. Wagner). Four months passed by, however, without any further word from Cohen, and as late as May 20 Janowsky wrote to Frankfurter regarding "a certain indefiniteness about the grant-in-aid." By June, he and wife Pauline decided to go abroad nonetheless, using their meager savings and, if necessary, taking a bank loan.[23]

In the meantime, Rosenberg had emphasized to Adler in early March the need to avoid any possible conflict among Jewish organizations in the appointing of a legal committee to explore the World Court and minority rights as far as Jews were concerned. He also thought that "a grand piece of work" by hired researchers, following the committee's guidelines, could be produced in about six months. Their findings would indicate what, if anything, could be done in the interest of "religious freedom and of non-discrimination, either for racial or religious grounds." The inquiry, he proposed, should deal not only with minority rights under treaties, but with all questions of international law under covenant, League of Nations or otherwise, which might be pertinent to the subject. Adler advised, in turn, that the proposed legal committee should consist of experts, not appointments made on a "Jewish political basis." A week to ten days' study, he concluded, should be given to decide on this important matter.[24]

Mack moved ahead on his own, advising Janowsky on May 9 to get in touch with Rosenberg, an "important member" of the AJC Executive, "in connection with work on the Minorities problem," Rosenberg offered to engage the young historian at $1,500 for several months on an analysis of international protection and diplomatic intervention on behalf of human and religious rights, the work to be done in Geneva and London for and under McDonald's direction. When Janowsky indicated that he would not like to delay his Conference study of the minorities problem, Rosenberg revealed in confidence that the project was actually to provide the evidence for a strong statement by McDonald to the League Council relating to the plight of the German Jews. That would be reason enough for him to postpone the minorities study briefly if Cohen agreed, Janowsky rejoined, but he could not accept an assignment from the AJC because Adler would seek to control his research. Janowsky suggested, instead, that the funds be paid to him through the Conference, an idea which gained the immediate approval of Mack and of an unaware but delighted Cohen. Janowsky also met with Melvin M. Fagen, whom Rosenberg indicated would conduct a similar study of the international law aspects of the project, and the two men took to each other immediately.[25]

For over a year, Fagen had been a member of the AJC staff, focusing as an assistant to Waldman and Harry Schneiderman on immigration issues, international relations, and legal questions. He had been awarded a BA and an MA at the University of Wisconsin in four years by pursuing independent studies as an honor student, and his master's thesis had dealt with "The Status of the Individual in International Law." A University Traveling Fellowship in International Law following graduation enabled him to spend 1933-1934 at the University of Paris's Faculté de Droit researching the political and legal aspects of "the Jewish question." Prior to returning home, he also helped the Comité with some translations and related matters before Motzkin's death in early November 1933. While then devoting nights to studies at Fordham

University Law School, Fagen served as secretary for the AJC Lawyer's Advisory Committee and the Joint Council on International Aspects of the German Situation chaired by Kohler, and represented the AJC at the Joint Conference on International Legislation. He also prepared memoranda on the occupational distribution of urban Jews in Hungary, Rumania, and Poland; Poland's current stance toward minorities; Congressional bills relating to immigration; a proposal to register all inhabitants of the United States; and Washington's obligation in 1935 to speak out against Nazi antisemitic persecution at a time when "religious freedom, human equality, and civilized progress are at stake."[26]

Following an AJC Executive Committee decision to consider Fagen for legal research connected to a McDonald resignation statement, Rosenberg summoned him to an interview on May 20. Laying aside Fagen's outline of the study to be undertaken on the minorities' question, he immediately began querying the twenty-three-year-old about his education and international law training and his knowledge of minority issues. In Fagen's view, legal grounds existed for the League to seek an Advisory Opinion from the World Court as to possible German violation of international law and/or treaty in the Reich's treatment of Jews, Catholics, or Protestants, but Germany would insist that this was a domestic matter and no state wished to offend Germany at present. The most desirable way of bringing the question before the League, Fagen opined, was to have McDonald or Cecil—"a neutral international official"—file with the League a brief, memorial, or petition covering Germany's contemplated denationalization of her Jewish citizens; the plight of current refugees from Germany; and antisemitic legislation that would drive more German Jews to leave, thereby presenting an increasingly serious international problem. Most experts, he added, had decided that certain German pledges and written memoranda not incorporated in treaties possessed no legal force. As to any cooperative effort with Protestant and Catholic groups, which Rosenberg sought, this should be done privately and unofficially, Fagen concluded.[27]

A first meeting of Janowsky and Fagen with McDonald in mid-June went well. McDonald knew from Rosenberg that Adler's personal objections to Janowsky's appointment remained a "troublesome point," but got the impression after chatting with the AJC president that he would not object seriously to Janowsky's "cooperation in the work JNR [Rosenberg] had so much at heart." On the 17th, Fagen submitted a twenty-page memorandum regarding recourse to the League and the World Court on behalf of Germany's Jews.[28]

Over luncheon at the Lawyer's Club in New York City three days later, the paper, which Rosenberg warmly praised, drew Chamberlain to note certain practical difficulties in the way of an Advisory Opinion. McDonald appeared to welcome the prospect of drawing up a detailed report for the League, pointing out Germany's responsibility for the failure to arrive at a solution of the refugee issue. When McDonald informed the group that he planned to resign his position the following January, it was suggested that he make this "his last will and testament," explaining and describing his efforts, and pointing to the Nazi regime's "Aryan" decrees and other specific causes for the refugee problem.

Rosenberg suggested that the report be drafted in the spirit of "a state document of high order," its effect wider than the immediate present. At best, the report could have only a moral or educational impact, he asserted, but hopefully it would stand as "a permanent record of the struggle for humanity and justice." All agreed that a thorough investigation of minority questions, principles, and precedents should be undertaken. Rosenberg observed that Janowsky was being sent to Europe by the Conference with Rosenberg's own financial support on the stipulation that he owe his primary obligation to McDonald for research, thereby allowing Janowsky to remain a full year in Europe. Assuming that Rosenberg could secure the AJC's permission, Fagen would serve as the legal specialist for this preparatory task. At the end, the group was in general agreement that Janowsky and Fagen would work under McDonald's direction along lines that he would indicate, and that prior to his using the result of their labors, they were not to publish it in any form without his approval. The High Commissioner still reserved judgment on the major question of issuing the ultimate statement, which would be preceded by the findings of the two researchers.[29]

The following day, at a luncheon with McDonald and Rosenberg, Warburg was not as enthusiastic as Rosenberg about the proposed declaration, but felt that it should be done. Informing Waldman that McDonald would be aided by Bentwich, Herbert May, and some British legal scholars regarding the statement of resignation, Rosenberg obtained the AJC's approval for utilizing Fagen's expertise as the Committee's representative. Not long thereafter, Sulzberger made McDonald a definite offer along with the request that he not come to the *New York Times* directly from the High Commission nor announce this prospective connection before resigning. Consenting to the latter, McDonald promised to let the publisher know his decision before the end of the summer.[30] He then boarded the *Ile de France* bound for Europe, where the last six months of his service as High Commissioner awaited.

II

Reviewing his activity to date on behalf of refugees, McDonald recommended at the Governing Body's public meeting on July 17, 1935, that the League assume direct responsibility for the pressing issue, and his office be terminated so that the refugees might be served more effectively. Cecil had privately agreed with this plan, but advised that liquidation by the year's end might have to be considered anew if the Assembly failed to take any action. Nevertheless, he felt, as did McDonald, that it would be better to have any work that was to be carried on placed in the hands of existing organizations. He also approved in principle the idea of McDonald's final statement and of utilizing the research by Janowsky and Fagen for this purpose. McDonald went on to announce the formation of the US Refugee Economic Corporation, and hailed Palestine as "the chief country of refuge" for having absorbed 27,000 out of the estimated 80,500 German Jewish refugees. Two-thirds of the Commission's work was done, in his view. The plight of the 15,000 still to be placed and others to follow would "soon become desperate," he concluded, if the present tendency to deny to unsettled refugees opportunities to work were not reversed.[31]

One week later, McDonald sent a long communication, to which Cecil did not object, to Eleanor Roosevelt. Harboring a deep "sense of impending doom" about Nazi intentions, he forecast a program to force Jews out of Germany gradually by creating conditions that would make life "unbearable," as well as the party's determination to establish a State church that would assume priority over loyalty to any of the country's established religions. With this "extreme form of statism" bound to have repercussions far beyond the German frontier, McDonald questioned if the time had not come, in harmony with other precedents in American history, for Washington to take the initiative in protesting against the "prevailing violations of elementary and religious rights in Germany." The First Lady informed him on August 1 that she was sending the document at once to the president. She did so, adding the handwritten notation "important." There is no indication that Roosevelt replied to McDonald's letter, which came to final rest in the chief executive's Official Files. A similar request concurrently from the AJC, American Jewish Congress, B'nai Brith, and the Jewish Labor Committee elicited Undersecretary of State William Phillips's bland reply that "the American people are always sympathetic" to the maintenance of "the concepts of religious freedom and liberty of conscience for all" in the United States "as well as in other nations."[32]

Nor did McDonald score any breakthroughs in the next two months. London was not prepared to ask that his final report to Avenol be made a Council document, although the Norwegians proposed in the Sixth Committee that the League create a new organization to take over the work of the Nansen Office, the High Commission, Assyrian refugees, anti-Nazis, and Jews from the Saar region. After hearing opposition to this step from various representatives and a bitter attack on McDonald and his activities from France's Bérenger, the Sixth Committee eventually rejected a coordination of all refugee work under the League, suggested that an Experts Committee investigate with help of a limited budget, and refused to accord the status of refugees to the "stateless people." More ominously, McDonald observed to Cecil, the shadow of an impending armed conflict in light of Italian ambitions against Abyssinia (Ethiopia) and particularly the growing conviction that Europe was "steadily marching towards a world war" stymied humanitarian efforts. Moscow firmly opposed any cooperation with an organization like the Nansen Office which included aid to anti-Bolshevik White Russian émigrés, while Germany's Nuremberg Laws of September 15, 1935, he warned Rosenberg, were only the "basis for the development of a wide range of anti-Jewish attacks."[33]

Writing to Warburg on September 9, McDonald provided a rough outline of his plans. He expected to be in Geneva during the period of the Assembly in October and perhaps for a few weeks afterwards to press forward the reorganization program, and to work on the resignation statement. Hoping that the latter, or at least his part of it, might be finished by then, he wished to go off with his wife Pauline to Palestine for a few weeks in November and December. A probable meeting of the Governing Body and the Advisory Council about the second week of December would call for his presence in London, allowing a departure on December 15 for New York, "to stay." Changing circumstances might seem to make it desirable for him to change his mind, but a number of factors had led to arriving at this conclusion. The letter closed with McDonald's certainty that Warburg would believe he had "not lightly" made up his mind to take this course.[34]

Janowsky and Fagen had lost little time after their conclusive meeting with McDonald on June 20 in preparing a detailed outline of the intended research. By July 8 Fagen could write Waldman that their report—"to be as scholarly as it must be forceful"—intended to direct the attention of governments to the plight of the refugees; to draw up a definitive record of the High Commissioner's work; and ("from our point of view, primarily") to place on record in a public international document "a strong indictment of Nazi Germany which will lay the foundation for some sort of diplomatic or judicial action in the future." It should put forward at least the possibility of a subsequent request for an Advisory Opinion from the World Court, persuade public opinion in civilized countries of the juridical and moral principles being violated daily by the Nazi government, and warn states like Austria, Poland, and Rumania against following Germany's example. Five chapters plus appendices were envisaged, demonstrating as well that the persecution of minorities has been considered "a matter of international concern under the law of nations, justifying the collective interest and intercession of the Powers." Fagen also prepared a brief, if an appeal were made to the Court, to proceed by means of a petition addressed to the Council under the regular minorities' procedure, and hoped to obtain the opinion of certain experts abroad as to the plan's advisability.[35]

To that end, prior to departing in mid-August for London and Paris, where he would collect documentation and then arrive in Geneva at the month's end, Fagen sent Laski his memorandum of June 17 for review. Laski shared it with Lauterpacht, the JFC's major legalist, who thought that requesting an Advisory Opinion would likely bring a negative ruling, and in addition probably be prejudicial to the Jewish cause inasmuch as it would "reduce an issue of obvious general significance to a small and highly debatable point." From the political point of view, Lauterpacht deemed this approach "inadequate, impracticable and highly dangerous" at present. A small possibility, he added, did exist for McDonald, "in a report of studied solemnity," to ask the Council to address once more an appeal to Berlin on the basis of the principles that had been unanimously, but for Germany's abstention, reaffirmed by the Assembly in October 1933 on behalf of minority rights. Informed of Lauterpacht's evaluation by Bentwich, who agreed with these views, Fagen replied that he, too, had dismissed Rosenberg's idea of an Advisory Opinion. He also pointed out that it might be of value to mention in McDonald's report the German pledges at the 1919 Peace Conference as regards minorities and to indirectly intimate the possibility of an appeal to the World Court.[36]

Bentwich transmitted as well McDonald's suggestion that Fagen travel directly to Geneva. There he could consult at the end of August with Bentwich before McDonald arrived. The Englishman advised, in addition, that Fagen and Janowsky summarize the League's past assertion of the right of equal citizenship (not minority rights) without distinction of religion or race, and discuss the possibility of an Advisory Opinion regarding Berlin's right to denationalize a large number of her subjects, whether or not resident in Germany. Fagen agreed to go to Geneva straight away, realizing together with Janowsky that "our project would not be quite so successful" without the benefit of Bentwich's knowledge and suggestions. Accepting Bentwich's point about the right of equal citizenship, he observed that the two researchers might also point to the recommendation in 1930 by the Hague conference on nationality that the League continue its work for the purpose of "arriving at an international settlement of this important matter." Fagen would set sail aboard the *SS Berengaria* on August 16.[37]

Janowsky's final travel arrangements did not go smoothly, however. He had meant to depart with his family for Palestine on July 13, arrive in Geneva in the latter part of August to work with Fagen, then proceed in January 1936 to Poland and embark on his study of the East-Central European "national minorities." Suddenly, on July 9 Rosenberg the advised Janowsky that the AJC would provide him directly $1,500 (which Rosenberg could not raise) for working on the McDonald statement, these funds being impossible for the AJC to pay via the Conference. Janowsky retorted that if Rosenberg repudiated their original agreement, he would revert to the initial plan of spending six months abroad under the Conference's sponsorship in order to study the minority rights question; he would be glad to aid the McDonald report at no charge with advice and assistance, which would not take up too much of his time. Prepared to drop entirely "this unpleasant project" but concerned that the Conference would then be mistakenly discredited, Janowsky reported back to Cohen. Cohen was ready to accept the terms, declaring that the projected minority rights study was more important than an affront to him, but Janowsky suggested that Rosenberg be told that the History assistant professor was resigning from the McDonald research team. Ultimately, Rosenberg honored the original understanding, the AJC and the Conference becoming co-sponsors of the private help rendered to the High Commissioner, and Janowsky departed on schedule.[38]

Janowsky and Fagen worked well together once they settled down in Geneva, but some personal apprehensions lingered about the task at hand. While their points of view meshed and each supplemented the other's knowledge, the two had reason to suspect that the established Anglo-Jewish leaders, along with their legal experts, might well resent the American initiative regarding McDonald's Letter of Resignation and treat the young men as interlopers. The cooperation of Bentwich, their only contact with the English in the first stage, was therefore essential. Yet McDonald's deputy had already asserted to Fagen in May that he considered the American project ill-advised, thinking that the Powers should not be bothered now with such "relatively small matters." Rather, energies ought to be concentrated "upon diplomatic efforts which would have a more far-reaching effect." Once he reiterated this viewpoint to Janowsky and Fagen on September 7, they resolved to adhere to the plan that Fagen had conveyed to Waldman two months earlier.[39]

The following day, after the researchers had a first discussion with McDonald, Janowsky wrote to Cohen that the no longer hesitant High Commissioner "seemed pleased" with the outline and exhibited "almost enthusiastic interest" in the proposed Letter. On September 14, Janowsky's diary read that McDonald, "cynical" about diplomats, was "anxious to resign" and "will be glad to attack Germany in a vigorous but reasoned statement." Having received his approval, and knowing that they had only about two months to accomplish their objective, they pursued the plan of research "with single-minded intensity." Janowsky focused on the historical and Fagen on the legal, but they discussed every point and shared every conclusion. The work went forward at an exhausting pace, augmented by depression at the "Aryan" decrees, meetings with Jewish refugees, and the "often downright" indifference of academics to the Nazi antisemitic persecution.[40]

By October, Janowsky and Fagen could provide an encouraging progress report to Rosenberg, who had continued to urge McDonald not to permit any consideration to deter him from carrying the final statement through. Parts I and II of their memorandum would analyze Berlin's policies and their effects, with Part III contending that the antisemitic legislation had become a subject for international concern. Citation of historical precedents would illustrate that the denial of human rights had long claimed the attention of Europe and America, while the League's activities in this regard and the position taken by enlightened public opinion, including the liberal pre-Nazi government, would receive their due. The conclusion would analyze the obligations, both legal and moral, of the Hitler regime, and the fact that persistent persecution could only result in a continued stream of refugees, which would mandate international action if this problem were ever to be solved. By means of "restrained language," they hoped to produce the effect of "a vigorous condemnation" of German policies. They also proposed to write a series of appendices or annexes, citing evidence for the points made. Finally, the writers hoped that besides submitting the memorandum to the League, McDonald would incorporate its substance in an address before some public forum. "We have found Mr. McDonald entirely sympathetic with our general plan," their letter ended, "and are much encouraged in our work."[41]

Fagen described his own labors over the past month in an extended communication to Waldman on October 3. As the time for McDonald's resignation drew closer, he began, it seemed that "what was originally a project introduced from the outside has become very much a part of him, that is, a way of finishing a rather messily done job in a final flash of glory." Attached to McDonald's Letter of less than 3,000 words to the Council would be a series of annexes or "explanatory chapters" sustaining and documenting the points that he had made, all bound together in the form of a book. At the appropriate time, the volume would be sent to newspapers and publications worldwide.

The ultimate document, as a result, might be made to "re-awaken concern" both among governments and literate public opinion as to the disaster which had overtaken Germany's Jewish population. Fagen sought to emphasize wherever possible the legal aspects of the German policies in the light of international law, wanting to show the Council and the Assembly that they were within their rights when concerning themselves with the situation in Germany. At the same time, he doubted that the League's possibly bringing the High Commission directly within its aegis would make it easier to find territories for Jewish settlement, especially as Secretariat officials would do nothing which might tend to "disturb the Reich."[42]

A frustrated McDonald spent the month lobbying for the League to assume responsibility for the refugees, emphasizing to Warburg that after the Nuremberg Laws "the need for immediate action is overwhelming." A "delayed or half-hearted solution of this problem by the League would be worse than nothing at all," he broadcast to the United States. At the Advisory Council meeting on October 15, McDonald sought to have Bentwich named as acting High Commissioner for the interim period, but some Jewish Colonization Association leaders backed their French government in advocating the complete dissolution of the Commission by the arrival of the next New Year. They treated him, wrote a JDC official, "like a small office boy whose services are no longer needed and who should be dismissed on the spot." London hesitated to make informal representations to the Reich authorities regarding antisemitic legislation, one Whitehall official privately noting that "Britain could be asked to take the Jews." Despite his own promises to do so, Roosevelt still had not given a speech protesting Germany's assault on her Jews. The major problem remained, McDonald urged Warburg: expediting the migration of some 20,000 younger Jews every year over the next decade, for "there can be no future for Jews in Germany." "I know what a very trying enterprise you are engaged in," Chamberlain wrote McDonald in an attempt at consolation, "and how little chance there is for any really happy thought in regard to it."[43]

The young researchers "plugged on," so that the end of their report was in sight towards the fourth week of October. Janowsky had completed his chapter on the "Aryan" decrees, and was working on "Precedents for International Action to Safeguard Human Rights," using the source materials as underpinning for a theme: "the studied effort to oust the Jews or destroy them" in the case of the racist legislation, and the growth and development of international concern and intervention in the case of the "Precedents." Fagen focused on the violations of the rights of other states and on promises and commitments made by former German governments. "I believe that this document will be stronger than we had expected even [*sic*]," he wrote to Waldman, hoping that "you will feel that the investment was worth while," On October 20, McDonald called the pair to come "as soon as we choose." His committee of review had evidently been selected. Janowsky and Fagen left Geneva on October 25, tarried in Paris for several days, and arrived in London on November 2, 1935.[44]

Two days later, they tentatively agreed with McDonald to complete the dictation of their first draft by the next week. This would be submitted to Lauterpacht, Laski, May, and London barristers Lionel Cohen (Board of Deputies vice president) and Vladimir R. Idelson, as well as McDonald's staff. While the High Commissioner emphasized at the time the possibility of centering his statement on Article II of the League Covenant, the researchers indicated that they were able to prove that the effect, if not the purpose, of the "Aryan" legislation was "to destroy the Jewish people in Germany," and that they had found some significant new material on non-Jewish aspects of the problem. The pair immediately set a frantic pace to get the book of some 200 typewritten pages into shape, Janowsky writing a conclusion of some 7,000–8,000 words in fifteen hours at a stretch. On the 15th, McDonald sent the first draft to Lauterpacht, noting that it would accompany as an annex the formal Letter of Resignation, the whole matter "in the strictest sense of the word confidential."[45]

Bentwich's sudden suggestion that McDonald's Letter state that two scholars had prepared the memorandum raised a fundamental problem immediately. As Fagen wrote to Waldman, the whole purpose of the report would be negated unless the argument in the memorandum was presented as an integral part of the High Commissioner's plea. Otherwise, the report would be viewed as "merely an academic investigation," which the League would regard as "irrelevant." Janowsky and Fagen's work had established that the League could not solve the problem of the actual refugees outside of Germany without considering the causes for the difficulty: "that within Germany there exists a reservoir of potential refugees whose ultimate emigration is only a matter of time—if the program of the German government is allowed to continue," The original purpose for their research had to be carried out, Fagen urged, particularly as this "may be our last chance of getting the German affair aired before the League." Laski supported the Americans, although McDonald later wished to say that a committee of Catholic, Protestant, and Jewish experts had drafted the memorandum. Janowsky and Fagen opposed this, too, arguing that everyone knew that an executive has his reports drawn for him by experts. Eventually, they appeared to have won this "skirmish."[46]

A "full dress" conference was held on November 18, McDonald first explaining the nature of his proposed Letter, followed by a discussion that began with "general principles." Lauterpacht, who stayed for only a half hour, made what McDonald' diary records as "the far-reaching and, I thought, unacceptable suggestion" that the memorandum should be considered as "raw material," and then the various parts be assigned to individuals for revision before being brought back to a drafting committee. Rebuffed when this and his follow-up suggestion to eliminate most of the legal argument found no support, Lauterpacht said impatiently (so reads Janowsky's diary): "Then send legal section for extended revision to an international lawyer and historical section to an historian." Idelson's view that leaving the legal sections as they were would open the group to the charge of indicting the Reich was not accepted. The material was then reviewed chapter by chapter, and at the end the attendees agreed to have additional conferences on details and another one on final form.[47]

As soon as Janowsky and Fagen completed the final revision of the last chapters, they read them to McDonald and Laski. At this time, on November 21, Laski praised the draft very highly. When the High Commissioner commented that Idelson had previously called the precedents cited by Janowsky a record of failures, Laski replied forthrightly: "No, this is not a record of failures, but proof of a continuous and persistent growth of international responsibility for the maintenance of human rights." Having personal memories of the violent Białystok pogrom of June 1906, Janowsky had already had a bit of a run-in with Idelson, whose pleasant recollections of Czarist Russia would not permit him to appreciate the American's inclusion of official US protests against the Romanov rulers' antisemitic policies among the desirable precedents for international intercession on behalf of human rights. Now, Janowsky and Fagen pointed out the additional fact that the chapter made evident an increase in the effectiveness of such action.[48]

The memorandum at this point was divided into two distinct parts, the first four chapters consisting of the "Aryan" decrees and other discriminatory Reich policies (Part I) and the remaining three chapters designated as Part II. The latter, more than half the total, included Fagen's long chapter on the legal case against Germany and two of Janowsky's chapters: "Precedents for International Action to Safeguard Human Rights" and a conclusion, "The Task of the League of Nations." Fagen's legal chapter had already been submitted to distinguished international law Professors James L. Brierly and Arnold D. McNair of Oxford and Cambridge Universities, respectively, whose critical comments were taken into account for the revised draft.[49]

On November 24, the opposition of the Anglo-Jewish establishment became manifest. To the amazement of Janowsky and Fagen, Lauterpacht opened the meeting of the entire group at Laski's office that Sunday morning with a proposal to eliminate all of Part II. Although this constituted their significant and innovative contribution, it was claimed that the memorandum would be stronger without Part II. The main issue was the legal argument made by Fagen, although the British members had not yet read the revised version of Fagen's chapter, and Professors Brierly and McNair did not suggest scraping this effort. Janowsky's two chapters were treated even more cavalierly, never having been discussed earlier in open conference. Laski and Idelson agreed fully with Lauterpacht, and a vote was called for.

McDonald's diary noted briefly that the long discussion which ensued became "a little ardent" at times, and that "J and F refused to yield." Indeed, they put up quite a fight. They read the letters from Brierly and McNair, and argued that the legal case was meant not for a court of law but for the League and public opinion. Furthermore, the "Precedents" gave justification for international concern; it was imperative to show the League's past action, and to describe how that organization was empowered to act again. Janowsky and Fagen maintained, moreover, that if only Part I were submitted to the Council as McDonald's memorandum, the charge would immediately be made that German internal sovereignty precluded the concern of the League, or even of the High Commissioner. It was therefore necessary to prove that League involvement would not constitute an innovation, thereby lending powerful support to McDonald's plea for its intercession on behalf of the refugees.

One of the Britishers rejoined, no doubt to mollify Janowsky and Fagen, that the gist of the "Precedents" of Part II in general would be included in the Letter of Resignation itself, and that they were merely reducing the size of the memorandum. "Why?" Janowsky countered. "Had they been directed to save a few shillings in printing costs?" The essence of Part II would necessarily be brief and generalized in McDonald's Letter, he noted, and their memorandum would be an annex, adducing the documentary evidence to substantiate the claims of the Letter's text. "Did they wish," his soft voice queried in a mix of passion and irony, "to eliminate pertinent evidence?" While Lauterpacht fidgeted with impatience, Janowsky concluded: "Why the haste in calling for a vote on the elimination of the 'Precedents' when the matter has not even been discussed? Why steamroller tactics?" Lauterpacht could not tolerate the defiant last phrase, also used by Fagen when challenging the rejection of his legal arguments, and the Britisher exploded with the observation that when dealing with international law and history, the group should get an international lawyer and an historian. Janowsky retorted immediately: "You have an historian, Professor Lauterpacht. The historical chapters were written by an historian." There was shocked silence, and then something of a hubbub, everyone murmuring at the same time. The mood of the attendees seemed to be that Lauterpacht had gone too far, provoked into a rude affront. That same day, he wrote the two men what Janowsky termed a "left-handed apology," to which Janowsky replied with the assurance that his letter was accepted "in the same generous spirit in which it was written."[50]

Lauterpacht then moved on to Part I, proposing that Dr. Ernst Cohn be asked, so McDonald's diary records, "to check references and first part generally." The entry adds: "This J and F gladly agreed to." Lauterpacht telephoned Cohn, who read the entire memorandum without delay. The former University of Breslau law professor, now a German exile, saw Janowsky and Fagen the following day, offering valuable criticisms of Part I while praising their overall effort enthusiastically. In a letter to Laski, Cohen particularly recommended that the "Precedents" not be eliminated. In addition, he queried: "Is it not sometimes politically advisable to present even a case which is legally weak if by that the opponent can be forced to resort to technical arguments which are always bad in view of public opinion?" When Janowsky pointed this out to Bentwich four days later, McDonald's deputy questioned Cohn's authority in international law. Janowsky responded that such authority ended with the decision that the legal argument was debatable. Thereafter, it was a question of submitting a debatable argument, "and on that we are all experts."[51]

By that time, however, Janowsky realized that the British and the Americans were "shadow boxing." The fate of the "Precedents" and of Part II as a whole had been decided by Lauterpacht and Bentwich, the British "experts", during the week preceding the crucial November 24th meeting. A vote, which Lauterpacht pressed for that day, was never taken in the Americans' presence. After the lengthy meeting, McDonald's diary reads that he and Wurfbain were "inclined to the view that the second part had better not be used." He also consulted that afternoon by telephone with Brierly and McNair, who agreed to eliminate that whole section. Cohn's letter to Laski also showed that the High Commissioner let him understand that Part II "should be left out entirely." And in a telegram on November 25, "anxiously" seeking Rosenberg's views, McDonald expressed his own predilection to summarize the argumentation of Part II as part of his Letter of Resignation "APPEALING WORLD OPINION AND ASKING LEAGUE ACTION ON GROUNDS GERMAN POLICIES THREATEN DESTRUCTION JEWS AND NON ARYANS OR IMPOSITION INTOLERABLE BURDEN OTHER COUNTRIES."[52]

That same day, Janowsky and Fagen spelled out to Rosenberg at length that the decision against them had been taken before the heated November 24 encounter "for reasons extraneous to the main issue involved." In their view, McDonald wanted a weak memorandum; the "timid" British experts and leaders felt that "the Powers should not be disturbed"; Bentwich and Lauterpacht probably felt slighted at the Americans' intrusion; Idelson did not favor an analogy between Czarist Russia and Nazi Germany; and Laski's JFC co-chairman, President Leonard Montefiore of the Anglo-Jewish Association, appeared to have been "sniping behind the scenes." With many liberal-minded non-Jews coming to accept the German situation as normal, the issue had to be raised again. The memorandum, conceived and drafted as a powerful indictment of racial and religious persecution in Germany or elsewhere, would constitute an urgent appeal to the League and public opinion for action. Having first proposed the project, Rosenberg alone could save the memorandum, they concluded.[53]

Rosenberg rose to the challenge, expressing the hope to McDonald on the 26th that "ABLE AND WEIGHTY RESUME PRECEDENT . . . A GRAND PIECE OF WORK WOULD BE INCLUDED," and getting Warburg to send a "gentle" cable to the High Commissioner in like vein. U.S. Supreme Court Justice Benjamin N. Cardozo asserted that the case established in the "Precedents" was "triumphantly complete," and that "indifference and timidity" would hold back the nations of the world if they were "silent after this noble call to duty." Janowsky drafted a long letter which Fagen co-signed on the 29th, the same day that Part I was approved by all concerned, pointing out to McDonald that Part II was "indispensable" if his resignation statement were not to be considered interfering with German internal affairs. No real criticism had been made of the "Precedents" and the conclusion, he observed, while the legal chapter had been revised in accordance with suggestions made by Brierly, McNair, and Bentwich. In fact, the intercession from Rosenberg and Warburg weakened McDonald to such an extent that he professed to have been greatly impressed with the Janowsky-Fagen letter, and wrote to the London office from Geneva: "in view of the possibility, but not now the probability, of eliminating Part II.[54]

For the Americans, a rare moment was at hand. With McDonald being advised by his friends and the leaders of English Jewry "not to cause too much of a stir," Fagen cautioned Waldman that unless advantage were taken of McDonald's imminent resignation, a great chance would have been lost. This represented the last stand, he felt, before Germany would be accepted "as a sister-state, as a normal government by the Powers."; Fully in agreement, Rosenberg tried to strengthen the researchers' hand with a telegram urging that unless McDonald "SQUARELY PRESENTS THE POINTS OF INTERNATIONAL LAW THIS WHOLE EFFORT WILL END IN A LAWYERS BRIEF TO WHICH NO ONE WILL PAY

THE LEAST ATTENTION." "WE HERE DEEPLY CONCERNED," he concluded as he alerted Laski on December 3, "THAT NEITHER WE NOR HE SHALL MISS WHAT IS NOW HIS GREAT OPPORTUNITY." Another cable advocated "THE STRONGEST POSSIBLE PETITION, WITHOUT PUSSYFOOTING."[55]

The denouement came on December 8, just after McDonald went over the Letter of Resignation with Bentwich. A few days earlier, Bentwich had vaguely warned the American researchers that it might be unwise to antagonize the Nazis in light of current negotiations regarding a loan to finance the settlement of 40,000 German Jews. McDonald's deputy, whom Janowsky considered the center of the opposition, now proposed once again that the last chapters be eliminated. McDonald tried to place the burden upon Janowsky and Fagen, saying that since they would not agree to a "mutilation" of their chapters, he could not incorporate Part II. Janowsky immediately countered that changes had been made, but sections could not be eliminated when the objective sought was not known. He did prevail on the High Commissioner to have Part II printed and to ask US experts for their opinion when he would arrive in New York. McDonald's Letter of Resignation, rewritten by Lauterpacht and Bentwich as their contribution to the text, incorporated "scraps" from the three chapters that had been cut. Consequently, Janowsky wrote to Rosenberg, the Letter "is too long for a concise and moving statement, and not long enough without the supporting evidence which Fagen and I have prepared."[56]

McDonald's diary states that Janowsky and Fagen took the decision not to use Part II "with good grace," but their experience greatly disillusioned both Americans. After four months of arduous labor and sharp opposition from the Anglo-Jewish establishment, Fagen privately decried the "rather petty methods employed, which leave a rather bitter taste." Janowsky reminded Rosenberg on December 11 that "what passes for Jewish scholarship among the existing Jewish organizations is really Jewish politics." He made an effort "to salvage what I could from this wreck" by obtaining McDonald' agreement to honor their original oral understanding that eliminated chapters would remain Janowsky's property and be turned over to the Conference. In a last private talk with McDonald on December 14, he minced no words in criticizing Lauterpacht's "arrogance" and Bentwich's "burrowing ways," especially their efforts to discard the materials prepared by the two researchers and then to use these ideas as their own. He rejected the possibility raised by McDonald of contributing to political action based on the Letter, observing that the historian's job was done and he was leaving in January for Eastern Europe in order to study minorities. If the Council would take note of the Letter and distribute it among the member states as a League document, Janowsky ended the *téte-a-téte*, this would be an achievement.[57]

Just before leaving for the United States the next day, McDonald informed Janowsky that he was sorry about Part II. Janowsky told him to forget about the matter, and declared that the High Commissioner's Letter was an act of "great courage and humanity." The editor of the London *Times* and the *New York Times*'s Berlin chief were enthusiastic when McDonald confidentially shared the final Letter and Annex (Part I) with them, but he was concerned how the American Jewish leaders who were involved would react to the excision of the three chapters. Indeed, Waldman had wired Fagen, departing along with McDonald aboard the *SS Manhattan* from Southampton, that the AJC and Rosenberg were in close contact: "REGARDING YOUR JANOWSKY SPLENDID REPORT WE SHARE YOUR VIEWS HOPE MACDONALD [*sic*] AGREES AFTER CONFERENCE HERE IMPORTANT MEN." Laski had also been lavish in praise of the two young men, adding to Rosenberg that McDonald, "a mind which had already come to an unalterable conclusion," did not consult him regarding the ultimate result.[58]

A long telephone conversation with McDonald on December 23 pretty well convinced Rosenberg that the High Commissioner's mind "is finally made up." Writing to Janowsky, he expressed a "deep sense of disappointment" that the plans and proposals of the two researchers were not accepted, and concluded that he was "very much in sympathy" with Janowsky's bitter communication of December 11. Waldman made one last attempt, suggesting that Rosenberg say the following frankly to McDonald: His lack of success, combined with his proposal for merging the future work for German refugees with other relief action, had weakened his prestige "substantially." Even if he did not feel the Nazi assault "as deeply as he should," McDonald's "delivering a body blow" through the presentation of the originally drafted document would go a long way toward restoring his reputation among Jews and, through them, the world at large. In many ways, the High Commissioner was a "splendid person." Waldman concluded: "He worked indefatigably and earnestly against overwhelming odds. The cards were merely stacked against him." Still unconvinced by McDonald but learning that he would not reconsider including Part II, Rosenberg concentrated on persuading him to hold a press conference where he would again stress the Christian aspects of the problem and, for McDonald's sake, "indicate that he was not withdrawing his interest." At the end of all their talk that Christmas Day, Rosenberg was "still rather gloomy."[59]

Bentwich continued to worry about the Letter's impact. Three days after McDonald had sailed for New York, he asked Janowsky: "Is there no danger of angering the Council by notices of the McDonald letter in the press?" Although the American replied that one of the chief aims was to appeal to public opinion, Bentwich began sending telegrams to the High Commissioner warning that the officials whom he had seen in Scandinavia thought that publication would be "disastrous." McDonald refused to yield, stirring Bentwich to repeat the need for delay and reconsideration, and to add his personal assent. It would have been extremely difficult for McDonald to modify his plans in any event because of advance preparations, but he remained unconvinced. On December 27, 1935, McDonald officially submitted his Letter of Resignation, together with a thirty-four-page printed Annex on German persecution of "non-Aryans" and its effect in creating refugees, to Secretary General Avenol.[60]

McDonald's long Letter, published in its entirety three days later by the London *Times* and the *New York Times*, described the "catastrophic" conditions which threatened "the pauperization or exile" of hundreds of thousands of Germans not considered "Nordic" by the Third Reich. More than half of the Jews remaining in Germany had already been deprived of their livelihood, he observed, the Jewish people used as "the scapegoat for political and partisan purposes." The Nazi concepts of "blood, race, and soil," propagated with "fanatical enthusiasm," menaced not only Jews, but "all those who remain defiantly loyal to the old ideals of religious and individual freedom."

"The doors of most countries are closed against impoverished fugitives," McDonald noted. Members of the League and other members of the community of nations should resort to "friendly but firm intercession" with the German government for a modification of policies "which constitute a source of unrest and perplexity in the world, a challenge to the conscience of mankind, and a menace to the legitimate interests of the States affected by the immigration of German refugees." During the past three centuries, the Letter went on, the principle of respect for the rights of minorities had been "hardening into an obligation of the public law of Europe," the League Assembly itself championing this cause. He emphasized that "protection of the individual from racial and religious intolerance is a vital condition of international peace and security," and closed with a personal plea that public opinion "move to avert the existing and impending tragedies."[61] The resignation of the first High Commissioner for Refugees (Jewish and Other) Coming from Germany became effective as of December 31, 1935.

III

Warmly endorsing McDonald's Letter of Resignation and annex as a "damning indictment" of Germany, a number of the world's leading newspapers called on Berlin to restore full equality to Jews and others oppressed by the Nazi government. The London *Times* thought it "scarcely credible" that Germany's leaders could remain much longer insensitive to public opinion abroad and to the injury being done to German interests abroad; the *Prager Presse* of Czechoslovakia characterized the German attempt to refute McDonald's accusations and shift the blame to the League as "far from convincing." A *New York Times* editorial judged that the accused in this case were bound "to answer at the bar of moral justice"; the *Boston Globe* considered McDonald's final statement "a service to the human conscience to which he appeals." Regarding the document as a parallel to the Lytton report on the Japanese invasion of Manchuria, the *Nation* wrote that McDonald's departure "may well prove to be the most effective action of his two years' service." Privately, the British Foreign Office thought otherwise, considering the Letter "an unwise document, which did a disservice to the real interests of the Jews in Germany," and in which "the guiding hand of Zionism was apparent."[62]

When *Christian Century* reprinted the entire Letter and annex, subsidized by the Joint Council, McDonald made arrangements to have a number of supplements shipped to England. The Board of Deputies of British Jews received 5,000 copies for distribution, thus precluding an earlier thought that the document be sold for the benefit of Great Britain's Jewish Refugee Committee. Having encouraged McDonald to "tell the truth as you see it" and "disregard the consequences," Cecil penned a strong statement for this publication. While "wholesale starvation is what these German citizens of Jewish blood are threatened with," he also observed that the "fugitives" constitute "centres of embittered human beings without money or employment." A first step to the solution, Cecil added, was knowledge of the facts, and "the McDonald Report states temperately and impartially what is actually happening. I trust all interested in public affairs or the sufferings of their fellow-men will make themselves acquainted with this remarkable document."[63]

After two days of silence, the Third Reich news agency commented that the nations of the world had no right to criticize Germany's treatment of her Jewish population while Germans were being persecuted in other countries. The *Völkischer Beobachter* laid the blame for McDonald's action on "the countless complaints from all countries of Europe about the German refugees, who were "human garbage." This official organ of the Nazi party resented the League's "insolence" in supposing that it could deal with domestic German conditions, and advised the League to occupy itself with the persecution by Jews of Christians in various countries outside of Germany. A number of other German newspapers attributed the Letter of Resignation to "Bolshevik circles," which had made Geneva "an instrument of their policy." After reports from foreign countries showing the strong positive reaction to the Letter, the *Völkischer Beobachter* charged that the real cause of the resignation was lack of funds, and that Soviet Russia, as well as the Freemasons, had inspired McDonald's action to hide this fact.[64]

Jewish leaders in Great Britain and the United States applauded McDonald's last formal act. The JFC appreciated his "plain language," and even Rosenberg telephoned McDonald on December 30 to indicate that he was "more reconciled." At Warburg's home, where the JDC "high command" gathered, Baerwald presented McDonald with a sterling tea service as a token of the philanthropic organization's gratitude. American Zionists inscribed McDonald's name at the opening in Jerusalem of a new volume of the Jewish National Fund's Golden Book. Albert Einstein, unable to attend a dinner in McDonald's honor, sent this tribute to the Philadelphia gathering: "What he at first took on as a job became a matter of the heart. His Letter of Resignation to the League of Nations is one of those irrefutable masterpieces, which a human being can only achieve when he is consumed by his mission. This letter will go down in the annals of history as a lasting appeal to humanity's conscience."[65]

McDonald's protest quickly sparked requests among American Jewish groups for action against the Third Reich. The AJC's annual meeting endorsed a resolution by Judge Joseph M. Proskauer, who lauded McDonald's "unstinted and courageous efforts," expressing the hope that the League "will act in conformity with its principles to call the German National Socialist government before the bar of international justice." The American Jewish Congress requested the United States, as well as the League, to "make itself felt in unequivocal terms with respect to the monstrous wrong which the German government" was inflicting upon German Jewry, upon Jews everywhere, and "against the moral sense of mankind." Wise called upon President Roosevelt to speak frankly to the Nazi regime.[66]

Before going off for a six-week vacation at his doctor's advice, McDonald himself sought one more time to obtain some intercession from Washington. A twenty-minute talk at the White House on February 6 with Roosevelt, who was as cordial as ever, did not result in a statement denouncing Nazi persecution, however. He tried another tack. McDonald had made an appeal to the Foreign Office the previous month about informal representations at Berlin, preferably in cooperation with the US government, to support the evacuation of 100,000–150,000 German Jewish youngsters within four to five years. He raised the same subject with Undersecretary William Phillips on February 7, repeating the point made earlier to London that Jewish groups would undertake the financing. Unbeknownst to McDonald, the British had already decided not to intercede. The State Department concluded soon thereafter that it could not do so for a non-American group, and that the immigration laws did not permit the extension of any preferential treatment.[67]

Avenol's office decided to circulate the Letter of Resignation in English and in French as a League document to its members. The last three pages of the original annex were deleted because doubts had been raised about a few statements therein. The League's *Official Journal* noted on January 20, 1936, that the Council "has now to take note of McDonald's resignation and it will certainly desire to thank him for his devoted labors in connection with this work." After doing so, the Council passed on the Letter to the Assembly, which would not meet until the following September. While the League soon reorganized the High Commission under its own auspices, the new agency possessed no power to deal with Berlin and would devote itself almost solely to juridical questions. As to McDonald's successor, Prime Minister William L. Mackenzie King of Canada "wholly" agreed with an aide's observation that while the Letter's criticisms "were well warranted and the cause is a fine one," it would "seem anomalous" to have a Canadian accept the "thorny task" of occupying the office unless Ottawa was prepared to admit a large number of Jewish immigrants.[68]

The nod eventually went to Britain's retired Major-General Sir Neill Malcolm, who reiterated Avenol's insistence that the League "has nothing to do with the domestic policy of Germany," and that his office dealt "with persons when they become refugees and not before." The High Commissioner was not to concern himself with settlement and relief. In addition, this sixty-six-year-old Scot refused to have the High Commission act as an unofficial clearing house on behalf of refugees as McDonald had done, and would form an International Liaison Committee only a year later, and then strictly for organizational purposes. Nor did Malcolm wish to receive funds from private sources. The secretary of the liaison committee subsequently wrote to Warburg that Malcolm, who had a total budget of $16,000 for the year, appeared "devoid of initiative and ideas." Bentwich, leaving his post to head the emigration program of the newly created British Council for German Jewry, lamented that it was "sad to see "what a comatose affair" the High Commission had become.[69]

The two American researchers, thoroughly disappointed at the treatment accorded their original effort, received messages of consolation from some who had tapped them for the task in the first place. Frankfurter congratulated them on "the admirable work" embodied in the annexes, while Rosenberg assured Janowsky that "the great objective" had been accomplished "in large measure" by the Letter's raising the issue of fundamental rights and the deprivation of these rights by the Third Reich, He and Cohen agreed that the deleted part of the Letter should be used as a book or, "much deeper than that," as a basis for "a direct appeal or petition to the League by a group of internationally prominent citizens" on behalf of all those persecuted in Germany. Cohen still wanted McDonald to be pushed to adopt the annexes and send them over to the League after additional experts had reviewed them, but Mack observed that McDonald "is now completely out of it." If, he added to Janowsky, the subject matter could be brought before the League, especially when offered by non-Jewish international lawyers, it would be highly desirable. Whatever defects in the legal part, concluded the judge, and while he thought that McDonald's statement would have been better had he adopted the entire document, "it is none the less a forceful and a valuable presentation."[70]

Indeed, on the first of the New Year 1936, the AJC joined with nine other sponsoring organizations without regard to race or creed in a Petition to the League to intercede on behalf of groups persecuted by the German government. The appeal, publicized simultaneously in New York and in Paris, supported McDonald's Letter of five days previous. Deeming further intercession by the League "imperative," these groups resorted to Janowsky's "Precedents" and Fagen's legal chapter in order to elaborate and sustain the Petition. Former New York State Governor Al Smith, social work pioneer Lillian D. Wald, and US Socialist leader Norman Thomas, among others, endorsed the calling upon the League to "take action on defense of those elementary human rights which are the very foundation-stones of civilization, continued international peace and good will." The Petition, announced AJC Chairman Sol Stroock in a WMCA radio station address on "German Persecution Before the League," was to be officially circulated to the member states of the League in advance of its eighteenth Plenary Assembly in September 1936.[71]

On February 5, Fagen prepared for his AJC employers a memorandum about an appeal to the League on behalf of the Jews of Germany. Noting that he and Janowsky had correctly predicted the necessity of overcoming "the defense of sovereignty or domestic jurisdiction," which Germany raised soon after the Letter's publication, he argued that the Petition would make this case by drawing upon the three eliminated chapters. The appearance of the

Petition was "immediately desirable" for additional reasons: serious antisemitic outbreaks appeared imminent in Poland and Rumania, both of which were bound by the post-World War I minority treaties; representations which had already been made by Czechoslovakia and Poland for the protection of their nationals in Germany could be strengthened by the Petition; and France and Czechoslovakia had recently challenged Berlin's racial policy and consequent refugee exodus as a threat to their countries' welfare. The question should be raised publicly on "a broad foundation," he suggested, including non-Jewish signatories as well as Jewish organizations, with the hope that states represented at the League would ultimately take up the issues raised.[72]

Meeting shortly afterwards with McDonald's regular secretary, Fagen informed Waldman of their agreement that certain states could be approached for a general exchange of views regarding an Assembly debate on the question. At least one state should agree to address a letter to Avenol early in the summer, asking that the Petition (by then made public) be distributed to the League's members and discussed on the Agenda in September in connection with the McDonald Letter and the general question of refugees. Waldman raised the subject at a meeting of the Joint Council, spurring Wise, who was suspicious that the self-perpetuating AJC oligarchy desired to undermine the democratically elected American Jewish Congress, to suggest to his associate Nahum Goldmann in Geneva that no Jew be around the League when the presentation got under way. Brought up to date by Rosenberg, Janowsky replied from Europe that, so far as he was concerned, the remaining chapters were at his and Cohen's disposal if they could serve "our cause."[73]

A few days later, Waldman and Fagen met Salvador de Madariaga, Spain's distinguished representative at the League, who advised that they go ahead with the Petition. He agreed that, even if the League did not take concrete action, it was important to do everything possible to prevent the present situation in Germany from becoming crystallized as "normal." With certain circles of the League Secretariat, as well as elements in Britain and France, anxious to conciliate the Hitler government, he believed that Canada would be an excellent choice to take the lead in placing the Petition on the Assembly's Agenda. If no state agreed to do so, the Spaniard suggested that some government representative could "as the last resort" mention it in the debate on minorities before the Sixth Committee of the next Plenary Assembly in September.[74]

Bentwich remained skeptical, thinking the Petition "not of value" from the point of view of Europe and the Anglo-Jewish community in particular. If it secured signatures from prominent individuals and organizations in America, he advised Laski and others in London, perhaps the U.S. State Department would informally communicate approval for the matter to be placed on the League agenda. As regards use of the Janowsky-Fagen document, he averred that it should be considerably abridged if it were given to representatives at the Assembly. As soon as the American organizations submitted a draft of their Petition and memorandum, the JFC would consider the best way of approaching sympathetic governments like the Irish Free State and Norway. The Foreign Office should also be consulted, although Bentwich apprehended that "there is no hope of the British government taking a lead in what must be a thorny political issue."[75]

Sponsorship of the Petition remained a problem within the Joint Council. The pro-Zionist, liberal, and militant American Jewish Congress wanted it undertaken by Jewish organizations alone, claiming that "self-respect" and "dignity" demanded that the case be presented to the governments of the world as the "Jewish people." The non-Zionist, conservative, and assimilationist AJC and B'nai Brith, on the other hand, pointed out that the inclusion of non-Jewish organizations and groups would carry more weight at the League. Waldman particularly feared that Wise, the philosopher Horace Kallen, and other Congress spokesmen sought thereby to "manouevre the enterprise from the angle of Jewish nationalism and within its framework," much as they were "going ahead full speed" on establishing a World Jewish Congress that summer. The activities of Zionist leader Nahum Goldmann, the Jewish Agency for Palestine's political representative in Geneva, filled the AJC with "profound disgust," as he had reneged on an earlier promise not to be active in "Diaspora" politics by working assiduously for the World Jewish Congress's creation. Reluctant to confess it to himself, Waldman warned Stroock that against the Zionist "nationalist juggernaut," the AJC had been "almost completely unavailing."[76]

Laski shared these fears completely. "Moving heaven and earth" in a successful effort to prevent the Board of Deputies from associating itself with the prospective World Jewish Congress, he considered the Zionist domination of Jewish life more than ever "likely to undermine our position in the countries of the Diaspora." To the sympathetic Felix Warburg, he concluded a long letter in early April 1936 with this credo:

> The bogey of the international Jew which finds its crudest form in the Protocols [of the Elders of Zion], is, if you will bear with me, definitely assisted both by Zionism and by its offshoot,— or, as I have termed it, facet,—the World Jewish Congress. We need, except in matters of philanthropy, which belong to humanity, and therefore may be talked of and acted upon in the

language of universals, to preserve, emphasize, and indeed reinvigorate, as individuals, our status as citizens of the particular state in which we live, and if, in accordance with the non-Zionist approach to Palestine, we pursue Palestinian work, no one will quarrel with us. If, however, we decline to take this stand, but say that the loyalty of the Jew is a divided or twin loyalty, we shall destroy the Jewish position the world over.[77]

Rosenberg, also a non-Zionist, weighed in on the matter the following month, writing to Wise and Louis Lipsky, vice president of the American Jewish Congress, that the World Jewish Congress gathering scheduled for August "threatens the gravest of tragedies in Palestine." Given the recent outbreak of violent Palestinian Arab attacks, he argued, the convening of such an assembly would stimulate and might bring about a widespread Pan-Arab movement in the entire region "with a special anti-Jewish purpose." If the "undisputed facts" presented in McDonald's Letter of Resignation were "so totally without result," he observed, not producing "a ripple of action" from the League or elsewhere, what in the practical matter of protecting Jewish rights did they expect from the nations or the conscience of the world as a result of a World Jewish Congress meeting in Geneva? Getting no satisfaction from Lipsky's reply, Rosenberg reminded Wise of the tremendous achievements over the years of various Jewish relief organizations worldwide, and charged that the projected Congress, also opposed by the Board of Deputies and the Franco-Jewish establishment's Alliance Israélite Universelle, contained "a grave menace to Jewish life."[78]

This wider ideological rift directly affected the fate of the Petition, released to the world press on August 4, 1936. Laboring in Geneva at Waldman's request to help in the lobbying campaign, Janowsky correctly predicted to Cohen that the JFC, "having appointed itself tail to the British Foreign Office," would not "wag or even attempt to wag the dog." With London reluctant to antagonize Berlin, the cautious JFC declined to join the sponsoring organizations. Hearing this, the Alliance withdrew at the last minute, fearing to "inject the Jewish issue" when there was a danger of war or conflict between Germany and France. Although assured of no objection from the Quai d'Orsay, the Alliance did not want to encourage the feeling among antisemites that the Socialist administration of Prime Minister Leon Blum was a "Jewish" one. The American Jewish Congress refused to join as well, and Goldmann showed, in Waldman' words, "rather amazing irresponsibility" in promising much but in fact doing nothing on the Petition's behalf. Having striven tirelessly abroad with Fagen to see the matter through, Waldman decided to issue a press release immediately after hearing on

July 29 that France had consented to request Avenol to circulate the document at the opening of the League's Plenary Assembly on September 21.[79]

Disgusted at "this latest bit of *shtadlanut*" and not having been consulted, Janowsky resolved never to meddle again in Jewish politics. Having cautioned Waldman that a clearly stated objective and at least one League member to put the Petition on the Agenda had to be finalized one month before the Assembly convened, he failed to understand the sudden haste. Publishing the Petition so soon gave the Secretariat and the British "more time to knife it," he wrote Cohen, while the publicity value would "simply be frittered away" so that by the time the Assembly met "the Petition will be as dead as Jewish hopes." If the AJC hurried to publish in order to forestall the Congress from possibly "stealing the idea," he wondered, "then petty jealousies and personal ambitions and politics still are the determining factors in the 'fight' for Jewish rights." With their good spy system, the Germans probably knew all about our plans, he ended. "If they had a sense of humor, they would laugh heartily at the wisdom of the Elders of Zion."[80]

Fagen's update on August 7, informing Janowsky that Paris had actually not given any assurance that the Petition would even be circulated among the League members, left his fellow researcher for the McDonald Letter "aghast." Its anxiety to prevent an increased refugee emigration from Germany after the Olympic Games that summer in Berlin, together with a generally firm attitude on the question of human rights, had disposed the French government to forward the Petition to Avenol. Yet, Fagen observed, the international crisis resulting from the outbreak of a civil war in Spain now made the French hesitate. To this Janowsky shot back that the French might well take offense at the premature publicity and refuse to send the Petition to the League. The document would then "simply become an unofficial yelp to which no one would pay attention." Suspecting that the Petition was published quickly and prematurely in order to prevent the World Jewish Congress "from stealing a march on its rivals," Janowsky was chagrined by the thought that an excellent opportunity had thus been thrown away. "I am afraid," he ended, that "the twin brother of our illegitimate baby is only an abortion."[81]

Fagen was not at all disheartened by the fact that the secretary to the French delegation at the League transmitted the Petition to Avenol "for any use which might be valuably made of it." The document's signatories themselves could circulate it, he observed to Waldman. The important thing was that the various liberal governments, in the course of discussing the refugee question at the Assembly, initiate a resolution asking for a modification of Germany's policies as a violation of their rights and of human rights. To this end, the lobbying of friendly governments should continue, including getting Washington to instruct the American consul in Geneva to make a favorable statement if such a resolution were adopted. Since he did not want to tell Janowsky of the AJC's desire to make the announcement before the World Jewish Congress, he had originally communicated only the efforts being made with the French government, which was not in the least embarrassed by the Petition. Janowsky was told further that his idea of asking a state to place the document on the League Agenda as such was "a utopian hope," and that the AJC had never gone so far as to consider asking a government to do so on behalf of "a private and highly political petition" directed against Germany. To explain the American Jewish Congress's non-participation, Fagen had written his co-researcher of Goldmann's failure to keep his promises to work for the Petition and of Lipsky's letter disavowing the Congress's support.[82]

Suddenly, a telegram from Fagen on August 13 stirred Waldman to wonder if it would not be wise to suspend the Petition effort, explaining to the public that the decision was taken in the interest of world peace. The French foreign minister had just overruled the country's delegation secretary at the League, arguing that "ENCOURAGEMENT INTERVENTION GERMANY WOULD EMBARRASS NONINTERVENTION SPAIN." In addition, the British Foreign Office had replied to the Board of Deputies that London opposed any Assembly discussion on McDonald's Letter. Fagen doubted that he could successfully obtain another government's commitment, especially before the August 21 deadline which Janowsky had advised. While awaiting Adler's response to this information, Waldman replied to Fagen not to disclose the "disappointing outcome" to their closest friends lest it be exploited by "unfriends." At best, Avenol would circulate the Petition. Failing that, the AJC would do so and persuade some member state delegates to bring in the Petition as part of the supporting material for discussion on the McDonald Letter, which was already on the Agenda. He believed, in closing, that the AJC officers would want Fagen to continue his efforts in every possible direction to the end that the Petition should come up before the Assembly "in some way or another."[83]

One day later, Fagen could report some promising news following a "cordial" visit to the League official in charge of the work of the international organizations, and particularly those relating to refugees. Gustave G. Kuhlmann had informed Fagen, Janowsky, and Franco-Jewish leader Raymond-Raoul Lambert of his having advised Avenol that the Petition should be officially "received," and that mention of this fact would probably be made in the League's *Official Journal*. The President of the Assembly could then receive a delegation of the representatives of the signatory organizations, the document would be handed to him, and it would be reprinted in the *Official Journal* (without the annexes because of considerations of space). Copies should be distributed beforehand to every Assembly delegate and journalist in Geneva, Kuhlmann suggested, so that a wide circulation of the contents would follow after the announcement were made concerning the reception by the President. If a state wished to bring up the McDonald Letter during the course of the discussion in the Sixth Committee on the general question of refugees, he added, the Petition and the question of the treatment of minorities in Germany could also be discussed at that time. Fagen immediately set out to gain as many additional signatories as possible and to organize such a delegation.[84]

On September 29, 1936, Carlos Saavedra Lamas, President of the Seventeenth Plenary Assembly of the League of Nations, received this delegation at the Palais des Nations in Geneva. On behalf of ten signatory organizations, Fagen presented the Petition in support of the recommendations made in McDonald's Letter of Resignation. The appeal was buttressed by the Janowsky and Fagen chapters that had been eliminated nine months earlier, comprising an annex of fifty-nine pages which established in detail the historical precedents and legal grounds for international action to safeguard human rights and to prevent the violation of the rights of States arising therefrom. In reply, Lamas noted his personal interest in the fate of refugees, and emphasized that the League's activity in this regard, carried out in "a spirit of international solidarity" and in "a humanitarian spirit," had to be freed from all "political implications." He could not officially include the Petition in the Agenda, but wished to assure the delegation that the League would continue to interest itself in the refugee question. They could be certain, he ended, that the "constructive program" presently being considered in the Sixth Committee would be put into effect by the High Commissioner and the Assembly in "a most beneficent and comprehensive spirit."[85]

With no member of the League prepared to raise the refugee issue or any other question which would be regarded as unfriendly to Germany, however, Fagen and Janowsky turned to publishing their excised chapters in book form. *International Aspects of German Racial Policies*, including appendices devoted to McDonald's Letter and its Annex, the Petition, and a selection of expressions of opinion against the German persecution of "Non-Aryans," appeared the following year. In a preface hailing this "excellent and careful study," James Brown Scott, former President of the Institut de Droit International, stressed that "if law is to justify itself in our world it must eschew injustice, inequity and inequality." Rosenberg and Cohen observed in their introduction that the League had taken no action since 1933 to remind the German government "of the wrongs inherent in its oppressive policies," but "these profound issues will not down."

When the second term of the new High Commissioner for Refugees expired in 1938, would the League recognize that "the mailed fist which has struck down helpless Jews and 'non-Aryans' and has destroyed all political and civil liberties is also hostile to all religious freedom?" As sponsors of the monograph, they concluded with the hope that this book, setting forth the humane precedents established by civilized nations during more than two hundred years, "may help toward the restoration of international sanity."[86]

Developments thereafter across the Atlantic until Germany's unleashing of World War II proved this hope misplaced. The newly established World Jewish Congress, like its AJC, JFC, and Alliance rivals, could do precious little to stem the onrushing tide of European Jew-hatred. The governments represented at the July 1938 Evian Conference on Refugees adhered to stringent immigration admission policies, while masking the unique Jewish catastrophe under rubrics like "political refugees" and "involuntary emigrants." The moribund League's minority treaty system collapsed, the Munich Conference delivering the *coup de grâce*. The West responded to Third Reich aggression against Austria and Czechoslovakia with appeasement, the United States hued to neutrality and restrictive immigration quotas, and His Majesty's Government aimed at closing the most obvious and accessible haven for imperiled Jewry—Palestine. McDonald, chairing the President's Advisory Committee on Political Refugees since its formation in May 1938 and deputy to the US representative at the Evian Conference, accurately sensed towards the end of August 1939 that no definite plan lay behind Roosevelt's sudden "inspiration" to dramatize the urgency of a "comprehensive settlement" for refugees. He concluded: "Should worse come to worse in Europe, all considerations of inter-governmental activity on behalf of German refugees would be abandoned."[87]

McDonald, those engaged in preparing his Letter of Resignation, and the advocates of the subsequent Petition—whatever their respective limitations—were all hamstrung from the start by the tumultuous realities of the international arena. Rosenberg added presciently that "people are concerned with their own immediate affairs and when it comes to the sufferings of other people, especially when the people are far away, most people . . . have not the imagination to be concerned." In the interests of preserving peace, Cecil continued to call without success for a permanent organization under the League having large powers to deal with the refugees. The International Federation of League of Nations Societies invited the League in July 1938, and again four months later after the "revolting excesses" of the Third Reich's *Kristallnacht*, to convene without delay a conference to help Jews in certain European countries create and develop "a National State in Palestine" and to promote Jewish settlement abroad. These appeals, too, fell upon deaf ears in a world grown indifferent and at times hostile.[88]

The insistence of Hitler's Third Reich and others on the absolute sovereignty of states rendered the League impotent and left the Jews, not masters of their own destiny, vulnerable to unimaginable tragedy. Immanuel Kant's inspiring essay on universal peace, offering the great German philosopher's thesis in 1795 that peace among nations could only exist if they were governed by republican constitutions that safeguarded individual freedom and equality, could claim limited adherents among the corridors of power in the perilous decade of the 1930s. Nor were most governments then prepared to accept Cohen's contemporary postulate that the rights of minorities "are sacred because they are essential human rights, and their denial to any minority is but a way by which the suppression of the rights of all of us begins." In the words of British parliamentarian Josiah C. Wedgwood's postscript to the Janowsky-Fagen volume, "a tragic acknowledgment of moral bankruptcy by what we are pleased to call the civilized world" ensued.[89] The McDonald Letter and the subsequent Petition in its support, each completely without result, reflected honorable failure. In a larger sense, the failure lay at doorsteps not their own.

CHAPTER 3

The Swastika's Darkening Shadow

On the eve of Hitler's rise to power as Chancellor of the Third Reich, the Jews of Europe numbered about 9.5 million, or more than sixty percent of world Jewry. They had lived on the continent for more than two thousand years, creating richly diverse, often dynamic, cultures in the face of degradation, expulsion, and pogrom. Although constituting less than two percent of Europe's population, Jews emerged as political and intellectual luminaries in many countries. Most resided in Eastern Europe, with about 5.5 million living in Poland and the Soviet Union. Other substantial Jewish centers included Romania, Germany, Hungary, Czechoslovakia, Great Britain, France, Austria, the Netherlands, and Lithuania. In a little more than a decade, however, this reality underwent a seismic shift. By V-E Day on May 8, 1945, Germany's systematic annihilation of European Jewry during World War II, aided by collaborator nations and not countered by an Allied will to save, had taken a horrific toll. In what has since been called the Holocaust, an estimated six million Jews, including one and a half million children, had been murdered in the Nazis' "Final Solution of the Jewish Question."[1]

How had this come about? The convulsive spasm of murderous violence which overtook European Jewry has been impressively examined by historians in the past several decades. My own *The Jews Were Expendable: Free World Diplomacy and the Holocaust*; *The Holocaust and Israel Reborn: From Catastrophe to Sovereignty*; and *Decision on Palestine Deferred: America, Britain and Wartime Diplomacy, 1939–1945* explored some aspects of this subject.[2] Yet it is essential to commence with an examination of the years preceding the near annihilation of the Jews of Europe. What exactly was known at the time of how this community struggled to breathe as the antisemitic noose tightened, and how did Jews and non-Jews respond? Much has been written about the steady corruption of daily life for the pre-war Jewish community under Third Reich rule, while individual studies have appeared about the crisis which Jews confronted in other countries. Yet an overview of the spread of Jew-hatred across the continent, rooted in numerous reports of that persecution, has eluded serious inspection. My volume *The Swastika's Darkening Shadow: Voices Before the Holocaust* seeks to do so while shining a lucid spotlight on the years between Adolf Hitler's ascension to the chancellorship of Germany on January 30, 1933, and his unleashing of the Second World War on September 1, 1939, also seeking to understand how Jews in peril navigated their world as darkness closed about. A generous selection of documents augments the volume.

In April 1939, with a poem published by the *New Yorker* magazine, W. H. Auden movingly captured European Jewry's singular plight prior to World War II. Four years earlier, the young British writer had consented to a marriage of convenience to Thomas Mann's eldest of six children (Erika), thereby giving her a British passport with which to escape the Nazi regime. Having moved in January 1939 to the United States, where he would take American citizenship seven years later, Auden lashed out in "Refugee Blues" against the consul banging the table and saying "If you've got no passport, you're officially dead"; the committee asking him "politely to return next year"; a public speaker remarking "If we let them in, they will steal our daily bread." Referring to the Jews of Germany, the author observes: "Thought I heard the thunder, rumbling in the sky. / It was Hitler over Europe, saying: 'they must die...'" David Ben-Gurion copied down in his diary all the verses of "Refugee Blues" after being shown a copy one month later in Jerusalem. Chairman of the Jewish Agency for Palestine's executive committee, he recorded that this poem by a non-Jew "is worthy of being publicized in every Jewish home."³

Two months later, the Berlin-born Gershom Scholem explained the reasons of his "uncommunicative silence" to his closest friend, Walter Benjamin. Writing from Jerusalem on June 30, 1939, the depressed Hebrew University professor of Jewish mysticism and Kabbala revealed "the boundless gloom and paralysis" that had come over him during the past several months because of the current state of affairs. Palestine had been turned into "a showplace of civil war," the labor movement as a revolutionary and political factor was "deader than a doornail," and the British mandatory authorities' "capitulation" in the face of Arab violence also led some within the Promised Land's *Yishuv* (Jewish community) to adopt the weapon of terror. Scholem found it impossible *not* to think about Jewry's general situation: "The dreadful catastrophe that has befallen Judaism, a disaster whose dimensions no one can fully grasp, and the utter hopelessness of a situation in which hope is manufactured only in order to taunt us (like the shameless 'project' to send Jews to British Guyana [*sic*] as 'colonists')—all of this strikes one down and destroys one's peace of mind."[4]

At the very heart of the "dreadful catastrophe" about which Scholem wrote strode Adolf Hitler. Hitler's first expression on the "Jewish question," addressed to German soldier Adolf Gemlich on September 16, 1919, had declared that "the final aim" must be "the uncompromising removal of the Jews altogether." That pronouncement of what can be termed eliminationist intent would receive initial scholarly mention only in 1959, in a German historical quarterly, but readers of the Jewish Telegraphic Agency (JTA) from 1923 onwards could entertain no doubt that antisemitism constituted the very core of Hitler's, and then of his acolytes', political passion. The Nazi regime's firm conviction, driven by a pathological view of the Jew as the incarnation of evil threatening German and world survival, was expressed and progressively implemented with shameless candor. Writing in his diary on September 5, 1944, Victor Klemperer, a Romance languages professor in Dresden who had converted to Protestantism and married an "Aryan" piano teacher, captured this reality in a telling metaphor: "The Jewish problem is the poison gland of the swastika viper."[5] Remarkably, but commonly overlooked, Poland and Romania were home to far more virulent assaults against Jews in the 1930s until *Kristallnacht*, while mounting legislation and brutal anti-Jewish attacks could readily be seen elsewhere in Central and Eastern Europe.

The drama unfolds well before Hitler finally decided in World War II upon a course of systematic slaughter for the one people whose crime, according to his dogmatic *weltanschauung*, was that of birth—expiated only by death. The voices of Jews and Gentiles, of appeasers and opponents of Germany, of haters and champions of Jews, of Zionists and universalists, of refugees and natives on both sides of the Atlantic could all be heard. The baleful effect of antisemitic aggression, however crooked the path to Auschwitz-Birkenau, left many with an understandable sense of grim foreboding as to European Jewry's future. In a letter from Warsaw on November 25, 1938, to Martin Buber, who had departed Germany a few months earlier for a professorship in social philosophy at the Hebrew University, an anxious thirty-one-year-old Abraham J. Heschel observed: "Concepts are suddenly regaining their unambiguousness—for everyone. Perhaps we can now bury relativism."[6] None could have foretold the *Shoah*, the Hebrew term since adopted to signify the Holocaust, but the precariousness of Jews' existence on the soil of Europe could not be denied.

Their options for survival decreased dramatically once Great Britain curtailed entry to the obvious haven of Palestine, joined by other nations who also closed their hearts and their doors to Jews in desperate need. Moreover,

US President Franklin D Roosevelt (FDR), British Prime Minister Neville Chamberlain, and other leaders masked the Jewish people's unique calamity. With ever thickening shadows of war clearly visible on the horizon, *realpolitik* reigned supreme in these corridors of power. As a consequence, Europe's defenseless Jews, facing unprecedented anguish, would find few allies to answer the call of conscience.

The storm clouds that burst over Europe with the start of World War II had begun to gather early on. Three weeks after Hitler obtained a majority (joined by the Nationalist bloc) in the Reichstag, former Princeton University president John G. Hibben presciently warned in the *New York Times* that "Adolf Hitler is a menace to world peace, and if his policies bring war to Europe, the United States cannot escape participating." By the end of April 1933, Horace Rumbold, then British Ambassador to Germany, and Hamilton Fish Armstrong, editor of *Foreign Affairs*, were among the first to realize that Hitler's uncompromising racism constituted the *raison d'être* of his program for conquest, and that he would not be overthrown. His subsequent triumphs deepened the sense among the overwhelming mass of the German people of a reborn *Völksgemeinschaft* (national community), binding each individual to the will and mission of the *Führer*. The everyday practice of exclusion destroyed the civil and constitutional order, and transformed the German nation into an aggressive and racist society.[7]

At the same time, various European statesmen, desperate to avoid another world war and often more fearful of the spread of Soviet Communism, as well as buoyed by American supporters like Joseph Kennedy, then US ambassador to Great Britain, clung to the mantra that a concession here and a concession there could check Nazi aspirations and keep world peace. The same reasoning lay behind the wish of France and a number of other delegations to the League of Nations not to alienate Germany, and the decision to accede when Hitler sent troops to reoccupy the demilitarized zone of the Rhineland, staged the Olympiad in Berlin, annexed Austria, and demanded the Sudetenland. All chose to overlook the patent fact that for Julius Streicher, Heinrich Himmler, Alfred Rosenberg, Walter Frick, Hermann Göring, Joseph Goebbels, Rudolf Hess, Reinhard Heydrich, Adolf Eichmann, and especially Hitler himself, the twin doctrines of *lebensraum* (living space) for a pure "Aryan" race engaged in struggle against its moral enemy—the Jew—and of warfare to attain this end were directly linked to concrete action. This dual program had been frankly declared in Hitler's political manifesto *Mein Kampf* (1925–1926), a two-volume credo that he wrote while serving a sentence in Landsberg prison for a failed coup against the Bavarian state government, intended to launch a larger revolution against the liberal Weimar Republic in Berlin.

The influential Lord Lothian, Philip Henry Kerr, offers a classic example of those who demonstrated their inability to comprehend Hitler's mind. A wartime assistant to Lloyd George who had later aided the former British prime minister considerably in drafting the Treaty of Versailles, Lothian pronounced in the London *Times* in early 1935 after an interview with the *Führer* that Germany sought not war but "real equality." Most importantly, Hitler told him that "he will pledge Germany not to interfere in his beloved Austria by force." Not having the "slightest doubt" that Hitler was "sincere," Lothian believed that the cruelty and "merciless oppression of weak minorities" characteristic of the Nazi regime were due, in large measure, to the fact that Germany had not enjoyed these rights "at any time in the last sixteen years." Urging his fellow countrymen to treat the Third Reich "as a friend," Lothian publicly asserted that Germany "is not imperialist in the old sense of the word.... Its very devotion to race precludes it from trying to annex other nationalities."[8]

Yet Hitler's war against the Jewish people, comprising the key to his Manichean ideology, had also commenced in the years between his rise to the Chancellorship and his initiating World War II. The JTA, in particular, carried stories almost on a daily basis of antisemitic violence in the Third Reich and in subsequent areas of Nazi domination, persecution in which, Michael Kater and Marion Kaplan later confirmed, Germans acquiesced and often, spontaneously, took an active role.[9] The JTA's coverage should have left no doubt as to Hitler's dogmatic views, as well as his ruthless determination to defend humanity against the menace of what he termed "international Bolshevik Jews." The constant Nazi demonization of Jews as "vermin," "bacilli," and "parasites"; the evolving repression and omnipresent threat that made life for condemned Jews increasingly unsupportable; the activity of zealous officials like Eichmann or Heydrich—none were hidden from public view. They were absolute prerequisites for "the Final Solution of the Jewish question," later Nazi code for getting rid of all Jews by methodical murder.

A growing awareness of European Jewry's ever-worsening plight did not spark a generous response on the part of governments to receive Jews in desperate need. As Jews were not a major issue or of no interest to statesmen who grappled with unemployment, rearmament, and popular antisemitism, Zara Steiner observes, "pressures for collective action gave way to policies of self-defense, neutrality and isolation." The specter that encouraging German Jewish emigration might well provoke the flight of countless other Jewish refugees (the highly regarded John Hope Simpson spoke in 1938 of "nearly five million threatened Jews"—excluding Russia—to the east of Germany) reinforced this attitude. The horrific nature of *Kristallnacht* on the nights of November 9 and 10, 1938, across the Third Reich, and the subsequent coordination in Nazi policy under Göring and the SS leadership continued to encounter but minor opposition in Germany, David Bankier has pointed out.[10]

That state-sanctioned pogrom, marking the culmination of a policy which had proceeded in less than a decade from defining Jews as a stigmatized, pariah race to social quarantine to disenfranchisement and economic strangulation to their ultimate physical removal from German *lebensraum*, wiped away remaining illusions for most. Nonetheless, on December 16, 1938, the very same day that *Le Temps* publicized Premier Edouard Deladier cabinet's willingness to allow the absorption of a contingent of refugee children, Minister of the Interior Albert Sarraut sent urgent telegrams to prefects of the northeastern border provinces instructing them to bar the entry of German Jewish children in particular. His Majesty's Government closed off wide entry to the most obvious haven of Palestine with the 1939 White Paper, and other countries sealed their borders. The search for alternative havens beyond Europe, notably championed by Roosevelt, proved a delusion—too little and too late.[11]

Anti-Jewish aggression elsewhere on the continent also received extensive coverage in the JTA, Jewish organizational reports, diplomatic correspondence, and other venues. The rapid spread of violent Jew-hatred and the rise to power of the radical right in Poland, Romania, Hungary, Slovakia, Germany, Lithuania, and Latvia, reflecting the confluence of economic distress, Christian indoctrination, the triumph of chauvinism, xenophobia, anti-Bolshevism, and the great prestige of Nazi Germany, could not be denied; nor could Nazi influence in Arab countries. The pages of *The Swastika's Darkening Shadow* record how this tragedy mounted and spread over the course of six years.

Taking a brief look at some countries outside of Germany during the very first month of 1933 is itself revealing. The Bishop of Linz (Hitler's hometown), Johannes A. Gfollner, while rejecting the Nazis' radical antisemitism and anti-Christian program, condemned in a pastoral letter the "destructive Jewish spirit" for carrying Capitalism, Socialism, and Bolshevism. Romania witnessed mass meetings of the virulently anti-Jewish Iron Guardists (also known as the Legion of the Archangel Michael or the Green Shirts) in Czernowitz (or Cernauti, now Chernivtsi, Ukraine), Kishinev (now Chişinău, Moldova), and Klausenburg (now Cluj-Napoca), with the local archbishop leading their demolishment of the home of a Jew near the Nicolae Domnesc Church in Bucharest. Cuzist Party students (followers of Professor Alexander Cuza, head of the League of National Christian Defense) assaulted Jewish students at Czernowitz University, then proceeded to attack the offices of two Jewish newspapers. Not one of those responsible for the pogrom in Jassy (Iaşi) was punished, while the murder of five Jews in Soroca (now in Moldova) was passed over even without a trial of the guilty.

For the second time within two days, Jews were murdered in East Galicia. Warsaw University authorities refused to enroll Jewish medical students for anatomic studies; anti-Jewish boycott inciters in the Posen and Pomerania districts distributed flyers with the inscription "Only swine buy from Jews." National Democratic Deputies in the Sejm called for the expulsion of Jews "because they rob the Poles of their bread," and objected to the placing of military orders with Jewish firms. Jewish language rights, guaranteed in the Minority Treaties at the Versailles Peace Conference, were practically abolished in Lithuania, while the government closed down the Jewish Teachers' Seminary in Latvia.[12]

In 1934, developments in Poland, where Jews constituted a tenth of the total population—the highest percentage of Jews in any land outside of Palestine—and formed over a quarter of the urban population, gave great cause for anxiety. Of the country's Jews, who were primarily concentrated on commerce and handicrafts, almost half were "bordering on economic ruin" according to a report that August from Joseph Hyman to the American Jewish Joint Distribution Committee (JDC). In September, Foreign Minister Józef Beck renounced the Minorities Treaty which his country had to sign at the Paris Peace Conference of 1919, guaranteeing religious freedom and civil equality for minorities (which included more than 3,000,000 Jews in Poland at the time). The British and French representatives immediately registered strong protests, but such sentiments carried little weight against aroused nationalistic feeling and intense antisemitic propaganda within Poland, much coming from Germany. Further reflecting the prevailing consensus, Cardinal Aleksander Kakowski responded to an appeal from four rabbis by accusing Jews of propagating atheism, supporting Communism, and publishing pornography, and implied that Jewish behavior provoked Polish youth to use "regrettable" Nazi methods.[13]

Nor were conditions promising elsewhere on the continent. The day after Austrian Chancellor Kurt Schuschnigg declared, following an interview with Jewish leaders Neville Laski and Nahum Goldmann, that Austria treated its Jewish citizens as equals, his government issued a decree segregating Jews from Catholics in the country's public schools. A new wave of antisemitism broke out in Romania, where hundreds of thousands of Jews faced "abject poverty." A right-wing dictatorship in Latvia placed its Jews in a "very unsatisfactory and threatening" position. Marie Schmolke, head of the HICEM emigration association's office in Prague, reported to the JDC in Paris that a new wave from Germany of stateless Jews of Polish and Russian origin, in "a state of indescribable misery," was arriving in Czechoslovakia. In Constantinople there was even an island on the Bosphorus for wild dogs, she noted, adding: "The time has come when a solution must be found for these hunted people. Everything should be set in motion to get the League of Nations to take up this question."[14]

In early 1935, persecution of Jews continued in and beyond the Third Reich's borders. All health officers in Germany were instructed to propagate "racial purity" in close contact with the Nazi organizations, while all wives of doctors and dentists had to submit proof of their "Aryanism." Nazi newspapers in Austria, where many Jews committed suicide because of rampant discrimination in the professions, demanded a complete boycott against Jewish lawyers. The majority of the Danzig (now Gdańsk, Poland) Senate, consisting of Nazi members, officially applied for the dissolution of the parliament and for new elections, which might eventually bring the status of the Free City's terrorized Jews to the same as that of the Jews in the Saar. Hundreds of Jewish families in Upper Silesia, who had for many years earned their living by peddling, were threatened by a law against that trade. Legislation in Romania, where anti-Jewish propaganda on a large scale was being financed by Germany, insisted that all economic and civil enterprises had to employ eighty percent Romanian personnel. This proved a particularly terrific blow to numerous Jews in Bukovina and Bessarabia, since the Romanian authorities refused to naturalize the Jewish population there despite the fact that they had resided in these territories since 1918.[15]

Nor did the situation improve throughout the year. A wave of terror and suicides occurred among Jews throughout Germany. Mass arrests, the closing of Jewish firms, and the stoning of Jewish houses by SA members were reported by the JTA. The Nuremberg Laws of September, separating Jews from the rest of the population by depriving them of political equality and prohibiting marriages or sexual relations between Jews and Germans, as well as the employment of German maids under the age of forty-five in Jewish households and the raising by Jews of the swastika banner—the new Reich Flag, led the London *Times* to note that, "after being denied the rights of citizenship," Jews are "coming to be denied the right to live." On the last day of the year, when submitting his resignation as the first League of Nations High Commissioner for Refugees (Jews and Others) from Germany, James G. McDonald noted that "the doors of most countries are closed against impoverished fugitives." He called on members of the League and other nations to resort to "friendly but firm intercession" with Berlin for a modification of policies "which constitute a source of unrest and perplexity in the world, a challenge to the conscience of mankind, and a menace to the legitimate interests of the States affected by the immigration of German refugees." McDonald's public letter of resignation received praise from some quarters, but no positive government response followed.[16]

While antisemitic legislation increasingly took hold in Germany throughout January 1936, a worrisome picture appeared in other European countries that same month. The anti-Jewish boycott movement in the German districts of Czechoslovakia gained in intensity, Karlsbad's (now Karlovy Vary, the Czech Republic) Jews also receiving regularly a replica of a railway ticket with the inscription "Free passage to Palestine, but no return journey." A gang attacked the only Jewish family in the village of Wola in Poland's Radom district, killing the mother and seriously injuring her four children, including a twelve-year-old boy whose hand was hacked off. Two bombs exploded in one of Kraków's Jewish areas, three Jewish shops were set on fire in the village of Moska near Lwów (now Lviv, Ukraine), and the entire Jewish population of the village of Dąbrówka Kościelna had to flee in the face of attack. Anti-Jewish demonstrations occurred in the Universities of Grodno (now Hrodna, Belarus), Lwów, and Warsaw. The Association of Catholic German Youth in Vienna called for a boycott of Jewish enterprises. In the townships of Krosna and Varniai in Lithuania, thirty-three Jews were injured, one seriously, in anti-Jewish riots by peasants. Chief Rabbi Jacob Niemirower of Romania narrowly missed death at the hands of three young assassins, members of the fascist Iron Guard.[17]

Some 50,000 Jews in Romania's Bessarabia province, suffering from their third famine in the last twelve years, were in a worse position than their Gentile neighbors because of antisemitic boycotts and lack of government relief. On February 13, the Socialist Party leader Léon Blum was dragged from a car in Paris and beaten by the *Camelots du Roi*, youth group of the antisemitic Action Française royalists. A Vienna court ruled that the German law prohibiting intermarriage between "Aryans" and Jews was applicable to Jewish subjects of the Reich living in Austria, the official gazette of the Vienna Archbishopric adding that neither register offices nor Catholic Churches in the country could wed Germans who had been refused marriage licenses in Germany. As they went on trial in Katowice, twenty-one adherents of the semi-fascist Endek party admitted to having bombed synagogues in several Polish towns. While admonishing Poles not to assault Jews, August Cardinal Hlond's pastoral communication of February 29 labeled Jews "free-thinkers" who "constitute the vanguard of atheism, of the Bolshevik movement and of revolutionary activity," supported a boycott of Jewish businesses and "pornographic" publications, and indicated a willingness on the part of the Catholic Church to accept the conversion of Jews. Prince Janusz Radziwiłł, president of the National-Conservative bloc, appealed in the Sejm for the forcible, mass emigration of the Jews, and proposed that Warsaw seek Palestine certificates from England: "If Germany has by anti-Semitism obtained a high quota of certificates, the Polish anti-Semites might wish to follow Germany's example."[18]

A pogrom against Przytyk's 700 Jewish families on March 9, 1936, which claimed three Jewish lives and involved the destruction of shops and the burning of houses, reflected mounting antisemitic terror in Poland. After Marshal Pilsudski's death the previous May, the Endek and extreme rightist Nara (National Radical) Parties had stirred the peasant masses to violent attacks on the country's Jewish citizens. Scores of Jews were murdered and hundreds more wounded. Separate "ghetto benches" for Jewish students, first instituted the previous December in the Lwów Polytechnicum, were installed in universities, while heavy taxes threatened the traditional practice of kosher slaughter. Premeditated riots after the Przytyk pogrom, where Jewish armed resistance had been repulsed by the police and the Jewish Labor Bund party called a half-day general strike in protest, followed in Nowa Wilejka (now Naujoji Vilnia, Lithuania), Świdnik, Częstochowa, Łódź, and elsewhere, with tragic results. Anglo-Jewish leader Neville Laski headed a Joint Foreign Committee delegation on March 26 to see Col. Józef Beck and present a memorandum of their grievances. The Polish foreign minister replied that they had to "face the fact of the uprising of chauvinist Nationalism in a number of countries, one of the results of which had been increased anti-Jewish activity."[19]

In the Third Reich, the comparative quiet which Jews had enjoyed from Nazi propaganda activities as a result of the Summer Olympics proved to be short-lived. Across the border to the east, Poland's Jews witnessed attacks of a more murderous nature. In September, more than fifty Jews were wounded in violent disorders in the town of Wysokie Mazovieckie. Two months later, ten Jews were seriously wounded by a peasant mob in the Białystok district township of Śniadowo, Endek agitators also instigating a bitter anti-Jewish boycott in the township of Czyżew. On November 27, Jewish stay-in strikes spread to Poznań, while the Jewish Labor Bund proclaimed a one-day general strike in protest against antisemitic activities in Polish universities. Donning gas masks, police stormed Warsaw University to eject several hundred Nationalists. A four-day strike at Wilno (now Vilnius, Lithuania) University over "ghetto benches," during which more than thirty Jews were wounded, including one who lost an eye, remained unresolved. The next month, a large number of Jews were beaten up by Endeks during the market day at Czyżew despite the presence of police reinforcements. In the non-Jewish districts of Warsaw, yellow bills were posted in front of Jewish shops to encourage boycotting of these establishments.[20]

In Romania, some 250,000 members of the National Christian party, led by the poet Octavian Goga and largest of the country's many anti-Jewish organizations, assembled in Bucharest on November 6. They paraded with large swastika banners throughout the city, shouting anti-Jewish slogans. Special Storm Troopers, wearing the forbidden blue uniforms with swastika armbands, flanked the marchers, who heard Goga and Cuza underline the necessity of a Romanian alliance with Germany. "The Jewish leprosy spread like eczema over the whole country," Goga declared. Returning home, the demonstrators promptly set about assaulting the Jews in their own villages. Grave riots would have occurred but for the timely intervention of the police. Interviewed by the Balkan correspondent of the London *Times*, a leader of the Green Shirts declaimed for about a half hour on the necessity of "exterminating" the 1,000,000 Jews who were citizens of Romania. In Danzig, Nazi rulers eliminated opposition parties, and instigated a boycott against the city's Jews and against Polish citizens. Goebbels's *Der Angriff* newspaper published an editorial imputing to the Jews the causes of Polish hostility towards the Nazis in this regard.[21]

Assaults against Jews did not abate throughout 1937. In Eastern Europe, declared Otto D. Tolischus in dispatches from Warsaw to the *New York Times* in early February, the spread of antisemitism was turning the Jewish tragedy there into "a final disaster of truly historic magnitude." The calamity in Latvia, Lithuania, Hungary, and Romania, "approaching its high-water mark" in Poland, confronted those Jewish communities with the choice of "repeating the Exodus on a bigger scale than that chronicled in the Bible, or "dying a slow death from economic strangulation." Describing "rowdy anti-Semitism" and "terroristic activities," Tolischus cited an unofficial toll that between May 1935, when Marshal Piłsudski died, and the end of January 1937, 118 Jews had been killed and 1,350 wounded; 137 Jewish stores were bombed; 35 Jewish homes were burned down, with more than 100 Jewish students injured in the last three months in university rioting. Jewish leaders, he continued, deplore the "ambiguous generality" of government pronouncements and especially the campaign for "evacuation" of Jews. "Altogether," said the Jews bitterly, "if a Polish Hitler should arise, there would be little work for him to do."[22]

Detailed JTA reports corroborated Tolischus's warning. In resolving that no more Jewish lawyers would be permitted to join the Romanian Bar Association, some speakers at the group's General Assembly on February 8 asserted that "the Jews are parasites that must be gotten rid of." Permits were granted a week later to three new antisemitic dailies, making a total of fifty-nine such publications in that country. With an unchecked wave of savage attacks reducing the Jewish population in the Białystok area townships to a state "worse than during the World War," Jewish Deputy Emil Sommerstein observed in the Sejm that few persons implicated in these excesses were put on trial. (According to the official figures reported to the Sejm by Premier Felicjan Sławoj-Składkowski, which Tolischus cited, 21 pogroms and 348 anti-Jewish outbreaks had taken place in 1936 in the Białystok region alone.) Severe restrictions were placed on kosher slaughter. Surrendering to Endek demands, Wilno University authorities quietly introduced on February 17 virtual "ghetto" regulations for Jewish students, and an ordinance now forbade treatment of non-Jewish patients at Jewish hospitals. Eight Jewish students were badly beaten on February 20 in renewed Nationalist attacks at Warsaw University, while Kraków University authorities approved the "Aryan paragraph" contained in the by-laws of the Law Students' Union. Three Jewish students were injured in rioting at Hungary's Budapest and Pécs Universities. Police halted attacks against Jewish shops in the area, but anti-Jewish students broke the windows of a synagogue, the Jewish community office, and a Jewish elementary school.[23]

Physical violence, in addition to other anti-Jewish action, prevailed in other European countries. Cuzists in Bucharest seriously wounded thirty Jews, including several women, in Bacau, Moldavia. Patriarch Miron Cristea, leader of the Romanian Orthodox Church, praised Cuza as an "enthusiastic nationalist fighter," his remarks seconded by the Orthodox Patriarchs of Bessarabia, Transylvania, and Bukovina. In the Hungarian town of Debrezin (Debrecen), rioters broke the windows of three synagogues and of Jews' homes, while budding antisemitic parties such as the Arrow Cross (so reported British Minister Geoffrey G. Knox in Budapest) were being "carefully wet-nursed" from Germany. In Wilno, fifty-four Jewish students were excluded from the university's Natural Sciences Faculty for boycotting laboratories in protest against the segregation of Jews carried out unofficially by professors. A quantity of anti-Jewish literature was distributed in Sofia, although Bulgaria had exercised tolerance until then towards the 50,000 Jews who lived in that country.[24]

That summer proved grim for Jews in Eastern and Central Europe. Six Jews were injured in Ostrów Mazowiecka. On August 24, fifty Jews were beaten, seven of them seriously injured, in a market day raid by hundreds of Endeks in the town of Brańsk. The same occurred the next day in Stoczek Węgrowski, Kolno, and Jedwabne, with many Jews beaten up and their property vandalized. Scores of Jews fled to Warsaw as disorders spread throughout the Białystok province. Anti-Jewish attacks by Nazi youths shouting "Heil Hitler!" also took place in Schwartzort (now Juodkrantė) near Memel (now Klaipėda), Lithuania, in which several persons were wounded while the German autonomous police refused to intervene. In a statement that all nationalist newspapers reprinted on their front pages, Patriarch Cristea described the Jews as "a plague," and wondered "why should we not get rid of these parasites who suck Romanian Christian blood?" On September 13, 1937, not long after Hitler had denounced the Bolshevik substitution of a race of "Jewish parasites" in place of real "intellectual nationals," and two days after Goebbels pointed the finger at the Jew as "the visible demon of the decay of humanity," the *Führer* publicly hammered home his consistent thesis about world Jewry being the force behind Bolshevism and the historic enemy of humanity.[25]

Greater physical outbreaks in Poland heralded the arrival the Jewish New Year. Widespread disorders and considerable property damage, assaults during which some Jews were killed and many injured, wrecked havoc in Wieliczka, Poznań, Tomki, Łomża, Drohobycz (now Drohobych, Ukraine), Bydgoszcz, and Małkinia. Twenty Jews were wounded and more than 100 beaten in Warsaw, Łódź, Łomża, and ten other localities, many of these attacks carried out by uniformed members of the National Radical Camp and National Democratic Party in what appeared to be prearranged plans. Eleven Jews were wounded in market-day riots in Sokołów Podlaski; three elderly Jews were taken to a hospital in Radom in critical condition. The Nara Party organ boasted of further attacks at Długosiodło, Branczyce (now Branchytsy, Belarus), Poręba, and Czwórka. Members of the Youth Section of Col. Adam Koc's Camp of National Unity called for mass Jewish emigration, while placards in Piotrków Trybunalski declaring "Death to the Jews" were not removed despite the intervention of the socialist mayor. Eight houses in Kielce were set afire and a number of elderly Jews stoned, while Jews returning from Yom Kippur prayers in Czeladź were set upon by Nara loyalists; a trampled Jewish child was taken to the hospital. More than fifty Jews were injured, at least eight seriously, in attacks on the streets of Częstochowa and other places in Poland on September 21. Endek and Nara groups wounded at least twenty Jews in Warsaw; pillage and destruction occurred in the Silesian towns of Biała and Bielsko. Bombs thrown on a crowded Bund club house and on a socialist parade in Warsaw wounded many, followed by bombs and shots fired on a Jewish club in Długa Street.[26]

Violence against Jews surged forward in Romania as well. A number of Jews were seriously beaten with clubs in Buhuși, a town in the Moldavia province, before police restored order. Archdeacon Jon Mota of Orăștie suggested on September 9 that Jews should be "isolated and burned out" like weeds, and compared the Jews to an attack of scabies, for which he suggested a disinfecting treatment. He added that the next best thing was to follow the plan of "the great master, Hitler" in dealing with Jews. In an article titled "The Jewish Plague," Bishop Tit of Hotin (now Khotyn, Ukraine) urged an anti-Jewish boycott under the slogan "not a pin from a Jew." Bishop Vartolomei Ramnic charged that all wars and revolutions were caused by the Jews, but that the victims were always Christians. This influential Church dignitary pressed for the expulsion of the Jews from the country and the confiscation of their property.

Several Ukrainian leaders in Cernauti (now Chernivtsi, Ukraine) appealed for permission to publish the antisemitic classic *Protocols of the Elders of Zion* in their language, intending to use Streicher's version and print 10,000 copies for distribution among the Ukrainians in the Bukovina province. Many Jews were injured in attacks in Suceava. The influential National Soldiers' Front ordered "spiritual mobilization of all Rumanians against the vast Jewish plot which paralyzes the normal development of the economic life of Rumania." Corneliu Zelea Codreanu, Supreme Commander of the Iron Guard, declared that the battle against "a foreign invading race" would now begin. Hitler conferred the Order of the Red Cross upon Patriarch Cristea.[27]

What options for emigration existed for Jews desperately in search of haven that autumn? Approximately 125,000 persons had fled from Germany since 1933 according to the JDC, of whom approximately 13,000 to 15,000 were non-Jews, and now the pressure was far greater. Director Marc Wischnitzer of the German-Jewish *Hilfsverein* noted that immigration into the United States and South America was limited at present, while good opportunities in South Africa, Rhodesia, Australia, and Kenya required considerable preliminary work before large-scale efforts could succeed.

Beck and other associates urged that Palestine be opened wide to Jewish immigration, but the staunchly anti-Zionist George Rendel, the British Foreign Office's Middle East expert, replied to First Secretary Michalowski of the Polish Embassy in London that Palestine "could offer no solution to the major demographic problems [sic] of Europe." Rendel privately added to his colleagues that "it is by no means inconceivable that if there was some turn of the wheel in Europe, a no longer actively Jew-baiting Germany might find a ready-made spiritual colony awaiting her in a key position in the Middle East." "Our policy of creating a Jewish State in Palestine for the sake of Jewish immigrants from Poland and Central Europe," he observed in a memorandum for Foreign Secretary Anthony Eden on October 20, "has provoked the uncompromising hostility of practically all the Arabs of Palestine and of the neighboring Arab territories."[28]

Developments in November 1937 were even bleaker. Attacks continued in Danzig, while a new Italian edition of the *Protocols* appeared in Rome.

Some Polish universities were closed after riots resulting from the attempt of Nationalists to obtain Jewish segregation in classrooms. A number of Jews were injured in Endek student demonstrations in all Polish universities on November 11; the Universities of Poznań, Kraków, and Wilno decreed separate "ghetto benches" for their Jewish students. Streicher's "The Eternal Jew" exhibit, also informing about the so-called Jewish "blood rite" of murdering Christian boys to use their blood for the baking of Passover *matzot*, opened in Munich as part of the festivities marking the fourteenth anniversary of Hitler's abortive Beer Hall putsch of 1923. "Prisoners are still tortured to death in German concentration camps," a special correspondent reported in the London *Daily Herald*. The Nazi Party asserted on November 16 that Jews should show "gratitude" that lynch law was not used to solve the Jewish problem, even as it sought to pursue "the complete segregation" of Jewry. In Budapest, the largest police raids in the capital's history rounded up more than 500 Jews, thirty of whom were detained for deportation when they could not produce proper identification papers. Assaults against Jews occurred in the Lithuanian towns of Memel, Wilkomir (now Ukmergė), and Shavli (now Šiauliai). The arrest of a Swiss citizen in Berne disclosed Nazi espionage efforts worldwide.[29]

Romania posed the newest danger. For the first time, one of the country's schools introduced "ghetto benches"; a "ghetto" section was decreed for Jewish reporters covering parliamentary sessions; serious anti-Jewish disturbances occurred in Bukovina. Jewish journalists were forbidden this occupation and denied train passes. "Can the Romanian people end its days . . . wasted by poverty and syphilis, invaded by Jews and torn apart by foreigners?" asked staunch Iron Guard supporter and historian of religion Mircea Eliade in a leading newspaper. On December 29, King Carol II invited Goga to form a new cabinet within twenty-four hours. As many Romanian Jews were believed to be preparing to flee before a series of antisemitic decrees planned by Goga's Nationalist government, the Bulgarian government quickly responded. On the last day of 1937, Sofia issued measures against Jewish immigration from its immediate, far larger neighbor to the north.[30]

As the months of 1938 went by, Europe's Jews rapidly approached the abyss of despair. In Wilno, the Association of Journalists adopted the "Aryan paragraph"; twenty Jews were beaten by demonstrators shouting "What happened in Rumania will happen here!" The pro-German Arrow Cross attacked Jewish skiers near Budapest. The spread of Nazi racial theories and literature in Italy drew the denunciation of the semi-official Vatican organ *L'Osservatore Romano*, but an authoritative Italian spokesman gave his blessing to "the great historical experiment started in Rumania," and *La*

Stampa declared that Jewish domination of democratic countries followed the methods outlined in the *Protocols*. German firms in Bulgaria complied with Berlin's request to dismiss all Jewish employees. Hitler's entry into Vienna on March 14 to a rousing public welcome and the ensuing *Anschluss* (Union with Germany), immediately followed by the ruthless extension of Nazi rule over Austria's 185,000 Jews, accentuated Jewry's undeniable sense of powerlessness.[31]

The Latvian government began taking over "Jewish enterprises "in the interests of the State," while the Bern Cantonal Court overruled the conviction of two Nazis for distributing copies of the *Protocols*, claiming that, while these writings "are particularly vile," they were not to be considered "immoral literature" in the strict sense of the Bern penal code. Fifty-two Jews were wounded in Poland on March 20, two of them seriously, as Nationalists rioted in apparent disappointment over the peaceful settlement of the Polish-Lithuanian crisis. Many Jews were beaten at the Lithuanian city of Kaunas (Kovno), when students prevented Jews from voting in university union elections. Czechoslovakia started to close its doors to refugees from Austria, as did Yugoslavia and Hungary; Italy was giving transit visas only to Poland. By a vote of 210 to 142, Great Britain's House of Commons turned down a bill giving the Home Office much wider powers for the admission of Austrian Jewish refugees; US Secretary of State Cordell Hull announced that no increase in the German and Austrian quotas could be contemplated. More than 500 Jews with their families left Danzig within two weeks, while others seeking to flee besieged foreign consulates every day for visas.[32]

The Evian Conference on Refugees, convened between July 6–15, 1938, to respond to European Jewry's growing crisis, witnessed delegate after delegate limiting official responses to sympathizing with the refugees and to deploring Nazi brutality. Australia's Thomas W. White exhibited no embarrassment in asserting boldly that "as we have no real racial problem, we are not desirous of importing one." France had reached "the extreme point of saturation as regards admission of refugees," stated delegate Victor Henri Bérenger, a sentiment repeated by his European counterparts. Switzerland insisted "it essential to exercise very stringent control over the admission of any further foreigners." Following US chief representative Myron Taylor's lead about his country's maintaining its strict quotas, the South American governments declared that their restrictive immigration laws could not be eased; the British Dominions sounded this tone as well. The one exception proved to be the Dominican Republic, which offered to accept up to 100,000 refugees on generous terms.[33]

The delegates unanimously agreed to create the Intergovernmental Committee on Refugees (IGCR), charged with approaching "the governments of the countries of refuge with a view to developing opportunities for permanent settlement," and seeking to persuade Germany to cooperate in establishing "conditions of orderly emigration." The final resolution employed "involuntary emigrants" for "refugees"; the words "Jew" and "Jewish" were markedly absent. Goldie Meyerson (later Golda Meir), outraged at not being seated among the delegates, called a press conference the day after the gathering ended. Speaking as head of the labor Histadrut's Political Department, this *Yishuv* representative announced: "There is only one thing I hope to see before I die and that is that my people should not need expressions of sympathy anymore."[34]

In the meanwhile, the Lower House of the Hungarian parliament set quotas limiting Jews (defined according to *religion*) to twenty percent of the positions in certain businesses and professions. In early June, seizures of Jews in Vienna had mounted into the thousands, and over 1,000 were sent to the Dachau concentration camp. At least 242 Jews were wounded and four killed in Poland during a month of murderous antisemitic assaults. On July 14, Benito Mussolini's fascist government announced that Jews did not belong to the "Aryan" Italian race. On September 2, the Italian Cabinet prohibited Jewish immigration, and decreed that all foreign Jews and those who had acquired citizenship since January 1, 1919, were required to leave the country within six months.[35]

In the Third Reich, *Kristallnacht*, the "Night of Broken Glass" on November 9–10, shocked Jewry and augmented its despair. An official Nazi report stated that ninety-one Jews had been killed, with hundreds wounded. The Board of Deputies of British Jews reported 500 destroyed synagogues. Hundreds of Jewish shops and dwellings were looted and destroyed. More than 30,000 Jews were sent to concentration camps, where several hundred would die in the following weeks. The Jewish community was fined one billion reichsmarks ($400 million), with an accelerated "Aryanization" of all remaining Jewish property—sold to non-Jews for ten percent of tax value—to follow. As Karl Schleunes's pioneering analysis has shown, the "experts" would now be in charge of the Third Reich's Jewish policy. Göring and the SS leadership would provide professional coordination at last, from which alone could emerge "a single direction and a clearly defined objective" how to get rid of the Jews.[36]

As the year drew to a close, serious attacks against Jews occurred in Bessarabia. The Endeks won a substantial majority in the Poznań municipal elections, while the country's right-wing press inveighed against the Polish Jews forcibly expelled from Germany. Netherlands branches of German firms dismissed Jews. The Finance Ministry of Romania, where *Kristallnacht* had "given strong fillip" to antisemitism, ordered 400 Jewish-owned inns and 800 tobacco shops to close on "sanitary grounds." Bratislava witnessed the burning of two synagogues and discriminatory measures against Jews. More than 800 Jewish families, fearing a Nazi election victory in Memel, evacuated that autonomous district for other parts of Lithuania.[37]

On January 30, 1939, Hitler announced the following during an address before the Reichstag:

> If the international Jewish financiers in and outside Europe should succeed in plunging the nations once more into a world war, then the result will not be the bolshevization of the earth, and thus the victory of Jewry, but the annihilation of the Jewish race in Europe![38]

Forcing the pace against Jewry could be found elsewhere in Europe as well. Nine Jews were injured, three of them seriously, when a bomb was thrown on the evening of February 5 into the principal synagogue of Hungary's Pest Jewish community during Sabbath services. In Hungary, Premier Bela Imrédy, who had just called for a fight against "the poisonous influence of the Jewish spirit in morality," had to resign for the announced reason that he had a Jewish great-grandmother. His successor, Pál Teleki, oversaw passage of the second Jewish Law (initiated by Imrédy to steal the thunder of the Arrow Cross), which further restricted the economic participation of Jews to five percent, and declared—adopting a *racial* definition of Jewishness—that baptized children who had at least one non-converted Jewish parent were Jewish. Hungarian authorities began a drive to deport all foreign Jews from Czech territories that were ceded to Hungary by Hitler's order. In the city of Munkács (now Mukachevo, Ukraine) alone, 300 Polish Jewish families were given a week's notice to leave, and another 200 families of Yugoslavian and Romanian Jews were ordered to depart within a fortnight. Of an estimated 80,000 Jews residing in that territory, the Hungarian authorities declared that at least 4,000 families had to leave because they were foreigners.[39]

After the German *Wehrmacht* took over the rump Bohemia and Moravia on March 15, 1939, to create a so-called Protectorate, thereby destroying the democratic Czech state, suicides of Jews and mass arrests by the Gestapo began. Jewish merchants sold their businesses to "Aryans" as quickly as possible at a fraction of the actual worth, Looting occurred immediately after the occupation; the largest synagogue in Brno (Brünn) was destroyed by a fire, as was the magnificent one in Olomouc (Olmütz), by Nazi instigators. Offices were set up in Prague, supervised by Eichmann as he had done earlier in Vienna and Berlin, to hasten Jewish emigration. The war against the Jews in Central Europe, declared Albert Einstein over the CBS network a week later, aims "to exterminate not only ourselves, but to destroy together with us that spirit expressed in the Bible and in Christianity which made possible the rise of civilization in Central and Northern Europe. If this aim is achieved Europe will become a barren waste." According to the Havas News Agency, well over 10,000 Jews were rounded up by the Gestapo in the Protectorate, most arrests reportedly made on the basis of a "blacklist" prepared over the years by Konrad Heinlein's Sudeten German Party.[40]

In May, the British issued the White Paper, which severely limited Jewish entry into Palestine for the next five years to 75,000—thereafter with Arab consent. Concurrently, unabated anti-Jewish terror raged in Slovakia. Lithuania's premier flatly pledged the government's support to the antisemitic merchants' association in its efforts to eliminate Jews from trade and industry. Unprepared to fundamentally question the United States' restrictive immigration laws at a time of massive unemployment and rising hatred for Jews, President Roosevelt at most extended the visitors' visas for some 15,000 refugees in the wake of *Kristallnacht*. The Coast Guard's barring from Miami more than 900 German Jewish passengers who had sailed from Hamburg to Cuba aboard the *SS St. Louis* with expensive landing certificates that President Frederico Laredo Bru had invalidated without their knowledge, as well as the failure of the Wagner-Rogers bill, calling for the admission of 20,000 Jewish children in 1939–1940 *under the quota system*, even to emerge from congressional committee, reflected the public temper which Roosevelt gauged so well. FDR's fascination with mass resettlement projects also offered little comfort to the Jews, an innovative gesture which, like the Evian Conference, suggested sympathy and possible long-term relief while, in effect, keeping America's doors shut.[41]

In Hungary, public opinion had shifted so far to the right that the Arrow Cross party garnered the second highest number of votes in the national elections and became the leading opposition party. At least 6,000 Jews in the Protectorate, where synagogues were being put to the torch almost every other day, depended for their maintenance upon welfare organizations. Aryanization of the medical profession in Austria "is now complete," reported the Vienna correspondent of the *Journal of the American Medical Association* on June 21. Two days later, any Jew living in the Protectorate was officially defined according to the 1935 Nuremberg Laws as regards the registration of Jewish property, Hitler appointee Konstantin von Neurath obtaining dictatorial power over its transfer of at least half a billion dollars in worth. Polish police began pushing Czech Jewish refugees into the Protectorate; the Reich resumed the expulsion of Polish Jews at the end of the month. British sea patrols continued their hunt for illegal Jewish voyagers to Palestine.[42]

Come August, the US embassy in London passed on to the State Department a report from the JDC that Eichmann had ordered Jews in the Protectorate to be prepared for emigration at the rate of 250–300 per day. The first concentration camp in the Danzig territory was opened on August 3 at Güttland with more than sixty Jews unable to work under the city's antisemitic laws. "In the interest of cooperation with the German nation," a branch of President Emil Hacha's party ordered that as of August 15 no Czech female citizen under the age of forty-five could be employed by Jews, and that all Jews be dismissed from Czech associations and commercial companies. The Belgian cabinet ordered all municipalities to draw up immediately lists of all foreigners residing in their districts. Three synagogues were sacked by mobs in Bratislava, which, along with other Slovakian towns, witnessed a pogrom through August 11–13 that injured many Jews, with many more arrested by the police. After at least 18,000 penniless Jewish refugees from Central Europe had reached Shanghai, a rare haven that required no entry visa, the Japanese naval authorities announced that no further refugees could reside in the International Settlement of the Hongkew (now spelled Hongkou) district. With the breaking of dawn on September 1, 1939, Hitler unleashed the Nazi *blitzkrieg* against Poland, bringing all the nations of the continent to the brink—a war, motivated by Hitler's obsession with racial purity, which would engulf the globe. The clock had run out on imperiled, isolated European Jewry.[43]

Some had come forward to answer the call to conscience. James G. McDonald, Lord Robert Cecil, Pope Pius XI, Cardinals Vervier in France and Mundelein in the United States, the author Romain Rolland, the Archbishop of Canterbury, British MPs Winston Churchill, Josiah Wedgwood, and Leopold Amery, and others denounced these vicious assaults, viewing them as, in American columnist Dorothy Thompson's words, "a human crisis." The eminent Protestant theologian Reinhold Niebuhr pleaded eloquently before the national convention of the Hadassah women's Zionist organization in October 1938 that Christians "owe the Jews a haven of a national home" in Palestine at "the precise moment when it is most desperately needed to offer asylum and the chance of rehabilitation to thousands of refugees from Europe," and that Britain could not "afford to make additional concessions to dictators without imperiling her physical integrity, just as she cannot afford to break her word without imperiling her moral prestige." Noted American publicist Raymond Swing, having just returned from the continent, warned the same gathering that the Jews of Europe had no place to turn but Palestine: "They face extinction after the most brutal torture and exploitation. The tide is against them. It is against all minorities."[44]

Yet such expressions of concern and appeals for action, fleeting flashes in the darkness, exercised little effect on national leaders who chose the role of bystanders in a world governed by what Ben-Gurion characterized as "power politics," rather than respond to the call of conscience. The Chamberlain cabinet's policy of appeasement that governed its stance vis-à-vis Hitler, for example, also determined its approach to the Palestine imbroglio: the first sought to avoid a potential war, the second to prepare for an inevitable one. (Jews would never support Hitler, and so were taken for granted; Arabs, whose loyalty to the democracies appeared questionable, were appeased.) For Roosevelt, the Great Depression, nativist sentiment, and rising antisemitism in the United States weighed heavily in the balance.[45]

In addition, the communal identity of world Jewry was regularly masked by these powers behind the term "refugees" (such as in the very title of the Evian Conference) or denied outright. This even occurred in the strong anti-Nazi denunciations that distinguished Thomas Mann's long letter of protest against the Third Reich on New Year's Day 1937 and Pius XI's *Mit Brennender Sorge* ("With Searing Anxiety"), branding the Nazi ideology of racism and totalitarianism "aggressive paganism," one year later. In an opaque observation, the draconian 1939 White Paper made but one reference to Jewry's beleaguered lot: His Majesty's Government was "conscious of the unhappy plight of large numbers of Jews who seek refuge from certain European countries." Even when oversimplifying by not admitting that the Nazis allowed Jews to emigrate only as practically penniless refugees, Goebbels's *Der Angriff*, as reported in the *New York Times* soon after *Kristallnacht*, told the truth this time:

> Clearly the possibility for Jews to emigrate has been greatly diminished. That is not the fault of Germany but wholly of the countries that on the one hand intervene with resounding speeches for "the pitiable Jewish people" and on the other hand, as the Evian Conference so clearly proved, do not think at all to take in Jews themselves.[46]

A political cartoon by Sidney "George" Strube, first appearing in London's *Daily Express* of June 20, 1938, with the single-word caption "WHITHER?," poignantly captured the escalating crisis. The noted editorial cartoonist of the *Daily Express* between 1912 and 1948 and the highest paid journalist in Fleet Street, Strube placed an elderly "non-Aryan" at the center of a large swastika.

Slumped over in sleep, the bearded Jew leans against a signpost with the word "GO" pointing to all four directions of the compass. The four ends of the globe, however, reached by the extending swastika, are each marked with the word "STOP." To the right of the frame, a sunrise heralds the imminent Evian Conference on Refugees. The Sunday edition of the *New York Times* on July 3 featured this cartoon, but with a different caption: "WILL THE EVIAN CONFERENCE GUIDE HIM TO FREEDOM?"[47] The answer was not long in coming. Culpability lay at many a door.

Jews understood early on, as Jewish Agency political director Moshe Shertok (later Sharett) put it to Palestine High Commissioner Arthur Wauchope in 1934, that they were "running a hard race against time." Already in April 1933, in bemoaning that FDR "has not by a single word or act intimated a faintest interest in what is going on" with respect to German Jewry, Zionist herald Rabbi Stephen Wise wrote to Judge Julian Mack that "none of us is quite alive to the fact that this may be the beginning of a world-wide movement against us, a world-wide conflagration, a world-wide undertaking against the Jews." Isaac Bashevis Singer's *Satan in Goray*, written two years before he migrated to the United States in 1935, had Jews foresee the gathering of Catholic Polish peasants "to exterminate" them. In the summer of 1936, famed poet Julian Tuwim's "The Ball at the Opera" delivered a bitter allegorical assault on a fascist, antisemitic Poland, and predicted an apocalypse. "The developments in Europe are unspeakably horrible," wrote Einstein to economist Otto Nathan that same year. "The Lord God appears to have appointed the devil to be the chief clerk of it."

Following his visit to Vienna in April 1938, World Zionist Organization official Leo Lauterbach considered that the German policy in Austria "may aim at a complete annihilation of Austrian Jewry." When calling that October for world Jewry, "God's chosen people," to unite and "erect an independent Jewish State," Austrian-born composer Arnold Schoenberg posed this question in an essay written from his home in Los Angeles: "Is there room in the world for almost 7,000,000 people? Are they condemned to doom? Will they become extinct? Famished? Butchered?" Four months later, delegate Emil Sommerstein denounced in the Sejm "the extermination policy of the present Government and system."[48]

Even establishment groups such as the British Joint Foreign Committee and the American Jewish Committee, with all their fears that a World Jewish Congress would affirm the bogey of the international Jew as most crudely expressed in the *Protocols of the Learned Elders of Zion*, sought without success to move their governments to action. The World Jewish Congress, like them and like the Jewish Agency for Palestine, could enjoy few triumphs after its creation in August 1936. Berlin Jewish leaders Leo Baeck and Wilfrid Israel found little official sympathy in London's Foreign Office when urging an emigration program to save at least German Jewish youth without delay. US Justice Louis D. Brandeis, who had immediately advised the departure of German Jewry in March 1933, told associate Robert Szold in early August 1939 that he remained certain of final Zionist triumph, except that "if the Germans would come in with their ruthless policy of extermination, it might be a different story."[49]

Still, they and all others could hardly forecast the depth of human depravity that would befall the Jews of Europe in the global conflict to come. While words like "annihilation," "destruction," "extermination," "starvation by death," "elimination," "physical extinction," *Shoah*, and "the onrush of lava" (the graphic phrase of Revisionist-Zionist leader Vladimir Ze'ev Jabotinsky) surfaced with greater frequency in these depressing years, no one could have foreseen the Holocaust, when Jewish hopes would be literally reduced to ashes. That unprecedented catastrophe was simply inconceivable. Before 1938, notes Avraham Barkai, even the most pessimistic Zionists, who "foresaw a complete end" to Jews in Germany, planned for an orderly emigration extending over a period of fifteen to twenty years, with no more than 20,000–25,000 emigrants annually. Jewish Agency official Arthur Ruppin spoke at the Evian Conference of an annual emigration rate of 50,000 Jews from Germany and Austria over a six-year period. Jabotinsky pressed in October 1938 for an immigration of 1,000,000 within three years, and he blundered badly when deriding Nazi Germany in May 1939 as an "inflated balloon." Even Ben-Gurion's call for an "*aliya* rebellion" without British approval after *Kristallnacht*, which he saw as "the signal for the extermination of the Jewish people throughout the world," referred to the entry of 1,000,000 Jews in a short time.[50]

The young Joachim Prinz, a charismatic Reform rabbi in Berlin, also failed to gauge fully the uniqueness of Nazi antisemitism. In 1934, his book *Wir Juden* ("We Jews") welcomed Hitler's regime on the grounds that it would force the assimilated Jews to show their colors and would alarm the strictly Orthodox who had opposed Zionism for religious reasons. Prinz's Zionist message along racial lines got him detained by the Gestapo on numerous occasions. When SS *Obersturmbahnführer* Otto Kuchmann warned Prinz that a final arrest was imminent, the thirty-five-year-old managed with Wise's help to reach the United States in the spring of 1937. Writing for the *New Palestine* that September, he astutely observed that "no one can doubt that German Jewry must die if the Nazi Government lives, and there can be little doubt that the Nazi Government is very far from dying." At the same time, while soon reminding an

American Jewish Congress convention that the hour had come of Heinrich Heine's warning a century earlier that "the German thunderbolt" would fall, Prinz went on to say this: "The attempt of the German Government is, after the attempt of Spain in 1492, the first attempt to expel a Jewry and to insult a Jewry instead of solving a problem which really is a problem in the world."[51]

Even Simon Dubnow, the Jewish people's preeminent historian at the time, misjudged the singular nature of Hitler's paranoid Judeophobia. Having left Berlin for Riga when Hitler came to power, the seventy-nine-year-old advocate of granting spiritual and cultural autonomy to the Jewish populations of Europe authored a confidential call in June 1939 for an International League for Protection of the Jewish People against Aggression. In his view, the Jewish people, lacking a state of its own, could not seek protection by "formal affiliation" with any Anti-Aggressors League that would be established. "Unceasing internal aggression" was leading to "the annihilation of a defenseless people." "Hitler Germany and its conquered territories," Dubnow continued, "are systematically carrying into effect the ancient program of the Biblical Haman: to exterminate, crush and wipe out all the Jews. . . . Those who have been unable to escape the Teuton Inferno face a truly dreadful prospect—forced labor after the fashion commanded by the Egyptian Pharaohs or in the event of war—the alternative of serving as cannon fodder." An international league for the protection of the Jewish people had to be created, he urged, with action on parallel lines to be undertaken by the World Jewish Congress in Paris and Geneva and the American Jewish Congress in New York. Yet, one month later, in an interview with a correspondent from the *Yishuv* labor newspaper *Davar*, Dubnow saw no fundamental distinction between totalitarian rule and previous absolutist regimes, and maintained his faith in autonomous Jewish life in the Diaspora.[52]

Mordecai ("Mordkhe") Gebirtig of Kraków probably came closest to articulating the enormity of the danger. This Yiddish folk bard, born in 1877 in Poland's second most important city, had become increasingly popular for his love songs, children's songs, and lullabies. In 1938, Gebirtig immortalized the Przytyk pogrom of 1936 in a poem. "*S'brent!*" ("Fire!") called out to his readers that "our poor town's on fire!" These lines of his hymn rang out with special force: "The dreaded moment may soon come / When the town with us included / Will be turned to flames and ashes." Brothers, Gebirtig implored, had to take pails and put out the fire! The shtetl, what David Roskies aptly calls "the Jewish collective presence in exile," could only be saved by Jewish solidarity. Much as the Zionist poet Hayim Nahman Bialik's "*B'Ir HaHareiga*" ("In the City of Slaughter") had made the 1903 Kishinev pogrom an archetype of modern Jewish calamity, "*S'brent!*" did so for Przytyk in warning that Jews could trust in no one but themselves when faced with a world in flames.[53]

Yet all sensed the screw press of history inexorably tightening about Europe's Jews. They "were actors in their own history" during these fateful years, Bernard Wasserstein has shown, but remained fundamentally powerless. Such was the hallmark of Jewish exile. Accepting the 1938 Nobel Peace Prize that December as president of the Nansen International Office for Refugees, Michael Hansson warned that "the Jewish problem in Europe" now included some five million people who were increasingly "outlawed in many countries" because "governments become more unfeeling and the people more fearful and suspicious." Hearing British Colonial Secretary Malcolm MacDonald's comment on May 13, 1939, that the Jews had made "many mistakes," Chaim Weizmann's sharp retort reflected personal bitterness and his people's angst: "Our chief mistake is that we exist at all."

The World Zionist Organization president's public *cri de coeur* in November 1936 to the British Royal Commission on Palestine, pointing to six million Jews living east of the Rhine "doomed to be pent up in places where they are not wanted, and for whom the world is divided into places where they cannot live and places in which they cannot enter," had not received a positive response. Jabotinsky fared no better when addressing that official body a few months later. "Dispersion becomes dismemberment," Buber observed to Mohandas Gandhi on February 24, 1939, when asserting that Jewish destiny was "indissolubly bound up" with "the possibility of ingathering" in Palestine. The Mahatma, who had publicly called on Jews one day after *Kristallnacht* to practice passive resistance even unto death, did not reply.[54]

War across the soil of Europe, a continent by then seething with fear and hatred, threatened the six million Jews "doomed to be pent up" in ways that none could rationally predict. Even when Vincent Sheean, musing about what Hitler would do with the Jews, concluded in 1939 that "the day of mass murder may not be so far off as we now think," the American journalist limited this rumination to the Jews of Greater Germany. If that day came, he added, "the democracies will have their share of the responsibility before the conscience of mankind, which must someday break through the clouds and assert its dominion, at least in retrospect, over the conduct of nations and prime ministers." His Majesty's Government, with King George VI on the royal throne, would grant a total of 13,700 Palestine certificates for all of that year.[55]

That March, carrying a suitcase stuffed with Franz Kafka's papers, Max Brod set out for Palestine on the last train to leave Prague, five minutes before the Nazis closed the Czech border. The same spring, having been ordered by the Nazis to sell their property and emigrate, the Danzig Jewish community succeeded in sending the sacred contents of its Great Synagogue museum in ten huge crates to the Jewish Theological Seminary in New York City. Thanks to a signed agreement in December 1938 with the Senate that they were willing to leave Danzig within several months, the remaining 4,000–4,500 of the city's Jews were saved from expulsion and death, the funds from the JDC's "purchase" of the more than 500 ceremonial objects going towards Jewish emigration.[56] Most Jews across Europe, however, remained trapped by nations that had bolted their doors, while dictators obsessed with antisemitic onslaught would not allow the luxury of orderly, long-range mass resettlement. The thunder, rumbling overhead (recall W. H. Auden's "Refugee Blues," 1939) was unmistakable. Implacable evil, resulting in the blackest of tragedies, loomed ahead.

CHAPTER 4

Vladimir (Ze'ev) Jabotinsky, Hillel Kook-Peter Bergson, and the Campaign for a Jewish Army

Viewed within the larger context of Zionist ideology and Zionist politics, the story of the campaign for a Jewish army in World War II must begin with Vladimir (Ze'ev) Jabotinsky. As early as 1923, the founder of the Jewish Legion in World War I and of the first Hagana units in Jerusalem against Arab attack in 1920, respectfully analyzing adamant Arab opposition to Zionist aspirations, advocated the only solution to be a Jewish majority with a formidable army in an independent Jewish state on both sides of the Jordan. The thesis of this pioneering essay, "The Iron Wall," was reiterated in the right-wing political platform of Jabotinsky's World Union of Zionist Revisionists two years later.

Jabotinsky was not, at the same time, prepared to embrace the maximalist trend in Revisionism, spearheaded in the early 1930's by Abba Ahimeir, Yehoshua Yeivin, and poet Uri Zvi Greenberg. While Greenberg had already called in 1923 for *biryonim* ("ruffians") who dreamt of "the Kingdom of Israel" and in 1928 for a Jewish armed force to conquer Palestine, and Yeivin blasted the World Zionist Organization (WZO) executive for relying on the British mandatory power, Ahimeir urged Jabotinsky to become Zionism's authoritarian Duce à la Mussolini. Ahimeir also called on Revisionist Betar youth to become the fighting avant-garde for Jewry's national liberation and, with Yeivin, even raised the possibility of political terror. Jabotinsky applauded Ahimeir's personal example of imprisonment, but his own abiding faith in British parliamentarianism, in liberal values, and in open diplomacy precluded the revolt demanded by Ahimeir's small *Brit HaBiryonim* circle; he refused to resign from the WZO. After the 1929 Arab riots, Jabotinsky pressed for a renewal of the Jewish Legion in Palestine, all the while preferring that a Jewish commonwealth become part of Britain's dominions as advocated by Josiah Wedgwood, MP.[1]

Ahimeir's influence extended to young Revisionists within the El-Al fraternity at the Hebrew University, who responded to his call to halt an inaugural lecture there in February 1932 by Norman Bentwich, because the former Attorney General for Palestine supported a binational state based on parity with the country's Arab population. Among the protesters was student David Raziel, also a member of the Hagana in Jerusalem. He, Ahimeir, M. A. Perlmutter, and Avraham Stern (then in Tel Aviv) were expelled for a time from the university as a result; the seventeen-year-old Hillel Kook, who had arrived in Palestine with his family from Ukraine in 1925, was arrested but released. Raziel, four years older than Kook, became his mentor after their first meeting at the yeshiva of Kook's uncle, the first Chief Ashkenazi Rabbi of Eretz Israel. When a faction within the Hagana, favoring a more militant response to murderous Arab assaults against the *Yishuv* (the Jewish community of Palestine), seceded to form the Hagana Bet in 1931, Kook followed Raziel and Stern into what also became known as the Irgun Tzva'i Le'umi B'Eretz Yisrael.[2]

Already in the first two issues of *HaMetzuda*, the Irgun's short-lived publication, Raziel and Stern made clear the new group's orientation. In a piece entitled "*L'Zekher Haver*" ("In Memory of a Comrade"), Raziel wrote of its hope "to absorb the bullet intended to destroy the Hebrew *Yishuv*." Stern's poem "*Hayalim Almonim*" ("Anonymous Soldiers") asserted that freedom from enlistment in the cause would only come with death, their dream "to die for our nation!" His original words about their flag heralding "war and conquest" were thought too extreme by the editorial board's Peretz Carmeli, so the final version read "defense and conquest." "*Hayalim Almonim*," performed at the first Irgun cadet class in the spring of 1932, quickly became the Irgun's anthem, but Kook found himself in the minority when opposing Stern's verses for "romanticizing death." As a protégé of Raziel's, he became an officer within the Irgun, and arranged for the clandestine printing of the first weapons manual by Stern and Raziel, *HaEkdach* ("The Pistol"), in 1935. One year later, at the start of the Arab Revolt, he commanded a group of Irgun fighters in Motza, outside Jerusalem.[3]

Jabotinsky, who played no part in the Irgun's secession from the Hagana, also called for sacrifice on behalf of the Zionist objective. His Betar anthem, composed in 1932, included the phrase "to die or to conquer the mountain!" He charged the labor Left, which secured a definite majority at the 1933 World Zionist Congress, with mounting a "blood libel" against the Revisionist-Zionists by charging them with the murder that June of the Jewish Agency's political director, Chaim Arlosoroff. He also clashed with the Jewish Agency for Palestine executive when launching a boycott of German goods and a worldwide petition in response to the Nazi Third Reich government's persecution of that country's Jews. Yet Jabotinsky still sought unity via a Round Table Conference of all Zionist factions, and he signed a preliminary peace pact with Mapai labor party leader David Ben-Gurion at the close of 1934. Menachem Begin, then a Betar commander in Poland, joined with the Palestinian delegation majority under Ahimeir's leadership at the sixth Revisionist World Conference in opposing the agreement, pointing out that Ben-Gurion had once called the Revisionist chief "Vladimir Hitler." Jabotinsky replied that Ben-Gurion and fellow laborites Yitzhak Ben-Zvi and Eliyahu Golomb had worn the uniform of the Jewish Legion, and would fight again if the Zionist cause demanded it. The World Union endorsed its leader's stance.[4]

Jabotinsky set off for a trip to the United States soon thereafter, meant to gain adherents for the World Union. His inaugural speech, delivered on January 26, 1935, at New York City's Mecca Temple, draw an enthusiastic audience of 4,000 which heard his warning of catastrophe in Palestine if immigration, settlement in Transjordan, and export of the *Yishuv*'s products were limited by the mandatory authority. Yet Zionist publications and spokesmen, especially Stephen Wise, pilloried Jabotinsky's militarist philosophy as close to Fascism; he received a cool, at times hostile, reception when addressing the National Board of Hadassah. Speaking engagements in other major cities did not draw large crowds and some potential allies sat "on the fence." America, Jabotinsky came to realize, was probably the hardest field to conquer for his movement: "Revisionism is 'dead earnest' because it was born in that European and Palestinian milieu where national ideals mean the actual salvaging of the nation, not the erection of flower-shops." American Jews, under the spell of President Franklin D. Roosevelt's New Deal domestic reform program, were drawn to what Jabotinsky called "salon Socialism." Finally, the Revisionist-Zionists in the United States lacked a hardcore group of supporters, one member admitting that no work had been done to build up an organization, even to create a central office with salaried staff. Jabotinsky's voyage having accomplished little, he discounted the United States as a political factor which could pressure Britain against retreating from its obligations under the Palestine Mandate.[5]

The labor Histadrut's overwhelming rejection of the Jabotinsky-Ben-Gurion agreement by an impressive majority in March 1935, coupled with the Zionist Actions Committee precluding Revisionist political action, convinced Jabotinsky that the time had come for "a clean and clear-cut *basta*" from the WZO. In April, following Hitler's decree of army conscription and

Mussolini's aggressive intentions against Abyssinia (Ethiopia), he sent former Colonial Secretary Leopold Amery a confidential letter. Guaranteeing that some 100,000 Jewish youth from outside Palestine would respond to England's need in wartime for any Eastern field of action, Jabotinsky wondered whether such an offer would be acceptable. The Jewish Legion, he noted, had become "a cherished legend" and an inspiring precedent, while military training had become extremely popular with the young men with whom he was in contact in "the deepest parts of the Ghetto." Amery, now a Conservative MP, replied to "Mr. J." that he would sound out the War Office, although he did not expect them "to take up your project with open arms." Indeed, the War Office turned the offer down.[6]

In September, one week after the World Zionist Congress witnessed Labor's becoming the decisive force in Zionism, its triumph crowned with Ben-Gurion's election as chairman of the Jewish Agency Executive and Weizmann's return to the WZO presidency, Jabotinsky formally broke with the WZO. At the congress in Vienna of the New Zionist Organization (NZO), Jabotinsky pledged a "war to the bitter end" against the Third Reich as a measure of Jewish self-defense. The NZO, he declared, would seek "not only to build Palestine, but to liquidate the Diaspora." To this end, the newly elected NZO president suggested a ten-year plan in order to secure a Jewish majority on both sides of the Jordan, providing for the settlement of 1,500,000 Jews in the next decade, and a bank capitalized at $500,000 to further Palestine's development. Following the exhortation from Col. John Henry Patterson, Irish-born organizer of the Zion Mule Corps (the nucleus of the Jewish Legion, which he commanded), to remind England that Jewish soldiers conquered Transjordan against the Turks in the Great War and that the NZO "pull the Jewish flag to the mast-head" in Palestine, the delegates also decided to appoint a special commission to deal with establishing "a Jewish Legion for the protection of Jewish peace."[7]

In early April 1936, a telegram from Jabotinsky to the British High Commissioner, Arthur Wauchope, called for "decisive action" in light of an "alarming report from Palestine voicing acutest apprehension of anti-Jewish outbreaks" on an "unprecedented scale." He warned that this would inevitably lead to bloodshed, especially considering "scarcity Imperial Troops inefficiency Police" and "absence legalized Jewish self-defense." Although Wauchope considered the British forces adequate for the present, the Arab Revolt broke out two weeks later. Mass meetings of the NZO in London and Paris urged reestablishing a Jewish regiment as a permanent section of the Imperial troops, without success. Jabotinsky initially supported the Jewish Agency's policy of forbearance and static defense (*havlaga*), whereas Ahimeir demanded that

Palestinian Jewish youth become "a generation of heroes" rather than one of "holy martyrs." By the end of August, the NZO president admitted that restraint had been harmful in the face of increased Arab rebellion. Come November, with Jewish casualties rising and His Majesty's Government (HMG) announcing the dispatch of a Royal Commission to investigate the disorders, Jabotinsky reluctantly concluded that "the British phase of Zionism is virtually over."[8]

One year later, the growing divide between Jabotinsky and the Irgun surfaced dramatically. Both rejected the Royal Commission's plan to partition Palestine into two polities, as well as the Agency's doctrine of *havlaga*. Whereas Jabotinsky, backed by Patterson, Amery, and Wedgwood, continued to champion a new Jewish Legion for defense to counter incessant and deadly Arab attacks, however, the younger commanders of the Irgun commenced on November 14, 1937, a series of retaliatory killings against Arabs in Jerusalem. Hailing this "first black day," Raziel stressed that only war in this fashion could end the Arab terror and achieve "the nationalist aspirations of the Jewish people." Jabotinsky agreed with their refusal to rejoin the Hagana and their declaration of independence that April as the Irgun Tzva'i Le'umi, but he harbored grave doubts about the killing of civilians who were not directly responsible, and he did not approve of individual political terror. While the Irgun's supreme commander, he held no official position of authority in this illegal organization. Living in the safety of London, he was further reluctant to approve large-scale Irgun action and its attendant hazards. Jabotinsky's stress on political action and faith in international conscience, in true Herzlian fashion, struck Irgunists Raziel, Stern, Kook, and Alexander Rafaeli, along with secretary of the NZO executive, Shmuel Merlin, as hopelessly naïve. Nor could the Irgun accept his insistence that Betar in Europe organize "illegal" immigrant transports, the Irgun only to act as "a landing agency" in Palestine.[9]

The hanging in June 1938 of Shlomo Ben-Yosef, who with two other Betarim attacked an Arab bus in reprisal for the on-going murder of Jews, brought out Jabotinsky's inability to stem the Irgun's influence and growing radicalism. At first condemning the action as an independent, badly executed effort, the Irgun subsequently hailed Ben-Yosef as having entered "the honored temple of the fighters for freedom." At the third Betar world conference that September, Jabotinsky lauded Ben-Yosef's calm, proud bearing in the face of death, and criticized Begin for insisting that "military Zionism" now become Betar's rallying cry. Jabotinsky dismissed Begin's well-received speech as unrealistic and the valueless "creaking of a door," but Israel Sheib (later Eldad) welcomed this "creaking" as a warning signal that the "thieves of surrender and opportunism" had stolen into the national Zionist movement. Ultimately, the conference voted down a resolution from Stern associate Uriel Halpern (later Yonatan Ratosh) declaring the Jewish State an immediately achievable aim and the conclusion mandated by Ben-Yosef's example, against Jabotinsky's principle that the Jews had to constitute a majority in Eretz Yisrael first.[10]

The showdown came in an elegant Paris mansion in February 1939, not long after Kook and Jabotinsky's son, Eri, commanders of the Irgun and Betar in Europe, respectively, signed an agreement regarding "illegal" immigration activities. Raziel, Stern, and Kook led the Irgun delegation, with Eri presenting Betar's position. Except for Raziel, the Irgun's chief military commander, his associates insisted that their organization existed as an entity free of Revisionist party control. A compromise was eventually arrived at, with veteran Ahimeir follower Yosef Katzenelson (now in the Irgun) to oversee the arrangement, but Jabotinsky realized that the conference was no longer a "family gathering." Together with Stern, who began creating separate Irgun cells in Poland, Kook and his colleagues in Europe soon disregarded the "Paris formula." Stern kept Jabotinsky in the dark about securing weapons and military training with the sanction of the Polish government. Yet Britain's White Paper of May, coming a few months after Ben-Gurion torpedoed a Jabotinsky's agreement with Hagana commander Golomb, brought Jabotinsky to openly endorse the Irgun's wholesale reprisals against Arab terrorism. With HMG now curtailing Jewish immigration to 75,000 in the next five years and promising an Arab state after ten, Jabotinsky concluded that the choice lay between "retaliating against the hostile population or not retaliating at all."[11]

In these same months, a small Irgun delegation arrived in New York. With letters of introduction from Jabotinsky, Robert Briscoe, the one Jewish member of the Government party in the Irish Free State parliament, began a two-month coast-to-coast tour of the United States in an effort to obtain the transfer of 1,000,000 Jews from Germany, Poland, and Rumania to Palestine within two years. He failed to fulfill Jabotinsky's request of securing an interview with Roosevelt, although he, Chaim Lubinski, and Patterson found a receptive audience in William Ziff, author of the anti-British *The Rape of Palestine*, and Rabbi Louis Newman of New York City's Reform Congregation Rodeph Shalom. Frances Gunther, the Jewish wife of well-known author John Gunther, and Wall St. banker Harvey Schwamm opened up various doors. In June, with the help of Yitzhak Ben-Ami, who was sent at Raziel's order to take charge of activities when the three emissaries were about to leave the United States, the group created the American Friends of a Jewish Palestine. This independent political arm of the Irgun soon began publicly to champion unauthorized immigration and a Jewish military force against the mandatory power.[12]

American Jewry received the new organization with caution. Non-Zionists such as New York Governor Herbert Lehman worried that its campaign embarrassed England. The American Zionist establishment also maintained a wary stance. Despite the bringing by the Irgun and Betar of more than 4,000 "illegals" into Palestine during the year following Hitler's *Anschluss* (annexation) of Austria in March 1938, Judge Julian Mack thought the seventy-two-year-old Patterson "over-enthusiastic," and US Supreme Court Justice Louis D. Brandeis agreed. The Zionist Organization of America (ZOA) released a statement in Brandeis's name, essentially approving the Weizmannite point of view. This official response mirrored Ben-Gurion's strong opposition to the Irgun, similar to that to be adopted by the Zionist Congress in August against the Irgun's membership as practitioners of terror who placed the WZO's ethical standard and its practical attainments in great jeopardy.[13]

A three-man Irgun delegation consisting of Kook, Lubinski, and Rafaeli arrived in Geneva to tell Zionist Congress delegates, and especially the foreign press, about the Irgun and the Revisionist movement's Af-Al-Pi "illegal" immigration. Their sudden appearance caught Jabotinsky unawares, but they received his green light to proceed with their mission. They joined forces with Irgunist Reuven Hecht of Switzerland, whose plan to dispatch Jewish refugees from Zurich to Prague aboard seven Swissair planes and then on boats via the Danube and the Black Sea to Palestine had been abruptly aborted by the Nazi invasion of Czechoslovakia. The youngsters plastered Geneva with colorful placards comparing William Tell and his fight for Swiss freedom with theirs against HMG. Journalists conveyed for the first time the Irgun's objective of concentrating in Palestine 100,000 fighters for Jewish sovereignty. Kook and associates also informed a packed press conference about the need to break with *havlaga*, which understandably sparked the WZO's irritation at this publicity triumph.[14]

By then, Jabotinsky had decided upon staging an armed revolt in Palestine. He had blundered badly in deriding Nazi Germany that May as an "inflated balloon," and then in June publicly dismissing the possibility of a global conflict, but the White Paper and British efforts to stifle *aliya bet* (unauthorized immigration) convinced him that the Irgun could carry out the rebellion with a bold plan. Through six coded letters that reached Lubinski, Jabotinsky proposed to arrive with other "illegals" in the heart of Palestine that October. While the Irgun would ensure their landing by all means necessary, Government House in Jerusalem and other key British locations would be occupied for at least twenty-four hours and the Jewish national flag hoisted aloft. A provisional state would be simultaneously announced in the capitals of Western Europe and the United States—all creating a political reality of inestimable value. The Irgun command, save for Stern, considered the plan seriously. The scheme was submitted to Raziel, in prison as of May, while his comrades carried out the first acts in the revolt against the mandatory by killing two British officers on August 26. Four days later, Stern and the entire Irgun command staff were arrested.[15]

Within an hour of England's declaration on September 3, 1939, of war against Germany for invading Poland, Jabotinsky excitedly asked Patterson to work jointly for "a fully mechanized Jewish Army, to fight side by side with the Allied forces." This, he confided to colleague Jeremiah ("Yerma") Helpern, would immediately fulfill the "Nordau Plan" of a Jewish State on both sides of the Jordan. Jabotinsky pressed French cabinet ministers in this regard, and sent off a letter—unacknowledged—to British Prime Minister Neville Chamberlain, suggesting the creation of such an army prior to the establishment of Palestine as a Jewish State. In his view, with East European Jewry inaccessible, and little to expect from "the Ghettos of Mayfair and the Faubourg St. Honoré," recruitment had to take place in the United States. Those selected would fight on all fronts and be represented at the peace table. The campaign would also support the intervention of Washington on the side of the Allies. Memoranda were prepared to this effect, while his book *The Jewish War Front* urged a Jewish force of at least 100,000 strong to fight the Third Reich, the transfer to Palestine of the first million Jews of his earlier plan within the first year after the war's end, and a Jewish State "as a war aim of the Allies." Completed in March, 1940, just before he left with a small NZO delegation for New York, the volume declared that these Jewish demands were to "prove just what some people would prefer to forget—that this is the Jew's war as much as Britain's and France's and Poland's." "We must all realize," he concluded, "that if the war is ever to develop in a direction leading up to real victory, it would have to follow a different line of development."[16]

Before leaving his wife in London and departing European shores in March, Jabotinsky sought to resolve a few other pressing matters. He invited two Jewish Agency Executive members for dinner, trying (unsuccessfully) to restore Zionist unity. Briscoe would initiate promising talks about the Jewish Army with Weizmann, who soon reversed his stand while expressing the intention of meeting with Jabotinsky in America. The Revisionist-Zionist avatar also initiated a campaign to allow more than 2,000 starving refugees from occupied Germany, stranded on four small steamers and barges in the Danube, to proceed to Palestine. When the United Palestine Appeal refused to finance the NZO transport under Eri's command, the American Friends of a Jewish Palestine obtained the funds for chartering a Turkish-owned steamer by releasing the facts to the press. John Gunther took the radio to lash out against the White Paper, while a letter by his wife to the *New York Times* charged that Britain's handling of the Palestine problem is "disturbingly reminiscent of Nazi methods at their worst." On February 13, the British halted the *Sakariya* miles away from Palestine's territorial waters, interned its cargo of 2,175 for six months, and put Eri behind bars. Wedgwood's demand for a court trial fell on deaf ears, and Eri was sentenced to one year's detention in the Acre Prison under the "Prevention of Crime Ordinance." Illegal immigration thereafter ground to a halt.[17]

Jabotinsky also asked Kook to travel to the United States. Operating from Warsaw at Raziel's order since 1937 in order to raise funds and help in illegal immigration for the Irgun, Kook had then been sent to London to serve as the Irgun central command's liaison officer with Jabotinsky. While there, aside from raising a slight blond moustache and improving his social skills, the twenty-four-year-old bachelor registered as a student of English at the London School of Economics. Now he wished to return home, adding that the imprisoned Raziel needed him. "If you go to Palestine first," Jabotinsky rejoined, "Raziel himself would ask you to go, but then you would not be able to get a visa." Further, he had told Raziel that Kook intended to go with Jabotinsky to the States. Eager to "plant a foot" there, Raziel favored the proposal and appointed Kook in charge of Irgun activity in America. As Kook recalled it years later, a letter in his pocket for Rafaeli in New York, including the directive not to answer to orders from the Revisionists but only from Raziel, was stolen and shown to Jabotinsky. In the end, John Gunther obtained the visa, and Kook would reach New York that July aboard the British vessel *SS Scythia* from Southampton.[18]

One week after crossing the Atlantic, Jabotinsky reiterated the thesis of *The Jewish War Front* to an enthusiastic crowd of 5,000 at New York City's Manhattan Center. Lord Lothian, the British Ambassador, swayed by his meetings with Jabotinsky and Patterson, cabled the gist of the program to the Foreign Office, and promised to second a consular representative to the NZO's second rally in mid-June. A Zionist delegation, led by Wise, objected strongly that Jabotinsky could not fulfill his plan; his agitation threw into question the loyalty of American Jews; and his activities only thwarted the effective help initiated by responsible Zionist and Jewish bodies. This opposition, coupled with Whitehall's directive that no encouragement be given Jabotinsky, caused Lord Lothian to back down. The mass meeting went ahead, Jabotinsky predicting to a packed hall that "the Yanks" are coming and Patterson declaring that if he were a Jew, nothing would give him greater pleasure than "to show the German criminals the Jews of today are capable of fighting just as their forefathers were

2,000 years ago." The fall of France to the German *Wehrmacht* in May lent extra force to this call, and inquiries poured into the NZO office from men prepared to serve. The ZOA's *New Palestine*, by contrast, deemed the Jewish Army slogan "misleading" and "obsolete" in light of the Agency's more limited request from HMG of a force for Palestine's defense and a Jewish division elsewhere.[19]

Yet mounting frustration and fatigue set in by that summer. American Jewish "leaders," Jabotinsky wrote to an associate in Buenos Aires, feared saying anything that might spark antisemitism. The Emergency Committee for Zionist Affairs, an umbrella organization created at the beginning of the war at the WZO's request, immediately turned down Jabotinsky's proposal to meet the crisis abroad with the formation of a World Jewish Committee. He ordered Rafaeli on June 12 to abide by the "Paris formula" and not have any Irgun representatives in the United States engage in independent political action, including with the American Friends or any other body, without his written approval. Ben-Ami was also directed by Jabotinsky to send copies of any outgoing correspondence from the Irgun office in New York. Living very modestly in a one-room brownstone apartment on the upper West Side, depressed about the European scene, concerned about his son's plight and unable to get his wife a visa to enter the United States, Jabotinsky looked worn out.[20]

On August 1, he sent out a lengthy *aide-mémoire* to various statesmen, explaining that a Jewish Army would provide military benefit, increase the moral weight of the Allied cause, and lead to "an adequate solution of the Jewish question." The next day, after a doctor confidentially confirmed his fears that he had *angina pectoris*, Jabotinsky called in Kook for what would be their last meeting. With a few other people present, including NZO representative Ben-Zion Netanyahu, he informed Kook that the break between the Irgun command and Stern's cadre in Palestine was final. Stern refused to abide by Raziel's decision to maintain a truce against the British during the war, and did not accept Jabotinsky's appeal "to maintain harmony" and recognize Raziel as the Irgun's chief commander once he and Stern were released from jail. "You are a cut-off battalion" having no connection to Palestine, the NZO leader went on. "Do all you can in the United States, first and foremost creating a committee for a Jewish Army." Confused, Kook did not reply. Two days later, Jabotinsky set off for a second summer visit to the Betar camp in Hunter, New York, where he died of a heart attack that same evening.[21]

The sudden death of Zionism's stormy petrel relieved some and saddened others. Lothian paid tribute to Jabotinsky's personal qualities and tenacity in opposition, Weizmann left it to history to judge the tactics of his "chivalrous opponent," and Ben-Gurion asserted that this "courageous fighter" saw the end goal clearly but not the necessary means. While more than 25,000 crowded the streets near Orthodox services in the Lower East Side's Gramercy Park Funeral Chapel, Kook and three other Irgunists stood as a guard of honor at his coffin. Those present included Patterson; NZO leaders Benjamin Akzin, Helpern, and Eliyahu Ben-Horin; John Gunther; secretary of the American Friends, William Stanton; and the legendary Yiddish actor Maurice Schwartz. Jewish institutions in the area and Yiddish theatres on Second Avenue were draped with black. There were no eulogies, following the precedent set by Herzl's funeral in Vienna in 1904; the ceremony concluded with the Zionist anthem *HaTikva*. Some 1,000 persons then boarded buses for the burial in the New Montefiore Cemetery's Max Nordau circle in Farmingdale, Long Island, "pending removal," the Jewish Telegraphic Agency reported, "after the war to Palestine."[22]

The Zionist right wing found itself in dire straits. The ten-man NZO delegation in New York had looked forward to expanding the Jewish Army, campaign that fall. As Akzin later recalled, it now was thrown into turmoil, and the movement foundered for a year without a helmsman while seeking its bearings. In Palestine, Stern soon formed the separatist *Lohamei Herut* Yisrael (LEHI), pledged to fight the British occupier of Eretz Yisrael. The Irgun emissaries to America were literally "hungry for bread," Kook reminisced, lunch often a nickel bag of peanuts and dinner the welcome largesse of some parlor meetings. He sought a monthly budget of $500, but only received small donations. Aside from colleagues Aryeh Ben-Eliezer in Philadelphia, Rafaeli in Chicago, and Ben-Ami in New York, the American Friends had an active group of no more than forty people. Its central office consisted of two rooms, with one secretary hired at $25 a week. Kook moved with Merlin, who had arrived in April at his request, to a rented room at $60 a month on New York's upper East Side, and then the pair transferred to an apartment on Central Park South. "The question of my subsistence confronts me each and every day," Merlin wrote to Stern at the close of 1940, the conditions for work here "as hard truly as the splitting of the Red Sea."[23]

Proposing to Kook that they work together for a Jewish Army, Akzin also invited Kook to join the NZO directorate. Jabotinsky had made an identical offer to Kook and Stern after the Paris meeting in February 1939. Both had refused at the time, wishing the Irgun to remain free of politics, and Raziel later refused as well. In light of the current crisis, Kook agreed to both requests. Two months later, he told Akzin that there was no point to continue their understanding. Explaining this refusal to NZO leader Aryeh Altman in Jerusalem, Kook argued that the NZO representatives in New York were not working hard and "creating" anything of significance. An eventual leadership would emerge from all this confusion, he believed. In the meantime, Kook sought to form "a non-political committee for the defense of Eretz Yisrael," its purpose to raise a large amount of money in an emergency campaign that would also be placed at the disposal of a similar committee in Palestine. If Pinhas Rutenberg, founder of the Palestine Electric Company and a supporter of Jabotinsky's call for unity within the *Yishuv*, could not head this effort, could someone else do so? Kook continued to seek agreement with the US Zionist establishment, their clear ideological differences notwithstanding, but most of their leaders had no sense of this need just when Palestine faced danger from a Nazi invasion of the Near East. "I doubt," Kook concluded, "if we ever had a more appropriate political conjuncture than now in America" to achieve "wonderful things," provided that a "united Jewish front" was created. To this end, Kook appealed to United Palestine Appeal chairman Abba Hillel Silver to take the reins from those supporting what he termed the "Weizmann spirit" of defeatist anglophilism.[24]

The NZO representatives in America, their arm strengthened by the arrival of Eri Jabotinsky, increased the drumbeat for a Jewish army. In January 1941, their convention urged the creation of a World Jewish National Committee for Jewish unity during the war, a "Jewish national army," and a Jewish state in Palestine. The group also welcomed the transfer of world NZO headquarters to the United States, endorsed Roosevelt's leadership in America's defense, asked international assistance for large-scale Jewish immigration into Palestine, and urged "the civilized states" to afford the endangered Jews of Europe temporary asylum. Reaching New York at the end of February, Eri Jabotinsky disclosed that a draft agreement between the NZO and Mapai, which took place after the *Patria* tragedy, called for the establishment of a Jewish Army to fight as a British ally and the immediate transfer after the war of all the Jewish masses desiring to emigrate to Palestine. In March, at a Betar reception, he again demanded that HMG form a "full-fledged" Jewish Army, and in April the NZO submitted to London an offer to form and equip a number of Jewish air squadrons as a first step towards the creation of a Jewish army.[25]

No Gentile matched Josiah Wedgwood's aggressive critiques of British policy vis-à-vis Zionism. Having asserted upon Jabotinsky's death that "no one can replace him but all will be better for the example of his life," the Labour MP soon objected during the House of Commons' debate on the Armed Forces bill to the exclusion of Jews as a unit in the other Allied armies, and to their being prevented from forming armies in Great Britain. Sir Edward Grigg, undersecretary for war, countered that the Jews did not have "a military system," and could render valuable help only as units of other national forces. In April 1941 Wedgwood charged that the Palestine administration was preventing formation of a Jewry Army, and he pointed to restrictions in land sales and immigration in Palestine. "The great American democracy," he warned, "pay the piper and they will call the tune." After asserting that Britain would have had at least two mechanized Jewish divisions if it had accepted the Jewish Agency's offer, Wedgwood proceeded to the States for a three-month tour, where he lost no time in urging that Palestinian Jewry be armed for its defense and that a home guard be set up along the lines of the Home Guard in England. The time had not yet come, he added, for establishment of a Jewish Army as an ally of Great Britain.[26]

Kook thought otherwise. He gathered to his cause Jeremiah Helpern, pioneer in establishing a Betar naval school in Italy who had also been sent by Jabotinsky to lobby the French for a Jewish Army once World War II erupted. Michael Berchin, co-editor of *Rassvet*, the Russian Zionist weekly that had moved to Paris and became a mouthpiece for Jabotinsky from the mid-1920s onward, also signed on. Before long, Eri Jabotinsky would join as well. On June 15, 1941, at the second annual convention of the American Friends, Congressman Joseph C. Baldwin of New York backed its resolution to have HMG register volunteers for a Jewish Army to fight with the Allies, and its petition calling for "restoration of the world's oldest democracy." Ten days later, the American Friends' rally in Manhattan Center demanded the immediate creation of a Jewish Army in Palestine, with registration for enlistment in the United States consistent with American laws. Journalist Pierre van Paassen, the Dutch-born author of the recent autobiographical best-seller *Days of Our Years*, told the crowd of about 3,000 that "there is no more important work in Zionism today than the effort to raise a Jewish Army." John D. Dingell, Congressman from Michigan, delivered remarks in the same vein, while Patterson called from Los Angeles to express his strong support.[27]

Pressure mounted from other quarters. Speaking before the Anglo-Palestine Club that September, Wedgwood insisted that the American habit of thinking that Palestine was exclusively a British affair had to change. Since the United States was, to a large extent, paying for the war while maintaining official neutrality, and since Washington would play a great part in any peace settlement, Palestine's future largely depended on America. Warning that Palestine was still in risk of invasion by German forces, Wedgwood charged that "it is the worst scandal in modern times" that the 500,000 Jews there were left unarmed, and he called for the creation of a Jewish Army in Palestine. Two months later, the Jewish Aviation League of America inducted twenty-five young men into the Jabotinsky Flying School, with officials present from Greece, Czechoslovakia and the Polish government-in-exile, and others interested in the plan for a Jewish Army. Col. Morris Mendelson, past national commander of the Jewish

War Veterans of America and now president of the New Zionist Organization of America, supported the proposal; Eri Jabotinsky sent a message of greetings for the occasion.[28]

All this appeared too late, for on November 9, 1941, Weizmann had to inform the public for the first time about HMG's ruling against the Agency's secret and extensive negotiations for a Jewish division. Great Britain's concealment of the distinctive service given on various fronts by 10,000 Jewish recruits (seventy-two percent of the Palestinians enlisted) under the anonymous rubric "Palestinians," together with its failure to live up to the War Cabinet's agreement in principle in September 1940 to a Jewish division, could no longer be denied. Newspaper editorials and a heated debate in the House of Lords decried the government's appeasement of the Arabs. Despite the pro-Nazi revolt in Iraq, the Hagana's help in Britain's invasion of Vichy Syria, the conspiracy of Anwar el-Sadat, Gamal Abdul Nasser, and the Egyptian chief of staff and the Muslim Brotherhood to support Hitler in return for their independence from British rule—all did not count in the balance for the anti-Zionist Colonial Secretary Lord Moyne, Foreign Secretary Anthony Eden, and the War Office. Prime Minister Winston Churchill could do no more than promise, in a public letter to the London *Jewish Chronicle* on the occasion of its centenary, that on the day of Allied victory, the sufferings of the Jews and their part in the struggle against the German *Führer* would not be forgotten.[29]

The breakthrough which Kook and company so desperately needed came in the person of Ben Hecht. Intrigued by that author's biting attack in an April column in the liberal-left newspaper *PM* against influential Jews who hid behind their pride in being neutral Americans, rather than speak out against Hitler, Kook sought an appointment with Hecht. The highly paid Hollywood scriptwriter of such films as *Wuthering Heights* and *Scarface*, and author of the popular play *The Front Page* (with Charles MacArthur) and the self-flagellating *A Jew in Love*, Hecht had been far removed from ethnic roots and from all contact with Palestine. Yet the Nazi purge of his people and the silence of the democracies regarding that persecution brought his Jewishness to the surface. As he put it later, in 1939, "I became a Jew and looked on the world with Jewish eyes." The author's *A Book of Miracles,* appearing on the eve of World War II, had prophesied a "great International Pogrom" against the Jews, whom he lovingly portrayed as the Lord's "little candle" in a world of cruelty of darkness. He subsequently wrote propaganda speeches and pageants for Herbert Agar's Fight for Freedom group, which sought to bring the United States into that global conflict. Kook's appeal therefore struck a warm chord.[30]

In the company of the tall, sunburned Helpern, who cut an impressive figure in a naval uniform, Kook sat down with Hecht at the author's usual haunt,

Club 21 in Manhattan. The celebrated writer ordered a third round of drinks for his guests, unaware that neither had eaten that day. The pair heaped praise on his feisty column "My Tribe is Called Israel," and then Kook, whose voice "inclined to squeak under excitement," proudly spoke of the "fine renaissance" begun by Jabotinsky and of matters in Palestine. Having never heard of Jabotinsky and feeling that Palestine's problems "confused the issue," Hecht responded that he wished to focus on the "cowardly silence" of leading American Jews towards the massacre of Jews started in Europe. They smiled politely at his irritation with their Palestine talk and maintained a mysterious air when asked about their activities. They left after the charismatic Kook received permission to call on him at his hotel. Hecht ate his dinner alone, unaware that "a Sinbad bringing greater riches than any of the diamond-mind peddlers who had preceded him" had entered his life. Before long, he agreed to join the campaign to mobilize the press and Congress for a separate army that could, as he later reminisced, "bring respect back to the name Jew."[31]

After months of planning, the Irgun emissaries under Kook's command launched the Committee for a Jewish Army of Stateless and Palestinian Jews on December 4, 1941, in Washington's Willard Hotel. The name was purposely chosen so as not to give the impression that Jews in the United States would join this entity instead of the US Army. Beneath the grouped flags of all the Allied nations, the conference of more than 250 representatives from across the land called for a force of 200,000 to be based in Palestine to "combat the satanic zeal" of Hitler and to fight under the British in the "evangelic hills of Galilee." Van Paassen stressed the army's invaluable strategic importance to the free world, certain that the issue of the war would be settled in the Near Eastern battle grounds, while Patterson declared that such a force would enable Britain to take advantage of great manpower resources now lying fallow because of administrative policies regarding Palestine. Samuel Harden Church, president of the Carnegie Institute and Honorary Chairman, went further in calling for an end to the 1939 White Paper and in forecasting the army's return to Jerusalem, where a Jewish government should be reestablished in Palestine with freedom for all peoples. Senators Claude Pepper (D., Florida) and Styles Bridges (R., New Hampshire) sent greetings, and, in a real coup, Secretary of War Henry Stimson called in his best wishes for the committee's future.[32]

America's entry into World War II following the Japanese attack on Pearl Harbor three days later, with Hitler and Mussolini joining Tokyo in a declaration of belligerency on December 11, appeared providential for the committee's success. Van Paassen, elected chairman of the Committee for a Jewish Army, announced that he would meet with members of Congress in order to facilitate the presentation of the new organization's cause on the floor of both Houses. He outlined a four-point program as the Committee's immediate objectives: (1) the mobilization of public opinion; (2) the registration of volunteers for the projected army; (3) the establishment of training centers for officers and enlisted men "wherever feasible"; and (4) a national fund-raising campaign. Three days later, Patterson, speaking as co-honorary chairman of the Committee, argued that with Hawaii, the Philippines, and Singapore now under Japanese assault, the 100,000 Australian troops engaged in the Middle Eastern campaign were vitally needed in the Orient. Formation of a Jewish Army in Palestine, he pointed out, would make possible the shifting of these Imperial forces to the new battlegrounds. The Committee quickly issued *The Battle for Jerusalem*, with contributions from the late Jabotinsky, Patterson, Wedgwood, and Van Paassen, explaining why a Jewish Army was indispensable to the survival of a Jewish nation and the preservation of world civilization.[33]

Kook followed this up with a masterstroke. A while earlier, he had Hecht solicit prominent citizens, their names drawn from *Who's Who in America*, to join the future Committee for a Jewish Army. Supporters, in turn, recommended others. On January 5, 1942, Kook (listed in small print as Peter H. Bergson of Palestine) placed the names of some of these politicians, professors, clergymen, and authors in a full-page advertisement in the *New York Times*. "JEWS FIGHT FOR THE RIGHT TO FIGHT," ran the headline on page 13, with a subtitle: "The Jews of Palestine and the stateless Jews of the world do not only want to pray—THEY WANT TO FIGHT!!!!" Quotations followed from Roosevelt ("The vast majority of the members of the human race are on our side. Many of them are fighting with us, all of them are praying for us") and from Churchill ("Any nation, any man who fights against Nazidom will have our aid"). The statement went on to demand that the Jewish people take their rightful place in "the ranks of the free peoples of the earth" by joining the Allied cause in a 200,000-strong force.

The unprecedented advertisement emphasized that the Committee sought to bring about, in according with US law, the formation of a Jewish Army based on Palestine "to fight for the survival of the Jewish people and the preservation of democracy." This army, composed primarily of Palestinian Jews and refugees, as well as volunteers from free countries, would "fight on all required battlefields side by side with the United States, Great Britain, and other Allied nations." The copy went on to point out that 135,000 "fearless Palestinian Jews," who registered as volunteers as soon as the war broke out, were still waiting to be called to the colors. Stateless Jews, whose relatives were "the most persecuted" under Hitler's yoke, as well as Jews from countries not yet involved in the war, also sought to unite in their own Freedom Army and fight under their own Liberty Flag under the supreme Allied command. With readers' help and cooperation (contributions to be sent to the national headquarters at 285 Madison Ave. in New York City, or to the Washington, D.C., office at the Willard Hotel and the regional offices in Philadelphia and Chicago), the signatories were certain that their cause would be victorious not only in the interest of the Jewish people, but also in the interests of world democracy: "Because ours is a struggle for right and justice—and right and justice are indivisible—they should be for all and everywhere."[34]

The $2,000 publicity gamble shattered the prevailing American consensus regarding Jewish affairs. A major proposal, as Eri Jabotinsky subsequently informed a friend in a letter which British censorship passed on to the Foreign Office, was now presented "as you would advertise Chevrolet motor cars or Players cigarettes." The Committee's forthright demand for a Jewish Army carried tremendous emotional power, appealing to non-Jews as well as to many Jews who had heretofore not identified with Zionist concerns. The very means of communication, bringing the message via newspaper and radio to the nation's breakfast tables, in turn generated further coverage. As Kook had estimated, the public found the substantial scheme, dramatically portrayed in non-partisan terms, more attractive than the Jewish Agency's limited request that HMG create a Jewish force of some 30,000 in Palestine.[35]

The American Zionist organizations found it difficult to counter this broad appeal. Upstaged by the young Palestinian mavericks and their innovative, activist orientation, the Emergency Committee for Zionist Affairs sought to co-opt the Committee for a Jewish Army's leadership. The attempt failed, while Ben-Gurion ordered an end to all negotiations with the dissidents. In his phrase, they were tied to the "fascist" Irgun. He intended to press, instead, for a Jewish commonwealth in Eretz Yisrael as part of both the war and peace aims of the entire Allied coalition. Aware through Zionist contacts of the US State Department's pro-Arabist line and of Roosevelt's skepticism about the Zionist endeavor, Ben-Gurion believed that a great possibility existed at present to create a united front of American Jewry on behalf of a Jewish State in Palestine. Having faith in the "justice and feasibility" of this cause, his diary read, he resolved to take up the task in Washington in the months to come.[36]

Kook's small circle took a very different approach. Their public "pitch," he reminisced, was not to conquer Palestine but to fight the Third Reich. Following Jabotinsky's earlier argument that a Second World War demanded a much larger Jewish force than a Legion of World War I vintage, and that Jews would be united against Nazi Germany, he doubled Jabotinsky's figure to

200,000. Although admitting years later that this number was "exaggerated," he reasoned that American public sentiment preferred to think in large terms. The overall "formula" had many more chances of success, Kook believed at the time, than what he termed "the wretched minimalism" of the Zionists. Without calling for a Jewish State or criticizing the mandatory government's policy regarding immigration, land sales, and other matters, or even discussing Eretz Yisrael's postwar situation, the Committee would demand that the British appoint a general (or an American general, if HMG preferred) and a staff to lead the Jewish Army on any battlefront required. This stance, taken "without any conditions or reservations," would also separate the issue from Palestine and the Arab question as much as possible. As he put it to Helpern, the group was only interested at this moment "that Eretz Israel would exist after the war and that the democracies would emerge victorious."[37]

Personal contacts gave hope to these plans. Hecht introduced Kook to Alfred Strelsin, an advertising tycoon whose brother had died while serving in the Jewish Legion. Strelsin became chairman of the executive board and paid for many of the advertisements. He paved the way to Kook's meeting with Donald Nelson, head of the War Production Board, and to the Jewish economist Robert Nathan. When the interview had to be stopped because of an appointment with Lord Halifax, Nathan suggested that the subject of weapon supply be raised with the new British Ambassador. General John Dill, then visiting Washington as Chief of the Imperial General Staff, showed interest. The sculptor Joe Davidson advised that Kook see Adlai Stevenson, then an Assistant to Secretary of the Navy Frank Knox. This also led to a meeting with Stimson, where Kook suggested that the proposed army be formed under American command and be based in North Africa. Knox, advocating that such a force stop the German threat towards the Mosul oil fields of Iran, openly declared on January 17 that "in Palestine Hitler faces the wrath of the people he has starved and tortured and degraded—Jews, over a half million strong."[38]

A concerted effort followed elsewhere. First, the aid of Senators, especially those with no sizeable Jewish constituencies, was sought. Aside from Strelsin's crucial opening of doors, Baruch Rabinowitz, a Maryland rabbi, had already left his congregation in 1940 to work full-time for the group as its chief lobbyist on Capitol Hill. Pepper, Edwin Johnson (D., Colorado), Elbert Thomas (D., Utah), William Langer (R., North Dakota), Guy Gillette (D., Iowa), James Murray (D., Montana), Harry S Truman (D., Missouri), and Scott Lucas (D., Illinois) signed on. A booklet entitled *The Fighting Jew* and a lengthy *Memorandum on a Jewish Army of Palestinian and Stateless Jews*, bearing the Bar Kokhba rebellion's symbol of the lion of Judea, were drawn up and distributed from the

Committee's new, larger headquarters at 535 Fifth Avenue in New York City. Radio programs carried the message still further. New advertisements, often bearing Hecht's biting style, appeared in such papers as the *Philadelphia Record*, the *Jewish Daily Forward*, the *Washington Post*, the *New York Herald Tribune*, and the *New York Times*. Britain's loss of Singapore on February 15 and more than 60,000 Allied troops there taken prisoner by the Japanese, for example, quickly sparked a Committee advertisement with the eye-catching headline "Suez must not be another Singapore!"[39]

Arthur Hays Sulzberger and his assimilated American Jewish circle would have none of this. As publisher of the world's most influential newspaper, he saw to it that a *New York Times* editorial quickly trumpet British anxiety about a Jewish Army and Arab antagonism to a Zionist state, and conclude that the full hopes of Jews could only be achieved by "the winning of a new world in which Jews along with other religions and national minorities may live peacefully and happily in every nation, enjoying the full rights of other citizens." The *Times* had already published with enthusiasm Hebrew University Chancellor Judah Magnes's credo for a binationalist Palestine, and defended Britain's 1939 White Paper by editorializing that the imposed settlement would "save the homeland itself from overpopulation, as well as from an increasingly violent resistance on the part of the Arabs." Sulzberger hosted a small meeting of anti-Zionists in his home to consider a statement favoring Palestine's economic and cultural development while rejecting Jewish sovereignty there, and he would help in the drafting of a statement (to be printed in the *Times* that August) of eighty-two Reform rabbis criticizing political Zionism for "diverting attention from our historical role to live as a religious community." Kook subsequently found out that one of these activists, American Jewish Committee executive member Col. Edward Greenbaum, appointed by Stimson to investigate the Jewish Army proposal, "buried it."[40]

By early April, Kook could report to Helpern, now back in London, that the Committee numbered 300 prominent intellectual leaders, together with 50 Senators and Representatives, and more than 75 important rabbis. They would certainly succeed, but would it not be too late? he wondered. With American military experts not understanding British objection to the scheme, it was vital for Helpern to open an identical campaign in Great Britain focusing only on the broad military proposal. A direct appeal to the intellectual class and the masses there had never yet taken place, and the British public was now capable of understanding "the Jewish tragedy." Aided by Lords Strabolgi and Wedgwood, and the backing of London *Jewish Chronicle* editor Ivan M. Greenberg, Helpern began to do so, just when the Zionists led by Ben-Gurion endorsed the Biltmore

Platform for all of Western Palestine as a Jewish State immediately after the war and "a Jewish military fighting force fighting under its own flag" and under the Allied high command. Helpern and Strabolgi were hardly prepared, at the same time, for Wedgwood's live message to the American Palestine Committee over the BBC airwaves condemning British appeasement, boldly calling for America to accept the Mandate and for the *Yishuv* one day to become partners in "a federal union of the free."[41]

Wedgwood's unexpected call, which surprisingly had passed BBC censorship, only stiffened the War Cabinet's opposition to a Jewish Army. A worried Colonial Office had applauded the *New York Times*'s January editorial as "most gratifying" in light of the "extreme Zionist demands now being made." Lord Moyne, saboteur of the Jewish division a year earlier and advocate to Churchill of postwar Jewish settlement in South America, Madagascar, and devastated areas of Europe rather that employing British bayonets to "force" 3,000,000 Jews into small Palestine, responded in Parliament to Wedgwood's "treasonable appeal" by comparing Zionist "aggression and domination" in Palestine to the Nazi spirit. While he departed for Cairo as the new deputy minister of state, Middle East, the Cabinet kept to the draconian White Paper despite the *Struma* tragedy and increasing reports of atrocities against Jews trapped in Nazi-occupied Europe.[42]

The Committee for a Jewish Army did not let up. Endorsing a House resolution by a fighting Irishman from Brooklyn named Andrew Somers which petitioned HMG to permit the formation of a Jewish Army in Palestine, Senator Johnson observed that the seventy-five miles east of the Suez Canal there "awaits in idleness a potential Jewish Army begging and pleading for the right to fight, to hold Suez." One month later, at a testimonial dinner in Van Paassen's honor, Senator James M. Mead (D., New York) stressed that the Axis forces were making "one gigantic effort to converge in the Middle East," and a Jewish Army would be fighting and defending Suez "only as a people who have real reason to hate would" if we understood "the meaning of total war." Senator Murray added to the 700 guests at the Waldorf Astoria Hotel that "no true Christian could withhold from these victims of Nazidom the privilege of fighting back at Hitler and fighting back as Jews."[43]

Churchill's presence in Washington sparked the Committee to publish an open letter on June 23 under Van Paassen's signature in the form of a three-quarter page advertisement in the *New York Times* and in other newspapers, calling for the creation of a Jewish Army in Palestine to fighting with the so-called United Nations. Citing the precarious position of the Allies in Libya and throughout the Middle East, it urged the mobilization of "an army of modern

Maccabees," 200,000 strong, on the shores of the Suez Canal at the side of the Allied troops now there under British Eighth Army General Claude Auchinleck. (Tobruk, with the surrender of 33,000 British troops and valuable military supplies there, had fallen to Erwin Rommel's *Panzerarmee Afrika* on June 21.) "We ask you, sir," the letter respectfully stated, "to grant the Jews of Palestine and stateless Jews the right to fight—and die, if need be—for democracy under the walls of Jerusalem."[44]

This advertisement, coming four days before Auchinleck retreated to El Alamein and when Weizmann sent a plea to Churchill for the *Yishuv*'s maximum self-defense on the grounds that "the actual physical existence of nearly 600,000 Jews in Palestine ... is at stake," led to Halifax's intervention with Whitehall. In the British ambassador's opinion, since "the Revisionists and their Committee for a Jewish Army set up a great agitation directed at the Prime Minister," "if any concession in the direction of a Jewish Fighting Force should be contemplated, we think it would be to our interest that the concession should be made to Dr. Weizmann personally so that he can gain credit for it and show that moderation pays." Yet the British military authorities refused Churchill's wish that the pro-Zionist Orde Wingate be appointed to lead a large Palestinian Jewish force, and the Prime Minister did no more than send a message to a Madison Square Garden rally on July 21, protesting the Nazi massacre of Jewry, of special tribute to the Jewish war effort in Palestine.[45]

In August, with Field Marshal Rommel threatening the Suez Canal against the British under the newly appointed General Bernard L. Montgomery, Secretary of War Edward Grigg announced in August the formation of a Palestine Regiment. This would consist of separate Jewish and Arab battalions for general service in the Middle East, bolstered by a few thousand additional Jewish rural special police and supernumerary police force. The battalions, at the same time, would not depart from the static mission, just as given the separate Arab and Jewish Buffs of two years earlier, of guarding military installations without modern weapons or new training. This limited step, the confidential Cabinet memoranda of the colonial and war secretaries revealed, was done specifically to check "extreme Zionists" like Jewish Agency political director Moshe Shertok (later Sharett), who sought to use the Jewish fighting force as "a valuable bargaining counter at the peace table" or to achieve a Jewish state by force after the war.[46]

Gentile stalwarts of the Committee for a Jewish Army hammered away at Britain's stance. While the British liberal *New Statesman and Nation* insisted that HMG's duty lay in preserving the Jewish population of Palestine "from Himmler's gas chambers [*sic!*] and firing squads," Strabolgi suggested that

Haifa be used as a base for Britain's Mediterranean fleet and the *Yishuv*'s Jews be relied upon to guard the hinterland. In a radio address, Johnson warned that "Suez must not become another Singapore, and the Holy City of Jerusalem not become another Lidice." Van Paassen decried Grigg's August pronouncement because it "merely sidetracks" the issue for which the Committee had been pressing for the last eight months in the United States and in Great Britain. "If the Germans reached Palestine the Britishers might retreat," Strabolgi observed, "but the Jews are doomed. What sort of government have we which refused these people the right to bear arms, and at least die fighting?"[47]

Following Montgomery's major victory at El Alamein (October 23–November 4, 1942), the British dug in their heels once again. The Hagana's Palmach striking force, allowed in early 1942 by the mandatory power to plan guerrilla activities in northern Palestine in case of a German conquest of the country, had to go back underground. HMG discouraged the *Yishuv*'s recruitment effort, and rejected Shertok's request to transfer Jewish volunteers in other units of the British Army to the Palestine Regiment, as well as to accept 5,000 recruits as a Jewish home guard in urban districts. Whitehall sent confidential reports to the State Department and to some leading Reform Jews in the United States against a Jewish fighting force. When State itself suggested that the Colonial and Foreign Offices receive a delegation from the Committee for a Jewish Army in order to allay American public sentiment, this was peremptorily quashed. While the former Grand Mufti of Jerusalem, Haj Amin el-Husseini, used the Axis airwaves to herald the Third Reich in the Moslem world and recruited thousands from the Balkans into Moslem Wehrmacht units, London censored the *Yishuv*'s impressive and varied contribution to the Allied cause.[48]

Most wrenching for Kook, however, was confirmation to him by Assistant Secretary of State Adolf Berle, Jr., on November 25 that half of the estimated four million Jews under the swastika had been murdered in an "extermination campaign." That headline above two brief paragraphs on page 6 of the *Washington Post*, citing Stephen Wise, galvanized Kook, Merlin, his chief lieutenant and the group's ideologist, and the Committee's executive board to shift their efforts towards the imperative of rescue. Their program for immediate action called on Roosevelt to clearly announce the country's determination to stop the mass slaughter and appoint a full-time team of military and political experts for the task. In addition, those "disinherited and stateless" Jews free of Hitler's clutches should be granted the right to form a Jewish Army in league with the Allied forces. "No Four Freedoms or Atlantic Charter or Democracy for the Common Man should be preached" before a democracy's collective conscience regarding

Hitler's first and primary victims was touched to the quick, Kook pointed out to radio broadcaster Raymond Swing four days later. Only thus, he added, could the murder of a people be shifted from the press's back pages and be interrupted by rescue action.⁴⁹

The Committee for a Jewish Army began its war for the rescue of European Jewry with a demand for action, not pity, against the "calculated extermination of the ancient Jewish people by the barbarous Nazis." Across a full page in the *New York Times* on December 7, 1942, Van Paassen's "Proclamation on the Moral Rights of the Stateless and Palestinian Jews" called on America, "the moral and military arsenal of World Democracy," to support the Jewish Army. Only with this military force, as suggested by celebrated Polish artist Arthur Szyk's accompanying portrait of a Jewish soldier with an automatic weapon and holding the body of an old, bearded Jew, could the survivors, "caught between the blows of Hitler's hammer and the anvil of our own passive sympathy," return to their rightful place among the free peoples of the earth. An end could then be put to "the scandal of history, of a great and ancient people compelled to haunt the corridors of Time as ghosts and beggars and waifs of every storm that rages." More than 3,000 distinguished Americans and European exiles would sign the document, among them Herbert Hoover, Clare Booth Luce, Eugene O'Neill, Taylor Caldwell, Aaron Copeland, Harry S Truman, Melvyn Douglas, Bruno Walter, and Sholem Asch.⁵⁰

When Van Paassen resigned as National Chairman from the Committee for a Jewish Army at the end of January 1943, officially "for reasons of health," Johnson soon took his place. At a testimonial dinner for the author after the Proclamation went public, the senator from Colorado had suggested that the United States gather Jews in North Africa into separate Jewish units within the ranks of the American army, and that this force be attached to the suicide squadron of the Allies for the bombing of German cities. Upon accepting his new post, Johnson released this statement to the press: "I refuse to believe that this world has grown so callous, so inured to the diabolical actions of the Nazi murderers that it can sit back and do nothing while four million human beings in Europe face the same fate that two million of their brethren have already experienced."⁵¹

With the "Proclamation" not generating mass public response, Ben-Ami suggested that Hecht be tapped to suggest something with greater impact to blast the spiritual lethargy of the world toward the Holocaust. Hecht's shrill full-page advertisement in early February about a Romanian offer of 70,000 in Transnistria's concentration camps, "AT 50 APIECE GUARANTEED HUMAN BEINGS," immediately drew fire from Wise and respectable Jewish organizations as unjustified in the absence of official confirmation. His article in the *American Mercury* (and abridged in the *Reader's Digest*), based on underground reports received from labor Zionist Chaim Greenberg of the *Jewish Frontier*, forced readers to confront the grim truth that only Europe's Jews ("reduced from a minority to a phantom") would not be represented in the judgment hall when peace dawned. Yet the country's writers of Jewish origin refused to join him in dramatizing to the United States and the world their people's unprecedented, darkest nightmare.[52]

One evening, sitting Buddha-like in his Nyack home, Hecht suddenly exclaimed to Ben-Ami: "Two tablets!" A dramatic presentation in Madison Square Garden, featuring two forty-foot tablets with the Ten Commandments inscribed thereon and an illuminated Star of David dominating the stage, would offer a memorial for the two million Jews already massacred by the Nazis and their helpers. Rabbis and cantors would lead the audience in last rites for these victims, who were tossed into rivers, funeral pyres, and common graves. The first part of the program would present a roll call of the Jewish contributions to civilization from Moses to Einstein, the second speak of Jewish participation in the Allied armed forces, and the third visualize the coming peace conference with the Jewish dead crowding around with a list of their experiences and sufferings. When a meeting in his Hotel Algonquin suite of all New York's major Jewish organizations failed to produce a united front, as Kook and Merlin had predicted, Hecht agreed to have the Committee for a Jewish Army coordinate the spectacle.[53]

"We Will Never Die" powerfully indicted the American nation on March 9, 1943, for its silence, and therefore its passive collaboration, in Hitler's systematic destruction of the Jews. Climaxing a day of prayer for the Jews "who have been brutally massacred," so read an official proclamation by Governor Thomas E. Dewey, the services began with the haunting call of a *shofar* summoning Jews to prayer. The Garden had to open its doors twice in one evening for 40,000 spectators, with thousands congregating outside in the hope of a third performance. The Hollywood actors Edward G. Robinson (originally Menasheh Goldenberg) and Paul Muni (originally Meshulem Meier Weisenfreund) starred as narrators alongside the chanting of several hundred members of the Cantors Association of America. For two hours, thanks to Hecht's script, the production by Billy Rose (originally William Samuel Rosenberg), Moss Hart's staging, and Kurt Weill's original music, the memorial reminded the free world, the city's papers agreed the next morning, that the four million Jews still alive in Europe were "helplessly waiting for death or deliverance."[54]

The "Bergson Boys," as they began to be called, followed this up with productions in Philadelphia, Boston, Chicago, St. Louis, and Los Angeles. On April 12, Eleanor Roosevelt, along with seven Supreme Court justices, two cabinet members, thirty-eight senators and hundreds of congressmen, as well as the representatives of forty nations, appeared at this bier of the dead. Johnson, an influential member of the Senate Military Affairs Committee, declared as a pageant sponsor that he wished to see "Jews raised to the dignity of a nation." He announced a threefold program of rescue: the immediate appointment of an intergovernmental commission of military experts to determine a "realistic and stern" policy to stop the wholesale slaughter; a Jewish Army, complete with commando teams and Eagle Squadrons, for retaliatory bombing of Germany; and the initiation of possible transfers of Jews from occupied Europe into Palestine and elsewhere. In April, the Committee's *Answer* magazine appeared, expressing its faith that the people of America and Great Britain (including the Jewish masses), once aroused, would demand action to stop Hitler.[55]

The Anglo-American Committee for a Jewish Army under Helpern and Strabolgi's direction continued to focus on the original mission. At its meeting in London to commemorate the twenty-fifth anniversary of the arrival in Palestine of the Jewish Legion, Field Marshal Philip Chetwode, under whose command the Legion had served, voiced support for a Jewish Army and stated that he had no doubt the Jews would fight "magnificently." Prime Minister Jan Smuts of South Africa sent a message emphasizing that since Hitler had made the Jews one of the main issues of the war, their fine contribution to the war effort must not be forgotten. Johnson, Patterson, and David Lloyd George, whose wartime cabinet had issued the 1917 Balfour Declaration pledging HMG to facilitate the establishment of a Jewish national home in Palestine, all sent messages of encouragement.[56]

The American-based Committee, however, concentrated on the impending Anglo-American Bermuda Conference on Refugees, convened after the public outcry at the UN Declaration on Jewish Massacres that had been issued on December 17, 1942. Johnson introduced into the Senate a resolution designed to put that body on record as favoring speedy action to aid endangered European Jewry. It provided that the conference "be advised that the Senate of the United States advocates an immediate and stern policy of action to save the remaining millions of the Jewish people in Europe, and that this humanitarian objective be consummated speedily in a manner that will restore to the helpless victims of Hitler the rights and dignity of a free people." He knew, at the same time, that colleague Scott Lucas had declared before departing with the

American delegation that only Congress could determine the government's immigration policy. ("He is not too hopeful," the Foreign Office privately observed.) Whitehall's Richard Law, heading the British contingent, insisted publicly that only the triumph of the Allied armies would help the refugees. His opposite number, Professor William Dodds of Princeton University, added that "the problem is too great for solution" by the two governments.[57]

The resultant "façade for inaction," Law's later characterization, led the Committee to blast the conference on May 4 with a full-page advertisement in major newspapers: "TO 5,000,000 JEWS IN THE NAZI DEATH-TRAP BERMUDA WAS A CRUEL MOCKERY." Its next line was equally stark: "When will the United Nations establish an agency to deal with the problem of Hitler's extermination of a whole people?" Ways and means of rescue were not undertaken at Bermuda, the statement read, and the word "Jews" had even been avoided in the conference's official title, giving Hitler a continued "carte blanche" at methodical murder. The Allies had not taken advantage of offers from Nazi satellite governments to release Jews. "Democracy cannot connive with the slaughter of millions of innocent civilian people—the Jews in Europe," the copy went on, and a UN agency or commission of military and diplomatic experts must create a realistic policy to save "the remaining five million Jews of Europe." All existing possibilities of transfer to Palestine or any temporary refuge had to be utilized without further delay, as well as the immediate creation of a Jewish Army of stateless and Palestinian Jews, including "suicide" commando squads and air squadrons for retaliation bombing deep inside Germany. The plea closed: "On the field of battle soldiers die. On the field of massacre civilization dies."[58]

Lucas took the Committee's open break with the State Department personally, and on the Senate floor insisted that "every possibility was carefully investigated and discussed" at the conference. After reading a letter from Johnson to Bergson that "the Committee and I must come to an agreement at once that greater care must be exercised," the Illinois representative then read the names of thirty-three senators listed in the advertisement as supporting the Committee's principles. Five of these members rose to repudiate any knowledge of the statement which had been printed alongside their names, including Democrats Truman, Albert B. Chandler (Kentucky), and Francis Maloney (Connecticut), and Republicans Alexander Wiley (Wisconsin) and E. H. Moore (Oklahoma). Some of his best friends were of the Jewish faith, Lucas continued, but he expressed the opinion that Jews were "injuring their own case with an advertisement of this kind," which "plays into the hands of Adolf Hitler." While Chandler then urged that the country "keep the commitments made to the Jewish people during the last war," Wiley deplored the advertisement as damaging to the cause it sought to further.⁵⁹

A spokesman for the Committee indicated satisfaction with the discussion on the floor as a step towards bringing the issue into the open, but leading American political figures began withdrawing their support. The left side of the advertisement had included a section of the Proclamation together with the names of senators and others who had signed it, giving the impression that these supporters endorsed this blunt statement as well. Truman quickly withdrew his name from the Committee, informing Bergson that while it did not mean that his sympathies were not "with the down-trodden Jews of Europe," he did not approve of Bergson's taking it upon himself without consultation to attack members of the Senate and House of Representatives who "are working in your interest." Johnson informed Bergson curtly that his name must not be used "in connection with any advertisement whatsoever." One month later, Truman would write to Wise that "it is fellows like Mr. Bergson who go off half-cocked in matters that affect strategy of the whole world that cause all the trouble." Such an advertisement, he explained, caused the Arabs in North Africa to stab American troops there "in the back." "We want to help the Jews and we are going to help them," he ended, "but we cannot do it at the expense of our military maneuvers."⁶⁰

Lucas followed up in the Senate by noting his particular resentment against Peter Bergson, the Committee's national director, as one of a group of "alien Palestinians" here on "temporary sufferance" who criticized the American Government with full-page advertisements, adding that he knew other colleagues would feel the same way. Senators Burnet R. Maybank (D., South Carolina) and James S. J. Davis (R., Pennsylvania) expressed their confidence in Lucas's work at Bermuda and their ignorance of the advertisement. The Committee could have been more circumspect in using senators' names, Langer agreed, but he pointed out that the names had not been appended to the actual text of the advertisement. While he would not pass judgment on the work of the Bermuda Conference before its records became available, the independent North Dakotan doubted that these documents would be made public soon enough to be of great use. He reiterated his belief in the necessity for concrete action, including the facilitation of entry into Palestine and the creation of a Jewish Army. Chandler added that he would be glad to furnish additional names of "aliens here" when Lucas wanted to pursue the subject further. Bergson responded that he would have no statement until he had a chance to read the Illinois senator's speech.⁶¹

That reply came in a letter to Johnson, which he inserted into the *Congressional Record*. "It was not the intention" of the Committee to use the names of certain senators for an unauthorized endorsement of the contents in that advertisement, Bergson asserted. "To our complete surprise," the list of signatories to the Proclamation, placed in a separate box, had been interpreted as using their names in this fashion. "Nothing was further from our minds," and on behalf of all the Committee's executive board he wished to express "our sincere regrets" to you and your "distinguished colleagues." Having transmitted this apology, Johnson stayed on as National Chairman, while Langer and Murray reaffirmed their support of the Committee's objectives. They could not know that both State and Whitehall were secretly delighted that the conference had yielded minimal results, or that Myron Taylor, Roosevelt's emissary to the futile 1938 Evian Conference on Refugees and later to the Vatican, had written privately to Secretary of State Cordell Hull and his subordinates that the Bermuda meeting "was wholly ineffective, as I view it, and we knew it would be."[62]

A far more incendiary advertisement was actually due to appear prior to the one about the Bermuda Conference, featuring Hecht's "Ballad of the Doomed Jews of Europe." In early 1943, the Hollywood scriptwriter had read a newspaper report saying that German Minister of Enlightenment and Propaganda Joseph Goebbels vowed to complete the Nazi objective of murdering all of Europe's Jews in time for Christmas. He responded with a poem which carried the refrain that the Christian world (including the State Department) was "busy with other news" than the killing of the Jews, and concluded that by Christmas all Christians would enjoy their "peace on earth" without the Jews—who would be killed by then. The advertisement was scheduled to appear in the *New York Times*, but the wartime paper shortage delayed publication. A staff member at that newspaper, which continued to universalize the singular Jewish tragedy and discounted the possibilities of rescue, leaked the text to officials of the conservatively inclined American Jewish Committee. Its president, the anti-Zionist Judge Joseph Proskauer, warned Bergson that it "could well bring pogroms in the U.S.A." Bergson agreed to withdraw the advertisement, but he insisted that Proskauer call a meeting of Jewish leaders to discuss how to press for government action to help European Jewry. Several organizations sent representatives, but these turned down Bergson's appeal that they jointly sponsor an emergency conference on the matter. Instead, the B'nai Brith delegate and others reiterated Proskauer's entreaty, urging that the provocative advertisement be shelved. Bergson agreed to hold back for several months, hoping that those present might yet take a more activist approach on rescue.[63]

The Committee moved forward on its own. Eri Jabotinsky began his duties to transform its ranks into a large membership organization. Working with sponsors of the Proclamation, the executive board decided to call an "Emergency Conference to Save the Jews of Europe." Senators Johnson, Langer, and Murray, along with colleagues Davis and Warren Barbour (New Jersey), jointly pledged their active support, publicly declaring the objective "urgent and timely." Meeting on July 20–25, 1943, at New York's Hotel Commodore, outstanding experts, after examining questions of international relations, military affairs, transportation, and relief, placed the tragedy in its place as a specific Allied problem capable of solution. The conferees urged the US government to create an official agency charged with rescuing this one people targeted for annihilation, the other "United Nations" free to participate if they so wished. The International Red Cross, neutral governments, and the Vatican, for their part, should oversee better treatment of Jews in the satellite governments and press for their emigration from Axis-held territory. Ample food and shipping was available, they observed, for limited feeding of the persecuted. In four months, 600,000 Jews from the satellite nations could be evacuated to Palestine, with an additional 150,000 brought to other temporary locations in neutral countries. Punitive raids and the threat of postwar reprisals would follow if Germany's satellites refused to let the Jews leave.[64]

From then on, the Bergson Boys abandoned the Committee for a Jewish Army campaign and devoted all their energies to the cause of rescue. Zionists and recognized Jewish organizations continued to challenge the youngsters—even discrediting them in government circles—for having no authorization to speak in the name of an established constituency, eliciting the retort that they relied on what Merlin termed "the mandate of conscience." With no united American Jewish front created to confront their people's horrendous calamity abroad, the Irgun emissaries pressed State for action, had Hecht's "Ballad" printed in the *New York Times* on September 14, arranged a rabbis' march on the capital just prior to Yom Kippur, and had Congressional resolutions introduced urging Roosevelt to establish a commission "designed to save the surviving Jewish people of Europe from extinction at the hands of Nazi Germany." In the face of the Holocaust, these and other innovative initiatives that were undertaken until the war's end met with meager success.[65]

On September 20, 1944, the British government announced that a Jewish Brigade group would be formed under the Jewish national flag and insignia, and assigned to active Allied wartime operations. Zionist leaders Wise and Silver, constantly worried that the Bergson Boys' crusade for a Jewish Army harmed their own confidential and public efforts in tandem with the Jewish Agency, extended congratulations to the Agency executive in Jerusalem for its "untiring efforts" towards the establishment of a Jewish military force. Certainly, Shertok's unremitting activities in this regard entitled him to first patrimony. Weizmann's diplomatic pressure in London and notably his strong influence on Churchill, without whom the project would never have gotten by the political-military British careerists in London and the Middle East, played the other chief role. Ben-Gurion's steps to have Palestinian and American Jewry back a Jewish fighting force and a postwar Jewish state contributed to its success. The *Yishuv*'s significant effort on behalf of the Allied cause, especially when compared with the Arabs, also could not fail to make some mark.[66]

The Committee for a Jewish Army, the only organization committed full-time until mid-1943 to the idea in question, did yeoman work in galvanizing public opinion for the Jewish combat force. With reason, Kook's newly formed Hebrew Committee of National Liberation cabled congratulations to Strabolgi for his unceasing work in this respect, and the NZO of America issued a statement recalling that the idea for a Jewish Army had first been advocated by Jabotinsky. The Committee's ability to arrestingly capture the public imagination in the United States and in Great Britain certainly allowed Churchill to assert in Cabinet that this cause enjoyed great support on both sides of the Atlantic. And in a way its founders never intended, the organization's large-scale, trenchantly put demands made it easier for Churchill and his colonial and foreign secretaries to deal with the established Jewish Agency, its smaller requests for a Jewish division and then a brigade, and (as Halifax had argued to Whitehall in June 1942) with the more moderate Weizmann. Thus, too, in ridiculing Strabolgi's continued insistence on a large Jewish Army, Undersecretary for War Lord Croft could intimate publicly for the first time in the House of Commons that a Jewish brigade might be in the offing. Curiously, the Jewish Telegraphic Agency's obituary notice on Kook's death at his home in Kfar Shmaryahu on August 18, 2001, carried no mention of his work for a Jewish Army, focusing on his efforts at "increasing awareness of the genocide [sic] through advertisements, rallies and plays."[67]

A later recollection by Van Paassen raised the possibility that perhaps more than a tacit understanding in this regard existed between Weizmann and Jabotinsky, the first the diplomat and statesman, the second the "critic, gadfly and public nuisance." When Ben-Gurion, while visiting Van Paassen's apartment on Upper Manhattan's Riverside Drive, heard the news of the Committee for a Jewish Army's formation, he exclaimed: "I won't have it! I will never consent to the setting up of such an army!" On the other hand, Van Paassen recalled, Weizmann received the news in the same city at the St. Regis Hotel "with a broad smile and with an expression of his entire satisfaction." Without a moment's hesitation, the WZO president (who alone among the Zionist leadership in London had volunteered assistance to Jabotinsky's drive for a Jewish Legion) dictated and signed a formal statement of assent—not for publication—which delineated the new Committee's purposes and objectives. Later, while serving as National Chairman, Van Paassen wrote *The Forgotten Ally*, a subsequent 1943 bestseller in the United States and Great Britain which first brought the *Yishuv*'s true military contribution to light.[68]

On February 1, 1940, the day that the *Sakariya* sailed, Henry Montor released a letter in his capacity as Executive Director of the United Palestine Appeal. This document explained that the Jewish Agency insisted on selective immigration in choosing young men and women trained in Europe for "productive purposes either in agriculture or industry" in Palestine. Many of those who had been brought into Palestine by the Revisionists, he went on, "have been prostitutes and criminals. This particular affair could be satisfactorily liquidated if the American Friends of Jewish Palestine would cease its separate fund-raising activities at which it had already proved unsuccessful, and if it were to agree to 'selectivity' in immigration." The five-page letter to the American Friends' Baruch Rabinowitz, carrying the endorsement of Wise, Lehman, Albert Einstein, and other American Jewish notables, served as the United Palestine Appeal's justification for refusing to finance the transport of more than 2,000 Jewish refugees then fleeing for their very lives from Nazi persecution.[69]

Twenty-three years later, Montor, the man whom Ben-Gurion had referred to as one of the top ten people "most responsible for the creation of the State of Israel," conveyed a very different message to his close friend Meyer Steinglas, National Publicity Director of the State of Israel Bonds since its inception in 1951. On December 29, 1963, he sent Steinglas a handwritten confession about his altered perspective on the Irgun, and on Kook in particular, since Israel's rebirth in 1948. The letter, which has eluded the historian's searchlight until today, contains a passage that deserves to be cited in full:

> My objections to the Irgun during the height of its activities were "moral" (whatever that may mean). But after the State was established, I recognized that Bergson in the U.S. and his colleagues had made a vital contribution to the establishment of the State. And that [the] Irgun had done the same. As time passes, I realize that the attitudes I once adopted were the result of historical fantasies in which I believed because I was a member—never an interested party—of the Establishment. But now that I see Ben

Gurion reexamined and various episodes of illegal immigration, among others, viewed in a new light, I realize that I may not have always have made judgments in the light of the real truth. How does one ever know?[70]

Shmuel Merlin ultimately judged the work of the Bergson Boys to be "a failure." Writing a long letter to Kook in July 1984, he observed that the European Jews were not saved; a Hebrew Republic of Palestine, which they had advocated as of July 1944, was not established; a Jewish Army of fifteen or twenty divisions was not created. "In all probability," he continued, "we were responsible for the British agreement to create the Jewish Brigade when the war was practically over, and the scope and composition of that Brigade it is better not to talk about—though a great many of them were active in illegal immigration and, of course, Dov Gruner came from the Brigade." Yet, Kook's chief lieutenant added bitterly, "Israel has become an instrument of death. It's the most exposed place in the world, where daily death stalks around the corner." Above all, he raised this question: "Does Israel outweigh the annihilation of 'Dos Yiddishe Folk'?" The latter personifying his own European-Jewish world, Merlin thought not.[71]

Seen from the historian's perspective, the failure lay elsewhere. Jabotinsky, Kook, and their associates, for all their unceasing efforts, could not translate ideas into action. The young, unheralded Palestinians particularly stirred masses of Jews, including those like Ben Hecht hitherto far removed from matters Jewish, and the generous impulses of the Gentile majority. They took the campaign for a Jewish Army and then one for rescue out of the back pages of the daily press and radio broadcasts, which had hitherto assigned coverage of Jews to rabbinical sermons and religious services, and brought them to the attention of millions. The Committee for a Jewish Army alone numbered almost 50,000 individual contributors and several active chapters of hundreds of members in the most major cities, thus taking on the proportions of a mass movement.[72] Yet fundamental decisions rested with Washington and London, who chose not to accord the one people lacking national sovereignty special consideration as an independent entity desperate for, and surely deserving of, help.

Financier Bernard Baruch telephoned Hecht and asked him on behalf of Roosevelt "for a respite" in the Committee's tactics. Samuel Rosenman, Roosevelt's lawyer and speechwriter, reported to Wise that the President and the Prime Minister had been "incensed" by its full-page advertisements, and particularly by the NZO's demand "Mr. Churchill, Drop the Mandate!" Roosevelt had also been "much displeased" at the rabbis' march on Washington, wondering "can nothing be done to liquidate [sic] Bergson? He was, after all, a

British Palestinian subject." London actually attempted to have Kook inducted into HMG's armed forces, but his Congressional supporters stymied this effort. Both warlords, nonetheless, continued to deem Hitler's primary victims expendable in Jewry's blackest hour.[73]

A mantle of "callous indifference" towards European Jewry's agony covered the two major Western powers, which discriminated against the Jews in the World War II years. Palestinian Jewry fought as Britain's nameless ally, while only one Jewish battalion and a tiny parachute unit from the *Yishuv* saw action, grudging concessions that were granted toward the end of the war. A joint Anglo-American statement was almost issued in July 1943 banning all talk of Palestine during the war; the White Paper remained in force; significant rescue action was never undertaken. In these same years, food reached Greece through Allied blockade; exchange of prisoners took place via the International Red Cross; Allied boats (other than ferrying some 430,000 enemy prisoners to camps in the United States) returned empty from theatres of war, although 20,000 Muslim pilgrims were brought by vessels from Cairo to Mecca and 40,000 Yugoslavs sent from Italy to refugee camps in Egypt. Churchill threatened to retaliate in kind if the Germans used poison gas on the Russian front; French Gentile youngsters in very impressive numbers were spirited to safety across the Pyrenees; Poles and Czechs received arms for resistance.[74]

In the sober war-torn world of *realpolitik*, political expediency proved decisive. The courteous but cold language of British official W. G. Hayter, speaking in Washington to Montor in December 1941, most aptly captured the tragedy:

> Yes, we have done badly in recent months. It is quite true we have overlooked the Jews. It has been called to our attention that the Prime Minister never has mentioned the Jews when he speaks of the yoke on Hitler's victims. But that is probably accidental. He looked over the map and could think only of specific countries seized by Hitler. The Jews, of course, were not on that map, and they were overlooked.[75]

Ten days earlier, the German *Führer* had sat down in Berlin with Haj Amin el-Husseini, the former Grand Mufti of Jerusalem. Asserting that the Third Reich's fight "without respite" against the Jews included "the so-called Jewish National Home in Palestine," and that he would continue the struggle "until the *complete destruction* [emphasis added] of the Judeo-Bolshevik rule has been accomplished," he promised that, when the Germans reached the southern

Caucasus a pro-Arab declaration would be issued and his guest would lead the Arab forces against Palestinian Jewry. In July 1943, following the Bermuda fiasco, California Congressman Will Rogers Jr. emphasized at the Emergency Conference to Save the Jews of Europe that Jewry's unique crisis had to be "taken out of the dossiers of the diplomats and placed in the hearts of humanity." Yet Roosevelt and Churchill had no intention of relinquishing control over major policy. Neither took up Hitler's challenge and made the rescue of a powerless people one of their war aims. The Jews, "not on the map" of sovereign nations, were "overlooked."[76]

In December 1980, my first public lecture on the Bergson Boys offered a conclusion which I have had no reason to alter in the four decades since.[77] I wrote then that propaganda and dissent, however impressive in the forthright and nonsectarian appeal used, proved to be limited in their ultimate effect. Even as Washington and London avoided the moral imperative to try to save an innocent people singularly marked for death in World War II, they declared their hopes of a postwar world ensuring Jews the full rights of citizens everywhere. Under the circumstances, these sentiments were noble but naïve. The Anglo-American alliance also cleaved to the line that Europe's Jews would be best served by the complete defeat of Germany. Alas, as the doomed Warsaw Ghetto chronicler Emanuel Ringelblum noted in his diary as early as February 1941, that eventuality might witness the victors' arrival, "declaring, 'We have conquered!'—to our graves."[78] The Jews could not wait for an Allied victory. Adolf Hitler would not let them wait. The kingdom of barbed wire and ashes, as a consequence, enjoyed an unbridled reign.

CHAPTER 5

The Steinberg-Lazaron-Frank Debate on Zionism and Jewish Survival

In early May 1945, forty-one-year-old Milton Steinberg, rabbi of Manhattan's Park Avenue Synagogue, looked forward to the publication of his latest book. After obtaining a doctorate in Philosophy from Columbia University, he had fallen under the strong influence of Reconstructionist Judaism founder Mordecai Kaplan at the Jewish Theological Seminary, from which he received ordination. While a disciple of Kaplan, Steinberg remained critical of his mentor's dismissal of metaphysics. Following five years of occupying Congregation Beth-El Zedeck's pulpit in Indianapolis, in 1933 Steinberg had joined the influential Conservative Jewish house of worship on New York City's Upper East Side. His eloquence and broad knowledge, displayed in sermons, many lectures, and the printed word, would contribute to a sixfold increase in the congregation's membership. Public recognition arrived with his first volume *The Making of the Modern Jew* (1934) and a best-selling historical novel *As a Driven Leaf* (1939), which revolved around the Talmudic characters Elisha ben Abuyah and Rabbi Akiva.[1]

As news of the Holocaust began to mount in the West, the Zionist cause particularly claimed Steinberg's concern. Under the initiative of the American Emergency Committee for Zionist Affairs and together with his cousin, Rabbi Philip Bernstein of Reform Temple B'rith Kodesh in Rochester, he spearheaded a campaign to develop contacts within the Christian clergy, which saw the first appearance of pro-Zionist articles by the likes of eminent Protestant theologian Reinhold Niebuhr and Methodist Bishop Francis McConnell. When a large group of Reform rabbis, opposing Zionism in favor of a post-war world governed by the universalist principles of Isaiah and the American Declaration of Independence, constituted themselves on

December 7, 1942, as the American Council for Judaism (ACJ), Steinberg and Bernstein helped found the Christian Council on Palestine one week later. On that occasion, Niebuhr championed a federation of Arab states "in return for a state in Palestine awarded to the people with historic claims to its soil and desperately in need of a homeland." In October 1943, a committee under Steinberg's chairmanship began to work to mobilize the assistance of American intellectuals to endorse Palestine as a Jewish Commonwealth after the war.[2]

Rabbi Morris S. Lazaron of Baltimore's Hebrew Congregation would have none of this, taking as early as December 1939 to the NBC radio airways to rally the nation's Jews to embrace the message of prophetic Judaism. For the Savannah-born, fifty-five-year-old clergyman, the Hebrew prophets called for "a universal religion which knows no land or people or race," the future lying with "the invincible dream of man—one humanity on earth as there is one God in heaven." Lazaron's accepting in principle Britain's restrictive May 1939 White Paper on Jewish immigration to Palestine greatly pleased Wallace Murray, anti-Zionist chief of the US State Department's Near Eastern Affairs division, as representative of "a large section of American Jewry" of whom little was heard. Some within the established American Jewish Committee rallied to his standard, as did older fellow Reform rabbis behind the ACJ's creation, objecting to calls for a Jewish Army to fight alongside the Allies and for Jewish sovereignty in Palestine championed by the young wing within the Central Conference of American Rabbis (CCAR). Lazaron's anxiety and those of a small minority within the CCAR regarding political Zionism's impact on Jewish existence surfaced in his public attack at the time on that movement's "philosophy of despair, which assumes that our present status is hopeless and that democracy is a failure." In his view, this stance delayed the Jew's integration into American life, made impossible a peaceful resolution of the thorny Palestine question, and challenged the universalist principles of prophetic Judaism.[3]

In November 1944, Lazaron brought his crusade to the general public through the pages of the prestigious *Atlantic Monthly*, founded in 1857 by the likes of famed literati Ralph Waldo Emerson, Harriet Beecher Stowe, and Henry Wadsworth Longfellow. "Palestine: The Dream and the Reality—A Survey of Jewish Nationalism," advocating for "the voice of American Israel," posited that when the Jewish communities of Europe were "threatened with destruction," and when the need to find homes for "the stricken wanderers is immediate and pressing," the "age-old land" of Palestine "has offered opportunity and hope." With so many doors closed worldwide, it was natural that Jews "should seek homes in the land which cradled their forebears," and that all Jews viewed with "keen disappointment" any policy that would sharply limit entrance to Palestine at this time.

Yet one group of American Jews opposed the establishment in Palestine of an independent Jewish State, fearing such a program as a departure from their tradition, as well as "not only unnecessary but dangerous." The inclusion of Jewish nationalist demands in both the current Republican and Democratic political platforms, Lazaron went on, carried the implication that Jews vote as a bloc to which special appeal must be made. Rather, believing that Israel has survived and will survive as a religious community, this group thought that a Jewish commonwealth would "build barriers" between Jews and their fellow citizens and give ammunition to the antisemite. Declaring that Palestine could absorb only a limited number of Jews, the vast millions continuing to live throughout the world, Lazaron also urged a positive program to promote among Jews in the United States a knowledge of Jewish history, literature, and tradition, and to deepen the religious life of the American Jew.

Only in our times, he warned, the religious community of Israel had been given "a secular basis and a political goal." Zionism arose out of the "apparent hopelessness" of the Jew's struggle for existence, security, and "the grievous and mortifying acceptance of himself as the hated wanderer never sure of a permanent home," and was rooted in a demand to be like other nations. This counsel of despair denied that there could be any progress, or that freedom and democracy will spread among humanity. "Brave spirits" arose in comparatively modern times, however, not hindered by theological or other prejudices against the Jew; "the progress of man is forward." The lines of "a new, happier order" were being drawn, as shown in the Atlantic Charter, the United Nations Relief and Rehabilitation Administration, the US War Refugee Board, and the unprecedented "Pattern for Peace" proclamation on the postwar world by Catholic, Protestant, and Jewish leaders in October 1943. The present antisemitism in some quarters was matched by an increased understanding of the Jew and of Judaism, and by sympathy and support of persecuted Jews in every country of the world. For the Jew, the preservation of his religious tradition in "the land of his habitation" was "the important object."

Jews should unite on a threefold program, Lazaron urged, submerging the present violence of partisanship in their ranks in the light of "the tragedy of our brother Jews." This included the international guarantee of the rights of all Jews to residence and citizenship anywhere; the rehabilitation of Jewish life, finding new homes as part of the international post-war reconstruction; and the international guarantee of "the largest possible Jewish immigration" into Palestine tied to a series of five or ten-year plans for economic growth.

Determining that country's political future must be postponed, however, until "more favorable conditions" had been developed, at which time "a democratic self-governing commonwealth" would be set up guaranteeing equal rights for all its citizens and "religio-cultural autonomy" for all groups which desired this. "It is not labels that count, but life," Lazaron concluded. Perhaps his essay was "an excursion into Utopia, but since when have dreams and visions been banned from Church and Synagogue?"[4]

A "thoughtful" article, Steinberg countered three months later in the same journal with his own *The Creed of an American Zionist*, but American Jewry has "turned overwhelmingly Zionist." The CCAR, once the fountainhead of anti-Zionism, had of late consistently voted pro-Zionist by approximately two to one, while the American Jewish Conference, an assembly of five hundred delegates, went on record in August 1943 with only four dissenting ballots in favor of a Jewish Commonwealth in Palestine. This "great transformation" reflected the "cogency and practicality" of the Zionist idea. While America was on its way to "new horizons of freedom and justice," in Steinberg's view, the Palestinian record of "impossible", superb accomplishment was clear wherein almost 600,000 Jews, free and self-reliant, had set about "incarnating an ancient dream" and introduced modernity and democracy into the Near East. About 35,000 of them had enlisted in the British military forces during World War II, while Palestinian Jewry gave refuge in ten years to 280,000 of their brethren, "who otherwise would now be dead to the last soul."

Yet "the core" of my case, Steinberg declared, was rooted in a religious conviction that at least a part of the House of Israel should be restored to its soil, an aspiration written deep in the Bible and inscribed boldly in the whole rabbinic tradition. His "even wilder vision," resting in the "historic confidence" of the Jewish religion, was an expectation of "some fresh word of God sounding in Jerusalem." Further, he advocated Zionism as "the most immediate and practicable answer to a vast, terrible and very tangible need." The Old-World House of Israel has been "trampled into blood-drenched splinters," as foretold by political Zionist founder Theodor Herzl and his associates, and Jewish Palestine shines as "a joy-bringing, hope-dispensing beacon." What is more, the need of a haven would in the future be more, not less, acute. No Jew, Zionist, or person of good will and democratic persuasion could tolerate the thought of any Jew being denied residence and equality status in the land of his birth or citizenship. There will be thousands of Jewish survivors for whom a return to former homes would be impossible, he declared, as antisemitism will not immediately vanish from Central and Eastern Europe and there will be those whose "last roots have been severed."

The July 1938 Evian Conference on Refugees had demonstrated that no government wanted homeless Jews, and now, with demobilization, reconversion, and the dread of mass employment, immigration barriers would almost certainly rise. As for undeveloped areas, investigations for possible havens for Jews had found that each suggested territory was either already overpopulated, unsuited for colonization by Europeans, or closed by political considerations. International covenant assigned Palestine to large-scale Jewish settlement; that country was ready now to receive the homeless Jews of the world. Walter Clay Lowdermilk, Chief of the Soil Conservation Service of the US Department of Agriculture, had recently concluded that the country could receive four million inhabitants beyond its present population.

But the needs of "my own spirit," Steinberg continued, impel to Zionism as Judaism also requires "infusions of the fresh, novel, and contemporaneous." There must be a place "where Hebraism will be a first culture, where it can flourish without hindrance, and whence transfusions of new value may emanate." The brilliant renaissance in Palestine, the revival there of Jewish music, art, letters, folkways, theaters, and the Hebrew language have "invigorated, stimulated, and enriched every Jew in the world." The claim of Zionism's opponents that Judaism is purely a religion was obviously not valid, for irreligious Jews remained Jews and some of the leading American anti-Zionists did not adhere to Jewish religious practice. The Jews of Palestine are "a nation in maturation"; the American Jew, bound to Palestine by ties of religion, sentiment and culture, has only one political duty—to America. The very prophets who conceived universalism loved Israel and Zion also. Judaism, religion and culture alike, needed Jewish Palestine "for its fulfillment."

In sum, Jewish nationalism meant no more than "recognition of the peoplehood of Israel, and of the propriety of that people's being a religio-cultural group in America, a nationality in Eastern Europe, and in Palestine an actualized nation." Without the Zionists' "commonwealth formula" there would be no further Jewish immigration to Palestine, limited by the "notorious" 1939 White Paper which still stood. That policy, "the misbegotten child of Chamberlain appeasement," had been denounced in Parliament by diverse politicians and the League of Nations' Permanent Mandates Commission, and had "contributed to the death of thousands of Jews." Jewish achievement decidedly benefited the Arab majority in Palestine, and all Arab rights would be guaranteed in the future Jewish Commonwealth—a safer solution than a Jewish minority in an Arab majority. As to urgency, the Palestinian Arabs were denied only a political aspiration, while Palestine was "truly a matter of survival" to millions of Jews. In the broader view, the Arab world had vast territories on which to realize political autonomy whereas Palestine was a mere five percent of that world. Where else could the people Israel "incarnate fully" its peoplehood and culture? The Zionist dream has been spoken to me "in almost every syllable of the religious tradition I cherish," Steinberg concluded: "It represents a desperate need, physical and spiritual, for world Jewry. It is fraught with promise for Israel and mankind."[5]

These themes would receive additional exposition in Steinberg's *The Partisan Guide to the Jewish Problem,* due to be published by the Bobbs-Merrill Company of Indianapolis that autumn, but one last matter had to be addressed before final galleys could go forward. He wished to quote from portions of an article by fifty-four-year-old Judge Jerome Frank, currently sitting on the United States Circuit Court of Appeals for the Second Circuit in New York City. "Red, White and Blue Herring," which had appeared in the highly popular magazine *Saturday Evening Post* one day before the Japanese surprise attack on Pearl Harbor that brought the country into World War II, would serve Steinberg in his sharp critique of the stance taken by American anti-Zionists. Accordingly, he sent the proposed chapter for Frank's approval, little anticipating the response to follow.

Those who claim that American Jews, as a group, have helped to build up interventionist sentiment in America, Frank's article had begun, "are using a red herring, or, rather, a red, white and blue herring." There is no such thing as a cohesive American Jewish group with a common body of opinion, and that was, and is, true with respect to World War II. He had been the strong isolationist who wrote *Save America First* (1938) on the subject, until Hitler's victories; the same change occurred in the thinking of many Americans including many Jews, and many now regretted their earlier opposition to "collective security." Most American Jews, like most German-Americans, were thoroughly devoted to America's interests.

"Unhappily," he went on to declare, a small, unrepresentative minority existed "who should not be described as American Jews but as Jews in America." What he termed "hyphenates" included Jews who were Communists or fellow travelers who had as little regard for Jewish as for American welfare. They were emotionally "merely sojourners in America," as were a small group of "fanatic Jewish nationalists" who have identified themselves completely with Palestine. The same could be said of a group of wealthy Fascist Jews in America who called for appeasing Hitler. These minorities were "out of step" with the great majority of American Jews.

An erroneous belief that American Jews think, act, and vote as a bloc, and were primarily interested in matters Jewish in America and throughout the world, gained plausibility because a majority of American Jews had adopted what Frank called a "hush policy." They had been understandably sensitive to criticism, and feared that any discussion of "the Jewish question" would activate antisemitic feeling. Consequently, they mistakenly had allowed the "more intense" Jewish nationalists among the Zionists and certain "professional Jews" to do most of the talking in public about American Jewish attitudes. That "hush policy" assumed that Jewish silence would prevent the American public from thinking about the Jews. It recalled Mark Twain's story of the little boy who was told to stand in a corner and not to think of a white elephant.

There were many shadings of attitudes even among the majority of American Jews. Yet their fundamental position could be simplified by considering what would be the answers given to these questions: Would you fight and die, if such sacrifices were necessary, to perpetuate the Jews as a separate people? The majority would say, "No." Would you fight and die to save American democracy? Almost all of them, without any mental reservations, would say, "Emphatically yes." Equivalent responses to equivalent questions would be received from most Polish or Italian Americans. Favoring a policy of speaking out, Frank charged that some persons deliberately, and others innocently, were aiding Nazi efforts to promote violent antisemitism in the United States of "the concentration camp variety." "If ever any Americans go to a concentration camp," he concluded, "American democracy will go with them."[6]

Frank's distinction between "American Jews" and "Jews in America," and particularly his labeling the country's ardent political Zionists as "Jewish sojourners in America," irked Steinberg. The author's reporting in that same article about the disintegration of Judaism and that most Jews born in America regarded as their "significant heroes" Thomas Jefferson and Abraham Lincoln, not Jewish folk heroes Moses and David, appeared reflective of assimilationism. Widespread condemnation from Jewish intellectual leaders echoed Steinberg's reaction, including American Jewish Congress leader Rabbi Stephen Wise denouncing the article as "treasonable to the Jewish people" and "simply inexcusable."[7]

These critics could not have known that Lazaron, secretly conveying both to US State Department and Whitehall officialdom at the same moment that some influential Jews were prepared to challenge the World Zionist Organization's objectives, recommended Frank's article to Undersecretary of State Sumner Welles as "completely right." Having studiously avoided Palestine when addressing an Inter-American conference, sponsored by the American Jewish Congress, about postwar resettlement, a receptive Welles also received from Lazaron news about the scheduled meeting of a small group of anti-Zionists including Lewis Strauss and Samuel Rosenman to meet in the home of *New York Times* publisher Arthur Hays Sulzberger. Their purpose: to consider a statement favoring Palestine's economic and cultural development while rejecting Jewish sovereignty there.[8]

Frank's very lengthy response on May 5, 1945, to the request from Steinberg, covering nine, single-spaced typed pages, charged that the rabbi's description of the article was replete with "misleading denunciations" and inaccurate conclusions. The projected chapter created the erroneous impression that Frank sought to indulge in a programmatic essay on "the desirability of the self-obliteration of the Jews," when in fact he had written the article to counteract the pre-Pearl Harbor propaganda of isolationists Charles Lindbergh and others picturing a unified American Jewry trying to induce the United States to fight fascism solely because of its selfish interest in matters Jewish. His accurate narrative aimed to have non-Jews understand that Jews were not "a nation within a nation," that to be an American Jew was not to be a "hyphenate", but overwhelmingly loyal to America. Most of the response mail which he had received came from gentiles, who, with very few exceptions, said that he had helped give them a sympathetic understanding of the unfairness of the Lindbergh propaganda. The point about Jefferson and Lincoln as primary heroes for American Jews was fact, Frank also having said that the results of this tendency "have not always been fortunate," counter to Steinberg's chapter stating that Frank wanted to "disavow Moses and David" and "discard those ancient Jewish worthies."

Tearing a phrase from its full context, Steinberg misleadingly charged that Frank impugned the patriotism of "some of his Jewish fellows," when he had actually criticized "a small group of fanatic Jewish nationalists." Nor had he questioned the loyalty of American Jews who adhered to Orthodox practice. As to "professional Jews" who purport to speak for "a solid group" on all occasions, Frank plainly meant those who "make a racket of Judaism," who by Jewish "chauvinism" get business or procure election or appointment to office. Steinberg's saying that Frank had, by "inadvertence," strayed from his theme and exhorted Americans to "slough off their differentiated heritage" by means of a program for the "suicide" of the Jewish group by which the Jewish community "shall seek to be swallowed up in oblivion" set up a straw man, and made Frank "a good deal of a fool." He was not attempting to do so, and had not offered such a program. His reporting of the "cultural assimilation" among American Jews was also fact, and should antisemitism substantially decline and continue to do so over a long period, total assimilation would be, he thought, "ultimately irresistible."

American Jews would for a long time have a problem concerning their attitudes towards the Jewish tradition, but Frank had not said anything of the sort, as Steinberg imputed to him the belief that the world would be better off if some day all cultural and religious differences were to vanish. Contrary to Steinberg's implication that antisemitism "loomed large" in Frank's life as an individual, which "approaches a hysteria", and that he was "not tempted to flight from myself, nor bitter, because I know in advance that it will prove futile," Frank retorted: I am no "escapist": "I have "never denied being a Jew or even thought of it."

Accordingly, Frank was "most reluctant" to give Steinberg permission to quote him as the rabbi proposed. One way to solve the problem would be to print the article in full as an appendix to the book. If that device did not suit, he suggested that they leave the problem's solution to Judge Bernard Botein, a member of Steinberg's congregation and a presiding justice of the New York State Supreme Court, Appellate Division, First Department. He was sending Botein a copy of this letter, emphasizing to Steinberg that it was not for quotation.[9]

"We are miles apart and are likely to remain so," Steinberg replied four days later. While the issues between them were "too large and involved" for exploration in writing," he wished to say only that Frank's argument left him "unpersuaded." Where he had offended critics including Steinberg was not in reporting actualities but the "spirit" in which they were reported, the conferring of approval or disapproval. The impression left was that Frank applauded the dissolution of the Jewish tradition, which is why the article was so generally assailed in Jewish religious and cultural "survivalist" circles, and why Steinberg still thought that it gave expression to the assimilationist viewpoint. Nonetheless, he would defer to Frank's preferences, and delete from the forthcoming book all direct quotation and discussion of the article. An "uncolored reference" to the article might be made, indicating to the reader that if he wanted what appears to be an assimilationist statement he may find one, as the author judges, in that article. Perhaps someday we shall have a chance to talk these matters over, he ended, both why Frank had been so widely understood (or misunderstood as they case may be), and "the objective, impersonal issues involved."[10]

Not mollified, Frank shot back with a five-page letter on the 15th, noting that he had received a huge "fan mail," including many Jewish "intellectual leaders," Joseph Proskauer and James Rosenberg among those giving warm approbation. A "distorted version" of his article by zealous, active Zionist propagandists going far beyond their own ranks, he pointed out, is common. The article, contrary to Steinberg's assertion, did not imply a feeling of pleasure in the possibility of complete assimilation of the American Jews. In the proposed chapter, Frank repeated, Steinberg, making important factual misstatements concerning what was actually in the article, "wrote irresponsibly," and if he spoke in like vein to his congregation, spoke irresponsibly. The chapter, unlike the letter, stated that Frank had (inadvertently) set forth a program for assimilation and arguments why Jews should adopt such a program—without offering a program.

As a government official, Frank had become an "experienced abusee [sic]." But while Steinberg's and other unfair Zionist criticism did not much disturb him, he worried that misrepresentation of statements made by a person with whose views one disagreed had been one of the chief tactics of the Nazis and other antisemites. At a time when American Jewry sorely needed leadership, it was "most unfortunate" that those who assert that they are Jewish leaders should employ such tactics. "Shockingly" misquoted by Rabbis Wise and Kaplan and Zionist adherents, that single Jew was vilified as "a slanderer" of thousands of other Jews. Should we meet, Frank closed, he wished to discuss the possibility of evolving a faith whereby Judaism would be "supplemented by non-Jewish factors." He did believe in one kind of healthy, objective escapism— that which sought, so far as possible, "to overcome difficulties without sacrificing indispensable values." For that reason, he wished to see Jews avoid the avoidable consequences of antisemitism. On that note, Frank returned the chapter herewith.[11]

"I'm afraid we've gotten into a routine of misunderstanding each other," Steinberg responded two days later. Perhaps we should let the entire matter slide until both of us could acquire "greater objectivity" concerning it. In the meantime, Frank was informed that all references to him were deleted from the chapter under discussion. He ended on a conciliatory note: "I hope that in our next encounter we may come to understand each other a bit better."[12]

Responding to, in Lazaron's depiction, the "unrestrained and unwarranted attack" of the Zionist Organization of America (ZOA) on American Council for Judaism adherents as anti-Zionists, he advised at the month's end that most of the Council's membership be classified as non-Zionists to evince their interest in Palestine development, as distinct from the whole concept of a Jewish State. In a draft memorandum, Lazaron stressed the group's "positive and constructive" attitude towards Palestine's growth, its opening hope for as large a Jewish immigration as possible, and the Balfour Declaration carried out "in spirit and in letter." Yet the Council, he added, was also concerned with the forces that "promise an extension of the process of emancipation for Jews wherever they live." It was concerned with Judaism, for the members believed that religious values "buttress our liberal civilization." The ACJ was concerned with American

Judaism, for it believed that "the center of Jewish life in the succeeding years" would be in America, and that Jewry must be strong and informed and have "a high faith" in its expression of Jewish life. The Council's moderate program, Lazaron concluded, was in keeping with the facts of the international situation, was destined to accomplish more for Palestine in the end, and represented more nearly the sentiments of the majority of the Jewish people of the United States than the "extremist" political demands of the ZOA, which went beyond the terms of the Balfour Declaration and rejected the spirit of the Atlantic Charter.[13]

A Partisan Guide to the Jewish Problem appeared that fall sans a reference to Frank's article but with a powerful critique of the American Council for Judaism. For Steinberg, "Zion shall yet be rebuilt, a haven for the outcast of the House of Israel, a lamp shining with the light of rejuvenated Judaism upon the many Jewries and the world, an embodiment of high Jewish vision, a tranquil Jewish community repeating and restating the timeless message of Judaism; in sum a free commonwealth in a new and better world order." Palestine could help American Jews by mitigating antisemitism in those lands that heretofore had been its chief breeding grounds. Let 2,000,000 Jews move from Europe to Palestine, and there would be improvement in the lot of Jews everywhere and in that of the native Arab population. Further, by its import and performance, Zionism stimulated Jews worldwide to persevere as Jews. Indeed, in the eyes of some Jews (a hint to the ACJ), herein lies the "unforgiveable sin of Zionism: that it is so clearly and vigorously a survivalist force." For those Jews who wished to play down their identities or desired not to live as Jews at all, Zionism was "an evil to be resisted to the last breath." Not every Jew who was happy to be a Jew was necessarily a Zionist, Steinberg concurred, but "without exception, every Jewish escapist is an anti-Zionist."

Notions that Zionism must be somehow unpatriotic and un-American were "grotesque," for the typical American Zionist had no intention except that he and his children would live out their lives in America. Steinberg's interest in Palestine flowed from his concern for his fellows abroad and for his own Hebraic heritage. That anti-Zionists were "timorous" in this respect was demonstrable from the simple circumstance that every US president from Woodrow Wilson onward had endorsed Zionism, as had both houses of Congress. The Jewish scene in recent years could not be misconstrued: On the one hand, "tens of myriads of Jews with the death mark on their foreheads," and, on the other, "only Palestine ready and capable of delivering them." The Jewish people possessed rights vis-à-vis that country which it did not possess elsewhere—the rights contained in the Balfour Declaration and Mandate: "And these boil down to a commitment to a Jewish Commonwealth." The urgency was great. Against the barriers pressed millions of homeless human beings "ridden hard" by suffering and want; against the walls beat the "inner needs" of world Jewry, "a culture seeking rebirth, a social idealism demanding incarnation."

Lastly, Steinberg declared, "the larger meaning." A Jewish Homeland in Palestine would likely make American Jews the stronger and better as human beings, "richer and more resolute in their Judaism." The success of Jewish Palestine (the *Yishuv*) may have "a salutary effect" on the moral position of Jews and "normalize" Jews in the eyes of the world, thus dissipating "the aura of the eccentric" hovering over them for millennia. This, together with the Jewish commonwealth drawing off a substantial part of the Jews of the "diseased" areas of Central Europe, would improve the condition of Jews everywhere. Palestinian Jews' now laboring in all fields of economic endeavor had begun to communicate its values to Jewish youth around the world. In addition, Jewish Palestine sought to realize the ancient dream of the "peoplehood" of Israel, as well as reviving and remolding Jewish ritual and culture. Thus, "root to branch, Zionism is survivalist," standing firm against "masked assimilationism." In one spot on the globe, things were "radiant with attainment and promise." This embodied the final gift of Jewish Palestine to American Judaism—the gift of *elan*, hopefulness, a conviction of worth, in sum, a confidence in the future of Israel and its way of life."[14]

A Partisan Guide to the Jewish Problem enjoyed quick success, a special printing of 5,000 copies selling out in advance. In October, a regular printing was exhausted, so the publisher rushed a second edition of 4,000. Reviewing it for the *Saturday Review of Literature*, the prominent Unitarian minister in New York City and crusader for civil liberties John Haynes Holmes declared that the volume contained everything one needed or desired to know about the subject. Eloquence, understanding, and compassion were evident in pages marked by no partisanship except as the author was "a partisan of decency, justice, and human brotherhood." Steinberg has no sympathy for cowardice, submission, or even mere patience and long-suffering, Holmes declared. Assimilation, in his eyes, "is as unworthy as it is futile." He would have Jews stand "straight and tall and in the full dignity of their manhood." Let the Jews be courageous, proud, stalwart in faith, hope, and resolute determination—to be true to themselves "and to their great and distinctive tradition." The book, Holmes concluded, "calls for high praise and gratitude."[15]

Lazaron did not stand idly by, writing a long letter, published in the *New York Times* on September 30, to warn "our Jewish fellow Americans" that Zionist pressures for Jewish statehood were "ill advised," and might precipitate violence and bloodshed in Palestine. They also embarrass those responsible for the conduct of our international relations, and complicate delicate negotiations now being conducted with Great Britain on many other important issues. Our Christian fellow-Americans should know that Jews were divided on this issue, and all should realize that "extremist action" might indeed jeopardize the "magnificent" achievements in Palestine, deprive thousands of "their one hope for a home," and trigger "religious and racial warfare" in the Near East.

The larger issue of the "stateless and dispossessed" Jews' need and desire for Palestine, with that country able to absorb such immigration within "the complex situation," is not debatable, Lazaron argued. Over and above is the basic question: what shall be the future of the Jewish citizens of America and the world? The philosophy of Jewish nationalism, he posited, would create "all sorts of emotional and psychological bars" between Jews and their fellow citizens, delaying or destroying the normal processes of integration in American life. To set us apart from our fellow Americans in any sense other than religious—for Judaism is purely a religious, not a national, communion—"is to ghettoize the great free community." The citizenship of two-thirds of the world's Jews, who now live in lands of freedom, should not be endangered by setting up a Jewish State, the latter always to be surrounded by Arab peoples, too small to protect even its own nationals, and always to be the "football of international politics."

In Lazaron's view, a key to the solution was contained in the 1919 King-Crane Commission's report, which had recommended to the victorious Allies of World War I "serious modification" of the "extreme" Zionist demand for the unlimited entry of Jews to Palestine and its finally becoming "distinctly a Jewish State." Neither a final decision nor a long-range solution was possible now, he believed, given the highly involved issues and intense feeling involved. Still, international guarantees to the Arabs against Jewish domination and a more generous Jewish immigration, with each community guaranteed local autonomy in cultural and fiscal affairs, should be possible. International supervision should be tightened over the mandatory power, the UN seeing to it that the rights and political status enjoyed by the Jews in any other country "are not prejudiced or jeopardized." Meanwhile, international authority must "repress the extremist, encourage the moderate, and give the land a chance." They who say they love Palestine should not insist on any other way. They who seek "the peace of Jerusalem," Lazaron concluded, will find it only in the way of "honorable compromise."[16]

Steinberg jumped to rebuttal on October 7 with an even longer communication appearing in the same newspaper. Rabbi Lazaron could not have "wrought greater harm" on the "wretched Jews of Europe," he began. He voices moderation and weaves "finespun, far-fetched reservations about

Zionism" at a time when it had been confirmed that 6,000,000 Jews were "butchered"; when those who survive are revealed to be "in the wildest extremes of need and despair," most sustained only by the hope of migration to Palestine; when the British government, in contravention of its pledged word, refuses these "lost souls" the fulfillment of their hope; and his letter appeared on the very day that publication of the Earl Harrison report confirmed both the survivors' desperation and Palestine's ability to absorb them. The effect, though unintended, "is relentlessly harmful."

The "vast bulk" of American Jews are solidly pro-Zionist, Steinberg observed, while the Arabs oppose all Jewish immigration. Whatever has been accomplished in Palestine has been wrought by Zionism and Zionists. Britain has not adhered to its promise, and there is "a terrible danger" that British bayonets and machine guns will be called into use against European Jews "so desperate" that death at the doors of Palestine is better than life where they are, and against Palestinian Jews engaged in giving asylum to their kin "trapped in the fiercest extremity." Palestine's doors should be open wide. The Arab League continues to threaten violence but that organization, the creature of a Britain that imposes its "dubiously moral will" on the millions of India, can surely be kept in order. Even if disorder should break out in Palestine, it would be violence directed against the saving of lives, carried out by native Arabs who have benefited by the establishment of the Jewish homeland.

History and experience, Steinberg observed, reveal that Jews are not only a creedal body, but an historic people as well. American Jews have one political loyalty—to the United States. Ninety percent of the Jewish chaplains in the US Army and Navy, like the late Supreme Court Justice Louis D. Brandeis, are Zionists or Zionist sympathizers. As for Lazaron's citing the King-Crane report, the late US ambassador to Germany, William Dodd, had quoted Charles Crane as saying to him in the 1930s, "Let Hitler have his way."

Ultimately, the central, twofold issues should not be obscured. First, the question is whether the Holocaust's survivors should remain in their confinement and "goaded to wild devices," or be allowed to enter Palestine, their desire. There alone can they be "transmuted" from the social problem arising from their current stay in Europe's Displaced Persons (DP) camps into "an asset for all mankind." Second, the deeper and more basic—the moral issue: whether the Mandate covenant made with "this harried people" shall be respected or unilaterally nullified. Will they who have been so long abused be abused still further by their supposed friends, or shall Britain act in "the light of the mercy and the justice to which it is pledged"? Between these two sets of alternatives, Steinberg ended, "no person clear in mind, forthright in purpose, humane in impulse, can long hesitate."[17]

These themes, pointing to the nexus between the Holocaust and Israel's sovereign rebirth, served as the basis of one of Steinberg's most memorable addresses, delivered in early 1946 at a Women's Division of the United Jewish Appeal (UJA) rally at the Waldorf Astoria hotel. Lighting an eternal candle in memory of the 2,000 Jews of Seirijai, birthplace of his father in the Lithuanian county of Suvalkija, he depicted a poor Jewish village of intense piety, books, a keen sense of justice, and a merciful place of "a great spiritual earnestness," very much like Boston and Concord "in the days when New England was in flower." Unable to think about the six million Jewish dead in Europe or the one and a half million "walking skeletons," Steinberg thought of tiny Seirijai instead, now all gone, "expunged by a ruthless hand almost to its last trace." As a Jew and as a human being, haunted by that hamlet's horrible fate, he cried out before the immense crowd of almost 2,000 women for justice and for the few survivors, not sound in body and all "touched with madness," to find a haven in their biblically covenanted Promised Land also pledged to them by the nations of the world. The nostalgia and grief evoked of the many little Seirijais that made up the "sum total" of Jewish life in Eastern Europe, now obliterated, moved his listeners deeply. Many personal letters praised the talk, which was reprinted in full on March 7, 1946, in the *Reconstructionist* magazine.[18]

Despite a third attack of chest pains the day after the address, convincing Steinberg that he would have to restrict himself henceforth to the rabbinate and to his writing, as soon as he was well enough he wrote to Eleanor Roosevelt on March 20 expressing his dismay that her speech on the same UJA platform about visits to the Displaced Persons (DP) camps for survivors in Germany failed to state her sympathy for these refugees' wish to get to Palestine. That county might become in time a British Dominion, a binational state, or a permanent UN trusteeship, but he believed her "too fine, too noble a human being" not to be on the right side of "so grave and so consequential an issue, or to avoid facing up to it."

The woman whom President Harry S Truman would call "the first lady of the world" replied two days later. She did not say Palestine was the answer because she thought one had to wait for the report from the Anglo-American Committee of Inquiry on Palestine. Its members would give every consideration to the wishes of the country's inhabitants and the available possibilities. She continued, to Steinberg's disappointment, with these reservations:

> Palestine, in spite of all the things which Mr. Lowdermilk and others have said, is not considered by everybody as a place capable of really becoming a home for self-supporting people beyond a given number.

If the commission after investigating makes that decision then I think we should try to find out how it can be accomplished with the minimum of bloodshed. I am quite sure it can be accomplished if the strong nations like Great Britain and ourselves decide it shall be done, but it cannot be accomplished by the Jewish people in Palestine alone. That is why I do not say that it seems to me the only answer.[19]

Meanwhile, Steinberg had asked the board of his synagogue to transfer its regular weekly advertising from the *New York Times* to the *New York Herald Tribune*. Aside from the former's not reviewing his new, best-selling book, he could not accept Sulzberger's newspaper regularly reflecting a negative orientation toward Jewish news in general and to Jewish Palestine in particular. "On that episode as on so many others," he wrote to Stephen Wise, "we get a much better deal from a straight-forward Gentile than from a sick-souled, scared and tied-into-knots Jew."[20]

Steinberg could take encouragement, at the same time, from growing, significant sympathy for the Zionist cause. Former Undersecretary Sumner Welles, in advocating the initial creation of an international trusteeship over Palestine to replace the British Mandate, wrote in the progressive journal *Nation* of "those who, like myself, know that the establishment of an independent Palestine as a National Jewish Homeland is an ideal which represents the spiritual conviction of many millions of people through the earth" and who "also believe that it is an objective inherently right and just." Welles then praised the "highest statesmanship" displayed by World Zionist Organization president Chaim Weizmann. President Truman, endorsing the Earl Harrison report, continued to call for 100,000 additional refugee Jews to be permitted to enter Palestine without delay. Mrs. Roosevelt criticized the British taking Jews bound for Palestine to detention camps in Cyprus, favored the 100,000 survivors "who must find homes immediately" and want to go to Palestine, and stated that the mandatory "have certainly had force in evidence in Palestine." A Roper poll disclosed that American Jews, whatever their age, economic level, or geographic area, overwhelmingly favored a Jewish state by an average of 80 percent.[21]

Frank, too, had begun to shift his ideological stance. In April 1946 he wrote to Lessing Rosenwald, president of the American Council for Judaism. that he had decided to withdraw from that organization. Until then a silent supporter of the ACJ, he pointed out to the former chairman of Sears, Roebuck and Company that he currently favored local autonomy in Palestine in some important areas, which would lessen Arab hostility to a large influx of Jews. He saw no other alternatives at this point, as the United States would not promptly open its doors and the Holocaust survivors were living "in misery and fear." No likelihood existed that a portion of Germany would be ceded to them. The risk of Arab antagonism, he thought, "must be taken."[22]

Frank was particularly concerned that the tragic plight of thousands of European Jews, the consequences of the British "mishandling" of Palestine, and the recent increase of antisemitism in the United States combined to put American Jews on the defensive. His long handwritten draft of a letter to the editor of *Commentary* at the year's end claimed that many minorities in such a position tended to treat defects as virtues, and to esteem "accidental" group values as "eternal and inherent." Yielding to those tendencies, American Jews doted on the "insidious flatteries" of non-Jews, a stance which blocked self-criticism. We American Jews need to do a deal of "self-probing" today, he concluded, to "demolish" (here came Frank's jab at militant Zionists) "many a chauvinistic Jewish mask," to avoid a "myopic" outlook on the world scene, to recognize that "we are part of a human race struggling to create a new civilization." The communication did not see print.[23]

Come 1947, Steinberg focused on his writing while Frank received an invitation to bolster the Zionist case. Steinberg's *The Common Sense of Religious Faith*, published by the Jewish Reconstructionist Foundation, and *Basic Judaism*, which *Christian Century* called "one of the best presentations of essential Judaism," were published that same year. As for Frank, he faced a dilemma soon after Britain requested in early February that the United Nations present a recommendation regarding Palestine's future. Simon Rifkind, former special adviser on Jewish affairs in the European Theater to General Dwight D. Eisenhower after World War II and currently US district judge of the Southern District of New York, asked his friend to join seven prominent American Jews practicing law in preparing a legal brief to the UN on behalf of Jewish statehood. Frank agreed to review the final draft, which reached him that summer.

With certain exceptions, he thought the brief "brilliant and as good as it possibly could be," the facts "most convincing." He was wholly in accord with its basic premise: Great Britain's 1922 Palestine Mandate from the League of Nations, adopting the "Zionist philosophy," had made a promise on which many Jews justifiably relied; with no other land open to homeless and oppressed Jews, it was "outrageous" not to keep that pledge. He disagreed with the memorandum's assertions that the Zionist position was wholly correct at the time of the Mandate and was wholly sound now, yet was ready to support the case made out in the brief.

Frank was not prepared to accept all the tenets of Zionism, however. At the time of the Mandate, the Zionists had maintained that, with almost complete unanimity, Jews throughout the world regarded themselves as a distinctive people with "a specific ethos and way of life" (to quote the brief), which could be preserved only through the restoration of a homeland in Palestine. In addition, they declared that such a restoration was at that time the sole way of meeting the problem of oppressed Jews, and that such a solution would also help to solve the problems of Jews everywhere, since nowhere were they adequately free and secure.

Frank thought that as of that date there was no such unanimous Jewish attitude, "far from it." Further, the amount of money spent on Palestine would probably have created other much safer places for oppressed Jews, and that such places might well now exist had it not been for "stubborn" Zionist opposition. Moreover, most American Jews have not been unfortunate, as the brief contended, and the Zionist philosophy might injure rather than improve the position of the American Jews.

Yet Frank also thought that most of that was now "irrelevant." No matter who was to blame, no matter what might be the effect on American Jews, the fact remained that no other place of refuge was now available to most of the "distressed and homeless" Holocaust survivors, and to afford them a safe haven "there must now be a Jewish Palestine." Nevertheless, "Jerome" went on to "Si," if he were to join in signing the brief he would want to see a few passages modified or deleted in order to avoid committing himself to ideas in which he did not believe. The pertinent pages with his suggestions for changes would be enclosed.

Frank also "earnestly" urged the insertion, at the very end of the brief, of something like the attached insert to meet the ideas of such as himself and to counter the possible inferences which could be drawn from the brief, especially the assertion that the Jews of the United States have "minority status", or that for their protection or welfare they need a Jewish state. With such changes, he would be "delighted" to sign the brief.

Whether he signed it was, of course, unimportant. But as he thought his views representative of those of "a considerable number" of Jews, it might perhaps be of value to obtain his signature, and to omit statements with which such Jews will disagree. A possible alternative would be to have the brief signed in its present form by some persons, and then, after their signature, to add Frank's proposed insert, in some form or other, below which he and persons of "like mind" could sign.

His suggested insert for the end of the brief (or for special suggestions) read as follows:

> Some of the undersigned do not accept the tenets of the Zionist philosophy i.e. that all Jews the world over are or should be a distinctive people having a specific ethos or way of life, that the effort to preserve or recreate that specific way of life is alone sufficient to require the establishment of a Jewish Palestinian State, one that the welfare of American Jews is dependent upon or will be bettered by that establishment. But whether or not one accepts the Zionist philosophy, there is now no feasible solution of the problem facing many thousands of homeless or oppressed Jews other than the creation of the Jewish State described above, since no other lands (such as the United States, for instance) where those Jews could live without unbearable fear are now ready to receive any considerable number of them and only in such a State can they be assured a humane future. Those reasons make it imperative that the clear promise contained in the Mandate should not continue to be broken.[24]

Considering that the small group behind the memorandum of what would be called *The Basic Equities of the Palestine Problem* wished to circulate their legal brief to the UN General Assembly delegates when the special session began its deliberations in mid-September, Rifkind and colleagues had little time to consider thoroughly Frank's letter and insert, sent on August 28 from Stamford, Connecticut. Frank would return to New York on the afternoon of September 2, only days before the Assembly would begin to take up the UN Special Committee on Palestine (UNSCOP) majority and minority reports. In the end, in place of his suggested insert, they decided on this formula to come at the end of the Preface:

> Some of the signers are Zionists; others, though non-Zionists, join in this memorandum because, owing to the tragic development of events, they see no other just or equitable solution of the Palestine problem than the full performance contained in the Mandate through the creation of a Jewish State in Palestine.

That paragraph satisfied Frank, and he consented to have his name placed on the brief.[25]

Once the General Assembly delegates voted on November 29, 1947, to accept the UNSCOP majority report recommending a Jewish and an Arab state in Palestine, eminent voices joined the tide that swung dramatically in favor of the Zionist camp. Aside from Steinberg, Frank, and the authors of *The Basic Equities of the Palestine Problem*, these ranks included Welles, Roosevelt, Sulzberger, Proskauer, leading internationalists associated with the American Association for the United Nations, and, for that reason and other considerations, even Truman himself.[26]

Not Morris Lazaron, long-time pioneer in interfaith dialogue with the National Conference of Catholics and Jews, who firmly stood his ground. His large and distinguished Baltimore congregation found this problematic after the Holocaust and particularly with the establishment of the State of Israel on May 14, 1948. His attitude led, in turn, to the severing of a relationship that had lasted thirty-two years, including his resignation in July 1949 after almost three years as rabbi emeritus when Lazaron refused the request of the synagogue's board of directors to avoid attacking Zionism in his sermons. His book *Olive Trees in a Storm* (1955), published by the pro-Arabist American Friends of the Middle East, and his pamphlet *In the Shadow of Catastrophe* (1956), published by the American Council of Judaism, reflected an unwavering anti-Zionist stand.[27]

In the *Shadow of Controversy*, delivered at the annual meeting of the AJC's Baltimore chapter on October 23, 1956, Lazaron charged that the Council came under "violent, vicious, and unwarranted" attack because it insisted on telling our fellow Jews "unpleasant truths," particularly because its "continued and growing influence" threatened those who had "conquered the Jewish communities" and linked the future of American Jews with Jewish political nationalism. The universal truths of Judaism for which the Council stood needed to be reaffirmed; "events have proved us right." With everyone living in the shadow of the possibility of nuclear war, the task of Jew, Muslim, and Christian today would seem to be an emphasis on the universal. The Jew could make a characteristic contribution here out of the universal insights of Judaism, to transform the pious phrase of "human brotherhood" into a passion of fellowship and "build an enduring peace." The general acceptance of Zionism resulting from an ignorance of Judaism, a religious tradition not composed of the prevailing secular-nationalist emphasis on particularism, but the consciousness of Jewish brotherhood in a universal hope and faith.

From Lazaron's perspective, the State of Israel's negative side was marked by chauvinism, a militant orthodoxy, a disregard for the basic rights of non-Jewish minorities, a tendency to regard world Jewry as obligated to support Israel not only financially but politically—all this to the detriment of relations between Israel and the nations and to the detriment of Jews as citizens of other nations. In the United States, nationalist Zionism had led to the intrusion of Jews as Jews into the American political scene, creating "discord and ill-feeling" among Jews and breeding anti-Jewish sentiment among others. The Zionist machine "ruthlessly" attempted to crush all opposition to silence it.

Today, Lazaron went on, the State of Israel and the Arab states were both guilty, inflexible, yet the United States dared not lose the resources of the Middle East and must win the sympathy of the Muslim millions, the millions of India, the neutral peoples of Asia. "No little nation can long endure," surrounded by hostile people, unless it makes sincere efforts to "dissipate" the suspicions and fears of its neighbors, and unless it makes sacrifices to win the friendship of its neighbors: "No nation can live long in the shadow of catastrophe." American Jews had given "unquestioning and unreserved" support to Israel's foreign policy, and encouraged "chauvinism" in Israel where it should have fostered "generosity and an appreciation of other points of view." They need "profound conviction" about their faith, themselves, their function in the world. He concluded: We need American Jews moving forward in a unity that serves not only themselves and Jews everywhere, but their country and all mankind. "Let us not tarnish the radiance of that vision!"[28] Lazaron held fast to this credo until his death on June 6, 1979.

In January 1939, Lazaron had advised Robert Goldman, president of the Union of American Hebrew Congregations (UAHC), that he did believe in rebuilding the "ancient homeland" from the philanthropic and cultural points of view. Yet, he quickly added, "the Palestine incubus will absorb us. We must release ourselves from it." Four years later, faced with staying or not in the American Jewish Conference after the adoption of its unequivocal call for a Jewish commonwealth led to prolonged applause from the delegates and the singing of the Zionist anthem *HaTikva* ("The Hope"), that lay Reform organization resolved to remain but to reserve its position on Palestine. When, however, the US State Department in February 1948 publicly moved at the United Nations to advocate an international trusteeship for Palestine, thereby reversing Washington's support in the General Assembly vote of November 1947 to partition the country into two independent commonwealths, Goldman agreed with a shocked Proskauer that the "very life" of the UN and the "good faith" of the United States were involved. With the State of Israel's establishment, the UAHC, like the other major American Jewish organizations, happily saluted the new reality.[29]

Albert Einstein captured the feeling harbored by most American Jews towards Zionism even before the undeniable grasp of the Holocaust would seize their consciousness. Lazaron sought to recruit him in early 1944 to the escutcheon of the American Council for Judaism. The world's most famous scientist turned him down, replying thus:[30]

> I do not like nationalism in itself. But I think that for us Jews a feeling of strong international solidarity is very important to make us independent in our inner life from the devastating influences of a more or less hostile social environment. There is no doubt, in my opinion, that Zionism has great merits in this respect and has saved many people from despair and from succumbing to an inferiority complex. This is true, I am convinced, also for our fellow-Jews in this country in the present situation and maybe still more in the times to come.

Steinberg, alas, did not live to witness the new Jewish commonwealth thrive. In his last years, he worked on a series of essays which he hoped would conclude with a book of Jewish theology while he struggled to find an adequate response to the Holocaust. Another project, a historic novel on the prophet Hosea and his wife intended to be a companion volume to his *As a Driven Leaf*, reached over 400 pages in draft. Neither came to completion. His worsening physical condition, which he had faced with wry humor after another attack of chest pains in March 1946 by saying "the handle of the potter must have shook when he fashioned my frame," came to its end at the age of forty-six with the heart attack that proved fatal on March 20, 1950.[31] Other volumes would appear thereafter: *Believing Jew: The Selected Writings of Milton Steinberg* (1951); *Anatomy of Faith* (1960), with an introduction by Arthur A. Cohen; *Only Human—The Eternal Alibi: From the Sermons of Rabbi Milton Steinberg* (1963); and *The Prophet's Wife* (2010). Some, especially *As a Driven Leaf* (in a new edition in 1996 with an introduction by Chaim Potok) and *Basic Judaism*, still in print and selling very well, continue to communicate the author's power after time has long passed beyond the bounds of living memory.

While endorsing both the legal justification and the human need for Israel's independence, Frank found the monotheism of the Jewish tradition "basically distasteful." As he wrote to the receptive Horace Kallen, ideological pioneer of cultural pluralism that articulated an "Americanized" version of Zionism which attracted Justice Brandeis, he championed William James's "polytheism" and diversity against "the totalitarian yearning for unity." This echoed his letter to Steinberg of May 15, 1945, where the secular Frank proposed that Judaism evolve into a faith that would be "sufficiently inclusive," drawing on Greek philosophy and other significant civilization values for religious inspiration.

Such thoughts were one with Frank's playing a leading role in the "legal realism" movement in America, arguing that the process of making decisions was in reality a composite of the psychological, environmental, and socio-economic factors that went into the development of the personality of the individual judge. This approach governed his classes at the Yale University Law School, his influential books, and decisions while sitting on the US Circuit Court of Appeals until his death on January 13, 1957.[32]

As Steinberg realized early on and Frank eventually came to advocate, the fires of the Holocaust seared American Jews and Jewry's communities worldwide, their ranks joined by many Christian allies in the United States and elsewhere. The *Shoah*, the Hebrew term for the methodical annihilation of Europe's Jews, converted them to a visceral understanding of the indissoluble link that existed between Jewish catastrophe and sovereignty.[33] Accordingly, they would hoist the Zionist banner after V-E Day and well beyond, seeing the reborn State of Israel as a bridge against their people's apocalyptic despair. Those few who did not were overwhelmed by the force of history.

CHAPTER 6

The Basic Equities of the Palestine Problem

On February 18, 1947, with a dramatic announcement by Ernest Bevin in the House of Commons, the fate of Palestine was about to be altered forever. Informing the Mother of Parliaments about the Cabinet's decision four days earlier, the British foreign secretary declared that London would ask the United Nations for its recommendation as regards a settlement for that highly contested country, first accorded a Mandate to Great Britain by the League of Nations on July 24, 1922. With both Arabs and Jews having rejected the binationalist plan of the Anglo-American Committee of Inquiry on Palestine (1946) and the cantonal suggestions in the Morrison-Grady Plan (1946) and the recent Bevin Plan (1947), the Labour government of Prime Minister Clement Attlee did not intend to advance any particular solution to the UN General Assembly. This "the only course now open to us," Bevin asserted, he called on all concerned to exercise restraint while the procedure involved further postponement in resolving the thorny problem. "After two thousand years of conflict another twelve months will not be considered a long delay," he declared, a statement which US President Harry S Truman later considered reflecting "callousness" and "a disregard for human misery."[1]

The thirty-third chief executive of the United States, without informing the State Department's pro-Arabists in the Near Eastern and African Affairs Division, had requested Churchill and then Attlee to admit into Palestine great numbers of Jewish survivors of the Holocaust (their true identity officially masked as "Displaced Persons"—DPs—by the Allied victors of World War II). Notwithstanding the restrictive immigration quotas of the Neville Chamberlain government's May 1939 White Paper, which also provided within ten years for a single Palestine state having an Arab majority, Truman had been deeply stirred by the unparalleled, methodical murder of European Jewry by the Germans and collaborator nations during the recent global war. The recommendation of Earl Harrison for 100,000 Jewish survivors to enter Palestine without delay, his mission to the DP camps sanctioned by Truman, only strengthened the president's inner convictions. He favored the Anglo-American Committee's conclusions, particularly its endorsement of the 100,000, and in a pre-Yom Kippur statement on October 4, 1946, called for "substantial" Jewish immigration into Palestine in light of "the terrible ordeal which the Jewish people of Europe endured during the recent war and the crisis now existing."[2]

Truman's recent correspondence with the staunchly anti-Zionist, first monarch of Saudi Arabia made his primary humanitarian concerns clear. On October 25, 1946, he wrote to Abdul Azziz bin Abdul Rahman ibn Faisal Al Saud (known in the West as Ibn Saud) that the US government favored Palestine entry for "considerable numbers of displaced Jews in Europe, not only that they may find shelter there but also that they may contribute their talents to the up building of the Jewish national home." Their plight, he averred, "is particularly tragic in as much as they represent the pitiful remnants of millions who were deliberately selected by the Nazi leaders for annihilation." When the Wahhabi king strongly objected, Truman reiterated on January 17, 1947, that "it seemed appropriate that this national home should be established in a land which for thousands of years had been regarded by Jews as their spiritual home." He went on to assert that "no people has suffered more than the Jews during recent years from aggression and intolerance. No people stands more in need of world sympathy and support at the present time." The failure of consultations with Arabs and Jews during the last year, Truman declared, served to emphasize "the urgency of this problem and the necessity that a solution of it be found without protracted delay."[3]

Others raised the issue of excessive postponement in Bevin's declaration of that Tuesday morning. Conservative opposition leader Winston Churchill wondered how the Rt. Honorable Gentleman could justify keeping 100,000 soldiers in Palestine who were needed in Great Britain, and spending Ł30–Ł40 million from the country's diminishing resources upon "this vast apparatus of protraction and delay," and now announce that mandatory rule would continue until the UN would solve the problem to which the foreign secretary admitted he could not offer any answer after a year and a half. Syrian diplomat Mardem Bey declared that the Arab League stood by its declaration at Bloudan in June 1946 to submit the question to the UN Security Council, the League uncompromisingly supporting the creation of an independent Palestine with the current Arab majority. Moshe Shertok (later Sharett), directing the political department of the Jewish Agency for Palestine, welcomed the turn to the UN despite the delay, but proposed that His Majesty's Government (HMG) should for the time being observe the mandate as it had done before curtailing Jewish immigration and land settlement as of 1937.[4]

Zionist avatar Chaim Weizmann instinctively understood the significance of Bevin's proclamation. Writing on February 21 to Eliyahu Epstein (later Elath), the Jewish Agency's representative in Washington, D.C., the chief architect of the Balfour Declaration that had pledged HMG on November 2, 1917, to "facilitate the achievement" of establishing in Palestine "a national home for the Jewish people," reached one conclusion. The UN offered "a great but last chance for the Zionists' appearance," he realized, as "there is no appeal from this tribunal." He realistically assessed that the financially strapped Labour Cabinet would pull out of Palestine if Arab-Jewish relations became more acute, as Attlee had announced on the previous day his colleagues' decision for withdrawing by June 1948 from the burden of mediating India's Hindu-Muslim divide, but thought that the Zionists would find little support among the great powers in the UN if terrorism in Palestine continued.[5]

The historic moment also seized Abraham Tulin, veteran stalwart of the Zionist cause. Born in Bezdezh, Russia (now Belarus), on March 26, 1882, he was brought to the United States as a child. His family settling as farmers in Connecticut, Tulin would receive a BA from Yale College with the class of 1903 and an LLB degree three years later from the Harvard Law School. Felix Frankfurter, the top student in the same law class, would later give him a letter of introduction to General of the Armies of the United States John J. Pershing in World War I. In 1918, Tulin was a captain of infantry in the army, serving as an American liaison officer and on the headquarters staff of Lt. General Robert Lee Bullard, Second American Army, until the Armistice. He then transferred to Paris as a liaison officer with the French Ministry of War.

After the Armistice, Pershing recommended Tulin to Herbert Hoover, then chief of the American Relief Administration in Europe. As an assistant to Hoover, Tulin traveled widely between March and May 1919 to survey the needs of the population of Southern Russia and Armenia. He returned to the United States that July to begin a legal career in New York City. On October 2, 1919, he testified before the Subcommittee on Foreign Relations about his tour of Armenia in April of that year. Vividly, he told of people dying of hunger, of "barely breathing skeletons of children." Continuing on a somber note, he noted the assaults against Armenians from Tartars and Turks, with the massacres renewed when British troops withdrew. Thanks to his efforts, the Hoover agency rushed food to the stricken Armenian survivors.[6]

Tulin's early interest in Zionism, kindled by the Dreyfus trial and its aftermath in France, continued while practicing law as a member of the New

York Bar Association. In turn, this confidant of Supreme Court Justice Louis D. Brandeis was selected as an American delegate to the World Zionist Congresses held in London in 1919–1920, in Basle, 1927 and 1931, and in Prague in 1933. Shepherding Albert Einstein during the former's first tour of the United States in 1921 and on other visits, Tulin developed a strong friendship that would last for decades with the most famous scientist in the world. In 1930 he became a member of the administrative committee to govern the Zionist Organization of America. Six years later, he married Anna Johanna von Lepel, a prominent leader in the Hadassah Women's Zionist Organization of America. That connection would eventually lead to his important *Analysis of British Policy in Palestine*, published by Hadassah in 1943. Three years later, Tulin was tapped to serve as the legal Counsel for the Jewish Agency before the Anglo-American Committee of Inquiry on Palestine. Together with Milton Handler, he prepared the evidence for Zionist witnesses before their testimony in Washington, D.C. to the Anglo-American Committee of Inquiry on Palestine.[7]

When Bevin announced in early 1946 the British government's proposal to establish the Emirate of Transjordan, its protectorate as of April 1921, as an independent state, Tulin pointed out to Abba Hillel Silver, executive committee chairman of the American Zionist Emergency Council (AZEC), that the Allied powers of the First World War, including the United States, had to consent to this transfer. HMG pressed forward on its own, creating the "Hashemite Kingdom of Transjordan" in May 1946, and awarding it full independence on June 17, 1946. Two months later, the AZEC Executive sent Tulin and Handler to meet with Undersecretary of State Dean Acheson to object to the new state's possible admission to the United Nations, an appointment arranged by the State Department's Legal Advisor, Charles Fahy.

A very troubled Acheson told Tulin and Handler that he thought the Jewish Agency's recent partition proposal "the first sign of reasonableness on either side," coming just when Washington had decided to "wash its hands" of the whole Palestine imbroglio, a matter he said was now one between the Agency, the British government, and the Arabs. He worried that "chaos and utter helplessness" would ensue if that problem, which he characterized as "a most complex and explosive question charged with emotion," were not solved within the next six weeks. In Acheson's opinion, it would then be thrown into the lap of the UN, where the Soviet Union would take the position that it was the protector of the Arab states and peoples, creating one more cause of discord between Moscow and Washington.[8]

In Tulin's view, Bevin's invitation now to the international community to weigh in on the Palestine conundrum for the first time offered the unique opportunity for "a lawyer's brief" to present the Zionist case. Believing that "justice and equity," the phrase later used in the Preface to the memorandum he had envisioned, lay on the side of the Jews, he wished to present "advocacy based on fair argument and unchallengeable facts." In the words of that brief, owing to "the tragic development of events," the only proper solution of the Palestine problem was "the full performance of the promise contained in the Mandate through the creation of a Jewish State in Palestine." Refusing along with like-minded colleagues to accept that the conundrum of Palestine belonged to that category wherein, as in the Greek tragedies, "two righteous protagonists proceed to inevitable disaster," Tulin immediately set out to recruit prominent American Jewish legal minds who would be prepared to endorse his vision.[9]

Simon H. Rifkind, judge of the US District Court, New York, and a long-time member of the Zionist Organization of America (ZOA), was a logical, instant choice. Personal advisor on Jewish Affairs to former SHAEF Commander Dwight D. Eisenhower and to his successor as heading the US forces in the European theater General Joseph T. McNarney, Rifkind had urged the Anglo-American Committee of Inquiry during its tour of DP camps in Europe to call for the entry of 100,000 survivors into Palestine. The Intergovernmental Committee on Refugees could not find "a single place which wanted these people," he recalled years later. Just before stepping down in April 1946 as McNarney's advisor on DP affairs, he reported that the "unwelcome" Jews of Central and Eastern Europe, escaping "a graveyard of memories," were converging on the US zone of occupied Germany in the hope of reaching Palestine. Unless the world was prepared to enable them to "strike permanent roots" there, Rifkind cautioned, this "handful of a decimated people" would be "driven to despair and disaster."[10]

Scouting among some of his friends, Rifkind soon tapped Lawrence R. Eno. A member of the New York Bar, Eno had served as Rifkind's aide-de-camp in Germany. Abraham (Abe) Fortas, former US Undersecretary of the Interior in President Franklin D. Roosevelt's administration who was appointed by Truman to delegations that helped set up the United Nations in 1945 before he entered private practice in Washington, D.C., was chosen for prestige. Joseph Proskauer expressed strong reservations, however. Elected president of the American Jewish Committee in 1943 on a platform which proposed free Jewish immigration into Palestine and an international trusteeship status but opposed a Jewish State, he thought the idea of a Jewish Commonwealth there "crazy." "If so," the former judge in the Appellate Division of the First Department of the Supreme Court of New York declared to Rifkind, "the streets of Jerusalem will flow with Jewish blood."[11]

The American Zionist Emergency Council, created in the beginning of World War II to represent Zionist leadership in the United States, was receptive at first. Tulin had been instrumental in getting the AZEC to sponsor the work. Arthur Lourie, secretary of the Council during the war and now director of the Jewish Agency's Office of the United Nations, wanted Milton Handler to lead the "enterprise" which Tulin had suggested. Roosevelt's chief advisor on antitrust matters had helped draft several landmark statues such as the Federal Food, Drug and Cosmetic Act and the National Labor Relations Act. Together with Benjamin V. Cohen, Handler had drafted the executive order that created the US War Refugee Board in January 1944. Yet he was not in a position to take on this "heavy assignment" prioritizing his teaching responsibilities at the Columbia University Law School and a private practice. While agreeing to become a member, he proposed that Rifkind chair the group. In agreement, Rifkind and he recommended that Murray I. Gurfein be retained for the task by the Jewish Agency as its Special Counsel to coordinate all the work necessary for preparing "the basic brief or briefs" to be submitted to the UN or the Special Committee on Palestine. Lourie made that appointment official on May 12 with a retainer of $10,000, it being understood that professional commitments required Gurfein, who would prepare the preliminary draft, to be relieved from all obligations under this retainer by August 1.[12]

Gurfein possessed impressive credentials. The Harvard Law School graduate and before long Assistant District Attorney in New York County (NY), as well as a member of the ZOA's executive committee, he went on to become a US Army Lieutenant Colonel in the Office of Strategic Services (OSS) overseas during World War II and serve as an intelligence officer at SHAEF headquarters, for which he won the Legion of Merit and the Croix de Guerre and was named an Honorary Officer of the British Empire. A visit to the recently liberated Dachau concentration camp, where many dead, naked corpses still lay on the ground, made a searing impression on Gurfein. In the fall of 1945, he served as the principal assistant to Robert H. Jackson, US Chief Counsel in the Nuremberg Trials of Nazi leaders. Retribution for "a handful of the worst criminals in human history," he subsequently reminisced, had to be followed by "a release of the trapped refugees, a mighty moral campaign against the British government." He soon realized that the survivors, "beleaguered in Displaced Persons camps that had become more like prisons," had no solution other than "ultimately the burgeoning of a Jewish National home into a State."[13]

Time was pressing, since an eleven-man committee excluding the Big Five, to be chaired by Canadian delegate Lester Pearson, was named on May 14, 1947, to make recommendations to the General Assembly not later than

September 1 as to Palestine's future. That date would allow the report of the United Nations Special Committee on Palestine (UNSCOP) to be circulated to the UN members in time for consideration by the second regular session of the Assembly. The committee was to conduct investigations in Palestine "and wherever it may deem useful," taking testimony from "the Mandatory power, from representatives of the population of Palestine, from governments, and from such organizations and individuals as it may deem necessary." Two days later, the fifty-five-nation General Assembly, with only the Arab countries, Afghanistan, and Turkey in opposition, approved the terms of reference. The session ended with Assembly President Oswaldo Aranha of Brazil declaring that a solution of the Palestine problem was "the most decisive test yet put to the U.N."[14]

Having received a voluminous quantity of materials sent to Gurfein from the Jewish Agency, Rifkind, Handler, and Tulin convened for several days that summer in Great Barrington, Massachusetts, where the chairman had a vacation home. Looking over the first draft from Gurfein, edited by Rifkind and Handler because Tulin had been involved in trademark litigation, the veteran Zionist advocate reacted sharply: "This is miserable!" Handler retorted: "If you think so, why don't you work on it?" Taking up the challenge, Tulin left with the manuscript for his apartment on New York City's Riverside Drive. While Handler visited him frequently, Tulin rewrote the entire draft in long hand. Seeing the lengthy manuscript, the chapters written by different members of the legal group, cut down "materially," Handler thought it a very comprehensive revision. Tulin was the perfect choice to do so. In Handler's characterization, his "elephant memory" and Zionist background enabled Tulin to give dates and places, even pages of books, on any subject discussed, already evident in a *Book of Documents* which he had prepared at the Jewish Agency's request for the Anglo-American Committee of Inquiry on Palestine and then for submission to the United Nations. Rifkind's great gifts were evident in what Handler called the judge's "great gift at purple prose" and lead sentences, while he concentrated on the legal aspects of the complex issue.[15]

One chapter had been written by a deft hand not on the legal team. Reading the first draft of the memorandum in April, Shertok cabled Aubrey (later Abba) Eban to fly immediately from London to New York to give the memorandum "the tang and flavor" of Palestine and of the Middle East. It dealt with the region more as a "problem" than as a physical reality, Zionism treated, in Eban's characterization, "as a learned argument rather than as a drama." The document should be supplemented by something "more impassioned and polemical," Shertok thought. The outstanding Cambridge University graduate in Oriental languages and classics, who rose to the rank of Major in the British Army as an intelligence officer in Cairo and Palestine during World War II, was asked to cross the Atlantic for the first time to undertake the task. Abruptly quitting his efforts in some Western European capitals to garner crucial votes for the Zionist cause in advance of the General Assembly's session on Palestine, Eban quickly arrived in the United States. Working in a room at Gurfein's New York City law office on 39 Broadway, he focused on the chapter dealing with Arab affairs. He could not do much more, given his selection as a Jewish Agency "liaison officer" along with economist David Horowitz to the UNSCOP delegation. The eleven members, Eban soon discovered, were "men of competence rather than of inspiration," not one of them involved in the past in any decisions as momentous as that in which he would now have to participate.[16]

Suddenly, the AZEC, in Handler's recollection, "got cold feet" about the whole project, and decided not to go forward at all. With the memorandum having reached galley stage, the trio of Rifkind, Handler, and Tulin decided to go forward on their own. They would pay the cost of publication and distribute it themselves to the delegates at the UN. Thinking that they required further sponsorship, Handler spoke to Stanley H. Fuld, a close friend then serving as a Judge of the Court of Appeals of the State of New York. Hearing Handler's invitation, he agreed to join the team.[17]

Finally, Handler went to see another good friend whom Rifkind also knew, Jerome N. Frank. Former chairman of the US Security and Exchange Commission and currently judge of the United States Circuit Court of Appeals, Second Circuit, Frank had been an early, if quiet supporter of the anti-Zionist American Council for Judaism. His article in the *Saturday Evening Post* one day before the Japanese surprise attack on Pearl Harbor that brought the United States into World War II, labeling Zionists "Jewish sojourners in America," had raised many hackles at the time, including American Jewish Congress leader Rabbi Stephen Wise denouncing it as "treasonable to the Jewish people" and "simply inexcusable." Perhaps, Handler thought, acceptance now would give Frank a chance to be rehabilitated in the eyes of Jews, while his joining would be "a big plus" for the team as representing a position that was not fully Zionist. He and Tulin met Frank in the Lawyers' Club at 115 Broadway, a hushed, leisurely lunchtime ambiance ever since 1912 for its members and their guests atop the Realty Building in the Wall Street area, in a room that looked like nothing so much as a medieval refectory. Frank examined the memorandum and made some points, to which the pair consented. His full review would be sent to Rifkind.[18]

With Gurfein, showed the changes by Tulin, giving his approval, a revised copy was brought to AZEC chairman Abba Hillel Silver and then to Shertok. Contemplating an address to the General Assembly, Silver, also chairing the American Section of the Jewish Agency, was "wildly enthusiastic." "I countermand whatever decision was made previously," he told Handler. Praising the work as the best ever done on the subject, he declared then and there that he would not allow them to pay for it out of their own pockets. The AZEC would foot the bill entirely. Shertok and his staff were also favorable. Final preparations now had to be made with alacrity in time to make distribution of the memorandum to the General Assembly session in September.[19]

While the eight-man legal team anxiously awaited the UNSCOP recommendations, Rifkind received two important requests from the Jewish Agency. Fearing that Near Eastern and African Affairs division head Loy Henderson, in collaboration with American military experts, would stymie Zionist aspirations by warning of an Arab *jihad* (religious war) and Arab sabotage of US oil lines and communications in the region, Eban and Shertok gave him a memorandum for Eisenhower's personal attention. On June 24, 1947, Rifkind presented the US Army Chief of Staff with its argument that a democratic Jewish State in Palestine would be in the strategic interests of the United States "against the contingency of war." It could mobilize three or four fighting divisions; provide heavy technical equipment through industrial and scientific capacities; and offer the only deep-water port in the Mediterranean at Haifa and a series of air bases in the Negev. The following month, Rifkind gave Eisenhower a memorandum by Epstein explaining that the Arab states, with their ill-trained, poorly organized and equipped armies, would not be capable of joining in any united military action unaided against the *Yishuv* (Palestinian Jewish community).[20]

Rifkind and his colleagues, as Gurfein later wrote, hoped that the United Nations would represent "the conscience of the world," and that it would be governed particularly on larger issues that transcended "bilateral confrontations by moral values and conceptions of justice." In their view, the Balfour Declaration and the Mandate should be read in that spirit, for Great Britain held Palestine only as a trustee. At this moment in history, one which might not recur, they considered two issues strongly favoring the Zionist cause. First, the tragic situation of the Jews in the DP camps. These Holocaust survivors were still prevented from moving, a condition which had to "touch the conscience of decent human beings everywhere." Second, the solemn promises regarding Palestine that had been made to the Jewish people everywhere for over a quarter of a century. A careful review of the difficult subject, the group believed, would be "a helpful moral and legal adjunct to purely political considerations."[21]

Come the last day of August 1947, their aspirations appeared on the cusp of fulfillment. That evening, the UNSCOP members sat down in Geneva's Palais des Nations for their fifty-second meeting to formally adopt the report. Most important, those assembled in the conference room on the fourth floor unanimously agreed that the Mandate must be replaced as soon as possible by independence. Seven delegates (Canada, Czechoslovakia, Guatemala, Netherlands, Peru, Sweden, and Uruguay), a majority, backed an Arab and a Jewish State with economic union after a two-year transitional period with British administration under UN auspices, and a *corpus separatum* of Jerusalem-Bethlehem under international control. During that time, Britain had to admit 150,000 Jews. Three (India, Iran, and Yugoslavia) voted for an independent federal state under Arab domination with Jewish and Arab provinces and a common capital in Jerusalem, following a transitional period not to exceed three years and entrusted during that time to an authority delegated by the General Assembly. Australia's John Hood abstained, explaining that, without having achieved unanimity, the Committee should send both recommendations to the General Assembly. All now looked to Lake Success, New York, the UN's temporary home in Nassau County on Marcus Avenue, for ultimate resolution.[22]

UNSCOP's majority report greatly heartened the legal team, which lost no time incorporating that recommendation in its ultimate memorandum for the General Assembly. In short order, the final version reached completion on September 10, 1947. Four days later, the US government announced that it would support the suggestion of UN Secretary General Trygve Lie of Norway that the Assembly, scheduled to open on the 16th, set up a special working committee to deal with the Palestine question. That same afternoon, Tulin distributed to the UN delegations and the Secretariat *The Basic Equities of the Palestine Problem*, which called on that body to implement the "creation in Palestine of an independent Jewish Commonwealth or State in control of its own immigration, land development and fiscal policies."

They endorsed in principle the partition plan proposed by the majority of the UNSCOP members. In their opinion, that report's recommendations were "a statesmanlike and sincere effort to provide a workable compromise solution of the difficult and complex Palestine problem." The majority proposal met two of the fundamental requirements of a just solution – insurance against governmental or administrative obstacles to immediate and continuing large-scale Jewish immigration and the establishment of a Jewish self-governing Commonwealth in Palestine. At the same time, the group expressed its disapproval of the territorial divisions suggested by the UNSCOP majority, since the Jewish National Home would be confined "to less than one-eighth of the territory originally set aside for it" in the 1922 Palestine Mandate. Specifically, the authors questioned the proposal to exclude the entire city of Jerusalem and western Galilee from the boundaries of the Jewish State.[23]

The Preface to the 107 pages of *The Basic Equities of the Palestine Problem* began by noting that the United States had a long association with the Palestine dilemma and a "deep interest" in its solution. Evidence of this included President Woodrow Wilson's active participation in the launching of the Jewish National Home policy in 1917 with his endorsement of the Balfour Declaration; the repeated Congressional Resolutions supporting that policy in 1922 and 1945; the Anglo-American Mandate Convention of 1924; American participation in the Anglo-American Committee of Inquiry in 1946; and numerous governmental and political pronouncements over the years.

The vast expansion in US responsibility for world peace emphasized, although it did not originate, the "present concern" of the American people with the Palestine imbroglio. This concern, the compilers of the memorandum were quick to add, had been made "acute" by the "shockingly long delay" in the liberation of "the surviving Jewish victims of Hitler's terror," now in Displaced Persons centers, "whose hopes for salvation are so passionately linked with Palestine." Setting down arguments in the form to which they were professionally accustomed – a lawyer's brief—they noted that the UNSCOP majority report's recommendations accepted the "major premises" for which they contended. The creation of a Jewish State in Palestine offered the only "just and equitable" solution, the signers ended, which this memorandum sought to advocate in the eight chapters to follow.[24]

Chapter one, making up almost half of the memorandum, begins with the authors asserting that the essence of "The Problem" is whether the "internationally covenanted" National Home for the Jewish people shall at last be made a reality for "the distraught Jews who seek to enter it, or remain "but a cruel and tragic mirage." The "uprooted survivors of the Jewish holocaust [sic] in Europe and the harassed and insecure Jews in some other parts of the world" now appeal to the United Nations to protect their "fundamental human and legal right" to resort to their promised Homeland for asylum and the "rebuilding of their shattered lives"—to that "National Home for the Jewish People" in Palestine. The latter phrase appeared in the Balfour Declaration, the 1920 San Remo Conference of the victorious Allied powers, the League of Nations Mandate, and the 1924 Anglo-American Palestine Mandate Convention. The British Mandatory Power, however, "in the hour of the greatest Jewish need," breached its international trust, its mandatory obligations, among others, to "facilitate Jewish immigration into Palestine" and to "encourage close settlement by Jews on the land, including State lands and waste lands not required for public purposes." This trust and specific obligations are surely "obligations arising from treaties and other sources of international law" within the meaning of the UN Charter.[25]

The 1939 White Paper, condemned by the League of Nation's Permanent Mandates Commission, by Churchill and other leading spokesmen of all British parties, was followed a few months later by mandatory restrictions on Jewish land settlement. With "irrefutable logic," the Labour Party Conference Resolution of 1944 had declared that "there is surely neither hope nor meaning as a 'Jewish National Home' unless we are prepared to let Jews, if they wish, enter this tiny land in such numbers as to become a majority" in Palestine. At its Conference one year later, Chancellor of the Exchequer Hugh Dalton considered the last assertion "irresistible" in light of "the unspeakable atrocities which Jews have suffered," and that "it is morally wrong and politically indefensible to impose obstacles to the entry into Palestine now of any Jews who desire to go there."[26]

International statesmen and organizations had acknowledged that the legitimate national aspirations of the Arab peoples of the former Turkish empire "had been provided for in full measure" by the very same post-World War I peace settlements which decreed the reconstitution of the National Home for the Jewish people. The Arabs received more than one million square miles of the richest territory of that empire with the stipulation of early independence. By contrast, Palestine, then comprising but 45,000 square miles before Transjordan was lopped off from that mandated territory in 1921, currently comprised only 10,000 square miles. The continuing intransigence of the Palestinian Arab leaders and the neighboring Arab states had been anticipated from the very beginning of the Jewish National Home policy, and Churchill had officially declared in 1922 as colonial secretary, when confronting Arab threats of violence against Jews, that he could not discuss the future of Palestine "upon any other basis than that of . . . the Balfour Declaration."[27]

President Franklin D. Roosevelt had declared on March 16, 1944, that "full justice will be done to those who seek a Jewish National Home," for whom the American government and people had the "deepest sympathy" in view of the "tragic plight of hundreds of thousands of homeless Jewish refugees." President Truman, supporting the entry of 100,000 Holocaust survivors towards establishing "the Jewish National home" in Palestine, had written to Ibn Saud in far stronger terms. Resolutions by the governors and legislatures of at least forty-four of the forty-eight states and statements by leading labor unions, as well as by Christian and Jewish organizations, culminated in a bipartisan Congressional resolution on December 19, 1945, which called for the "free entry" of Jews into Palestine to its maximum potentialities with full opportunity for colonization and development, so that they may proceed with up-building Palestine "as the Jewish national home" and establish Palestine, "with all elements of the population," as "a democratic commonwealth in which all men, regardless of race or creed, shall have equal rights."[28]

After the Jewish Agency announced on August 16, 1946, its willingness to sacrifice a part of the promised Jewish National Home if there were immediately created "a viable Jewish State in control of its own immigration and economic policies in an adequate area of Palestine," the American government immediately made known its support of this proposal along with economic assistance if a workable solution for Palestine should be devised. The Mandatory power ignored this compromise as well, as it would when Truman on October 4, 1946, again publicly said that substantial Jewish immigration into Palestine "should begin at once." To date, more than 20,000 Holocaust survivors had crammed into hulks and boats that barely float in their desire to reach Palestine, only to be stopped through "violence and bloodshed" by the Royal British Navy and transported to "new concentration camps" in Cyprus. Over 4,000 at this moment were actually being forcibly transported in "stifling prison ships" back to Germany, "land of the crematoria and gas chambers."[29]

The Mandatory's "ruthless policy," the first chapter went on, provoked what Churchill called "a squalid war" between despair-driven Jews and the repressive British armed forces, resulting in bloodshed, loss of life, and "barbarous reprisals on both sides." Palestine has turned into "a police state" with 100,000 armed British troops, which deprives the Jews of their elementary civil rights and is "suffocating" them economically. In Europe, the "overwhelming majority" of desperate Jews want to go to Palestine, the only organized community ready to receive them. Facing "Nazi-inflamed" antisemitism and shrinking with horror from the countries where "nearly six million Jewish men, women, and children" had been "fiendishly exterminated," the surviving Jews regard the DP centers as only "wayward stops on the road to Palestine. As the Anglo-American Committee of Inquiry on Palestine, the US Military Government in Germany, Earl Harrison, and others have attested, a steady "human demoralization" in these camps can only lead, if not promptly checked, to "complete disaster." Other than Palestine, where the survivors' "psychic wounds can heal" and their desire "to live a Jewish life together" can be fulfilled, there were only "the most meager" immigration possibilities elsewhere. The majority of the 800,000–900,000 Jews in Moslem lands, and particularly the younger generation, facing the permanent threat of violence at the hands of the "unrestrained and often incited mob," look to Palestine for salvation as well.[30]

The victorious Allies of World War I, understanding profoundly that "the fundamental affliction" of many Jews was due to "their minority and depressed status in many parts of the world," meant the "National Home" to signal a state for Jews everywhere. Balfour, Prime Minister David Lloyd George, Wilson, Prime Minister of South Africa Jan Smuts, and others said so explicitly at the time, perhaps none as clear as Churchill who, when attacking the White Paper in the House of Commons on May 2, 1939, charged that the Balfour Declaration was made to "that vast, unhappy mass of scattered, persecuted, wandering Jews whose intense, unchanging, unconquerable desire has been for a National Home." It was to include Trans-Jordan, reflecting "the whole of historic Palestine" in the judgment of the 1936–1937 Royal Commission under Lord Peel, which had called for Palestine's partition into an Arab and a Jewish State. This was later confirmed by Leopold S. Amery, one of the secretaries of the British War Cabinet that approved the Balfour Declaration, in his testimony before the Anglo-American Commission of Inquiry.[31]

The Preamble to the Palestine Mandate notes that the Balfour Declaration recognized "the historical connection of the Jewish people with Palestine and to the grounds for reconstituting their national home in that country." Churchill went further, asserting in his attack on the 1939 White Paper that HMG as a consequence and on the basis of that pledge received "important help" in World War I and then the Mandate for Palestine. The British representative to the 1925 League Permanent Mandates Commission officially declared that his government was in Palestine because of the Balfour Declaration, and ten years later Rapporteur M. Palacios of the Commission stated that the Balfour Declaration "is the very soul of the Mandate." That British pledge was given to the Jews in broad terms as "an act of justice and historic reparation," and the legal rights given world Jewry by this international commitment, formalized in Mandate and treaties, could not now be dissolved either by new interpretations or by "unilateral action which changes the substance of those rights."[32]

A careful reading of the Mandate unquestionably indicates that the establishment of the Jewish National Home is its "primary object." The second clause of the preamble established that the Mandatory was responsible for putting the Balfour Declaration into effect, securing the establishment of the Jewish National Home in Palestine by political, administrative, and economic means. The subordinate clause repeating the Declaration's condition that nothing should "prejudice the civil and religious rights of existing non-Jewish communities in Palestine," not referring to Arabs at all, simply implied that there should be no impairment of these rights. Yet the "political conditions" that HMG had recently been suggesting meant "the strangulation" of the Jewish National Home, "and are, on their face, illegal." As Baron van Asbeck of the Permanent Mandates Commission observed in 1939, the Palestine Mandate is *sui generis*—and did not provide that the Mandatory was to establish a national Palestine government by an Arab majority. The Peel Commission's observation was certainly true in 1947 as it was in 1937: "To put it in one sentence, we cannot—in Palestine as it now is—both concede the Arab claim to self-government and secure the establishment of the Jewish National Home." The Mandate was, therefore, carefully framed to preclude independence for Palestine until the Jewish National Home had been "fully established."[33]

The meaning of "political conditions" in Article 2 of the Mandate was further illuminated by the preamble's recital of world Jewry's "reconstituting" their National Home in light of their "historical connection" to Palestine. In doing so, they were to be regarded "not as an alien element imported into Palestine and dwelling there on sufferance, but as a people returning to the soil from which it sprang, there to rebuild the fabric of its national life." The Zionist Organization was recognized in Article 4 as the appropriate Jewish Agency, and directed to secure the cooperation of all Jews, in order to advise and cooperate with the mandatory government towards the Jewish national home's creation. The affirmative obligations to "facilitate" Jewish immigration, as well as "close settlement" on the land (Article 6), so recognized by a British Note to the Holy See on July 1, 1922, a British White Paper of the same year, and various HMG official statements, was "a dynamic concept" based on the economic absorptive capacity of the country. Nowhere did the Mandate provide for, or even refer to, any special political or national or, indeed, any other rights of the Arabs or of the non-Jewish communities in Palestine which could possibly conflict with the Jewish National Home objective.[34]

Concluding this first chapter, the authors of *The Basic Equities of the Palestine Problem* submitted that the Mandate did more than provide for the establishment of the Jewish National Home. It represented an international grant of rights to those Jews who desired to immigrate there to the limit of economic absorptive capacity, to acquire and settle there and, by thus becoming a majority of the population, to "reconstitute Palestine as a Jewish Commonwealth." The "flagrant breach" of these specific Mandatory obligations regarding Jewish immigration and land settlement "has not abrogated and cannot abrogate or affect these rights of Jews under international law."[35]

The juridical and moral principles of estoppel, chapter two proceeded, forbade the nullification now by Great Britain and other nations from abrogating or abridging their pledge to the Jews regarding Palestine. Referring in his speech against the 1939 White Paper to the "great experiment and bright dream" of the Jewish National Home policy, Churchill had wondered how the Chamberlain government could strike Jews "a mortal blow" after they had remarkably succeeded to date in Palestine with great benefit to the Arabs. Their sacrifices and achievements relied on the promises of the Balfour Declaration and the Mandate. To say that anyone engaged in framing the National Home favored an artificial restriction of Jewish immigration to ensure that the Jews should be a permanent minority in Palestine, Lloyd George wrote in his memoir about the World War I peace treaties, would have been regarded "as unjust and as a fraud on the people to whom we were appealing." In the House of Lords, the Archbishop of Canterbury presented the moral aspect of the situation when stating his feeling that the 1939 White Paper did not hold out "a prospect of reasonable justice" to the Jews, the National Home pledge surely not meaning their return to "that minority status which has been their lot through long centuries in every part of the world."[36]

The actual achievements of the 600,000 pioneering Jews greatly strengthened the moral case. Although owning a mere 6.4 percent of the land of what is actually Western Palestine, they have created a varied and rich agriculture, often on rocky hills and dry land. Jewish immigration, the 1937 Royal Commission observed, increased economic absorptive capacity. Electrification, building, a marked increase in agricultural settlements, and specialized industries marked by steady expansion aided by the war effort—all attested to impressive growth. Arab economic life and health, concluded that Commission and the mandatory's own 1946 report to the Anglo-American Committee of Inquiry on Palestine, much benefited in the process, as was also evident in the marked Arab population increase in urban areas affected by Jewish development. The *Yishuv* had created social, cultural, and educational institutions of a high order, such as the Hebrew University, the Haifa Technion, the Weizmann Institute, the Palestine Symphony Orchestra, and the Habima Theatre, and revived the ancient Hebrew language. These "heroic" efforts, reclaiming the land from its "millenial [sic] stagnation," should not be stopped or even interrupted midway. The "conscience of mankind" demanded this, and also that the incoming Jews be permitted to establish there "their promised Jewish Commonwealth."[37]

How had the Mandatory "flouted" the obligations of the Mandate? Rather than faithfully discharging its international trust, chapter three pointed out, HMG began from 1937 on to "subvert" that charge altogether. The Arabs, to quote the Royal Commission, "inevitably interpreted the Palestine

Administration's lack of sympathy for the Zionist enterprise as showing that the British determination to implement the Balfour Declaration "is not wholehearted." The Chamberlain government adopted a policy of "wooing the Arab agitators" in Palestine, notably Mufti Haj Amin al-Husseini and his circle, even extending its appeasement to the neighboring Arab countries by inviting them to weigh in at the 1939 London Conference on the country's future. This unprecedented action, "plainly illegal" under international law after the Allied and Associated Powers of the First World War and the League of Nations in the years 1917–1925 had "definitively" decided that question, was challenged by the chairman of the 1939 Permanent Mandates Commission. The "betrayal" of the Jews, culminating in the White Paper's limiting Jewish immigration for the next five years to 75,000 (thereafter with Arab consent), effectively foretold Palestine's becoming an Arab state. It signified, in Churchill's flaming words, "a breach of faith."[38]

Firmly shutting Palestine's doors just when European Jewry fell victim to Hitler's "Final Solution of the Jewish Question" led to disasters at sea like the *Patria* and *Struma* and to the deaths of "certainly tens of thousands" of Jews murdered in the Holocaust. British policy continued after the world war to prevent the "harassed and desperate" survivors from reaching Palestine. What HMG terms these "illegal" immigrants are, in fact, "pathetic and unfortunate" refugees who disregard the Mandatory's "*own illegal ban*" upon immigration. So, too, the continuing, restrictive ban from 1940 onwards concerning Jewish land settlement, reflecting the Mandatory's "*political*" purpose to preserve the Arab character of 94 percent of Palestine. Forcing the Jews to remain mainly town dwellers, it actually creates "a pale of settlement or ghetto for the Jews," reminiscent of Nazi Germany's legislation of a strictly racial character. The Mandatory, ignoring the "burning and unanswerable condemnations" by League and parliamentary representatives of its actions had thus "flagrantly breached" its international trust and obligations, and "subverted" the Mandate with which it was entrusted by the League of Nations and the United States of America.[39]

Palestine could absorb the mass immigration of Jews now in Europe, Africa, and Asia who wish to make their home there, chapter four pointed out. The past record and the studies of economic absorptive capacity made by competent, impartial experts like Walter Lowdermilk, Robert Nathan, and Tennessee Valley Authority (TVA) irrigation engineers demonstrated that between three and four million additional immigrants could be integrated into the country's economy if the water resources, now going to waste, were properly harnessed and utilized. The Mandatory had consistently underestimated Palestine's capacity for future development, with "waste lands" actually cultivated and reclaimed by the Jews in Rehovot, Hadera, the Vale of Esdraelon (Jezre'el Valley), the Kabara, and the Huleh (Hula) swamps. This growth did not and would not dispossess Arabs, whose rural population increased from about 400,000 in the 1920's to 793,000 in 1944. Jewish industry trebled in 1930–1937 and doubled in 1941–1945. Not only not a single Arab need be displaced or lose his occupation as the result of Jewish agricultural and industrial development, but not even a single acre of Arab-owned agricultural land which is not given up *"without very satisfactory remuneration"* need pass out of Arab lands. The memorandum's authors were confident that "ample" absorption capacity existed for all Jews desiring to settle in Palestine in the immediate future and would continue to expand as the country would be developed further.[40]

Drawing upon materials submitted to UNSCOP by the Jewish Agency, chapter five asserted that "a Jewish Palestine will contribute to the welfare of the Arab world." Arab spokesmen and their supporters claimed that any expansion of the Jewish National Home was an "act of aggression" against the Arab nation, violating the principle of self-determination and the spirit of the UN Charter. Yet the actual promulgators of the principle of "self-determination" had drawn up the Palestine Mandate while granting the Arabs of the former Turkish Empire that principle to "a greater extreme" than it has ever been followed in any other case both before and since. In 1918, King Hussein bin Ali al-Hashimi, King of the Hejaz and Sharif of Mecca, himself welcomed the return of the Jewish *jayila* (exiles) to their homeland, which he thought would "prove materially and spiritually an experimental school for their brethren," while his son Emir Feisal, meeting with Weizmann on January 8, 1919, signed an agreement which spoke of the acceptance by the Arabs of the Balfour Declaration and the encouragement of Jewish immigration to Palestine, Feisal prepared (so wrote the Royal Commission) to "concede little Palestine to the Jews" if his father and he secured "their big Arab state." Significantly, the Commission had reminded the Arabs that the Balfour Declaration brought HMG important Allied support, whose subsequent victory resulted in the emancipation of the Arab countries from Turkish rule.[41]

Palestine could not be considered on the same basis as the surrounding Arab countries. What the Jews have already wrought in the land in recent years "stamps it" as Jewish, although they constitute but a third of the current population. Moreover, Palestine owes its "lustre in the history of mankind" to its Jewish connections, as confirmed by the Royal Commission and the Mandate. It would not be a "major catastrophe" if a "minute fraction of the Arab peoples" lived outside the area of Arab independence, provided that their personal status in Palestine were secure, what M. Pierre Orts of the Permanent Mandates Commission deemed a "slight sacrifice." A minority status there for the Jews, on the other hand, would mean "imminent and ever present danger" for themselves and "the end of all hope" of a Home for their "homeless, uprooted and persecuted brothers of Europe and the Moslem world." Moreover, the minority position of Palestine's Arabs in a Jewish state would be "formal rather than actual," inasmuch as they would still be an integral part of a race "exercising unchallenged predominance" throughout the rest of the entire Middle East. No Jewish authority established in Palestine, interested in good relations with its neighbors, would show neglect or lack of consideration for the rights of Palestinian Arabs.[42]

Recalling the slaughter of 3,000 unarmed civilian Christian Assyrians in Simele, northern Iraq, in August 1933 by Iraqi soldiers and Muslim Kurd militia, as well as Arab leaders (including Haj Amin al-Husseini) who plotted with Nazi Germany for the destruction of Palestine's Jews and the National Jewish Home, the promise of international guarantees for Jews in a minority status offered scant hope. Nor did the depressed status of Jewish communities in the existing Arab countries, and their "recurrent violent persecutions" in those countries, offer any encouragement. Arab claims that the High Commissioner of Egypt, Sir Henry McMahon, had pledged Palestine to Hussein in 1915–1916 were publicly denied in 1937 by McMahon himself, while then Colonial Secretary William Ormsby-Gore announced at the same time that "the McMahon correspondence was fully in the mind of his Majesty's and the Allied Governments when the Balfour Declaration was made." The Hogarth message to Hussein in January 1918, supposedly giving a British pledge of Palestine to the Arabs, actually reaffirmed HMG's Jewish National Home policy, and simply reassured the Arabs that Jewish settlement in Palestine would be allowed only insofar as was compatible with the political and economic freedom of the "*existing*" population. Hussein and Feisal never referred to that message, while Churchill affirmed Lord Balfour's pledge when writing in 1922 as the colonial secretary to an Arab delegation, to the Holy See, and to the League of Nations.[43]

Jewish development in Palestine would influence the surrounding Arab countries, as recognized among others by T. E. Lawrence and Amery. With the Arab outlook "converging" towards the European concepts of the laws of change and the inevitably of progress which the Jews represented, the authors of *The Basic Equities of the Palestine Problem* were hopeful that the Arab-Jewish "deadlock" was "superficial and not profound; transient, not enduring." This would "likely pass," they believed, as soon as a political settlement "is imposed which banishes from the Arab heart all hope that the Jewish foothold can be reduced and eliminated by intransigeance [sic] and aggression."[44]

Finally, Jewish sovereignty in Palestine would not isolate that country from the unifying movements in the Middle East. Although currently a minority there, the Jews have given that country its "distinctive aspect, culture and level of civilization." Moreover, committed to establishing on its soil "a distinctive national polity," they would never be content to be a "mere collection" of individual citizens under a predominantly Arab government. Arab-Jewish cooperation would exist only when the conditions of equality and finality were achieved, including "a Jewish State within adequate boundaries," between the two peoples. With friction thus removed, mutual cooperation could follow.[45]

A brief chapter six put forth the legal team's solution: an independent Jewish Commonwealth or State. Two fundamentals, meeting the demands of the situation and in accord with the requirements of justice and international law, had to be ensured. Any thwarting of continued large-scale Jewish immigration and land settlement, as well as of the reclamation and development of "the backward country" agriculturally, industrially and culturally "for the benefit of all its inhabitants," would not resolve the pressing problem of "the uprooted Jews" of Europe, Africa and Asia, or the needs of Palestine itself and of the world. Short of this, the fulfillment of the international pledge of a Jewish Homeland would be "rendered impossible." In addition, the tragedy of the homeless Jews would continue to "harass the civilized world and might, indeed, unfold to a dreadful climax from which the imagination recoils."

The authors could do no better in defining a Jewish Commonwealth than to cite the official Jewish Agency memorandum to the UNSCOP delegation in July 1947. It meant "an independent self-governing Palestinian State with a Jewish majority in which all citizens regardless of race or creed will enjoy equal rights and all communities will control their internal affairs. . . . This state will have the special function of serving as a National Home for the Jewish people and providing a refuge for oppressed Jews." Equal rights would be embodied in the organic law of the State, but Arab rights guaranteed by the fact that the Jewish Commonwealth, surrounded by Arab states much superior in numerical strength, would depend for the maintenance of its security and economic interests on good neighborly relations with those states. On the economic side, it would again be "a matter of self-interest" for the Jews to raise the Arabs to their own level. The Jewish State would also devote special attention to safeguarding the rights of Christianity and Islam in Palestine, and propose the special appointment of a special UN Commission to supervise all holy shrines. When the Arab citizen of the new state realized that the solution was final, he would become "a healthy part of its electorate" and join in that "constructive effort" which would enable the new State to take its place "proudly in the family of nations."[46]

The two other principal solutions recently suggested for Palestine came under review in chapter seven. Cantonization, whether the Morrison plan's providing for only seventeen percent of Western Palestine for the Jewish province or the minute unconnected Jewish enclaves in an Arab land proposed by Bevin, meant that HMG would for some years, if not permanently, retain "supreme" control of the country. The Jews would still be required to cover the deficits of the "restricted region." In effect, these two plans would, if adopted, result merely in the legalization and perpetuation of "the unlawful and discriminatory" White Paper of 1939. The only effective change would be that the "inconvenient" original Mandate, with its positive obligations to the Jewish people, would be formally "got rid of." The Royal Commission itself had concluded that cantonization presented "most, if not all, of the difficulties presented by Partition without Partition's one supreme advantage—the possibility it offers of eventual peace." Further, local autonomy would become an illusion, the UNSCOP noting that the existing conditions of Arab and Jewish "diffusion" in Palestine might easily entail "excessive fragmentation" of the governmental process, and in its ultimate result "would be quite unworkable." In addition, "insoluble questions" would arise as to the allocation of public revenues, particularly with respect to development schemes for increasing absorptive capacity.[47]

The creation of a bi-national or parity state would complicate the problem and render it "insoluble, except by violence." With both Arabs and Jews having equal power, immigration policy and all matters relating to it, including industrial expansion, water supply, annual budget, and land settlement, would be subject to the "bitter opposition" of a co-equal political unit. No constitutional guaranty was self-executing; especially if affirmative in nature, both legislative and executive action were required to implement it. Moreover, immigration policy itself could not be divorceed from fiscal policy, nor, indeed, from economic policy generally.

Further, such a state would function only with difficulty, representing "two divergent political forces" whose outlook was bound to be different "for some time to come." The Jewish aim is "dynamic," the Arab, in many respects, "static." The former would continue its interest in industrial and agricultural development according to the best methods known to science; the latter would continue to resist change, to perpetuate existing methods of agriculture and to distrust industrial development. While some progress would inevitably be made, as there had been already through emulation and cooperation, the pace would nevertheless be "slow" and the "dead hand of tradition would remain a limiting force." The two opposing sides would actually be "pulling apart" on the major problems of national development.

Although the Jews had no doubt about the ultimate amelioration of the lot of the Palestinian Arabs nor, indeed, of the progress the Jews hoped they would make, it would be unwise to take out of perspective the true picture of the two populations today. For showing even "slight inclinations" in support of Jewish immigration and land settlement, too many Arab leaders had been assassinated in Palestine by the Mufti's followers. Both sides strongly disagreed on immigration, and there has never been "so sharp a cleavage" between two peoples on the general aims of government. The problem of internal security must also be considered as difficult, if not impossible, in a parity state, with police action questionable in terms of loyalty to one's group and difficulties arising over a security budget. Such a state would encourage the continuance of strife, "born in confusion and doomed to sterility." Its creation would dissolve the "irrevocable" pledges to the Jewish people." The consequences might be "civil war and chaos."[48]

Reviewing in chapter eight the UNSCOP minority recommendations, the memorandum noted that the essential attributes of true statehood were all reserved to the federal government, which would be Arab. The Jewish "state" would in effect have no control over immigration or development. The constitutional scheme would inevitably have an Arab majority in one chamber of the legislative body and strife in the second chamber's equal representation of the Arab and Jewish citizens of Palestine. Even worse, legislation under the minority report's recommended scheme could only be enacted "when approved by majority votes in both chambers of the legislature." When faced with "hopeless stalemate," an arbitral committee would always have an Arab majority. A federal court of appeal would likewise have an Arab majority. Moreover, after a transitional period of three years, Jewish immigration would be closed owing to the federal legislature's Arab majority. Finally, the all-important matters of national defense and administration would be controlled by the Arabs. Indeed, the minority report frankly declared that the federal state solution would permit the development in Palestine of patterns of government and social organization which would be "more harmonious" with those in "the neighboring states," thus making of Palestine another absolute Arab state with Arab governmental and social patterns. The "utter and complete unacceptability" of these proposals to the Jews is "so plain as to need no further argument."[49]

The UNSCOP majority recommendations, by contrast, represented "a statesmanlike and sincere effort to provide a workable compromise of the difficult and complex Palestine problem." 150,000 Jewish immigrants from Europe could enter their future state during the next two years, and thereafter at a rate of 60,000 per year until the Jewish State has been set up. Partition of the country into two states would permit each one to have plenary control over its own immigration and development save for matters like railways and interstate highways, as well as a common customs tariff and joint economic development as regards irrigation, land reclamation, and soil conservation. The territory of the Jewish State would be approximately one-half of the National Jewish Home under the Mandate and less than one-fourth of that promised in the Balfour Declaration. Still, partition would end "the festering situation now prevailing, and thus conduce to the peace and progress of the entire Middle East."[50]

Two reservations to the majority report remained. The exclusion from the Jewish State of the nearly all Jewish city of Jerusalem outside the Old City walls should be questioned. Containing almost 90,000 Jews and thriving modern institutions, with relatively few non-Jews, it constituted "an almost compact unit." As for the Western Galilee, it is acknowledged that the mountainous and sparsely settled area is predominantly Arab. At the same time, this territory was capable of being developed so as to support a large additional population by the employment of very substantial non-profit yielding capital sums and modern scientific methods. The Jews would develop this territory for the benefit of all its inhabitants. If included in the future Jewish State, it would obviously provide "a more adequate area" for the economic absorption of the hundreds of thousands of Jews "who so ardently wish and, indeed, must go to Palestine."[51]

Concluding their memorandum, the legal team declared that "every consideration of fairness, equity and law supports the case in all of Palestine," as pledged in the League of Nations Mandate. In a spirit of compromise, the Jewish Agency in February 1947 had expressed its willingness to accede to a partition of Palestine and the establishment there of a viable Jewish State in an adequate area of the country. A fair partition, in bringing finality to the present "impossible" situation, would satisfy in "reasonable measure" the aspirations of both the Jewish and non-Jewish populations of Palestine. It would open the doors to the Jews of Europe, Africa, and Asia who look to Palestine "as the only land where they can renew and rebuild their lives." The Jews in their new state would also be provided with an international status, permitting them to join the councils of the family of nations—"as a member and not as a supplicant for a hearing."

A state adequate to meet Jewish needs and hopes would bring to a close "the unhappy chapter in world history," which opened with Hitler's advent, proceeded with the "unjust and unforgivable" 1939 White Paper, and had culminated in the "unbearable tensions and dangers" of today. With such a commonwealth once sanctioned by and immediately implemented by the United Nations, the authors were confident, the present tensions and difficulties "should evaporate and peace again reign in the Holy Land." World public opinion would support such a solution, as had the United States in 1946. Given the opportunity, rang the ultimate, last sentence of the memorandum, "the Jews now and in the future in Palestine will meet the challenge—peacefully, constructively and fairly, consonant with their rich traditions and their genius for home-building."[52]

The Basic Equities of the Palestine Problem made its mark on the General Assembly's seminal deliberations. It "lay the groundwork," as Handler put it, for Zionist lobbyists to push for the partition resolution. James G. McDonald, a staunch pro-Zionist on the Anglo-American Committee of Inquiry and Truman's appointee some months later as the first US ambassador to the new State of Israel, praised the memorandum highly. He sent a message to Tulin: "It is an outstanding piece of analysis, brilliantly put together the whole case. It has had great—perhaps decisive—influence on the thinking of most members of the United Nations Assembly." After the Assembly adopted Resolution 181 (II) on November 29, 1947, in favor of the UNSCOP majority recommendations by a vote of thirty-three in favor, thirteen against, ten abstentions, and one absent, Silver wrote to Gurfein, along with similar letters to other authors of the legal brief, thus:[53]

> Among those in favor of the establishment of a Jewish State in Palestine, a very special word of thanks is due to you and to other members of the group associated with Judge Rifkind who were responsible for the publication of "The Basic Equities of the Palestine Problem." This clear, concise and cogent study appeared at the psychological moment and undoubtedly played an effective part in winning for our cause the sympathies and intelligent understanding of many men of influence in the United Nations and in American public life generally.
>
> On behalf of my colleagues and personally, I would ask you to accept this expression of our very deep appreciation for your valuable collaboration in this admirable document.

Tulin merited a separate letter from Silver, who acknowledged "the particular responsibility which devolved on you in connection with the writing and public action of this memorandum." I wished, he added, to add "a more personal word of thanks and appreciation for your splendid and deeply valued services" in this regard. Seven months earlier, the Executive Committee of the American Section of the Jewish Agency, which ordered 1,000 copies of his revised *Book of Documents*, had passed a resolution expressing its thanks and gratitude for his "immense effort" in producing that hefty volume as "as an outstanding and invaluable addition to Zionist literature on the subject," with Lourie writing on a personal note his certainty that even he had only a partial idea of "the thought and painstaking attention to detail" which went into this "admirably executed piece of work."[54]

Two days after the historic General Assembly vote favoring Palestine's partition into a Jewish and an Arab state, Handler congratulated Shertok, noting "what a strain these past few days must have been!" "You have won the admiration and warm regard of the entire Jewish community," he declared, "for your statesmanlike and skillful representation of the Jewish Agency before the United Nations." "Your expressions of appreciation are deeply gratifying to me," the Agency's political director responded. "However," he was quick to add, "the struggle is far from over and the road ahead is a long and hard one. Now, more than ever, do we need the whole-hearted support of all who like yourself have our cause deeply at heart."[55]

Of the eight who had a hand in preparing the memorandum for the General Assembly session on Palestine, the oldest, who also had first proposed the idea, subsequently devoted much of his time to advancing the American Society of the Israel Institute of Technology, the Technion. Abraham Tulin was instrumental in obtaining a gift to that institute of about $8 million in the form of a bequest by Gerard Swope, president of the General Electric Company. Swope had been so impressed by a speech which he gave at a fiftieth-anniversary class reunion at Yale University that the contact of college days was re-established. As a consequence, Swope visited Israel and the Technion in 1957. When he died some time afterward, he left $8 million to set up the Swope Fund of the American Technion Society. Just short of his ninety-first birthday, Tulin, then Honorary Board Chairman, was the first recipient of the Albert Einstein Award of the American Technion Society, the unit's highest honor, bestowed by Israeli Supreme Court Justice Moshe Landau for Tulin's thirty-year contribution to the institute's achievements. He passed away in his New York City apartment on January 24, 1973, having over a long Zionist career lived up to the inscription on the Einstein award—"a man of valor and great deeds."[56]

The three other major signatories to the memorandum returned full time to the law. Simon H. Rifkind (1901–1995), achieving fame as a versatile trial lawyer whose clientele included Pennzoil, Jacqueline Kennedy Onassis, needy Holocaust survivors, and (at the request of the US Supreme Court) the individual chosen to sort out Western states' rival claims to water from the Colorado River, was at his death the senior partner in the New York-based firm of Paul, Weiss, Rifkind, Wharton, and Garrison. Milton Handler (1903–1998), a partner in the firm of Kaye, Scholer, Fierman, Hays, and Handler, set a record of teaching for forty-five years at the Columbia University Law School while helping draft the GI Bill of Rights and preparing amendments to the US Social Security Act that later became the foundation for Medicare. Murray I. Gurfein (1907–1979) served as president for ten years in the US HIAS immigration service and was a partner in various law firms until appointed to the United States District Court by President Richard M. Nixon in 1971 and elevated to the Appeals Court in 1974. While presiding over scores of complex cases and trials, Gurfein achieved the hallmark of his judicial career by affirming the *New York Times*' right to publish the *Pentagon Papers* when the Nixon Administration sought to block the newspaper on the grounds of jeopardizing national security.[57]

The remaining four also followed in the law. For almost fifty years, Lawrence R. Eno (1914–1997) was counsel to and a former partner in the firm of Rosenman and Colin. Jerome N. Frank (1889–1957), whose many influential books played a leading role in the "legal realism" movement, taught intermittently at the Yale University Law School and continued on the US Circuit Court of Appeals until his death. Stanley H. Fuld (1903–2003) served for fourteen terms on the Court of Appeals of New York, including his elevation in 1967 to become chief judge of the State of New York and of the Court of Appeals. Known in that capacity for his concern for personal civil liberties in what he believed was infringement by the state, Fuld retired from the bench in 1973 and returned to private practice until his death.

Abe Fortas (1910–1982), while a founding partner in the influential Washington, D.C., firm of Arnold, Fortas, and Porter, was appointed an associate justice of the Supreme Court of the United States by President Lyndon B. Johnson in 1966. As a member of the then dominant liberal bloc, perhaps his most important opinion came the following year in a highly important case called *In re Gault*, which established that children facing court proceedings were entitled to many of the constitutional protections enjoyed by adults. In May 1969, he became the only Supreme Court member to resign, this amid an uproar over disclosures that he had accepted a $20,000 fee from a foundation controlled by a friend and former client who at the time was under Federal investigation for violating securities laws, Fortas practiced law until his death with the firm of Fortas and Koven.[58]

The work of Tulin, Handler, and Eno on *The Basic Equities of the Palestine Problem* received a brief mention in their respective obituary notices on the pages of the *New York Times*. Thirty years after publication of that memorandum, the America-Holy Land Project of the Hebrew University's Avraham Harman Institute of Contemporary Jewry issued a reprint through the Arno Press, a Manhattan-based publishing house founded by Arnold Zohn in 1963 to specialize in reprinting rare and long out-of-print materials. Any analysis of the memorandum's genesis or of its significance went wanting. Curiously, neither did a single reference to that comprehensive document appear in numerous scholarly books and articles on the rise of the State of Israel. In the conclusion to my five-volume study of Israel's sovereign rebirth between Adolf Hitler's appointment as Chancellor of Germany on January 30, 1933, and David Ben-Gurion's declaration of the Jewish State's independence on May 14, 1948, I devoted one sentence to that important legal brief, the best juridical defense for the Zionist objective before the UN General Assembly's historic vote of November 29, 1947.[59] For more than seventy-five years, *The Basic Equities of the Palestine Problem* eluded the searchlight of history—until now.

CHAPTER 7

Poland's Distortion of the Holocaust

In the second week of August 2022, Poland's attempt to rewrite the nation's involvement in the Holocaust was revealed in leaked emails between Polish Prime Minister Mateusz Morawiecki, right-wing journalist Bronisław Wildstein, and two political advisers, according to a report by the Polish news site Wyborcza.

In one email from 2018, Wildstein told Morawiecki that "the basic problem we have in our relations with the Jews is that our enemies have monopolized all contact with them." Wildstein went on to explain that "our enemies" referred not only to political adversaries but also "enemies of the entire Polish nation." As an example, he named the Center for Holocaust Research, which he said "presents an almost obsessive hatred of Poles." (The Polish Center for Holocaust Research was established on July 2, 2003, as a section of the Institute of Philosophy and Sociology of the Polish Academy of Sciences. It is the first and, so far, the only research institution in Poland dealing exclusively with Holocaust studies.) Wildstein also named historian Jan Grabowski of the University of Ottawa, who "says that the issue of Poles helping Jews can be addressed only after our own [Polish] crimes have been investigated," and sociologist Barbara Engelking, co-founder and director of the Center for Holocaust Research, who has "taken over relations with Yad Vashem."

The email ended with Wildstein telling Morawiecki that it might be necessary to analyze the status of institutes such as the Jewish Historical Institute and the POLIN museum, both in Warsaw, "and the possibility of introducing our people into their midst." In another email revealed by Wyborcza, the journalist tells the prime minister that it is important to promote Poland both locally and internationally by equating Polish suffering in the Holocaust years to that of the Jews.

"The media issue you mention is important, not just in Israel, but all over the world," Morawiecki wrote in response, according to Wyborcza's report. "We must map out journalists sympathetic to Poland. This is a job to be done right now by the Foreign Ministry and the Polish National Foundation." (The Polish National Foundation, founded in 2016 and financed to the tune of 400 million złoty (€93 million) from the country's leading state-run corporations, was created to combat the deluge of bad press about the country's right-wing Law and Justice (PiS) Party, which came to power that year.) The prime minister's advisers responded to this email, suggesting "sympathetic journalists" who could be good for the job. Other emails sent between the four contained similar messages.[1]

Poland has consistently insisted that it was not involved in Nazi crimes during the Holocaust, and refuses to take responsibility for any of these. Phrases such as "Polish death camps" have been controversial in the Central European nation over the past decades, with former US president Barack Obama being heavily criticized when he used the term while awarding a posthumous Medal of Freedom to Polish World War II resistance fighter Jan Karski in May 2012. Poland demanded an apology from the White House after President Obama spoke of a "Polish death camp" while awarding a posthumous Medal of Freedom to Karski, the man who alerted the world in the fall of 1942 to the Nazi Holocaust in occupied Poland. Obama's words "touched all Poles," Prime Minister Donald Tusk said in a statement. "We always react in the same way when ignorance, lack of knowledge, bad intentions lead to such a distortion of history, so painful for us here in Poland, in a country which suffered like no other in Europe during World War II." Foreign Minister Radosław Sikorski wrote on his Twitter account that the White House should apologize "for the outrageous mistake." A spokesman for Obama's National Security Council, Tommy Vietor, responded in turn that the president "misspoke" while referring to "Nazi death camps in Poland."[2]

The Polish search for creating a "usable past," reflecting a modern desire to make sense of national experiences in ways that unify citizens rather than separate them, actually commenced early on. In *The August Trials: The Holocaust and Postwar Justice in Poland*, Andrew Kornbluth recently examined a series of trials (over 800 out of a total of 32,000) of collaborators that were held in Poland during the decade or so following the end of World War II. Kornbluth demonstrates that far from being a tool in the hands of the Soviet authorities, these trials of "Fascist-Nazi Criminals Guilty of Murder and Torture of Civilians and Prisoners and of the Traitors of the Polish Nation" began as a genuine attempt to come to terms with the violence and murder committed by Poles under the German occupation. With the passage of time, however, the trials became a site for downplaying or even erasing Polish responsibility for the ethnic cleansing of Polish Jewry, the legacy of two decades of the Second Polish Republic, namely the propagation of political antisemitism by right-wing nationalist movements, most prominently the pre-war National Democracy Party (Endecja) combined with a similar trend in the Polish Catholic Church.

As the process of retribution began to unearth evidence of enthusiastic local participation in the Holocaust (later called "the hunt for Jews," an unambiguous case of ethnic cleansing by the village self-government, the Polish "Blue" Police, and the underground), the hated authorities, traumatized populace, and fiercely independent judiciary all struggled to salvage a purely heroic vision of the past that could unify a nation recovering from massive upheaval. The "essence of the radical apologia," writes Kornbluth, "is that Poles were helpless to resist German commands regarding Jews." The trials, most of which took place from 1944 to 1953, became the crucible in which the Communist state and an unyielding society forged a foundational myth of modern Poland that the Germans alone had perpetrated the crimes of the Holocaust. They left, at the same time, a lasting open wound in Polish-Jewish relations. Postwar retribution largely came to an end with the process of de-Stalinization initiated by Poland's "thaw" of 1956, when the Holocaust reckoning of the August trials, however imperfect, became associated with the period of violent Sovietization and dismissed as illegitimate.[3]

Mirosław Tryczyk's *Miasta Śmierci* (2015), an English translation appearing in 2021 as *The Towns of Death,* presented a documentary collection of more than 700 cases that had been examined in those same court trials together with survivor memoirs, Soviet archives, and investigations carried out by the Polish Institute of National Remembrance. Mainly focusing on the German-occupied Białystok region, this independent researcher found that tens of thousands of Jews were murdered in 1941–1942 by neighbors operating on their own initiative, mainly headed by people who belonged to the prewar Polish elites, in fifteen different towns and villages in the Podlasie province of northeastern Poland. That area was one of the strongholds prior to World War II of the right-wing, deeply antisemitic National Democracy Party, supported by lower-ranking priests but also by the bishop of Łukom. In some cases, the German forces left the murders to the local perpetrators, who regularly resorted to axes, pitchforks, and hammers—rarely firearms, and burning Jews alive, while in other cases the locals cooperated with the killers. It was a landscape of fear, betrayal, and death.[4]

Justice was poorly served. According to Kornbluth, more than 20,000 guilty verdicts were issued over the course of twelve years, including 1,835 death sentences, although fewer than 130 may have been carried out. He adds that while the overall rate of conviction for crimes covered by the decree was likely around fifty percent, the conviction rates of persons accused of crimes against Jews may have ranged as low as fourteen percent. More than 80 percent of the cases conducted under the "August decree" regarding those who had committed crimes against Polish citizens of Jewish origin ended with acquittals or sentences within the lower range of punishment, concludes Tryczyk. In the case of the pogrom in Szczuczyn and its vicinity, for example, seven Poles were sentenced to prison terms, the President of the Republic of Poland changed the sentence of the only Pole facing death to imprisonment, and twenty-one were acquitted.[5]

The one Pole convicted of "crimes of genocide" as a German collaborator, Henryk Mania for serving as a member of the *Sonderkommando Kulmhof* in the Chełmno death camp, was sentenced by the District Court of Poznań on July 6, 2001, to eight years imprisonment. As the convict did not appear to serve his sentence voluntarily, Mania was arrested on December 1, 2005, and placed under arrest in Szczuczyn. Due to the constantly deteriorating health of the accused, on January 13, 2006, after only one and a half months in prison, the court ordered a break in serving the sentence until the health obstacles ceased to exist. This never happened, however, and thus Mania did not cross the prison threshold again, spending only a few months out of his original sentence behind its walls.[6]

The Polish government's first commemoration of the Holocaust, dedicating on April 19, 1948, the iconic bronze sculpture of the Warsaw Ghetto Revolt by Warsaw native and survivor Nathan Rapoport, actually received official status. The many representatives present, aside from a Palestinian Jewish delegation and some 20,000 spectators, included Premier Josef Cyrankiewicz, Minister for Justice Henryk Swiatkowski, and Minister without Portfolio Władysław Baranowski. As I have described elsewhere, Swiatkowski paid tribute during this impressive ceremony "to the heroic deeds and battle of the Jews of the Warsaw Ghetto." Rapoport was awarded the government's Order of Polonia Restituta; a special postage stamp was issued; the government contributed the land and one-tenth of the memorial's considerable cost of $250 million; and all attendees received a silver medal struck by the Jewish Central Committee of Poland. The same day, a Museum of Jewish Martyrdom was opened by the Jewish Historical Institute. Polish stamps would, in time, feature the monument and themes of armed revolt.[7]

Thirty-five years later, Rapoport's monument would become the scene of an especially bitter struggle between the Communist-led government and the Solidarity trade union movement. At the stroke of noon on April 19, 1983, the Polish authorities began the fortieth anniversary commemoration of the Warsaw Ghetto Revolt. Before a crowd of 1,000, a military guard of honor slowly marched forward, banks of red and white Polish flags and wreaths brought to the base, led by a member of the state-controlled veterans association Union of Fighters for Freedom and Democracy. This was followed by the mingling of the Polish anthem with Israel's *HaTikva*. At the close, the Jewish mourners' *Kaddish* prayer was intoned after the many soldiers disappeared, and the Zionist national anthem was again sung.[8]

At the same time, with hundreds of Polish police having outlawed an unofficial gathering there one day earlier to mark the anniversary, Solidarity supporters flashing victory signs before being forcibly dispersed, more than 1,000 people then gathered at the memorial to the Jewish armed resistance headquarters on 18 Miła Street. They turned it into a rally for the Solidarity union before being scattered by jackbooted policemen armed with submachine guns. Sixty-two-year-old cardiologist Marek Edelman, the Bund Jewish socialist representative on the ŻOB (Jewish Combat Organization) and the only known survivor of the revolt still living in Poland, had called in Solidarity's newspaper for a boycott of the official ceremony. The well-regarded human rights activist, placed under police surveillance and ordered not to leave his home in Lodz, declared that in light of the suppression of Solidarity and our "social life in its entirety overshadowed by degradation and oppression," the state commemoration would be "an act of cynicism and scorn."[9]

The American Jewish Committee announced that it would not attend the official commemoration either. The Polish government had chosen to politicize the event, it declared, "as manifested in a spate of vitriolic anti-Israel editorials" and the "presence in positions of prominence of people associated with the anti-Semitic campaign during the time of the [Władysław] Gomulka regime." The latter objection, hinting to what had led to the departure of almost 13,000 Jews in 1967–1968, the result of a domestic assault aimed to purge Jews from all positions of influence and leadership that had evolved from a Cold War anti-Israeli policy in reaction to the overwhelming Arab defeat in the Six Day War, was strengthened especially with the recent news that a representative of the Palestine Liberation Organization (PLO), dedicated to Israel's destruction by armed struggle and recognized by the United States and Israel as a terrorist organization, would be present to lay a wreath at the memorial to the martyred victims. "Given this flagrant insult to the dead as well as to the living," the

Committee's statement ended, "we have recalled our representative and cancelled all plans to participate."[10]

The same day, some of the heads of delegations met with Prime Minister Wojciech Jaruzelski in a private two-hour session. It was reported that Jaruzelski had given them unqualified assurances of total support for Jewish institutions, places of worship, cemeteries, and the cultural aspects of Jewish life. In the end, four members of the Israeli delegation cut short their visit, forty others remaining to visit four Nazi death camp sites in Poland. The delegation officially protested the PLO's placing of a wreath, calling it a "cynical act and a desecration of the memory of the victims" of the Nazis. Warsaw media ignored the incident, while government officials explained in private contacts with the Israelis that the PLO's action had been done without the knowledge of the authorities, and that a PLO wreath placed on the monument on the morning prior to the memorial ceremonies had been removed before the ceremonies began.[11]

Jan Błoński's "Poor Poles Look at the Ghetto," published in January 1987 in the country's most influential Roman Catholic weekly magazine *Tygodnik Powszechny*, opened new venues in Polish historiography vis-à-vis the Holocaust. Inspired by Nobel laureate in literature Czesław Miłosz's two wartime poems criticizing the apathy of Poles during the Warsaw Ghetto Revolt, the Jagiellonian University professor decried his society's "indifference and moral paralysis" in Jewry's darkest hour and called for acknowledging Poland's antisemitic past in order to "gradually cleanse this doomed land." In the extensive controversy which erupted, some supporters went further in charging Poles with complicity in murder. Others, defending their fellow gentile compatriots' record, offered what Shmuel Krakowski characterized as "biased, apologetic, distortive and anti-Semiticly [sic] flavored traditional approaches."[12]

The following year, tensions over the political reality in Poland and its connection to Rapoport's iconic monument had escalated. Pressing for a site to commemorate the Warsaw Uprising of August-October 1944 against the Germans, painfully aware that the Red Army had camped quietly across the Vistula River while 180,000 Poles died in their valiant resistance, Solidarity leader Lech Wałęsa pointedly enlarged the Poles' national sense of themselves to include memory of the Jews. "In this land of so many uprisings," he declared in a letter before a crowd of 10,000 who assembled at the Warsaw Ghetto Revolt statue to commemorate the rebellion's forty-fifth anniversary despite a government ban, "the uprising of the Jewish fighters was perhaps the most Polish of all uprisings," and he begged forgiveness for the "painful excesses" of antisemitism in Poland. Earlier, at Warsaw's Jewish cemetery at Okopowa Street, several thousand Poles and Jews, some of them ghetto survivors, gathered to unveil a monument to the preeminent Bund leaders Henryk Erlich and Wiktor Alter, who were murdered during World War II at Stalin's order. On that occasion, Edelman asserted that the cenotaph in their honor made the cemetery "a symbol of the shame of inhuman totalitarianism all over the world."

Several hundred representatives of world Jewish organizations chose to attend a week of government-sponsored ceremonies, including the dedication of a memorial at the location of the *Umschlagplatz*.[13] Edelman had refused to take part in these official events, saying that participation dishonored the ghetto fighters in light of the repressive character of General Jaruzelski's dictatorial government. Yet Kalman Sultanik, a Holocaust survivor from Poland and vice president of the World Jewish Congress, declared: "I respect everyone's right to commemorate as he sees fit. But we came here for a commemoration, first of all, of the ghetto. This is such a broad and important issue, and this is unfortunately taking away from that importance, by directing it to something that is only minor." At about the same time, meeting in the Polish parliament to award ninety-seven Yad Vashem's Righteous among the Nations of the World medals to non-Jews who had rescued Jews during the Holocaust, Moshe Bejski, a justice of the Israeli Supreme Court and another Polish survivor, told the recipients: "You, just people, were unknown and you acted secretly. Risking your lives, you performed your duty toward other people—you contributed to saving the conscience of mankind."

Virtually none of the several thousand Israelis currently in Poland for a government-sponsored commemoration took part in the unofficial events, after the Polish authorities warned them that they could not guarantee their safety. The Communist authorities denounced the independent gatherings, charging that Solidarity leaders exploited them for political ends. They feared apparently that that banned movement would commemorate the Warsaw Ghetto Revolt "by actually re-enacting it." Indeed, the Polish Workers' United Party's *Trybuna Ludu* editors viewed the ghetto revolt commemoration occurring "at a time of wide upsurge of interest in Poland in the centuries-old Polish Jewish history, in the role of Polish Jews in cultural, economic, and social life, *in our common fate*." As James Young later observed, that is what precisely happened in 1988, when the ceremony at Rapoport's monument ended in an anti-government strike at the Gdańsk shipyards six weeks later.[14] And on December 9, 1990, Wałęsa won the presidential election, defeating Prime Minister Tadeusz Mazowiecki and other candidates to become Poland's first freely elected head of state in sixty-three years, and the first non-Communist head of state in forty-five years.

In April 1993, Pope John Paul II had defused a major controversy by telling fourteen Carmelite nuns to move from their convent at Auschwitz-I, opened in

1984 in the same building that had stored canisters of Zyklon B for the gassing of more than one million Jews at Auschwitz-II (Birkenau) three kilometers away, and where a twenty-three-foot wooden cross in front of torture site Block 11 had dominated the skies since 1985. The protests of Jewish and other leaders had until then achieved nothing, Józef Cardinal Glemp even taking the occasion of a visit in August 1988 at the Jasna Góra Monastery in Częstochowa, the shrine of the country's most revered religious icon, to warn Jews, whose "power lies in the mass media that are easily at your disposal in many countries," not "to talk to us from the position of a nation raised beyond all others" and "to offend the feelings of all Poles, and our sovereignty." This brought to mind the utterance of Cardinal August Hlond at the time of the violent Kielce pogrom on July 4, 1946, where Poles, spurred on by the medieval blood libel charge, killed forty-two Jews and seriously wounded forty others, that that savage attack and antisemitism in Poland were due to a great extent to Jewish cooperation with the postwar Communist regime. The persistent Catholic strain of Jew hatred, together with Polish officials still claiming Jew and Gentile in Occupied Poland as equal victims of the Nazis' "Final Solution of the Jewish Question," each losing three million lives, could not be easily dismissed.[15]

The first Polish-born Pope seemingly aimed, in Sergio Minerbi's phrase, to actually "Christianize" the Holocaust. While visiting Auschwitz-Birkenau as Pope in June 1979, John Paul II (originally Karol Józef Wojtyła) called it "the Golgotha of the modern world," and spoke of "six million Poles who lost their lives during the Second World War: the fifth part of the nation." Referring on that occasion to Jews indirectly, he even connected them to Christianity as "the people originated with Abraham, who is the father of our faith as was expressed by Paul of Tarsus." In May 1987 the same Supreme Pontiff beautified and later canonized the convert to Catholicism and Carmelite Order nun Edith Stein, gassed there in 1942 for being Jewish, claiming that she died as a daughter of Israel "for the glory of the Most Holy Name" and at the same time as "Sister Teresa Benedicta of the Cross." In the March 1998 Vatican document "We Remember: A Reflection on the Shoah," its preface written by Pope John Paul II himself, the Holocaust was declared "the world of a thoroughly modern, neo-pagan regime. Its anti-Semitism had its roots outside of Christianity." Rather than acknowledge the Christian roots of antisemitism in what Jules Isaac termed the Church's historic "teaching of contempt" for Jews, that document only admitted that Nazi persecutions "were made easier by the anti-Jewish prejudice imbedded in some Christian minds and hearts."[16]

In 1995, a monument was unveiled near Rapoport's statue in Warsaw to honor those Poles who had risked their lives in the ŻEGOTA relief council, sponsored by the London-based Polish government-in-exile, to rescue Jews from December 1942 onwards. Righteous among the Nations of the World medalist Władysław Bartoszewski, Poland's Foreign Minister and the last surviving member of ŻEGOTA's executive, stressed that the group's creation had been a common activity of Christians and Jews, helping "the most vulnerable." American and Israeli ambassadors spoke, with prayers offered by Chief Rabbi of Warsaw Menahem Joskowicz and Bishop Stanisław Gądecki, president of the Polish Episcopate's Commission for Dialogue with the Jews. The modest black stone, with inscriptions in Polish, Hebrew and English summarizing the organization's activities, had been commissioned by a group of Americans, mostly Polish, and designed by Warsaw artists Hanna Szamlenberg and Marek Moderau.[17]

Jan Tomasz Gross's *Sąsiedzi* (*Neighbors*), a study by the Princeton University historian of the massacre on July 10, 1941, of almost all of the 1,600 Jews in Jedwabne village in northeast Poland by their gentile neighbors, forced the country to examine a significant aspect of its past. That introspection had begun with the showing of Claude Lanzmann's documentary film *Shoah* in 1986 and Jan Błoński's article the following year. What to say about a distinct people that had vanished from its soil after living there for close to 1,000 years, one-tenth of Poland's population of thirty-five million on the eve of World War II and the highest percentage among the general population in Europe? The question stands apart from the fact that as many as 1,000-2000 Polish Jews of the approximately 380,000 who survived the Holocaust were murdered after the war by Poles.[18]

A vigorous two-year debate ensued from the time that Gross's slim book appeared in Polish (2000) and then in English translation (2001), with local historians divided over its factual charges and the mainstream Polish press expressing consensus regarding the basic accuracy of the author's findings. The volume inspired film director and screenwriter Władysław Psikowski to produce his 2012 fictional thriller *Pokłosie* (*Aftermath*), claiming that Gross's book "was the source of my knowledge and shame." Cardinal Glemp described the book's thesis as "incontestable" and Polish President Aleksander Kwaśniewski asked his countrymen to "seek forgiveness for what our compatriots have done." In 2011, President Bronisław Komorowski also publicly apologized for the crime. Other Polish publications, on the other hand, accused Gross's book of being a "part of international campaign aimed at damaging the image of Poland and preparing ground for restitution of Jewish property."[19]

Gross's subsequent study, *Fear: Anti-Semitism in Poland after Auschwitz* (2006) also raised hackles in Polish nationalist circles. His discussion of the deadly 1946 Kielce pogrom and other instances of the murder of Jews following World War II was later followed by *Golden Harvest* (2011), co-authored with his wife Irena. It drew similar native ire with its account of Polish peasants who pillaged the mass graves of Jews buried at the sites of historical pogroms. (That same year, a 2001 monument to the Jews killed in 1941 in Jedwabne was vandalized with swastikas.) His charge, in an essay published in 2015 in the German newspaper *Die Welt*, that during World War II "Poles killed more Jews than Germans," followed in 2016 by his declaring that Poles killed "a maximum 30,000 Germans and between 100,000 and 200,000 Jews," was dismissed by a Foreign Ministry spokesman as "historically untrue, harmful and insulting to Poland." Polish prosecutors, having opened a libel inquiry against Gross in October 2015, closed their investigation in November 2019, claiming that the establishment of the numbers of Germans and Jews killed as a result of actions committed by Poles during the Second World War "is still the subject of research by historians and the subject of dispute between them."[20]

For years to come, controversy over Holocaust commemoration in Poland continued unabated. At the seventieth anniversary of the Warsaw Ghetto Revolt, an official ceremony was held in the vast plaza square between the Rapoport statue and POLIN, the new Museum of the History of Polish Jews. Sirens wailed and church bells rang throughout the city to mark the date. In attendance were Polish President Komorowski and Prime Minister Tusk, as well as Israeli Education Minister Shai Piron and the legendary ghetto fighter Sima Rotem. Three years earlier, the government had erected a monument over the manhole at 51 Prosta Street, where Rotem had emerged from the sewers with the fighters he had led out of the ghetto. My comrades and I, Rotem declared now, launched the uprising to "choose the kind of death" they wanted, the rest of the ghetto's remaining Jews expecting the same fate as the majority who had been killed by then. Yet to that day, he added, he kept thinking whether we had the right to make the decision "and by the same token to shorten the lives of many by a week, a day or two." Although first feeling "utterly helpless" when facing the tremendous German firepower and a huge infantry force of 2,000 men, Rotem confided, "an extraordinary sense of spiritual uplifting" followed, the moment we had been waiting for . . . to stand up to this all-powerful German."

At the same hour, a half mile away, a small group gathered under leaden skies at the entrance to Warsaw's huge Jewish cemetery for an alternative memorial. Carrying bunches of bright yellow daffodils, they laid the flowers on the grave of Marek Edelman, who had died at the age of eighty-eight in October 2009. The group, most now in their sixties and seventies, had come together for decades to mark the anniversary of the uprising. Until his death, the Łódź doctor was usually with them, laying a bunch of daffodils at the dark, towering monument to ghetto heroes. For years, he had received yellow flowers, usually daffodils, from an anonymous person on the date of that anniversary. Eventually the flowers became a symbol of remembrance. The group placing flowers on Edelman's grave this year included several Polish Jews forced to leave the country during the Communist regime's antisemitic campaign of 1968 under Gomulka, along with former dissidents and Solidarity activists. Throughout the city, young volunteers handed out paper daffodils for people to wear on their jackets or lapels. All over Warsaw, people could be seen sporting the symbol, which was reminiscent of the yellow Star of David that the Nazis had forced Jews to wear.[21]

POLIN, the new museum facing the Warsaw Ghetto Revolt monument, which was officially opened on April 22, 2013, had also sparked controversy. While celebrating the rich millennial history of Polish Jewry, its future permanent exhibits were also intended to confront the country with its own dark chapters of Jew-hatred. Many citizens preferred an image of Poland as a model of heroic resistance to centuries of past oppression, both by Germans and Russians. Many grew up under a communist regime that dictated whose suffering should get attention. Further, historian Krzystof Jasiewicz of the Political Studies Institute of the Polish Academy of Sciences, although provoking widespread academic protest, drew considerable support in online forums for recently claiming in a magazine article that "the Jews worked for centuries to bring the Holocaust about . . . the scale of the German crime was only possible because the Jews themselves participated in the murder of their own people." Another debate arose over the idea of raising a memorial to Polish Righteous among the Nations of the World (6,000, the largest number from any country, officially recognized by Yad Vashem) right next to the museum, critics arguing that it would lead some to falsely believe that most Poles acted as rescuers of Jews during World War II. That June, a monument to revolt commander Mordechai Anielewicz's last stand at 18 Miła Street was vandalized, the words *"Jude raus"* ("Jews out") crudely painted there.[22]

The grand opening ceremony of the POLIN museum with its multi-media core exhibition on October 26, 2014, drew Polish President Komorowski, Israeli President Reuven Rivlin (on his first foreign visit), Polish Prime Minister Ewa Kopacz, Sejm members, several foreign delegations, and well over 1,000 guests. The museum's name in Hebrew means "here you will rest," Komorowski observed, appropriate because until its partitioning in the late eighteenth century, the country was "a safe haven and a generally friendly place." Ever since Poland won its freedom twenty-five years ago, it strove to "put right the account of history that has been corrupted, manipulated and distorted in so many ways during the non-democratic communist era." Only "parallel stories of greatness and smallness, heroism and cowardice, sacrifice and crime, life and death," Komorowski concluded, "can bring the idea of Polin back again." Although Jews were torn away from Poland, Rivlin responded, "it is difficult or even impossible to tear Poland away from Jews." Polish society was becoming "more and more courageous" in confronting its past and its future, he declared, and only through this kind of courage "shall we be able to write—and we have already started that process—a new, promising chapter of our mutual history which we have shared throughout centuries."[23]

In 2015, Andrzej Duda, in the course of defeating presidential incumbent Komorowski in the country's elections, resolutely rejected the painful truth of Jedwabne and proclaimed "a new historical policy strategy to enhance the perception of Poland in the world." He sought to have the Ministry of Foreign Affairs rescind Jan Gross's second Polish Order of Merit. Poland's most prominent intellectuals, in return, produced letters of protest, and historian Timothy Snyder of Yale University announced that he would renounce his own Polish order.[24]

Jan Grabowski confronted even more significant criticism from groups associated with the Polish right-wing political spectrum, which attempted to have him fired from his University of Ottawa professorship, death threats leading to increased security patrols in his department. This began with the publication of his *Judenjagd* (2011), with an English translation (*Hunt for the Jews: Betrayal and Murder in German-Occupied Poland*) two years later by the Indiana University Press and awarded the Yad Vashem International Book Prize, which focused on the "Hunt for the Jews" in a rural county in southeastern Poland by their neighbors. Grabowski, whose Jewish father participated in the 1944 Warsaw Uprising, estimates that about 200,000 Jews were killed by Polish police and local citizens during the Holocaust. His study *The Polish Police: Collaboration in the Holocaust* (2016), published by the US Holocaust Memorial Museum, furthered this contention. In June 2017, the Polish League against Defamation issued a statement signed by 134 Polish academics protesting his "false and wrongful image of Poland and Polish people." Some 180 historians worldwide soon signed an open letter in his defense, praising Grabowski's scholarship and asserting that the Polish League puts forth "a distorted and whitewashed version of Poland during the Holocaust era."[25]

On March 8, 2018, President Duda made an emotional plea for forgiveness for the Gomułka government's violent purge against the country's Jews, placing flowers on a memorial at Warsaw University. Poland was not to blame, asserted

Prime Minister Mateusz Morawiecki, saying that it was the Communist regime forced on the Polish people "that treated the Jews so badly back then." At the same time, this fiftieth anniversary of the mass expatriation of half of the Jews then living in Poland coincided with the controversy surrounding the government's Holocaust law. The latter decreed that suggestions that Poland bore responsibility for Nazi crimes in the country were a criminal offense. The Institute of National Remembrance, created in 1998 to prosecute crimes against the Polish nation, had its mission statement amended to include "protecting the reputation of the Republic of Poland and the Polish Nation." Historians in Israel, the United States, and Poland feared that this new stance could lead to a complete denial of Polish crimes against their fellow Jewish citizens during World War II.

The current Holocaust debate had triggered a new wave of agitation against Jews in the media and the internet, declared historian Dariusz Stola, then director of the POLIN museum. There were similarities to the antisemitic slogans and lies perpetrated in 1968, Stola told DW, Germany's international media outlet. Comments on social media had included such assertions as "The Jews and Israel have the liberal lobby in Brussels [headquarters of the European Union's executive branch] on a leash," and "Too bad, that not all Jews emigrated in 1968. Now they are showing off again."[26]

The following month, Poland marked the seventy-fifth anniversary of the Warsaw Ghetto Revolt, daffodils again widely worn throughout the city. Open Republic, an association fighting antisemitism and xenophobia, announced that it would stage an "independent" gathering in opposition to what it called the "hollow nationalist pomp" of the government, recalling how the prime minister, allied with the ruling Law and Justice Party's illiberal, nationalist policies, had paid tribute earlier that year to a Polish wartime insurgency unit which had collaborated with the Nazis. That commemoration in Warsaw was the first major anniversary without any survivors of the revolt in attendance, although several surviving noncombatants who had been in the ghetto as children commemorated the loss of their loved ones and their community.

Among those present that day was eighty-seven-year-old Marian Kalwary, a Polish survivor of the Warsaw Ghetto. In an interview with the Associated Press, he said that he was horrified to see violence in the world today and what he asserted was the rise in Poland of the same nationalistic views that drove Nazi Germany into starting World War II and the Holocaust. "I am terrified by the rebirth of fascism and nationalism, and I can see nationalism being glorified and put on a pedestal as something noble," Kalwary declared. "Nationalism is being confused with patriotism."

A separate ceremony, held on July 22, 2018, honored Szmul Zygelbojm, the Bund representative on the National Council of the Polish government-in-exile, who had committed suicide in London on May 12, 1943, when word came of the liquidation of the last Jews in Warsaw, among them his wife Manya and son Tuvia. In a "cry of protest" against the world's "indifference" during the Holocaust, his final letter read, Zygelbojm had hoped that taking his life would "shock" the Allied governments into action now, perhaps "the last moment for the remnants of Polish Jewry." The head of the local Jewish History Institute, sociologist Paweł Śpiewak, asserted that Zygelbojm's name needed to be recalled because it was not found in major Holocaust history books and there was no street in Israel named after him. The March of Remembrance, held by the Institute each year since 2012, began at Warsaw's *Umschlagplatz* Monument, participants placing yellow ribbons with Jewish names on a barbed wire fence that symbolized the ghetto's isolating wall. Joining hundreds of residents that Sunday, Israeli ambassador Anna Azari remarked that the memory of Zygelbojm should be a lesson for the present and for the future.[27]

The march came one month after the fallout over an agreement, signed by Israeli Prime Minister Benjamin Netanyahu and his Polish counterpart Morawiecki on June 27, which Poland saw as exonerating it of accusations that Poles had any meaningful role in corroborating in the Holocaust. The declaration, which drew sharp international criticism and was castigated by Yad Vashem, Netanyahu's coalition partners, President Rivlin, and opposition members of the Israeli Knesset, was part of an agreement that ended the diplomatic spat between the two countries over the controversial Holocaust Law passed by the Sejm in February that made any individual accusing the Polish nation of being "responsible or co-responsible for Nazi crimes committed by the Third Reich" open to a prison term of up to three years. The declaration was issued just minutes after the Polish parliament passed amended legislation to make such accusations a civil (facing major fines) rather than a criminal offense. President Duda signed it into law, right-wing Prime Minister Morawiecki conceding that his government had to take into account the "international context". The declaration also stated that the term "Polish death camps" was "blatantly erroneous," and that the wartime Polish government-in-exile in London "attempted to stop this Nazi activity [the killing of Jews] by trying to raise awareness among the Western allies to the systematic murder of the Polish Jews."[28]

Three months later, the Polish government handed over the site for a future Warsaw Ghetto Museum, the former children's hospital that had been within the ghetto's walls and was now to be found in the capital's main business district at 61 Śliska Street/60 Sienna Street Scheduled to be opened in 2023 to mark the eightieth anniversary of the ghetto uprising, the key was ceremoniously given by a government official to historian Albert Stankowski, who signed a long-term lease. Fragments of a plaque could be found on the floor, listing the names of donors of the original Bersohn and Bauman Children's Hospital, which had been established in the late nineteenth century by the two Jewish families. One of the stories which the future museum would tell was of the harrowing decision that some Jewish doctors had made to give many children fatal overdoses of morphine in order to spare them worse deaths in Treblinka. "This museum will be very important for all Jews because it is a symbol of the Shoah and the extermination of the Jewish people," director Stankowski remarked. "But even more importantly, it has a universal message important for the whole world. It shows what can happen when people are dehumanized."[29]

As the seventy-fifth anniversary of the liberation of Auschwitz-Birkenau by the Red Army on January 27, 1945, approached, marked since 2005 by the UN General Assembly as International Holocaust Remembrance Day, it was clear that the Polish government had not come to peace with commemorating the Holocaust. After being told that he would not be allowed to speak at a related event in Yad Vashem but Russian president Vladimir Putin would, Duda chose to stay home. His move came amid anger in Poland over Putin's recent comments accusing Poland of complicity in the start of the Second World War, purposely neglecting the Soviet Union's August 23, 1939, Non-Agression Pact with Nazi Germany and the subsequent invasion of Poland by both powers on September 1.[30]

On April 19, 2020, Warsaw sirens wailed and Jewish prayers were said for the heroes of the 1943 ghetto revolt, but the annual memorial observances were scaled down that Sunday and moved to the internet. The worldwide coronavirus pandemic and the need for social distancing "forced us to change the formula" for commemoration, declared POLIN museum director Zygmunt Stępiński. Poland's chief rabbi since the early 1990s, American-born Michael Schudrich, recited prayers at the monument to the ghetto fighters. Prime Minister Morawiecki and representatives of Jewish and Polish organizations laid wreaths. They all wore face masks and kept themselves at a distance from each other. President Duda and Warsaw Mayor Rafał Trzaskowski also sent wreaths. History lectures and virtual visits to ghetto sites were offered on the internet, mainly by the POLIN museum. Commemorative concerts were broadcast on Radio POLIN and on Poland's state radio.[31]

In July 2020, Duda, supported by the media and the influential Roman Catholic Church, running a radicalized nationalist campaign that had homophobic and antisemitic overtones, narrowly won a second five-year term in a bitterly fought election against Trzaskowski, the liberal mayor of Warsaw. Three months later, the Polish Senate passed a law, authored by the ruling right-wing Law and Justice party leader Deputy Prime Minister Jarosław Kaczyński, to end its $1.8 billion kosher and halal meat export industry in 2025. The same October, the former governor of Lublin, Przemysław Czernek of the Law and Justice Party, was selected to become Poland's education and science minister. He had called in 2019 for the removal of the memorial created by artist Dorota Nieznalska. The memorial, which Czernek deemed "a Polish scandal," featured a heap of charred logs arranged in the shape of a burning stake with signs denoting places where Poles had killed Jews during and after the Holocaust.[32]

With internecine warring between political factions in this predominantly Catholic country of thirty-eight million, including some 20,000 Jews, a reality that coarsens the public discourse and results in more public acts of vandalism and verbal abuse, the Polish Jewish Museum in Oświęcim (which the Germans had renamed Auschwitz) decided to conduct a month-long program in November of educational activities to sensitize teachers and activists to the dangers of exclusion. Announced two days after dozens of people from more than forty-nine countries sent greetings on his 101st birthday to Józef Walaszczyk, one of the last surviving Righteous among the Nations of the World who had saved more than fifty Jews in Poland during World War II, this initiative aimed via the internet to warn that "Auschwitz did not fall out of the sky" and to teach responses to discrimination and intolerance.[33]

Come February 2021, world-renowned Polish historians of the Holocaust Jan Grabowski and Barbara Engelking, who had co-edited the two-volume *Night without End: The Fate of Jews in German-Occupied Poland* (the Polish edition had appeared in 2018, later in English in conjunction with Yad Vashem), were ordered by a judge to apologize to an elderly relative of the mayor of Malinowo whom they had slandered as a pro-Nazi collaborator while allegedly "disseminating false information." Stanisław Żaryn, a spokesman for the Polish Minister-Coordinator of the Polish State, defended the decision in *Why Poland Is Trying to Control Holocaust Memory* (sic!) as part of what he deemed a "truth campaign" to counter a supposedly dire "security threat" to the welfare of the Polish nation. His false, egregious assertions included that "the Poles were the first nation the Germans had selected for extermination in the Auschwitz death camp"; the Polish Underground State "actively and resolutely punished those who took side of the German aggressor" when, in fact, the notorious blackmailers who contributed to the deaths of uncounted thousands of Polish Jews (*szmalcownicy*) remained practically unpunished; there were "many more 'righteous' people than traitors" among the Poles; "the majority of Poles adopted a passive attitude to what Germans brought upon the Jews" when, in fact, masses of Poles took part in German liquidations, went looking for Jewish property, and continued to look for hidden Jews during and after the war. In August, an appeals court overturned that ruling and dismissed the claims against the historians.[34]

Aside from this political use and abuse of history, in July 2021 Poland passed another law effectively preventing Jews from receiving restitution for property stolen from their families during the Holocaust. Two years earlier, Prime Minister Morawiecki had declared that paying compensation to Jews for property seized during World War II would represent "Hitler's posthumous victory" if "the victim and the executioner switched places," the ruling PiS Party arguing that as a victim of invasion and occupation by Nazi Germany, Poland should not be saddled with financial obligations in providing such payments to Jews. The 2021 ruling caused a diplomatic crisis between Poland and Israel, with Prime Minister Yair Lapid, who was foreign minister at the time, recalling the Israeli envoy to Poland, advising Poland's ambassador to Israel to remain on vacation in his homeland, and instructing Israel's new ambassador to Poland, Yaakov Livne, to remain in Israel. In Lapid's view, the legislation was "antisemitic and immoral." Poland "turned into an anti-democratic, illiberal country that doesn't respect the greatest tragedy in human history," Lapid charged. Poland responded by accusing Israel of "baseless and irresponsible" behavior.[35]

Slowly, the two sides deescalated the tensions. Poland is part of the four-member Visegrád Group, a bastion of support for Israel within the European Union. The Poland-Israel group in Poland's parliament is the largest such caucus in the legislature, with 127 out of 460 deputies in the group. Livne took up his post in Warsaw in February 2022 to coordinate Israeli efforts to extract citizens from Ukraine fleeing Russian invasion and to provide aid to Kyiv. Two Polish lawmakers visited the Israeli Knesset in June, the first to do so since 2017. Russia's invasion is driving the two countries back together, Polish MP Marek Rutka told the *Times of Israel* in June. Two months earlier, denouncing Russia's war against Ukraine when joining more than 2,000 young Israelis and others at the March of the Living in Auschwitz-Birkenau, President Duda had declared that "we are here to show that every nation has a sacred right to life, has a sacred right to cultivate its traditions, has a sacred right to develop." At the same time, he took the occasion to add this: "We come here to show that while during World War II, Nazi Germany managed to wipe my country off the map, wipe it out and murder Poles, including Polish Jews (*sic*), we will never again allow something like this to happen."

Presidents Duda and Israel's Yitzhak Herzog shared a telephone call on July 4, 2022, speaking in English. Duda indicated that in the coming days Poland would send its ambassador-designate to present his letter of credence. Their call, during which Herzog requested the return of a Polish envoy, was part of a months-long joint initiative with the Foreign Ministry, according to Herzog's office. "Both presidents expressed their hope that any future issues between Poland and Israel will be solved through sincere and open dialogue and in a spirit of mutual respect," read a statement from Herzog's spokesman. Livne presented his official credentials to Duda the following week.

On September 20, Chief of the Israeli army's General Staff Aviv Kochavi held meetings in Warsaw with the Chief of the General Staff of the Polish Armed Forces, Rajmund Andrzejczak, and additional senior officers. After Kochavi received a ceremonial honor guard at the Ministry of National Defense, a discussion was held on the strategic relationship and operational and intelligence cooperation between the two militaries and the plans for their expansion. A joint wreath-laying ceremony then occurred at the Tomb of the Unknown Soldier. Kochavi also visited the Warsaw Jewish Cemetery, in which approximately 200,000 Jews are buried, took part in a wreath-laying ceremony at the Rapoport memorial alongside a delegation of Israeli army commanders and Israel's Ambassador to the Republic of Poland, and visited the POLIN Museum. In closing remarks, Kochavi declared that "the existing reality requires and enables the ever-increasing cooperation between our militaries and our strengthening ties. The tragic past will forever be remembered and is another reason for mutual cooperation, given the present and future regional challenges."[36]

Disagreements remain, however. In June 2022, Lapid banned educational trips to Poland for thousands of high school students this summer, charging that the Polish government sought to control the Holocaust studies curriculum taught to Israeli children. The Polish government sought formal rules to regulate the terms under which Israeli schoolchildren conduct Holocaust study visits to the country, including the presence of armed Israeli guards, Deputy Foreign Minister Marcin Przydacz responded. Przydacz declared that young Israelis were receiving a "negative image" of Poland because of the armed guards accompanying the youth groups, the visits' focused on the Holocaust only, and there was a lack of contact with Polish youth. Four months later, Warsaw would uphold the ban on Israeli armed security guards for a trip long considered a milestone in Israeli education prior to the COVID-19 epidemic, some 40,000 Israeli students having come each year.[37]

On September 1, 2022, eighty-three years after the German invasion of Poland unleashed World War II, leader of the Law and Justice Party Kaczyński announced that the government would seek the equivalent of $1.3 trillion in reparations from Berlin for the cost to the country of five years of Nazi occupation. Most of this sum "is compensation for the deaths of more than 5.2 million Polish citizens," he added. The right-wing government, noting that Poland was the war's first victim, argued in a multi-volume report that the country had not been fully compensated by neighboring Germany, which is now one of its major partners within the European Union. The war was "one of the most terrible tragedies in our history," President Duda declared. "Not only because it took our freedom, not only because it took our state from us, but also because this war meant millions of victims among Poland's citizens and irreparable losses to our homeland and our nation." Once again, the victims of the Holocaust were conflated, now anonymously, into the separate tragedy of their Polish neighbors.[38]

Shamelessly, volume three of that same report, whose authors stated that it was the result of several years of research, included Jedwabne among the 9,292 places where German atrocities had occurred against Poles. Radziłów, Bzury, and Szczuczyn, additional sites witness to Jews being killed in the summer of 1941 by their Polish neighbors, received mention in those pages as well. The Lux Veritatis Foundation, which compiled the list, is headed by the controversial Rev. Tadeusz Rydzyk. The archconservative Catholic priest, who delivered millions of votes for the Law and Justice Party and, in turn, received from the government tens of millions of dollars in tax breaks and grants for his business empire, is known for spreading antisemitic statements over decades. In his Facebook account, Professor Grabowski called these inclusions "grotesque," and he asked in Polish on Twitter "what kind of restitution does Poland want from the Germans for the 200,000 Jews murdered by the Poles or with Polish participation?" The tweet drew angry responses, with comments calling him "Jewish bastard" and "Jewish swine," among other things.[39]

Professor Michael Fleming's review of the recent publication by the Polish Institute of International Affairs (PISM) *Confronting the Holocaust: Documents on the Polish Government-in-Exile's Policy Concerning Jews 1939–1945* places this large volume in the context of the current government's determination to highlight Polish heroism and martyrdom during World War II—particularly "to aid and rescue Jews during all stages of the war." Yet the work "obfuscates" exactly when that government in London became aware that Germany was murdering Jews, thereby deflecting "awkward questions" about its response in the second half of 1941 and early 1942. A relative paucity of documentation is given about any efforts of some in the Ministry of Foreign Affairs to transform information about atrocities into knowledge of war crimes (inter alia, to facilitate prosecution).

The Polish government-in-exile was unable to reconcile the affirmation of equality for all its citizens with Prime Minister Władysław Sikorski's advising British Foreign Secretary Anthony Eden on January 19, 1942, that a future Poland could not have over three million Jews: "room must be found for them elsewhere." An explanatory footnote to a document from the wartime Front for the Rebirth of Poland does not highlight that a censored version in the Polish emigrant press excised its affirmation that Jews were "the political, economic and ideological enemies of Poland." Editor Piotr Długołęcki does not mention the involvement of Polish soldiers in pogroms against Jews in 1918 and 1919. Anti-Jewish assaults in the interwar period go wanting here as well. Finally, the thorny issue of why it took almost five months for the Polish Ministry of Foreign Affairs to wait until November 1942 to formally share reports with the Allies of the German mass killing of Jews at various camps is not addressed.[40]

On the evening of February 7, 2023, Foreign Minister Eli Cohen spoke with his Polish counterpart Zbigniew Rau, the first such talks between foreign ministers of both countries in two years. Prime Minister Benjamin Netanyahu's new government has sought to restore the country's frayed ties with Poland, including the resumption of high school educational trips to concentration camps in the country. It also wants Poland to return its ambassador to the country's embassy in Tel Aviv. Warsaw had recalled its envoy there in 2021 and had downgraded the mission to Israel in November of the same year.

"The ministers discussed ways to warm relations between the countries, inter alia through the completion of the outline for the return of the Israeli youth delegations to Poland," the Israeli Foreign Ministry declared. Poland has said it would examine the "possibility of appointing a new Polish ambassador, this after an extended period in which there has been no Polish ambassadorial presence in Israel," "The conversation was conducted in good spirit," concluded a Foreign Ministry representative, "and the ministers expressed a desire to maintain direct and continuous contact, and even to hold a direct meeting in Poland or Israel in the near future."[41]

That same month, Father Michał Woźnicki, a Catholic priest from the city of Poznan with a long track record of antisemitic comments, was sentenced by a judge to thirty hours of community service a month for the next six months after being convicted of insulting Jews and inciting hatred against them. Woźnicki was on trial for comments made during a sermon in October 2021, including "Jews in the world have assumed the role of a leech, a tick, a body that lives on the host's body, swells, leading the host's body to death, moving on to the next one." He also said that Jews were in league with the devil and responsible for the spread of sexual impropriety in Poland.

Woźnicki was already facing sanctions from the church because of his record of controversy, and he delivered the sermon online because he has been suspended from his pulpit. But because he remains an ordained priest, his conviction is groundbreaking, according to the civil society group that pressed for him to face charges. Otwarta Rzeczpospolita (Open Republic), devoted to fighting antisemitism and xenophobia in Poland, asserted that "this is a precedent case. It was not Woźnicki's first hateful sermon, but the first one that the prosecutor's office dealt with." Poland's chief rabbi, Michael Schudrich, declared that "the Polish court has handed down a clear verdict that antisemitic hate speech is illegal in Poland. We are hopeful that the Polish courts will continue to find others guilty of this crime." After the verdict, Woźnicki lashed out in comments to journalists. "I am convicted of preaching," he reportedly said. "Apparently, the Jews do not like me very much because I love the Lord Jesus. As a non-Jew, I concede to the Jewish king, while the Jews do not so much to their king."[42]

The skewed version of history touted by right-wing Polish nationalist groups has found some allies in a group of committed editors on the English-language Wikipedia, the world's largest encyclopedia online. Their systematic, intentional distortion of history minimizes Polish antisemitism, exaggerates the Poles' role in saving Jews during the Holocaust, insinuates that most Jews supported Communism and conspired with Communists to betray Poles (Żydokomuna or Judeo-Bolshevism), blames Jews for their own persecution, and inflates Jewish collaboration with the Nazis. A review in early February 2023 in the *Journal of Holocaust Research* by Grabowski and Professor Shira Klein of twenty-five public-facing Wikipedia articles and nearly 300 of Wikipedia's back pages, supplemented by interviews with editors in the field, reveals the digital mechanisms by which ideological zeal, prejudice, and bias trump reason and historical accuracy. While nothing ties these distortionist editors to the Polish government, the two historians conclude that Wikipedia's "inadequate safeguards will encourage state-sponsored agents to enter the scene, as has already happened in other cases."[43]

An announcement from the office of Israel's prime minister on March 7, 2023, that Israeli high school trips to visit the death camps in Poland are set to resume after a three-year hiatus was seen by Israeli as a sign of thawing relations with that country. "The lessons of the Holocaust can be learned in many ways, but there is nothing better than seeing it with one's one eyes," said Binyamin

Netanyahu. Foreign Minister Eli Cohen added that resuming these trips "is of great importance in shaping the national identity of the youth, and familiarity with the history of the people of Israel in general, and preserving the memory of the Holocaust in particular." The announcement made no mention of how the matter was resolved, and whether Israel had agreed to changes to the curriculum that would strengthen the Polish narrative of the historical events. The Ynet news site reported that an agreement had been reached that Polish security would protect the trips, while Israeli guards would be allowed to attend in cases of specific threats.[44]

At the month's end, Warsaw's acting ambassador to Israel, Agata Czaplińska, declared that Jerusalem's decision last year to reinstate its ambassador to Poland, coming three days after the outbreak of Russia's war against Ukraine, played "an instrumental role" in improving relations between the two countries. The "circumstances" on our eastern border with Ukraine required the presence of the "very helpful" Israeli ambassador, she noted, with Poland serving as the key gateway from Ukraine during that war and Israel helping extricate citizens and refugees from the war-torn nation. It was agreed that Polish security will provide protection for Israeli youngsters visiting her country in coordination with Israeli security officials, and each side presenting recommended sites to visit in their respective countries for youth to get a "broader understanding of the centuries of history that their two peoples shared" before the Holocaust. More interaction between young Israelis and Poles will be included "to counter prejudice and stereotypes," which Czaplinska felt was "the perfect vehicle for understanding and cooperation."[45]

Three days later, Poland's deputy prime minister, Piotr Gliński, told a conference in the European Union parliament in Brussels commemorating the eightieth anniversary of the Warsaw Ghetto Revolt that "in Poland, antisemitism is not allowed and there is no place for it in our country." "Jewish people can feel safe in Poland," Glinski added. He also described antisemitic incidents in Poland as "isolated" and "fifteen times less numerous than in Germany," the *European Jewish Press* reported. Glinski told the conference, which was organized by the European Jewish Association (EJA) and the Social and Cultural Association of Jews in Poland (TSAZ), that antisemitic incidents "must be combated, including through education, both about the Holocaust and the many centuries during which Poles and Jews have coexisted."[46]

Yet a close look at the agreement to have Israeli teenagers resume visits to Poland reveals the stipulation that they will be required to visit sites related to "other crimes of World War II." This refers to museums and memorial sites that document crimes committed by the Germans against non-Jewish Poles.

The agreement also includes an appendix with a list of such sites, from which the Israeli student delegations must select at least one to visit. Some of these sites "ignore documented aspects of Poles' involvement in the murder of Jews," and others, observes Professor Havi Dreifuss of Tel-Aviv University, actually "glorify Poles who were involved up to their necks in the murder of Jews."

Highlighting the Markowa Ulma-Family Museum because that family hid eight Jews and paid for it with their lives, for example, distorts the far more common phenomenon of Poles killing Jews and aiding the Germans. Further, museums dedicated to Poles who fought the country's communist occupation obscures some, such as Jozef Kuras ("Ogień"), who were involved in murdering Jews in Poland. Professor Grabowski, even more scathing in his description of this list, responded thus: "What you have here is the 'Polish wish-list' of where Israeli youth should go. It reads like a Holocaust denier's dream." The fact that Israeli and Polish youth are being jointly called upon in this agreement to combat hatred of the other is highly controversial as well, confusing antisemitism, one of the causes of the *Shoah*, and anti-Polonism, which derives, in part, from the actual role played by Poles in exacerbating Jew-hatred and participating in the Holocaust. Yad Vashem called these additions "inappropriate" and "problematic." Together with Israel's education ministry, it declared that tours to Poland can take place exactly as in the past, with no changes in the future.[47]

Talking about the "Jewish problem" remains a great challenge in Poland. Antisemitism has not disappeared, while prevalent universalizing of the Holocaust refuses to acknowledge that the Jews, not the Poles, faced annihilation, and that the majority of Poles were either apathetic or overtly hostile to their Jewish neighbors when one people was targeted in World War II for death with no reprieve by the Third Reich and its collaborator nations. "There can be no reconciliation without remembrance," declared Federal President Richard von Weizsäcker, the son of convicted Nuremberg war criminal Ernst von Weizsäcker, to the West German Bundestag in Bonn on May 8, 1985, convened that day to commemorate the fortieth anniversary of the end of World War Two in Europe and of "National-Socialist Tyranny."[48] With the twenty-first century proceeding apace, decades after Nazi terror darkened a continent and, fueled by racist ideology, destroyed European Jewry, it is time for a full, honest healing to begin.

CHAPTER 8

The Jews Were Expendable: Free World Diplomacy and the Holocaust – Forty Years Later

———————

At first, I had no intention of researching and then writing what would eventually become *The Jews Were Expendable: Free World Diplomacy and the Holocaust*. Having completed my dissertation in June 1970 for a doctorate in US history, a study which focused on the Federal Writers' Project within the Works Progress Administration during the Great Depression, I turned to my Columbia University mentor for advice. Aware that I was keenly interested in Zionism, William E. Leuchtenburg suggested that I proceed to an examination of Harry S Truman and Israel's creation. I soon discovered that the papers at the Truman presidential library were not yet fully available for inspection, and so returned to Professor Leuchtenburg's office on the sixth floor of Fayerweather Hall. He proposed, as an alternative, that I shift my attention to Franklin D. Roosevelt in this regard. So began my next major scholarly effort.

The choice was a fortuitous one. Other than knowing a good deal about FDR as the result of seven years of graduate study, I had just obtained a full-time assistant professorship to teach American history at Bard College in Annandale-on-Hudson. This bucolic academic retreat lay but a half-hour drive away from the Roosevelt presidential library in Hyde Park, New York. I could thus spend a full day each week sifting through document after document, uncovering much that had long been awaiting an historian's eye. I also put the final touches on a revised and expanded dissertation for my first book, *The Federal Writers' Project: A Study in Government Patronage of the Arts*, which would be published by the University of Illinois Press in 1977. As for Roosevelt and Palestine, my first significant contribution to this contentious subject surfaced a year later. "The 1943 Joint Anglo-American Statement on Palestine," appearing in volume eight of the *Herzl Yearbook*, revealed in depth how Roosevelt and Churchill seriously considered issuing a proclamation that would rule out public discussion of the Palestine conundrum until the end of World War II.[1]

By then, in addition to visiting numerous archives and interviewing individuals across the United States, I had made two forays during the summers of 1972 and 1976 to archives in Israel and in Great Britain. My initial visit to the Public Record Office in the heart of London had the added benefit of a first conversation with Yehuda Bauer, who was then combing through the newly opened wartime records of the British government for his own analysis of the Holocaust years. I continued to concentrate on my study of the Palestine question during World War II.

What altered this focus? Or, to be more exact, what broadened it? The answer actually rests in a miniseries by Gerald Green for the NBC TV channel. Green (born Gerald Greenberg in 1922 in Brooklyn), a Columbia College graduate who edited the US Army's *Stars and Stripes* newspaper during World War II, had achieved literary prominence with his best-known novel, *The Last Angry Man*. In 1978, his four-part teleplay *Holocaust* appeared in April and went on to win eight Emmy Awards, including one for "Outstanding Writing in a Drama Series." However criticized by some, beginning with Elie Wiesel in the *New York Times*, for trivializing the singular horror of the *Shoah*, the intertwined stories of two German families, Weiss and Dorf, captivated an estimated 300 million viewers in the United States and elsewhere. Like Alex Haley's TV series *Roots* a year earlier, which portrayed a family saga of the American slave tragedy and its aftermath, *Holocaust* alerted many to something of which they were ignorant. This nine-hour series, with a transatlantic cast featuring an early appearance by Meryl Streep, soon saw print as a best-selling novel.[2]

In January 1979, the TV series was aired in West Germany. Watched by twenty million people or fifty percent of that nation's population, it first brought the matter of the systematic slaughter of European Jewry in World War II to widespread public attention in a way that it had never been before. After each part of *Holocaust* was aired, a panel of historians in a companion show answered questions from people calling in to the TV station. Thousands of telephone calls arrived from shocked and outraged Germans, a great many of whom stated that they were born after 1945 and this was the first time they learned that their country had carried out the mass murder of Jews in World War II. The German historian Alf Lüdtke wrote that the historians "could not cope," as they were faced with thousands of angry callers asking how these things could happen or why they had never learned about them at school. Subsequently, the *Gesellschaft für deutsche Sprache* named the term "Holocaust" as German Word of the Year. Green's teleplay was also credited with persuading the West

German government to repeal the statute of limitations on Nazi war crimes. In recognition for his effort, Green was awarded the Dag Hammarskjöld International Peace Prize for literature in 1979. That same year, he edited *The Artists of Terezin*, which would be followed by his receiving an Emmy nomination for the 1985 TV script *Wallenberg: A Hero's Story*.[3]

I had known something of the Holocaust. Although no courses on the topic were then available in undergraduate study at Yeshiva College or in Columbia's graduate faculties, and no member of my close family was killed in Nazi-occupied Europe, two books in my parents' library had first sparked my interest and concern. *The Black Book, The Nazi Crime Against the Jewish People*, published in 1946 by the World Jewish Congress, the Jewish Anti-Fascist Committee, the Va'ad Le'umi, and the America Committee of Jewish Writers, Artists and Scientists, presented a most damning indictment. So, did, in a far different fashion, Ben Hecht's autobiographical *A Child of the Century*. Nothing prepared me, however, for Arthur Morse's searing critique of the US government's response during world Jewry's most tragic hour. *While Six Million Died: A Chronicle of American Apathy*, a best-seller when it first appeared in 1967, opened my eyes to the need for rigorous analysis of the *Shoah* in its various dimensions that would be rooted in primary documentation. Slowly, I made my way through Raul Hilberg's magisterial *The Destruction of the European Jews* (undertaking this with a one-volume paperback edition!) and Lucy Dawidowicz's well-received *The War against the Jews*, reading Holocaust memoirs along the way. Important volumes by David Wyman, Henry Feingold, and Saul Friedman on the American government, with an admirable study by Bernard Wasserstein about its British counterpart, took their place together with *Yad Vashem Studies* and many others on my rapidly growing bookshelves.[4]

I came to realize, to my surprise, that, while numerous works ably reviewed the actions of German and other killers and of their Jewish victims across the European geography of grief, a broad analysis of what could be termed the world of "bystanders" had yet to be written. Green's *Holocaust* TV series scarcely touched on this vital third leg of a triad, but the attention which it garnered worldwide convinced me that the effort had to be made. With some trepidation, and hardly aware of what such an endeavor would entail, I contacted Richard L. Wentworth, formerly editor-in-chief and now director of the University of Illinois Press. Prepared to postpone my commitment to examining the Palestine dilemma, I suggested that taking a wider perspective, covering various aspects of bystander reactions, could present a much needed and welcome contribution. Wentworth readily agreed, and I set out on a demanding journey of exploration.

Re-reading now my first essay on the Palestine dilemma in World War II—published back in 1978!—I am struck by these lines in the concluding paragraphs:

> Hitler's paranoid rantings to the contrary notwithstanding, the Jews were anything but a powerful international force. Having no state of their own—the Zionists had always grasped this—Jews could conveniently be considered expendable in the war years. The democracies' silence about the rescue of European Jewry and Palestinian Jewry's war contribution was also exemplified dramatically in the joint statement, even though that statement did not appear....
>
> Adolf Hitler had won his war against the Jews: the 4,000,000 victims reported in August, 1943, were joined by an additional 2,000,000 when the Third Reich's *Götterdammerung* sounded. Against his determination and the failure of his opponents to meet the unparalleled crisis of the Holocaust with extraordinary measures, the Zionists' rare success regarding the joint statement ultimately counted for nought. It would be up to the post-war world, stricken by a guilty conscience after the event, to try and make some amends.[5]

Herein, as it would turn out, lay the kernel of the thesis for the subsequent volume. The future title itself surfaces as well: the Jews were expendable. Yet all this remained in embryo. Countless hours of research would be mandatory before I could commence to paint a very broad but much detailed canvas. How to set out? What issues merited scrutiny?

Quickly understanding that the subject at hand was too vast and complex for inclusion between the covers of one book, I came to choose nine case studies on the diplomacy of the Holocaust. I hoped that the conclusions of these separate studies, when taken together, would possess an underlying unity. Chronology would guide the chapters. As month after month rolled by, I became especially mindful of Fustel de Coulanges's trenchant observation that "years of analysis are required for one day of synthesis."[6] Fortunately, a few grants, buttressed by the support of family, friends, and helpful archivists, made both exercises possible. Several hitherto closed archives and private collections were opened to me as well.

I began with the struggle during World War II for an Allied Jewish fighting force and the "illegal" immigration of Jewish refugees to the national home in Palestine. These issues appeared paramount for many concerned about Jewry's fate under the swastika before the tragedy's true nature was realized beyond the borders of Hitler's *Festung Europa*. The unveiling in the free world of what the Third Reich leadership deemed to be the "Final Solution of the Jewish Question," as well as the immediate responses that followed, was traced in the third chapter. A fourth examined the 1943 Bermuda Conference and its aftermath once the Anglo-American Alliance had officially acknowledged on December 17, 1942, the relentless annihilation of European Jewry. The genesis of the US War Refugee Board in January 1944 was then described at great length. Succeeding chapters explored various attempts to rescue Jews from the Balkans and the martyrdom of Hungarian Jewry—the Holocaust in microcosm. The final stage in the murder of Europe's Jews was then viewed from two distinct perspectives: the confrontation between the World Jewish Congress and the International Red Cross, and the overtures to *Reichsführer* SS Heinrich Himmler by the Sternbuchs of Montreux and Hilel Storch of Stockholm. The epilogue presented an overview of the *Shoah* and its implications for human survival.

The understandable anguish that a historian of the Holocaust experiences proved palpable, but significant revelations throughout made the arduous task worthwhile. Four examples among many will suffice. A letter in the Hagana Archives disclosed that Moshe Shertok (later Sharett), then the Jewish Agency for Palestine's chief political officer, gave the signal in November 1940 to place a small bomb on the ill-fated French liner *Patria* in an attempt to halt the British deportation from Haifa Bay of more than 1,700 Jews who had fled Nazi persecution and lacked Palestine immigration certificates. A reading of Leon Kubowitzki's overlooked diary in the Yad Vashem Archives uncovered, for the first time to the public, the identity of Eduard Schulte, a highly placed German industrialist who transmitted word to the West of a program discussed in Hitler's headquarters to build huge crematoria in order to eradicate all of Europe's Jews with prussic acid in the autumn of 1942. With trembling hands, I held a forgotten memoir in the YIVO Archives, written in Yiddish in a Polish forest by a man who escaped during the Treblinka death camp revolt of August 2, 1943. I was also able to trace the remarkable activities of a group of young Palestinian Jewish emissaries in Turkey who, discarding legal convention and political differences, brought a few thousand souls to the Jewish homeland and safety in 1944.[7]

What ultimately emerged from the years of painstaking labor? This first overview of the free world's failure to respond decisively to the Holocaust revealed a fundamental reality. The confluence of disbelief, indifference, antisemitism, and, above all, political expediency that obtained in Western counsels helped doom a powerless people to the diabolic realization of the Nazis' mechanized kingdom of death.

Allied callousness toward the Jewish people reflected a different elementary failure of perception. Having at first misjudged the dimensions of the Holocaust, London and Washington continued to deny Jewry the sense of communal distinction that had accounted for its mysterious survival these past 4,000 years. Heir to the Enlightenment's emphasis on personal freedom and the good inherent in all human beings, the West concluded that according the one people lacking national sovereignty special consideration as an independent entity would mean the vindication of Hitler's philosophy of *das Volk*. The postwar world, these officials publicly declared, should ensure Jews the full rights of citizens everywhere. Paradoxically, this meant that the unique fate of European Jewry was either concealed under "Poles," "Belgians," etc., or refused sympathy because Jews were classified as "enemy aliens" when found in countries loyal to the Axis. In either instance Hitler—who thought otherwise—secured his primary objective.

Thus it never occurred to the Anglo-American Alliance, which alone could have checked the tempo of slaughter and rescued thousands of innocents whose paramount crime in Nazi eyes was that of birth, that Europe's Jews, like other peoples opposed to the Third Reich, should be assigned any role in the general war strategy. Greeks would obtain relief to avert famine, Poles and Czechs arms for resistance, but not Jews. French youngsters in very impressive numbers could be spirited to safety across the Pyrenees, but not a targeted people to haven in neutral Spain and Turkey. Tens of thousands of Yugoslavs and Greeks received a cordial welcome in Middle East refugee camps, yet His Majesty's Government in London continued the draconian 1939 White Paper limiting immigration to Palestine throughout World War II for those most needing their accessible homeland. The two major Western powers, worried lest the German leadership "embarrass" the Allies by "flooding" them with unwanted Jews, sought to stifle public discussion of Palestine's future as long as the war lasted. For the same reason, they mutually consented not to alter their respective limited immigration quotas. Enemy prisoners fared far better: boats were found to ferry some 430,000 to camps in the United States during the world conflict.

Churchill and Roosevelt, along with Stalin, omitted the Jewish people from the 1943 Moscow Conference's lengthy formal statement about those who were victim to Nazi atrocities. Neither leader, in the course of their secret correspondence with one another, raised the possibility of rescuing the particular targets of Hitler's obsessive hatred. Both focused on the period after the war—too late for those found on a globe, to cite World Zionist Organization president Chaim Weizmann, "divided into countries in which the Jews cannot live and countries which they must not enter." Not a word of the infamous SS death marches from the fall of 1944 onward appeared in SHAEF directives or in the Western press. The Intergovernmental Committee on Refugees, the Bermuda Conference on Refugees, and the War Refugee Board all omitted mention in their titles of the one group for which each had been principally created. For most of World War II, these officially designated nonpersons did not fare better with self-professed guardians of humanitarianism and morality like the International Red Cross and the Vatican, or with the five neutral governments. Moscow ignored the entire matter.

Only one Jewish battalion and a tiny parachute unit from the Jewish *Yishuv* in Palestine saw action, and these grudging concessions from 10 Downing Street and 1600 Pennsylvania Avenue were not granted until toward the end of the war. Nineteen RAF de Havilland Mosquito bombers escorted by Spitfires successfully attacked an Amiens prison in "Operation Jericho" on February 18, 1944, to free nearly 100 members of the French resistance, but the Auschwitz crematoria and the railroad lines leading to them, near which Allied bombers regularly flew to bomb German oil factories that summer, never became prime targets. The director of the War Refugee Board gave an account of the Amiens assault to the US undersecretary of war in a failed effort to have the lines to Auschwitz-Birkenau bombed.

Reprisals on German cities expressly for atrocities against Jews, the dispatch of funds for underground rescue, and delaying negotiations over the Adolf Eichmann "goods for blood" offer were all ruled out by the West. Responses to specific, practicable evacuation proposals concerning Jews in Transnistria, France, Romania, Bulgaria, and Hungary were not commensurate with the urgent need. Szmul Zygielbojm's suicide, meant to move Churchill, Roosevelt, and the free world to action in mid-1943, went unheeded. FDR fled from 400 Orthodox rabbis who marched on Washington that October; the British prime minister avoided Weizmann. Instead, to defeat the enemy and have the Jews return to their European "homes" after the war served as the fixed philosophy for the duration. Alas, that policy proved bankrupt to the one people singled out for death in the war years.

The Jews Were Expendable, whose title was soon to become part and parcel of the lexicon of Holocaust Studies, drew much praise. Professor Richard Polenberg of Cornell University declared the volume "a major work and one upon which all future studies of the Holocaust will rely. It is an impressive and admirable achievement." "A tour de force... written in dispassionate yet vivid prose," concluded a reviewer for *American Jewish History*. The book, a finalist for the National Jewish Book Award in Holocaust Studies that year, received the B'nai Brith Anti-Defamation League Merit of Education Distinction and Yeshiva University's Belkin Memorial Literary Award. It went into a second hardcover printing one year later, with a paperback issued by Wayne State University Press in 1988.

Few scholarly volumes, however carefully prepared, are without their flaws, and *The Jews Were Expendable* is no exception. Rising antisemitic sentiment in the United States, the apathy or negligence of various government agencies besides the State Department (Treasury and Interior proved to be the exceptions), and why American Jewry overwhelmingly supported Roosevelt deserved more focus. Sustained explanation for the moral collapse of the free world at large in the face of on-going mass murder was necessary. The same is true for other concerns which pressed in upon the bystanders during World War II, preventing a full grasp of the reality of the Holocaust and the taking of possible action.

The conclusion to chapter three, in particular, should have been rephrased. Its last paragraph stated that European Jewry "would fall victim to the democracies' procrastination and unsurpassed callousness, as well to the Nazis' prussic acid, first mentioned to London and Washington in [Gerhart] Riegner's cable of August 8, 1942." No. As Richard J. Evans recently observed, losing one's moral compass is not the same as setting it to mass murder.[8] Rather, the sentence should have read that European Jewry "would fall victim to the Nazis' prussic acid...." The final sentence of that chapter can stand: "And from Allied and Axis camps alike, thunderous silence."

The Jews Were Expendable also details how a few courageous souls attempted to shatter the Allied conspiracy of silence, as well as the prevailing illusion that nothing could be done. Yet their valiant race against calculated mass-production death wrested only limited successes. Hitler, Himmler, Eichmann, Ion Antonescu, Miklós Horthy, and others like them believed with apocalyptic certainty that a demonic international Jewry controlled Germany's opponents; the West, in whose councils the stateless Jews commanded no political leverage, consigned the Third Reich's primary victim to one category: expendable. Behind the mask called twentieth-century civilization, as a consequence, countless more worlds were destroyed.

In the four decades since the volume's publication, many studies have appeared on the world of the bystanders. Some are outstanding, others less so. Most add to our understanding of responses by those who stood by while outside of Hitler's grasp. They include governments, organizations, and individuals who had to confront the call of conscience while the German *Führer* resolutely created hell on earth in ways surpassing at times even Dante Alighieri's fevered imagination in the tortured vision of the *Divine Comedy*.

Heading the list is David Wyman's magnum opus, *The Abandonment of the Jews*, which appeared one year after *The Jews Were Expendable*. This extensive study of US government policy during the Holocaust enjoyed enthusiastic reviews and garnered several awards. It went through seven hardcover printings and a paperback edition, was translated into German, French, Hebrew, and Polish, and sold more than 150,000 copies worldwide.[9]

Wyman, the grandson of two Protestant ministers, issued a *J'accuse* against the Allied wartime leadership, and the Roosevelt administration in particular, for passive complicity in the Holocaust. His charge had first been leveled in "Why Auschwitz Was Never Bombed," to be chapter fifteen in this book, which appeared in the May 1978 issue of *Commentary* and aroused a major controversy in the press. Wyman's meticulous account explored how many segments of the American population—including the churches and segments of the Jewish community except for small groups like the one led by Hillel Kook (Peter Bergson) and the Orthodox Va'ad HaHatzala—did little to aid European Jewry. It exposes the failure of the State Department for leaving ninety percent of the US immigration quotas unfilled, and the continuous pattern of deceptions by which the government rejected proposals for relief and rescue that were made, no matter their feasibility.

What might be called the "Auschwitz Bombing Controversy" claimed the most headlines. James H. Kitchens III, an archivist at the United States Air Force Historical Research Center, argued counter to Wyman that the Allies did not have sufficiently detailed intelligence about the location of these facilities to reasonably target them, and the logistics of bombing would have been too difficult to reasonably expect a successful result. Richard H. Levy, a retired nuclear engineer, supported Kitchens' position. Many historians, however, including Martin Gilbert and Stuart Erdheim, pointed out that the Allies not only flew near Auschwitz-Birkenau to bomb nearby oil refineries and over the rail lines leading to that death center in 1944, but they had opportunities to acquire sufficient military intelligence on potential Auschwitz targets; Dino Brugioni and Richard Breitman added that no concerted effort was made to gather and evaluate such information. Others have observed that Allied bombing missions which were just as difficult proved successful, and these were supported by comparably incomplete intelligence. Yet Michael Fleming has shown that the Allies had extensive knowledge already in 1942 of the mass killing of Jews at

Auschwitz, but publicizing of this vital information was actively discouraged by the authorities in Great Britain and the United States.[10]

Several historians observe that a considerable number of Jews were saved, and argue that even more could have been rescued. *The Jews Were Expendable* had previously shown that persistent pressure in Congress on the Roosevelt administration by the "Bergson Boys," coupled with crucial support from Treasury Secretary Henry Morgenthau, Jr., led to the establishment of the War Refugee Board. The board supported, among other actions, the heroic mission of Raoul Wallenberg in Budapest and Ira Hirschmann's successful efforts from Turkey to save Jews in Transnistria. David Kranzler noted that protection papers handed out from Switzerland by George Mantello (a Salvadorian diplomat) and Recha Sternbuch saved large numbers over the objections of some US officials. Mantello publicized what has now been called the Wetzler-Vrba Report included in the Auschwitz Protocol, which helped lead to successful appeals from some leaders that Horthy halt the transports leading to Auschwitz. Horthy's offer to permit emigration of all Jewish children under ten who possessed visas to other countries, and all Jews of any age who possessed Palestine certificates, failed due to the month-long delay in negotiations by the Allies and neutral governments; in the end the Nazis took control.

Sharon Lowenstein showed that Roosevelt's single approval in mid-1944 of transporting fewer than 1,000 Jewish refugees from Europe to Ft. Oswego, New York, where they had to remain behind barbed wire and then return "home," represented but a "token refuge." The "dilatory treatment of the Jewish catastrophe evolved into a steady practice," concluded Hilberg in a chapter on the Allied powers, who negated the requests of Jewish leaders for rescue "even though the requested actions were within the realm of the possible."[11]

William Rubinstein took an extreme position in his rejoinder to Wyman, pointedly calling his book *The Myth of Rescue*. With little archival research, Rubinstein even went so far as to assert that "not one plan or proposal, made anywhere in the democracies by either Jews or non-Jewish champions of the Jews once the mass murder of the Jews of Europe had begun, could have rescued one single Jew who perished in the Nazi *Holocaust* [sic]." For this specialist on Britain's economic elites, the Western powers had a creditable record, Palestine was not a potential refuge, and effective allied action against the death camps was not possible. Not the British government but Jewish Agency Executive head David Ben-Gurion and other Zionist leaders in Palestine are primarily to blame for not giving refuge to European Jews, in his opinion, an accusation that David Cesarani rightly dismissed as unscholarly polemic. Historians of Allied responses to the *Shoah* blasted Rubinstein's book as extremist and filled with arguments that, in the words of Walter Laqueur, "are flatly and often outrageously wrong."[12]

Far more judicious and balanced studies came from Israeli scholars. Yehuda Bauer's volume on the American Jewish Joint Distribution Committee's activities during the war years, as well as his fascinating book *Jews for Sale?*, added new facets to Holocaust Studies. Dina Porat's *Hanhaga b'Malkod*, later translated as *The Blue and the Yellow Stars of David: The Zionist Leadership in Palestine and the Holocaust, 1939–1945*, deservedly earned the Yad Ben-Zvi Prize. Sensitivity and perception were also evident in Dalia Ofer's study of "illegal" immigration to Palestine; examinations by Hava Eshkoli and Yechiam Weitz of the Mapai labor party during the Holocaust; Hava Eshkoli Wagman's review of the Mizrachi religious Zionist party in that time; Tuvia Friling's two-volume work on Ben-Gurion in World War II; Efraim Zuroff's book on the activities of the US-based Orthodox group Va'ad haHatzala; Zohar Segev's study of the World Jewish Congress's efforts; Shlomo Aronson's *Hitler, the Allies, and the Jews*; and Judy Tydor Baumel-Schwartz's books on the Bergson group and on the *Yishuv*'s parachutists to Europe.[13]

Wyman's description of the callous neglect of the Roosevelt administration in the face of history's most monstrous evil, going so far as to call FDR's indifference the worst failure of his presidency, triggered an outburst of understanding and support for the American chief executive. Richard Breitman and Alan Kraut's study of US refugee policy and European Jewry from 1933 through 1945 first ascribed most importance to preexisting restrictive immigration laws that were hewed to by a rigid State Department, an antisemitic and pro-restrictionist American public, and Roosevelt's reluctance to accept "the inherent political risks of humanitarian measures on behalf of foreign Jews."

Ten years later, examining closely what the British and Americans knew of Nazi plans, Breitman concluded that the West could have made a "considerable difference" in saving lives before the War Refugee Board's creation "if there had been a will to do so." Yet in their recent *FDR and the Jews*, Breitman and Allan Lichtman seek almost every possibility in order to vindicate the president's stand. For example, they assert that he "broke the logjam on Jewish refugees in 1936," although Breitman had asserted in the 1980s that no evidence exists that Roosevelt issued instructions to liberalize immigration policies in 1936–1937. Neither savior nor bystander, in their view, this supreme pragmatist had to make compromises, but he reacted "more decisively" to Nazi crimes against Jews than did any other world leader of his time. (This is "damning with faint praise," Jerold Auerbach responded.) Robert Rosen, a divorce lawyer in Charleston,

South Carolina, went far further than Breitman and Lichtman in the lengthiest defense of FDR, calling his book *Saving the Jews, Franklin D. Roosevelt and the Holocaust*.[14]

None were more steadfast champions than administrators of the Roosevelt Institute and the Franklin D. Roosevelt Presidential Library. William vanden Heuvel, an attorney and founder of the Franklin and Eleanor Roosevelt Institute, argued in articles and lectures that the only way to help the Jews was to win the war. Faced with Wyman's relentless moral judgments in retrospect, New Deal historian Arthur Schlesinger, Jr. also took vanden Huevel's stance, and defended FDR against any suspicion that he was unsympathetic to Jews. Vanden Heuvel endorsed Gerhard L. Weinberg's claim that the United States accepted about twice as many Jewish refugees as the rest of the world put together ("about 200,000 out of 300,000"), although Breitman and Kraut's figure for German and Austrian immigrants totaled under 75,000 for the years 1933–1939.

In 1996, a volume entitled *FDR and the Holocaust*, edited by Verne W. Newton, director of the Roosevelt library, came to print with essays that favored the president. The following year, Schlesinger's posthumously published diaries revealed that vanden Heuvel's secret campaign had successfully persuaded the US Holocaust Museum to revise its original accurate text in a major exhibit: "American Jewish organizations repeatedly asked the U.S. War Department to bomb Auschwitz" became transformed to "A few Jewish leaders called for the bombing of the Auschwitz gas chambers; others opposed it. . . . No one was certain of the results. . . ." The Resident Historian at the Franklin and Eleanor Roosevelt Institute David B. Woolner lauded the Breitman and Lichtman volume in the *Journal of American History*; this reviewer, not a Holocaust specialist, erred significantly therein, for example, by crediting an actually reluctant Roosevelt and Zionist herald Stephen Wise with the creation of the War Refugee Board.[15]

The increasing defense of Roosevelt, as well as of Allied inaction, moved Wyman and Rafael Medoff, founding director of the David S. Wyman Institute for Holocaust Studies as of 2003, to "shine a spotlight on those Americans who had not abandoned the Jews." The staff of the Institute, based in Washington, D.C., interviewed rabbis who had participated in the march to the White House on October 6, 1943, three days before Yom Kippur—the only such effort during the *Shoah*—to stir FDR to action. One year later, Wyman and Medoff published *A Race against Death*, highlighting the incessant efforts of the "Bergson Boys" to alert the American public to the Holocaust and to the possibilities for rescue. Subsequently, a portrait of the march on the capital and materials about the Bergsonites appeared in the permanent exhibit of the US Holocaust Memorial Museum; in July 2011, Yad Vashem hosted a joint conference with the Wyman Institute, celebrating the seventieth anniversary of the Bergson group's creation. With the Institute's involvement, Harry Bingham IV, a rogue US diplomat who, with Vivian Fry, smuggled over 2,000 Jews out of Vichy France, was honored with his likeness on a US postage stamp. The American boycotters of the 1936 Olympics in Berlin were honored at numerous events in the Jewish community, and their children and grandchildren followed in their footsteps by taking part in human rights protests related to the 2008 Olympics in China.

A petition organized by the Wyman Institute asked US newspaper publishers to acknowledge their moral failure for having downplayed coverage of Hitler's tyranny and of Nazi assaults against Jews. It was signed by eighty leading journalists and editors, including *New Republic* editor-in-chief Martin Peretz, Marvin Kalb of "Meet the Press," and Columbia Journalism School dean Nicholas Lemann. Many publishers publicly apologized for their actions in that decade, and invited Laurel Leff, a member of the Institute's academic council, to address their board of directors. Leff's analysis of how and why the *New York Times* buried stories of the Holocaust in its back pages offered yet another key aspect of bystander response. In so doing, her volume followed in the wake of related books by Haskel Lookstein, Robert Ross, and Deborah E. Lipstadt.[16]

Medoff went on to author a series of related books. In the spirit of his first study of the American Jewish leadership in the Holocaust years, *The Deafening Silence*, the Wyman Institute's director authored a volume on Josiah DuBois, Jr., a member of the Treasury Department staff who successfully pressed in the latter half of 1943 for an activist government response. With David Golinkin, Medoff wrote about three rabbinic students who sought to shatter the silence regarding European Jewry's unmatched tragedy. He then edited an autobiographical account by Samuel Merlin of the Bergsonites' campaign to save Jews. A study of Herbert Hoover and the Jews, co-authored with Sonja S. Wentling, appeared the same year as Medoff's creative examination with Craig Yoe of American political cartoonists who used their art to have the public demand the rescue of Hitler's primary victims.[17]

All this culminated in Medoff's *FDR and the Holocaust: A Breach of Faith*. A first chapter charges that Roosevelt's private wish to restrict the number of Jews entering some professions and universities, joined to his belief that Jews should be "spread thin all over the world" so they would quickly assimilate, helped shape the president's attitudes towards immigration and rescue during the Holocaust. (200,000 US immigration quota places were left unused in that period.) Requests to bomb Auschwitz or the railway lines leading to it were made directly to Secretary of State Cordell Hull and Secretary of War Henry Stimson, both of whom misleadingly claimed that the proposal did not fall within their area of responsibility. Although a futile effort, individuals and editors did press the administration to undertake relief and rescue. Senator and Democratic presidential candidate George McGovern, a twenty-two-year-old B-24 Liberator bomber pilot in World War II, claimed years later that an ordered strike against Auschwitz could have slowed down the killing process there; a strong majority of Jewish leaders in the United States and Palestine favored such an assault. A later chapter in the book points out several assertions by Roosevelt defenders that are not warranted by the actual record. The assumptions—then and much later—of the president's humanitarianism, Medoff concludes, "proved to be unfounded."[18]

The debate over Roosevelt and the Allied powers vis-à-vis the Holocaust, at times acrimonious, gained a momentum all its own. Lucy Dawidowicz regularly denounced the Bergsonites (whom I had praised in 1981 when writing the first documented overview of the group's various activities) as hampering the cause of rescue, and she noted that America focused properly on winning the war against Germany. This did not sit well with some who contributed to an investigatory report, edited by Seymour M. Finger, which castigated both American Jewish leaders and the Roosevelt administration. In a collection of essays, Henry Feingold argued that the constraints of the domestic political system and the extraordinary events of the time made it virtually impossible for the government and American Jews to react differently. Yet other historians countered, for example, that the United States brought more than 400,000 enemy soldiers to the safety of its shores, where they fared far better than the few Jewish refugees in Ft. Oswego; that the British, who made virtually no attempts at the rescue of Jews, provided ships to bring 20,000 Muslims on a religious pilgrimage from Egypt to Mecca in the middle of the war; that General George Patton even diverted US troops in Austria to save 150 of the famous Lipizzaner dancing horses.

So disgusted was Leon Wieseltier with Dawidowicz's defense against Wyman's withering indictment of US government passivity—even accusing Wyman of anti-Americanism, that he refused to publish Dawidowicz's piece in the *New Republic*. (It would appear elsewhere.) "My conscience would not allow it," the literary editor told her. They never spoke again.[19]

To replace heat with light, all interested in assigning these topics their proper historical context would do well to begin with the primary record itself. A thirteen-volume set of documents upon which Wyman drew for his work appeared some years later under the title *America and the Holocaust*. Robert H. Abzug, author of a riveting account of soldiers who reached the major concentration camps in Germany at the war's end, offered a brief annotated documentary history, which demonstrated the variety of American understandings of the Holocaust as it occurred. Dina Porat and Yechiam Weitz edited a representative collection of primary documents dealing with the *Yishuv*'s contemporary responses to the *Shoah*. The Vatican, censured in books by John Morley and John Cornwell, has released ten documentary volumes of its activities during World War II. A multivolume series of documents and photographs, edited by Henry Friedlander and Sybil Milton under the title *Archives of the Holocaust*, draws on an internationally representative group of archives in five countries on three continents. Finally, a very useful collection of articles on bystanders, written by many specialists in the field, can be found in a three-volume collection edited by Michael Marrus. From here onwards, with diligent research in the pertinent archives, analysis and synthesis may begin.[20]

Many aspects relating to bystanders still await scrupulous investigation, some of which were suggested in an international conference entitled "Rescue Attempts during the Holocaust" that Yad Vashem sponsored in 1974 and published three years later. For example, Meir Dworzecki, in a last article before his death, wrote about the policy of the International Committee of the Red Cross regarding Jews under Nazi rule. I explored this further with the benefit of the archives of the World Jewish Congress, then stored in a dank warehouse on New York City's upper East Side, that Gerhart Riegner opened to me in the late 1970s.

In 1988, Jean-Claude Favez's official study of the ICRC, *Une Mission Impossible?*, was first published in French and later translated into German and English. At the close of 1996, the ICRC in Geneva turned over copies of its files—25,000 microfilmed pages—to the US Holocaust Memorial Museum. Some of the documents provided verification that the ICRC knew of the persecution of Jews in Nazi camps but felt powerless to speak out. ICRC inspectors wrote positive reports after visiting the Nazi "model ghetto" of Theresienstadt. For the most part, its assistance came late in the war and had limited effect. Admitting that his organization "has shared responsibility for the silence of the world community," archivist Georges Willemin replied to a question why it had taken more than fifty years for the ICRC's information to be released: "Because it takes time to face your own history." The time has decidedly come. This treasure trove of original documents awaits extensive scrutiny.[21]

The Soviet attitude to the rescue of Jews, a topic that Dov Levin raised at Yad Vashem's first international conference on rescue, calls for considerable study once access is fully given to many archives in the former USSR. Joseph Kermish and Yisrael Gutman spoke then about stances in occupied Poland towards Jews, but David Engel's later scholarship on the Polish government-in-exile indicates much which can be explored further. Haim Avni's essay in that same volume regarding the Zionist underground in Holland and France and the escape to Spain, soon fleshed out for his book in Hebrew about Spain and the Holocaust, does not exhaust the subject. This is also the case for Portugal's position vis-à-vis the *Shoah*, discussed years later in a biography of Aristides de Sousa Mendes and Avraham Milgram's extensively researched volume. Switzerland's stance was treated in Carl Ludwig's pioneering study for the years 1933–1945, Alfred Hasler's popular *The Lifeboat is Full*, and Jacques Picard's *Switzerland and the Jews, 1933–1945*, but various cantonal records remain closed while that country has yet to approve Serge Klarsfeld's request for a new commission to study its attitude to Jewish refugees reaching the Swiss border during the war years. As for the other neutral governments in Europe during the Second World War, interested readers can begin with Corry Guttstadt's *Turkey, the Jews, and the Holocaust*, W. M. Calgren's study of Swedish foreign policy during the Second World War, and biographies of Raoul Wallenberg.[22]

The position of some other countries beyond occupied Europe remains to be delved into. Irving Abella and Harold Troper did justice to Canada's sorry record. As for the three remaining members of the British Commonwealth, Australia received just treatment from Michael Blakeney; New Zealand and the Union of South Africa, with Holocaust centers in Wellington and Cape Town, go wanting. The same is true for Ireland, home to a Jewish Museum in Dublin. The response of the South American governments, which maintained a closed-gates policy during the war despite broad expanses of vacant territory and their need for development in a number of areas, ought to be studied. Jeffrey Lesser's volume on Brazil's response is a welcome start in this direction Books by Marion Kaplan and Allen Wells disclose that Dominican dictator Rafael Trujillo's offer at the 1938 Evian Conference on Refugees to accept 100,000 Jews on generous terms was stymied by State Department hostility, this owing to fears that the Jews would serve as spies for the Third Reich. The reception of Jewish refugees in Shanghai, the one place in the world where one could land without a visa, is well told by David Kranzler; what occurred elsewhere in Asia has yet to be revealed.[23]

Additional subjects readily come to mind. Members of the US Congress and the Houses of Parliament deserve more attention, as do coverage about the Holocaust (including when compared with different wartime atrocities) in major newspapers and magazines and the private musings of their editors. Governments-in-exile aside from the Polish one in London, particularly those such as the Czech and the French having good contacts in countries under the swastika, ought to be examined. Prominent intellectuals and churchmen can be studied, as well as those cabinet members and advisers who served at the time in Allied capitals. Following the lead of Richard Bolover's *British Jewry and the Holocaust* and Ariel Hurwitz's *Jews without Power, American Jewry during the Holocaust*, specific Jewish communal leaders merit further review.[24] More information on what was then known in intelligence circles about the *Shoah*, the subject of a colloquium at the City University of New York in June 2003, would be welcome. That would include German intelligence messages scattered throughout various archives, especially in Central Europe, the former Soviet Union, and in the Vatican's diplomatic files (opened up until 1939).[25] The same is true for reactions within various ethnic groups to the unique plight of Europe's Jews. My argument that the Allies discriminated when helping other captive peoples under German rule but not the Jews, made in the final pages of *The Jews Were Expendable*, deserves more evaluation.

Having spent a number of demanding but rewarding years on this overview of bystanders, I chose after 1983 to pursue other, if related, subjects for research, beginning with the two archetypal symbols of Jewry's unprecedented destruction and revival. *The Holocaust and Israel Reborn*, a collection of essays published in 1994, demonstrated how British and American indifference during the *Shoah* confirmed Jewry's need for independence in its historic homeland. The tone was set with the first chapter, looking at how the newly created World Jewish Congress, which lacked the reality of Jewish sovereignty, could not check the ruthless antisemitism of dictators and the heartless apathy of democracies between the two world wars. The remainder of the volume focused on the growing public perception, by Jew and Gentile alike, that Palestine was the answer to the Jewish people's fundamental powerlessness and consequent victimization over the centuries. An exploration of some current implications of the *Shoah* and of the establishment of the State of Israel, which included an essay on the Auschwitz convent, Pius XII's role in the Holocaust years, and Poland's "Jewish problem," brought the book to a close.[26]

I then returned to my original interest in the Palestine question. *Decision on Palestine Deferred: America, Britain and Wartime Diplomacy, 1939–1945* was published in 2002. The book related in detail how these two governments' policy of drift and delay only aggravated the natural breach that had emerged by September 1939 between the two claimants to Palestine. The postponement by London and Washington during World War II of confronting the vexing quandary also meant death for trapped Jews in Europe facing liquidation. The impact of the Holocaust, with both governments breathing the very spirit of defeatism and despair, surfaces throughout. Intrigue, cynicism, and competing interests dominated Anglo-American diplomatic involvement in Palestine. Political expediency reigned supreme in these war counsels. The greatly restrictive 1939 White Paper legislation stood, Churchill's pro-Zionist inclinations notwithstanding. Roosevelt temporized, exhibiting his penchant for studied ambiguity when faced with yet another controversial issue. Moreover, this substitute for policy drove the two major communities in Palestine to greater militancy. With neither Arab nor Jew giving any sign of willingness to compromise, irrepressible confrontation and bloodshed loomed closer on that country's horizon.[27]

Twentieth Century Jews: Forging Identity in the Land of Promise and in the Promised Land, a series of essays that appeared eight years later, looked at how members of the ever-beleaguered tribe grappled with their Jewish selves in the last century. Felix Frankfurter and Arthur Hays Sulzberger continued to struggle with the pull of their ancestral roots, their prolonged anxieties affecting personal conduct both as regards the Holocaust and Israel's sovereign rebirth. The same held for the founders of the anti-Zionist American Council for Judaism, who greatly feared possible charges of dual loyalty. The fires of the Holocaust seared the young Reform rabbinical wing, however, as it did their fellow Jews, to rally to the Zionist standard after V-E Day and beyond, seeing the State of Israel as a bridge against their people's apocalyptic despair. The struggle for domestic political control in the biblically covenanted Promised Land, on the other hand, weakened efforts to unite the political left and right wings within the *Yishuv*. This sharp divide bore unfortunate results, both prior to the *Shoah* and long thereafter.[28]

All the while, I pondered what exactly was known of European Jewry's increasingly acute plight in the pivotal years between Hitler's ascension to power and his unleashing of World War II. Much had been written about the steady corruption of daily life for the prewar Jewish community under Third Reich rule, and individual studies had appeared about the crisis which Jews confronted in other countries. Yet an overview of the spread of Jew-hatred across the Continent continued to elude serious inspection. Newer studies, such as Bat-Ami Zucker's *In Search of Refuge*, and Stephen Norwood's *The Third Reich in the Ivory Tower*, added much to a comprehension of how America and its Jews responded as the antisemitic noose tightened abroad.[29] Ample evidence, I came to understand, was available from Jewish Telegraphic Agency dispatches, newspapers, diaries, diplomatic correspondence, Jewish organizational reports, private letters, and a host of other materials in order to analyze the dreadful drumbeat of events that befell Europe's Jews in the nineteen-thirties. A generous selection of primary documents, appended to the text, could augment the picture.

The Swastika's Darkening Shadow: Voices before the Holocaust presents this survey. It recounts the ways in which European Jews navigated their world as darkness closed about, even as individuals and organizations tried fervently to command the world's attention and mobilize others to action. The storm clouds that burst over Europe and its Jews with the start of World War II had begun to gather well beforehand. Appeasement of Nazi Germany prevailed even though that regime's uncompromising racist hatred of the Jew was publicly expressed and progressively implemented with shameless candor. Jews were not a major issue or were of no interest to statesmen who grappled with xenophobia, anti-Communism, unemployment, rearmament, a fear of global war, and popular antisemitism. Poland and Rumania were home to far more virulent attacks against Jews until *Kristallnacht*, while mounting legislation and brutal anti-Jewish attacks could readily be seen elsewhere in Central and Eastern Europe.

Yet leaders like Roosevelt, Chamberlain, and Daladier chose the role of bystanders in a world governed by what Ben-Gurion characterized as "power politics." The communal identity of Jews was regularly masked by these statesmen behind the term "refugees" or denied outright, as even occurred in strong anti-Nazi denunciations by Thomas Mann and Pope Pius XI. Doors to refugees were closing before and after the Evian Conference. None could foresee the Holocaust, but Jews understood that they were, as Shertok put it to Palestine High Commissioner Arthur Wauchope in 1934, "running a hard race against time." With September 1, 1939, the clock ran out on imperiled, isolated European Jewry.[30]

Palestine in Turmoil: The Struggle for Sovereignty, 1933–1939 provided further context. Published in 2014, its two volumes examine the growing political conflict between Arab and Jew in Palestine, which first surfaced clearly in these years and which proved to be an irreconcilable rift once the leadership of both peoples refused to accept minority status. The Palestinian settlement of sizable numbers of Jewish refugees, escaping Germany's descent into barbarism as well as poverty and attack in Central Europe, galvanized an Arab Revolt which began in April 1936 and only guttered out in early 1939. The various suggestions advanced at the time for resolving the Palestine conundrum, especially within the Arab and Jewish camps (both in and outside the country's borders), are given close inspection as well. The narrative is set within the larger framework of the intervention of Arab states in the region and the reaction of foreign statesmen to Third Reich aggression.[31]

The nationalist passions that surged at the time through both communities in Palestine witnessed the establishment even before the Holocaust of the basis of Jewish statehood, as well as internecine rivalries within Palestinian-Arab clans which signaled the beginning of that society's collapse. Nonetheless, His Majesty's Government chose to deflect attention on Palestine as essential refuge just when European Jewry faced grave danger. Echoing Arab claims, London came to refuse the right of the Jewish people to self-determination in a distinctly Jewish Commonwealth. Certain of Jewish loyalties but not of Arab sympathies, the Chamberlain government concluded that Imperial strategic priorities trumped all of Weizmann's appeals to moral values, to British honor, to history, and to international obligations. European Jewry's singular calamity, as well as the *Yishuv's* novel strength and firm resolve toward achieving ultimate freedom, carried scant power in a world girding for world war.

For Roosevelt, the Great Depression and rising domestic antisemitism weighed heavily in the balance. Ever cautious, FDR privately condemned the White Paper and focused on post-war settlement on a large scale in the Americas and Africa for Jews in dire need. After the 75,000 Jews would arrive in Palestine under the 1939 White Paper quotas and the British plan for administration began to work during the next five years, FDR advised State Department officials, the whole problem could be reviewed again. Patience, however, was a luxury denied to the Bible's Chosen People.

A firmer grasp of the nineteen-thirties is crucial to our understanding of the Holocaust. Hitler's war against the Jewish people, comprising the key to his racist, Manichean ideology, had commenced in the same years. Those leaders capable both of halting his early drive for *lebensraum* and of aiding Jews in distress chose to stand silently by, and thus turned away. Many nations on the Continent began their own deadly assault against Jews. These defenseless human beings found few allies. Well before Babi Yar and Treblinka, the future killers demonized Jews, while future bystanders depersonalized them. Their separate stances, carried on throughout World War II, marked innocent lives for unmitigated disaster.

The bimillennial disability of Jewish powerlessness, which resulted in the denouement since called the Holocaust, is well captured in the courteous but cold language of W. G. Hayter of the British Embassy in Washington to the United Palestine Appeal's Henry Montor on December 5, 1941.

Yes, we have done badly in recent months. It is quite true that we have overlooked the Jews. It has been called to our attention that the Prime Minister never has mentioned Jews when he speaks of the yoke on Hitler's victims. But that is probably accidental. He looked over the map and could think only of specific countries seized by Hitler. The Jews, of course, were not on that map, and they were overlooked.

Two days earlier, Hitler's personal newspaper organ had announced that "it is the *Führer's* policy to exterminate the Jews by whatever means possible." On December 8, in the small Polish village of Chełmno, forty-seven miles northwest of Łódź, the first death camp in which the Final Solution was carried out by means of gas began its secret horrific operation.[32]

What of today? Ever since May 14, 1948, the Jewish people are on the geopolitical map, an independent commonwealth located on a sliver of land hugging the Mediterranean Sea. Yet the State of Israel is the one national community whose right to exist is questioned. Despite all the remarkable successes wrought by the Zionist revolution in dramatically transforming Jewish life, the only democracy in the Middle East has become a stigmatized outcast. Ritual condemnation at the UN and boycotts throughout the world are commonplace. Aside from daily facing lethal incitement and terrorism from implacable neighbors, Israel is threatened by Iran with total extinction. In addition, almost eighty years after the Red Army reached the gates of Auschwitz-Birkenau, virulent antisemitism—the most sustained chronicle of enmity in history – has returned to rage across significant parts of Europe. And Holocaust denial remains a staple of official media across the Middle East and North Africa.

Additional crimes against humanity occur elsewhere. Islamist zealotry, bent on a *jihad* of war against non-Islamic countries, threatens the West. At stake are the cardinal values of freedom, individual dignity, openness, and pluralism. The persecution of Christians in Muslim lands is on the increase. On the 100th anniversary of the start of the Turkish genocide against Armenians, a state-sponsored slaughter not acknowledged to this day by the perpetrator nation, the slaughter of civilians in Bosnia, Rwanda, Sudan, Cambodia, Syria, and Nigeria should remind everyone concerned about truth and decency that the Holocaust was not the last chapter in the triumph of evil. We have seen that in Kosovo, Sierra Leone, Kurdistan, and, later, eastern Congo and Yazidi areas of Iraq outside efforts sometimes can make a difference. "But, in general," Nicholas Kristof recently observed, "the world is typically less galvanized by mass atrocities than paralyzed by them."[33]

Mankind has forgotten too soon. "Something terrible had fallen like a meteorite into history," as Vilna partisan Abba Kovner expressed it years later, when the Holocaust showed the whole world that the blood of a people could be shed with impunity. Radical humanist action, perhaps taken through transnational constituencies, is needed to rescue blameless victims from oblivion and to have complacency give way to personal commitment. The concluding thoughts expressed in *The Jews Were Expendable* appear as relevant in the twenty-first century as they did more than forty years ago: "Once and for all, the calamitous fallacy that what happens in one part of the globe is not another's affair must be shed, lest one day a brother's keeper be again found wanting in the face of extremity. . . . The cancer of bestiality is the concern of us all, and the infinite preciousness of life requires daily affirmation."[34]

In the years after my delivering a briefer version of this essay at an international conference on "The Allied Powers and the Holocaust," held at the Menachem Begin Center, Jerusalem, in March 2015, a number of significant publications appeared on this broad topic. Laurel Leff tells the riveting full story of the hiring decisions that American universities made during the Nazi era, deeming many Jewish refugee scholars in Europe not "well worth saving," thus leaving them to face the horrors of the Holocaust. Thorsten Noack showed how famed journalist William L. Shirer publicized early reports on the Nazi "euthanasia" program (Aktion T-4), but the US State Department rejected appeals in March 1940–March 1941 from its third secretary at the US embassy in Berlin to publicly condemn the mass murder. Paul R. Bartrop contributed a comprehensive study of the fruitless 1938 Evian Conference on Refugees. The appeasement of Hitler's Germany by the US and British governments in the early years of the Third Reich even as Nazi annihilationist intentions were clearly discernible, challenged by boycott movements and mass demonstrations at the grassroots level in both countries, is detailed in Stephen H. Norwood's *Prologue to Annihilation*. In a related study, he had exposed the Quakers' "dark side" of antisemitism and appeasement of the Hitler regime in this same period, that humanitarian relief organization failing to grasp the extent or uniqueness of the Nazi persecution of the Jews.[35]

The efforts of a few individuals, hitherto lost to history, who sought to counter the murderous Nazi design received their due. Peter Duffy offered an account of the acquittal after a much-publicized trial in 1935 of William Bailey and his small group for cutting down in New York harbor the Nazi flag from the *SS Bremen*, the flagship of Hitler's commercial armada, and the ensuing brawl, which exposed the *Führer*'s aggression for all of America to see. Steven Pressman's narrative, first related in an HBO documentary, related how

Philadelphia's Gilbert and Eleanor Kraus rescued fifty Jewish children from German-occupied Vienna in the spring of 1939. Biographies of Ben Hecht by Adina Hoffman and Julien Gorbach told of the famed Hollywood screen writer who mobilized pressure on the Roosevelt administration in wartime for an Allied plan to rescue Europe's trapped Jews. The story of Rudolf Vrba (Walter Rosenberg), the eighteen-year-old Slovak Jew who escaped the Auschwitz-Birkenau death camp in April 1944 along with Fred Wetzler in order to alert the world about its horrors, only to have those in power have reactions ranging from lack of interest and disbelief to outright antisemitism, was grippingly described by Jonathan Freedland. Sara Kadosh revealed the ceaseless efforts of Shaul Weingort, a young Polish rabbi operating from neutral Switzerland, to save fellow Jews during the Holocaust with food and false passports.[36]

The indefatigable Rafael Medoff continued to publish strong critiques of the Roosevelt administration, as well as of some Jewish leaders in the United States, when confronted with Jewry's systematic slaughter across Europe under Third Reich control. Joining other historians, the David S. Wyman Institute for Holocaust Studies under his direction presented chapters on the War Refugee Board which confirmed that the fixed approach of FDR's circle (shared by His Majesty's Government in London) to defeat the enemy and have the Jewish remnant return to their "homes" after the war proved bankrupt for European Jewry. Three essays on antisemitism in the White House, reflections on American Jewish political power in the 1940s, and the October 1943 march of Orthodox rabbis on Washington, D.C., just before Yom Kippur were followed by a volume faulting Rabbi Stephen Wise for not strongly pressing Roosevelt. Medoff then joined with other historians in a monograph which details how the US Holocaust Memorial Museum's laudatory exhibit "America and the Holocaust" distorted the true facts. His documentary history on America's response during the Holocaust appeared in 2022.[37]

That same year, Medoff and I joined in critiquing Ken Burns's three-part *"The U.S. and the Holocaust"* PBS series for faithfully accepting the US Holocaust Memorial Museum's narrative of absolving Roosevelt from blame while focusing on the antisemitism of a citizenry opposed to Jewish immigration even while aware of the extent of what was happening during the *Shoah*. As an example, we observed, it is not surprising that the April 1943 Bermuda Conference on Refugees, wherein the American delegation—with Roosevelt's prior approval—joined their British counterparts in rejecting all feasible options to rescue Jews, receives no mention in this documentary film. The same is true for the president's stand on Palestine, Jewry's most obvious haven, prepared as he was to issue with Churchill a statement at the same time that forbade against any further public discussion of that contentious issue until after the war.[38]

The postwar plight of survivors of the *Shoah* came under additional scrutiny. Resorting to archival sources and especially on eyewitness testimonies, Dan Stone revealed the complex challenges which these Jews faced and the daunting tasks undertaken to help them reclaim their shattered lives, as well as the efforts of their liberators as they contended with survivors' immediate needs, then grappled with longer-term issues that shaped the postwar world and ushered in the first chill of the Cold War years ahead. Andrew Kornbluth's study of the 1945 August trials in Poland and Jan T. Gross's earlier books on antisemitism in that country during and after World War II signaled a scholarly movement opposed to that government's distortion of Poland's role during the *Shoah*. My own *After the Holocaust* examined some aspects of that subject, along with the Earl Harrison mission to the Jewish "Displaced Persons" (DPs) camps, the effort to keep the continent's Western borders open to Jews fleeing Eastern Europe, and the first official killing of a Jew in Germany after World War II.[39]

Pioneering scholarship on Poland's response in the Jewish people's most anguished years also appeared at this time. Jan Gross and wife Irina G. Gross had already, in *Golden Harvest*, examined a photograph of peasant "diggers" atop a mountain of ashes at the Treblinka death center who were actually seeking gold and precious stones that the Nazi executioners had overlooked when killed Jews en masse, followed by their study of the ravaging of Jewish assets across Europe. Jan Grabowski explored the "hunt" for Jews by ethnic Poles during the German occupation, as well as the collaboration of the Polish police in this respect. Similar findings came to light in *Such a Beautiful Day* by Barbara Engelking, the first Polish researcher since the early 1990's to work from the Jewish victims' perspective, detailing how Jews desperately seeking refuge in the Polish countryside when the process of mass murder was mostly complete rarely found safe refuge. The documentation in Mirosław Tryczyk's *The Towns of Death: Pogroms against Their Neighbors* added to this indictment.[40]

Recently, a few scholars associated with US government institutions seek, in the phrase of Laurel Leff, "to inch more to the middle" in claiming that the State Department was not as callous towards aiding endangered Jews as previously asserted by critics of the Roosevelt administration. The president is cleared of responsibility by Richard Breitman, former editor-in-chief of the US Holocaust Memorial Museum's official journal, and Museum archivist/curator Rebecca Erbelding. The former's *The Berlin Mission* follows the tone of his *FDR and the Jews*. The latter's book on the US War Refugee Board (WRB) omits a reluctant Roosevelt forced to establish the Board in January 1944 because of political pressure in an election year; his allocating it a small staff and little funds from his executive budget; his temporizing on Palestine as haven; and his very limited response to rescue options for European Jewry facing death on a daily basis. Continued resistance to the WRB in the State and War departments, which hampered its success, is also glossed over. While failing to take note of the existing literature about the Board, Erbelding's statement that the claim of some that FDR and his administration were complicit in European Jews' murders is "preposterous" is odd, given that the WRB's founding document was titled *A Report to the Secretary on the Acquiescence of This Government in the Murder of the Jews*.[41]

In addition to Breitman and Erbelding, three journal articles by Melissa Jane Taylor of the Office of Historian, US Department of State, set forth the case that US consuls in Vienna and Marseille pursued a middle-ground—never defined—approach in handling the flood of visa applications received in the wake of German conquests in 1938 and 1940. A close review of her evidence, however, does not justify revising the consensus view that State officials insisted on limited immigration to the United States in the Nazi period to levels well below what statutory quotas allowed, advising consuls abroad not to fill their quotas (and they did not). She pays scant attention to Bat-Ami Zucker's important critique of US consuls in Nazi Germany in the years 1933–1941. Taylor does not offer a single example of an American diplomatic rescuer, even trying to discredit vice consul in Marseille Hiram Bingham IV, the one American diplomat who defied State's restrictive policy toward European Jewish refugees.[42]

Perhaps the most damning indictment of the free world's judging Europe's Jews in the Holocaust to be "expendable," using the term that I had coined forty years ago with regard to the *Shoah*, appeared in 2022 with Daniel Kertzer's *The Pope at War: The Secret History of Pope Pius XII, Mussolini, and Hitler*. Having examined thousands of documents about the actions of Pope Pius XII and the Vatican at that time, released in 2020 after sixty years to open scholarly inspection thanks to Pope Francis I, Kertzer revealed that within weeks of Pius XII being elected pope—he was elected by the College of Cardinals in March 1939—Hitler saw an opportunity and decided to send a personal envoy, the great-grandson of Queen Victoria of England and a Nazi prince, son-in-law of Italy's King Victor Emmanuel III. Philipp von Hessen would shuttle back and forth between Hitler and Pius XII over the next two years, engaged in secret negotiations. These centered on the treatment of German Catholics while ignoring the *Wehrmacht*'s invasion of Poland on September 1, 1939, among other matters, as well as reports from the pope's nuncios across Europe that reveal just how much he knew about the Holocaust.

Kertzer also found additional evidence that on October 16, 1943, the Nazi SS elite guard, in charge of carrying out the "Final Solution of the Jewish Question," tried to arrest all of Rome's Jews, thousands of them. They found about 1,260 and brought them to a military college just outside the walls of the Vatican, where they were held for two days. The Vatican worked very hard to show that some, having been baptized and therefore not considered Jews from the point of view of the Catholic Church, should not be transported to Auschwitz with the rest of the group. About 250 of those originally rounded up were freed. Two days later, the others were herded onto a sealed train for Auschwitz-Birkenau. Of these 1,007, 16 would survive. Pope Pius XII had sent Cardinal Secretary of State Luigi Maglione to meet with the German ambassador to the Holy See to ask if something could be done about the deportation. When Ernst von Weizsäcker, informing Maglione that the action had been ordered by the highest level (Hitler), asked if he really wished to protest on the Vatican's behalf, the cardinal basically replied that he did not insist on that point.

Kertzer also discovered that the Holy See ordered the official Vatican newspaper *L'Osservatore Romano* to suppress clear evidence about German massacres during the war as "in apparent contrast with the supreme interests of the country." The authoritarian pope wanted to ensure the Vatican's neutrality during World War II and protect Catholic interests across Europe. Despite the urgent pleas of priests, rabbis, and Allied diplomats, Pius XII refused to condemn "the Nazis' ongoing extermination of Europe's Jews." Kertzer acknowledges that the pope initially had legitimate concerns that the Axis dictators would soon be in control of Europe, and therefore needed to tread lightly, but as the tide turned and evidence of German atrocities against Jews mounted, his approach never changed. Rather, the Supreme Pontiff then feared that communism would spread throughout the Continent, with Catholics to suffer thereafter. "As a moral leader," Kertzer concludes, "Pius XII must be judged a failure."[43]

The same can be said about the free world powers and humanitarian organizations in the years when Europe's Jews lived in the half-life between rescue and death, with the darkness of the latter claiming most. What explains this moral collapse in the face of the on-going, methodical slaughter? Regrettably, the question has hounded the inhabitants of this planet ever since then, with genocides, terrorism, and baseless hatreds continuing to stigmatize certain human beings as "the other." Our troubled world can reap an invaluable lesson from the mantra of Ira Hirschmann, who had helped save the surviving 40,000 Jews in Transnistria and ameliorate the plight of Bulgaria's Jews while working in neutral Turkey on behalf of the US War Refugee Board: "Never indulge in hesitant mercy."[44]

Endnotes

Notes to Chapter 2

I wish to express my special thanks to Ms. Bernhardine Pejovic, now retired, for her help as director of the League of Nations Archives and Historical Collections Section consultation room in Geneva.

1 *Advocate for the Doomed: The Diaries and Papers of James G. McDonald, 1932–1935*, ed. Richard Breitman, Barbara McDonald Stewart, and Severin Hochberg (Bloomington: Indiana University Press, 2007), 766–767; Rosenberg to Waldman, June 26, 1935, RG 23, file 1/33, American Jewish Archives (hereafter AJA), Cincinnati, Ohio; James Rosenberg, *Painter's Self-Portrait* (New York: Crown, 1958), 74.
2 Norman Bentwich, "The International Problem of Refugees," *Foreign Policy Reports* 9:25 (February 12, 1936): 306–311.
3 Carole Fink, *Defending the Rights of Others: The Great Powers, the Jews, and International Minority Protection, 1878–1938* (Cambridge: Cambridge University Press, 2004), 328–330; Feinberg to Robinson, April 5, 1933, A306/73, Central Zionist Archives (hereafter CZA), Jerusalem.
4 Leo Motzkin, "The Question of the Persecutions of the German Jews before the League of Nations," n.d., A126/612, CZA; Cecil quoted in *Palestine Post*, April 3, 1933; League of Nations, *Official Journal* [Geneva] 14 (1933): 835–849, 930–935; J. W. Brugel, "The Bernheim Petition: A Challenge to Nazi Germany in 1933," *Patterns of Prejudice* 12:2 (1983): 17–25; Natan Feinberg, *HaMa'arakha haYehudit neged Hitler: Al Bimat Hever haLe'umim* (Jerusalem: Mossad Bialik, 1957). Article 67 of the Upper Silesia Convention declared that "all German nationals shall be equal before the law and shall enjoy the same civil and political rights without distinction as to race, language or religion." The Joint Foreign Committee represented the Anglo-Jewish Association and the Board of Deputies of British Jews.
5 *New Judea* (May–June 1933): 138–139; Motzkin speech, June 4, 1933, A261/622, CZA; Mossinson speech, June 4, 1933, A45/29, CZA; *La Question des Juifs Allemands devant la Societé des Nations* (Paris: Librairie A. Rousseau, 1933), 81–101; Blanche Dugdale, "Notes from London," Zionist Review, February 21, 1941, 3.
6 *Manchester Guardian*, May 22, 1933; Laski and Benwitch-Vansittart interview, June 22, 1933, file 75, David Mowshowitz MSS, YIVO Archives, Center for Jewish History, New York City; Laski-Montefiore report, July 7, 1933, Minutes, Board of Deputies of British Jews Archives, London; Laski-Vansittart interview, June 29, 1933, Joint Foreign Committee files, American Jewish Committee Archives (hereafter AJCA), Center for Jewish History, New York City; Lauterpacht to Bentwich, June 21, 1933, A255/477, CZA; Laski to Vansittart, July 7, 1933, League of Nations Bentwich file, AJCA.
7 Feilchenfeld memorandum, September 22, 1933, Feilchenfeld file, Cyrus Adler MSS, AJCA; Morris D. Waldman, *Nor by Power* (New York: International Universities Press, 1953), 52–53. Concurrently, Sidney E. Goldstein, Assistant Rabbi at the Stephen Wise Free Synagogue and Professor of Social Service at the Jewish Institute for Religion, proposed that the Council of the League of Nations work to have member states ratify an International

Convention that would outlaw "all acts of intolerance and injustice practices against every Minority group in any country." Sidney E. Goldstein, *The League of Nations and the Ground for Action in Behalf of the Jews of Germany* (New York: Press of Correct Print, 1933).

8   *Advocate for the Doomed*, 47–48; Wise to Mack, April 8, 1933, and May 4, 1933; both in box 115, Stephen Wise MSS, American Jewish Historical Society (hereafter AJHS), Center for Jewish History; Diary, May 2, 1933, James P. Warburg MSS, Special Collections, Columbia University, New York City; McDonald Town Hall address, May 4, 1933, box 137, Felix Frankfurter MSS, Library of Congress, Washington, D.C.; *Advocate for the Doomed*, 73 and 76.

9   Rosenberg to Baerwald-Warburg, July 14, 1933, microfilm 1920, Felix Warburg MSS, AJA; Meeting, August 10, 1933, Chronos file, AJCA; Feilchenfeld memorandum, September 22, 1933, AJCA; *Advocate for the Doomed*, 73–75, 80–95, 125; Bentwich-McDonald interview, September 5, 1933, A255/397, CZA. The Concordat guaranteed the freedom of Catholicism in Germany, in return for which Catholics abandoned political activity there. Pacelli would become the next pope in February 1939, taking the title Pius XII.

10   Draft petition and draft resolution, August 30, 1933, A264/145, CZA; McDonald address, September 6, 1933, Chronos file, AJCA; McDonald to Ogden, September 25, 1933, microfilm 1916, Warburg MSS; Diary, September 23, 1933, Jay Pierrepont Moffat MSS, Houghton Library, Harvard University, Cambridge, MA; Feilchenfeld memorandum, September 22, 1933, and October 2, 1933, AJCA; Kohler to Cohen, September 22, 1933, box 11, Max Kohler MSS, AJHS; September 29, 1933, League of Nations, *Official Journal* [Geneva] (1933): 47–49; *New York Times*, October l, 1933.

11   Bentwich to Kohler, October 5, 1933, League of Nations, Bentwich file, AJCA; League of Nations, *Official Journal* [Geneva] special supplement 120 (1933): 22–57, 59–60, 70–72; League of Nations, *Official Journal* [Geneva], special supplement 114–121 (1933), 22–29; file R5718/50/7100/7100, League of Nations Archives (hereafter LNA), Geneva. For Motzkin's influence one week earlier on Czech Foreign Minister Eduard Benes's anti-German speech at the League, see Azriel Carlebach, *Sefer haDemuyot* (Tel Aviv: Modi'in, 1959), 186–187.

12   *Advocate for the Doomed*, 125–135; Schiff to Warburg, October 16, 1933, microfilm 22, Louis D. Brandeis MSS, University of Louisville, KY; Bentwich report, November 5, 1933, Paris files, AJCA; Laski to Adler, October 24, 1933, file 23, Morris Waldman MSS, AJA; Weizmann to Cecil, October 31, 1933; Cecil to Weizmann, November 3, 1933; both in L13/154a, CZA; Avenol to McDonald, October 26, 1933; McDonald to Avenol, October 28, 1933; both in file R5718/50/7912/7100, LNA. The JDC eventually paid for more than ninety percent of the administrative outlay of McDonald's office, and when two other Jewish organizational sources fell short of their commitments, the JDC met the deficit. Barbara McDonald Stewart, *United States Government Policy on Refugees from Nazism, 1933–1940* (New York: Garland, 1982), 125.

13   *Advocate for the Doomed*, 145, 148–149, 152, 166, 185, 205n, 209–213, 216, 218; November 28, 1933 meeting, file R5722/50/11748/7564, LNA; Stewart, *United States Government Policy on Refugees from Nazism, 1933–1940*, 133; December 5, 1933 meeting, file C1616, LNA.

14   *Advocate for the Doomed*, 162–165, 168, 183–184, 189, 205–206, 208, 231–235, 238n; Bentwich-McDonald interview, November 10, 1933, McDonald file, Oscar Janowsky MSS, AJHS; Hyman to Warburg, November 13, 1933; Hyman to Warburg, December 11, 1933; both in microfilm 1918, Warburg MSS; Jewish delegation meeting, November 15, 1933, A306/26, CZA; Weizmann report, December 18, 1933, ZOA assorted MSS, Zionist Archives (ZA), New York City (now at CZA).

15   *Advocate for the Doomed*, 268, 388, and chaps. 9–14; Rosenberg to Flexner, March 22, 1934, box 69, Lewis Strauss MSS, AJHS; Wurfbain to Dieckhof, February 21, 1934; Bentwich-Barandon correspondence, April-June 1934; both in file C1609/60, LNA; February 25,

1934 meeting, Refugees folder, Janowsky MSS; McDonald to Rosenberg, April 6, 1934, file 111, Julian Mack MSS, ZA; McDonald to Warburg, April 10, 1934, April 12, 1934, and, May 5, 1934; all in microfilm 1923, Warburg MSS; McDonald statement, May 2, 1934, F38/537, CZA; McDonald to Bentwich, June 9, 1934, PAC files, James G. McDonald MSS, Herbert Lehman School of International Affairs, Columbia University, NY.

16 *Advocate for the Doomed*, 459–460, and chaps. 15–19; McDonald to Warburg, July 17, 1934; McDonald to Warburg, September 18, 1934; both in microfilm 1923, Warburg MSS; Liebman to McDonald, July 30, 1934; Bentwich to Warburg, August 22, 1934; both in PAC files, McDonald MSS; Laski to Brotman, September 15, 1944, JFC, Adler-Laski files, AJCA; McDonald to Fuld, September 15, 1934, file AR7162, box 1, Leo Baeck Institute, Center for Jewish History; Laski memorandum, September 1934, file 76, Mowshowitz MSS; Schmolke to American Joint Distribution Committee, October 13, 1934, file C7610/67, LNA; McDonald to d'Avigdor Goldsmid, November 17, 1944, file C1609/62, LNA.

17 McDonald to Warburg, August 16, 1934, PAC files, McDonald MSS; Warburg to McDonald, August 28, 1934, microfilm 1924, Warburg MSS; Warburg to Oungre and to Kahn, September 5, 1934, microfilm 1925, Warburg MSS; *Advocate for the Doomed*, 460–461.

18 *Advocate for the Doomed*, 498, 521, 559–560, 571. To Zionist official Arthur Ruppin, who hoped that McDonald would make plans for the annual evacuation of some 20,000 younger Jews from Germany in the next decade, McDonald opined that the High Commission should be, if possible, wound up by October 1, 1935. McDonald to d'Avigdor Goldsmid, September 29, 1934, file AR7/62, Leo Baeck Institute.

19 *Advocate for the Doomed*, 617–618, chaps. 20–25, and 765–766; file C1610/SAAR, LNA; Chamberlain to McDonald, January 23, 1935, file C1611/76, LNA; McDonald report, February 12, 1935, A255/382, CZA; Inman report, February-June 1935, High Commissioner files, McDonald MSS; McDonald to Cecil, March 14, 1936, file C1609/62, LNA; McDonald to Cecil, April 12, 1935, box 68, Strauss MSS; Bentwich to McDonald, May 24, 1935, PAC files, McDonald MSS. McDonald joined the *New York Times*'s editorial staff, then went on to become president of the Brooklyn Institute of Arts and Sciences. After serving as chairman of Roosevelt's Advisory Committee on Political Refugees (1938–1945), he became one of six US delegates on the Anglo-American Committee of Inquiry on Palestine, and ultimately was appointed the first US Ambassador to the State of Israel. On the occasion of this last diplomatic appointment, the former French delegate to the Intergovernmental Committee on Refugees (an ineffectual group that had been created after the 1938 Evian Conference on Refugees) warmly saluted McDonald's "realistic idealism" as symbolized in his "vigorous, outspoken" Letter of Resignation. Coulon letter to the *New York Times*, February 27, 1949.

20 *Advocate for the Doomed*, 624–625; Chamberlain to McDonald, February 5, 1935, High Commissioner files, McDonald MSS; Robert Dallek, *Franklin D. Roosevelt and American Foreign Policy, 1932–1945* (New York: Oxford University Press, 1979), 95–97; Rosenberg to Adler, February 18, 1935, Fagen file, AJCA.

21 Adler to Rosenberg, February 21, 1935, Fagen files, AJCA; Oscar I. Janowsky, *The Jews and Minority Rights (1898–1919)* (New York: Columbia University Press, 1933).

22 Oscar I. Janowsky autobiography (hereafter JA), chap. 15, Janowsky MSS; Janowsky to Baron, June 26, 1932, Salo Baron MSS, MO580, Department of Special Collections, Stanford University, Stanford, CA. For Hayes's assault on Zionism, see Carleton Hayes, *Essays on Nationalism* (New York: The Macmillan Company, 1926), 118–119, 213–220. For the first summary of Hayes's obstruction, when US ambassador to Spain in World War II, regarding the rescue of Jews during the Holocaust, see Arthur D. Morse, *While Six Million Died, A Chronicle of American Apathy* (New York: Hart, 1968), 268–270. For the support at the Peace Conference of Mack and especially his successor, the non-Zionist AJC President Louis Marshall, for "national rights" (which US President Woodrow Wilson rejected), see *Louis Marshall: Champion of Liberty, Selected Papers and Addresses*, ed. Charles Reznikoff (Philadelphia: Jewish Publication Society of America, 1957), 552–553, 563.

23 JA, ch. 16; Morris R. Cohen, *A Dreamer's Journey, The Autobiography of Morris Raphael Cohen* (Boston: Beacon Press, 1949), 225–228, 237–248; Oscar I. Janowsky, "The Problem of Minorities," *Conference on Jewish Relations Newsletter*, April 1935. Horace Kallen, who transmitted Brandeis's thought to Cohen, had wished the American Jewish Congress to sponsor the study, but the Congress lacked the necessary funds. For Janowsky's research proposal, see "The Operation of the System of Minorities Protection," n.d., Janowsky file, Baron MSS.
24 Rosenberg to Adler, March 5, 1935; Adler to Rosenberg, March 11, 1935; both in Fagen files, AJCA.
25 Mack to Janowsky, May 9, 1935; Janowsky to Mack, May 14, 1935; both in Janowsky MSS; JA, chap. 16.
26 Fagen to Waldman, February 20, 1934; Schneiderman to Fagen, April 5, 1934; Fagen memoranda; all in Fagen files, AJCA.
27 Memorandum, "The Refugee Problem as the Result of National Socialist Policies"; May 22, 1935 memorandum; Fagen to Waldman, May 24, 1935; all in Fagen files, AJCA.
28 JA, chap. 16; Fagen memorandum, June 17, 1935, Fagen MSS. Janowsky had subsequent access to McDonald's diary, and cited in his own (unpublished) autobiography entries that have been omitted in the published McDonald diaries.
29 Fagen memorandum, June 20, 1935, RG 23, file 1/33, AJA; *Advocate for the Doomed*, 772.
30 Waldman to Rosenberg, June 20, 1935, Fagen files, AJCA; Rosenberg to Waldman, June 26, 1935, RG 23, file 1/33, AJA; *Advocate for the Doomed*, 773, 775. Warburg also continued to meet McDonald's financial needs. Warburg to McDonald, June 21, 1935, microfilm 1927, Warburg MSS.
31 July 17, 1935 cable dispatch, RG 90, file 10/6, AJA; *Advocate for the Doomed*, 778.
32 McDonald to Eleanor Roosevelt, July 24, 1935; Eleanor Roosevelt to McDonald, August I, 1935; both in Official Files 198A, Franklin D. Roosevelt Library, Hyde Park, New York; *Advocate for the Doomed*, 786n; American Jewish organizations to Phillips, July 26, 1935; Phillips to organizations, July 29, 1935; both in Chronos, AJCA.
33 Bentwich to McDonald, August 17, 1935, PAC files, McDonald MSS; *Refugees and Rescue: The Diaries and Papers of James G. McDonald, 1935–1945*, ed. Richard Breitman, Barbara McDonald Stewart, and Severin Hochberg (Bloomington: Indiana University Press, 2009), 12–13; McDonald to Cecil, September 9, 1935, file C1609/61, LNA. The first of the Nuremberg Laws made Jews state subjects, as opposed to "Aryan" Germans, who were declared citizens of the Reich. The second prohibited marriages and extramarital relations between Jews and Germans, the employment of German maids under the age of forty-five in Jewish households, and the raising by Jews of the Nazi German flag.
34 McDonald to Warburg, September 9, 1935, file AR 7162, box 1, Leo Baeck Institute.
35 Fagen to Waldman, July 8, 1935, Fagen files, AJCA.
36 Lauterpacht to Laski, July 3, 1935, file AR 7161, box 1, Leo Baeck Institute; Fagen to Bentwich, August 6, 1935, Fagen files, AJCA.
37 Bentwich to Fagen, July 24, 1935, file C1606/4, LNA; Fagen to Bentwich, August 6, 1935, Fagen files, AJCA.
38 Janowsky to Cohen, July 9, 1935, McDonald file, Janowsky MSS; JA, chap. 16.
39 JA, chap. 17; Fagen to Waldman, May 14, 1935, Fagen files, AJCA.
40 JA, chap. 17.
41 *Refugees and Rescue*, 32; Janowsky and Fagen to Rosenberg, October 1935, file C1606/4, LNA.
42 Fagen to Waldman, October 3, 1935, German Jews and AJC file, AJCA.
43 *Refugees and Rescue*, 37–38, 41–42, 46n, 49–51, 58, 64; Stewart, *United States Government Policy on Refugees from Nazism, 1933–1940*, 161; McDonald to Warburg, October 10, 1935, Warburg file, McDonald MSS; McDonald statement to Permanent Committee, October 16, 1935, A306/59, CZA; Bentwich to Warburg, October 21, 1935, file C1604/24, LNA; Warburg to McDonald, October 21, 1935, microfilm 1927, Warburg MSS; Chamberlain to McDonald, October 21, 1935, file C1611/76, LNA.

44 Fagen to Waldman, October 21, 1935, Fagen files, AJCA; JA, chap. 17.
45 *Refugees and Rescue*, 74; JA, chap. 17.
46 Fagen to Waldman, November 16, 1935, Refugees files, AJCA.
47 *Refugees and Rescue*, 78–79; JA, chap. 17. Janowsky's diary regarding this meeting reads November 18, while McDonald's diary gives an entry for the next day.
48 Janowsky to Rosenberg, November 26, 1935, Janowsky MSS; JA, chap. 17.
49 JA, chap. 17.
50 JA, chap. 17; Fagen to Rosenberg, November 26, 1935, McDonald file, Janowsky MSS. McDonald's published diary for November 24 omits all entries, but Janowsky, who cites from it in his memoir, had access to the diary years later.
51 JA, chap. 17; Cohn to Laski, November 27, 1935, Janowsky MSS.
52 JA, chap. 17; McDonald diary, November 24, 1936, US Holocaust Memorial Museum, Washington, D.C.; McDonald to Rosenberg, November 26, 1935, RG 23, file 1/33, AJA. McDonald's consulting with Brierly and McNair is noted in his diary. I thank Benton Arnovitz and Stephen Mize of the US Holocaust Memorial Museum for sending me a copy of this and other unpublished diary entries for November-December 1935. The latter confirm that McDonald's diary is accurately quoted in Janowsky's autobiographical memoir.
53 Janowsky and Fagen to Rosenberg, November 26, 1935, McDonald file, Janowsky MSS. McDonald's diary later indicates Montefiore's involvement, which, with Weizmann's support, led to cutting the whole subsection entitled "The Refugee Reservoir." McDonald diary, December 13, 1935. Lauterpacht went on to become a professor of international law at Cambridge University (1938–1955), then served on the International Court of Justice at The Hague until his death four years later.
54 JA, chap. 17; Janowsky-Fagen to McDonald, November 29, 1935; Janowsky to Cohen, December 11, 1935; both in Janowsky MSS; Rosenberg to Warburg, December 5, 1935, microfilm 1929, Warburg MSS; Waldman to Stroock, December 16, 1935, Fagen files, AJCA.
55 Fagen to Waldman (and memorandum attached), November 29, 1935, microfilm 1929, Warburg MSS; Rosenberg to Janowsky-Fagen, December 3, 1935, RG 23, file 1/33, AJA; Rosenberg to Janowsky-Fagen, December 12, 1935, microfilm 1917, Warburg MSS.
56 *Refugees and Rescue*, 97; Janowsky to Cohen, December 11, 1935, Janowsky MSS; Janowsky to Rosenberg, December 11, 1935, McDonald file, Janowsky MSS. Bentwich had earlier informed the High Commissioner that Janowsky and Fagen did not like the "mutilation" which he had suggested for Part II. Bentwich to McDonald, November 28, 1935, file AR 7162, box 1, Leo Baeck Institute.
57 McDonald diary, December 8, 1935; Fagen to Waldman, December 13, 1935, Fagen files, AJCA; Janowsky to Cohen, December 11, 1935, Janowsky MSS; Janowsky to Rosenberg, December 11, 1935, McDonald file, Janowsky MSS; JA, chap. 17.
58 JA, chap. 17; *Refugees and Rescue*, 100–101; McDonald diary, December 16–22, 1935; Waldman to Fagen, December 14, 1935, Fagen files, AJCA; Laski to Rosenberg, December 15, 1935, RG 23, file 1/33, AJA.
59 Rosenberg to Janowsky, December 23, 1935; MDW (Waldman) to Janowsky, December 24, 1935; both in Janowsky MSS; McDonald diary, December 25–26, 1935. Fagen later informed Janowsky that when Rosenberg renewed "the agitation" for including Part II, McDonald threatened not to release Part I at all. Rosenberg then backed down. Fagen to Janowsky, March 31, 1936, Janowsky MSS.
60 JA, chap. 17; *Refugees and Rescue*, 101–102; McDonald to Secretary General (Annex attached), December 27, 1935, file R5718/50/7593/7100, LNA.
61 London *Times* and *New York Times*, December 30, 1935.
62 "Repercussions of the McDonald Letter of Resignation," n.d., box 55, Morris R. Cohen MSS, Special Collections Research Center, University of Chicago Library, Chicago, IL; *Nation*, January 15, 1936; Ari Joshua Sherman, *Island Refuge, Britain and Refugees from the Third Reich, 1933–1939* (London: Paul Elek, 1973), 65. The Report of a League of Nations commission

of inquiry under the Earl of Lytton, signed on September 4, 1932, found that Japanese action one year earlier was not self-defense, and that Japan' creation of the Manchukuo puppet government did not flow from "a genuine and spontaneous independence movement." It recommended the establishment in Manchuria of an autonomous administration under Chinese sovereignty with international advisors and recognition of Japanese economic interests.

63 Waldman to Rosenberg, March 2, 1936, RG 23, file 1/33, AJA; Wurfbain to Battsek, January 18, 1936; McDonald to Bell, January 17, 1936; Cecil preface, January 1936; all in file C1611/80, LNA; *Refugees and Rescue,* 80.

64 "Repercussions," box 55, Cohen MSS. For one pro-German response by an American citizen against "Hebrew-made Bolshevism," and Hitler "fighting the battles of all progressive men," see Ehlers to McDonald, January 3, 1935 (should be 1936), McDonald MSS.

65 January 15, 1936 report, Joint Foreign Committee, Board of Deputies of British Jews Archives; *Refugees and Rescue,* 103, 105, 110. In a JDC address that same month, Warburg lauded McDonald's "self-sacrificing" work, and emphasized: "None of us had any right to expect tangible results with unemployed everywhere, but the very fact that a very real Christian spirit has fought our battles as valiantly as he has done deserves recognition." Warburg address, December 8, 1935, microfilm 1926, Warburg MSS.

66 *American Jewish Year Book* (1936–1937): 596, 645–647; *Refugees and Rescue,*105.

67 *Refugees and Rescue,* 111–112. For the Foreign Office's perspective at this time, see Sherman, *Island Refuge,* 61–63.

68 Montenach to Wurfbain, January 18, 1936, file C1611/80, LNA; Skelton memorandum, January 7, 1936 (and King notation), MG 26, J4, vol. 173, Public Archives of Canada, Ottawa. Canada had from the outset, before the first meeting of the Governing Body in 1933, regarded the plan of refugee settlement as "a European effort to 'break down' North American immigration restrictions." Stewart, *United Slates Government Policy on Refugees from Nazism, 1933–1940,* 133.

69 League of Nations, *Official Journal,* January 20, 1936, file R5719/50/22122/7100, LNA; Bentwich to McDonald, February 8, 1936, microfilm 1935, Warburg MSS; Stewart, *United Slates Government Policy on Refugees from Nazism, 1933–1940,* 230–232. For the creation of the Council, which McDonald had encouraged before his resignation, see David Silberklang, "Jewish Politics and Rescue: The Founding of the Council for German Jewry," *Holocaust and Genocide Studies* 7:3 (Winter 1993): 333–371; *Refugees and Rescue,* 79, 99–100; McDonald to Warburg, November 13, 1935, High Commissioner files, McDonald MSS. For a brief evaluation of the subsequent work of the High Commission, which continued to be "bound and shackled" until the office closed with the outbreak of World War II, see Michael R. Marrus, *The Unwanted: European Refugees in the Twentieth Century* (New York, 1985), 164–166.

70 Frankfurter to Fagen, January 1 l, 1936; Cohen to Janowsky, January 4, 1936; Rosenberg to Janowsky, January 3, 1936; Mack to Janowsky, January 10, 1936; all in Janowsky MSS. In telling Janowsky how work on the Petition began, Fagen referred to McDonald as "the Blessed Virgin," "the unwilling Mother," and "MacDuff." Fagen to Janowsky, March 31, 1936, Janowsky MSS.

71 American Jewish Committee news release, January 1, 1936, Digital Archives, American Jewish Committee.

72 Fagen memorandum, February 5, 1936, Digital Archives, American Jewish Committee.

73 Fagen to Waldman, February 11, 1936, Digital Archives, American Jewish Committee; Wise to Goldmann, February 11, 1936, file 76A, World Jewish Congress Archives, New York City (now at the American Jewish Archives); Janowsky to Rosenberg, February 20, 1936, Janowsky MSS.

74 Waldman-Fagen interview with de Madariaga, February 21, 1936, file P-13/2/13, Central Archives of the History of the Jewish People (hereafter CAHJP), Jerusalem.

75 Bentwich to Laski, March 3, 1936, Foreign Countries/Germany file, AJCA; Conference in Laski's chambers, May 12, 1936, Chronos, AJCA.

76 Waldman to Rosenberg, March 2, 1936, RG 23, file 1/33, AJA; Waldman to Laski, March 6, 1936, file P-13/2/13, CAHJP; Waldman to Stroock, March 19, 1936, Foreign Countries/ Palestine file, AJCA. From the same perspective, the AJC and the Board of Deputies, reflecting the stand of their respective governments, opposed the American Jewish Congress's endorsement of a boycott of German goods and articles. See Naomi W. Cohen, "The Transatlantic Connection: The American Jewish Committee and the Joint Foreign Committee in Defense of German Jews, 1933–1937," *American Jewish History* 90 (December 2002): 363–365.

77 Laski to Warburg, April 9, 1936, microfilm 1933, Warburg MSS. Also see Laski letter, March 18, 1936, file P-13/2/11, CAHJP; Laski to N. Laski, March 24, 1937, Foreign Countries/ Palestine file, AJCA. The *Protocols of the Elders of Zion*, an antisemitic forgery which sought to demonstrate that an international Jewish conspiracy was bent on world domination, was authored anonymously in Paris by a Russian secret police officer at the end of the nineteenth century. The text, widely circulated during the Russian civil war of 1919–1921, was publicized in the West by Russian émigrés associated with the anti-Bolshevik White armed forces. While Philip Graves exposed it in the London *Times* as closely similar to a French political pamphlet that attributed ambitions of world power to Napoleon III, it was translated into many languages. The *Protocols* found the largest number of adherents in Germany, and the Nazi Party propagated this theme from the start.

78 Rosenberg to Wise and Lipsky, May 18, 1936, PAC files, McDonald MSS; Lipsky to Rosenberg, May 22, 1936, file P-672, box 3, Louis Lipsky MSS, AJHS; Rosenberg to Wise, May 18, 1936, PAC files, McDonald MSS. Rosenberg would expand on these convictions in a forty-page letter six years later, by which time he had become an anti-Zionist. Rosenberg to Waldman, July 22, 1942, Rosenberg file, AJCA.

79 Janowsky to Cohen, June 16, 1936; Waldman to Janowsky, July 13, 1936; Fagen to Janowsky, July 21, 1936; Waldman to Jacobs, July 31, 1936; Fagen to Waldman, August 5, 1936; all in Janowsky MSS. A copy of the Petition is in the American Jewish Committee's Digital Archives. The signatories were the AJC, B'nai Brith, the Conference on Jewish Relations, four French human rights organizations, the Women's International League for Peace and Freedom, and the American Christian Committee for German Refugees.

80 Janowsky to Waldman, July 13, 1936; Janowsky to Cohen, August 7, 1936; both in Janowsky MSS. Throughout Jewish history, the *shtadlan* was a representative with access to Gentile dignitaries and legislative bodies. From the late nineteenth century onward, the term for this exercise of power (*shtadlanut*) was used to decry Jewish representatives who showed timidity and an eagerness for compromise.

81 Fagen to Janowsky, August 7, 1936; Janowsky to Fagen, August 8, 1936; Janowsky to Cohen, August 8, 1936; all in Janowsky MSS. When right-wing Insurgents led by General Francisco Franco revolted against the Republican Loyalist government of Spain in July, thousands of Italian and German "volunteers" joined the Franco forces. Great Britain and France attempted without success to unite the Powers on a policy of non-intervention, fearing lest the war expand into a general conflict. By early 1939, the Loyalist forces were defeated, with the war costing about 700,000 lives in battle, 30,000 executed or assassinated, and 15,000 killed in air raids.

82 Fagen to Waldman, August 11, 1936, Janowsky MSS. The State Department had already informed Avenol, however, that the US government would not participate actively in a Council-sponsored conference that July to discuss the legal status of Jewish and non-Jewish refugees coming from Germany, would not become a party to any convention which might be drafted at the conference, and did not wish to comment concerning the agenda. Hull to Avenol, April 7, 1936, file R5759/50/23441/23011, LNA. In the end, a junior US consul in Geneva was sent with the instruction not to speak on the floor.

83 Waldman to Adler, August 13, 1936; Waldman to Fagen, August 13, 1936; Waldman to Fagen, August 19, 1936; all in Janowsky MSS.

84 Fagen to Waldman, August 20, 1936, Janowsky MSS.
85 Press release, September 29, 1936; Declaration by the President of the Assembly, September 29, 1936; both in Fagen files, AJCA. The ten organizations were the AJC; the B'nai Brith of the United States; the American Christian Committee for German Refugees; The International Federation of Trade Unions; the Women's International League for Peace and Freedom; the League for the Rights of Man (France); the French National Committee for Aid to German Refugees; the French Central Committee of Assistance to Jewish Refugees; the Committee for the Defense of the Rights of Jews in Central and Eastern Europe; and the Committee for General Jewish Questions (Amsterdam). Sixty-seven prominent Americans also endorsed the Petition. Their names were later published in Oscar I. Janowsky and Melvin M. Fagen, *International Aspects of German Racial Policies* (New York: Oxford University Press, 1937), 234–237.
86 Janowsky and Fagen, *International Aspects of German Racial Policies*, v–x, xv–xxi, and *passim*. For favorable reviews, see Hans Kohn, *Yale Law Journal* 47:3 (January 1938): 510–511; J. P. Chamberlain, *Jewish Social Studies* 1:1 (1939): 131–132. Also see Bentwich to Janowsky, November 29, 1937, Janowsky MSS. For Cohen's chairing a dinner in honor of Rosenberg's "vision and courage" regarding the McDonald Letter and his "persistent generosity" which made the Janowsky-Fagen book possible, see Cohen to Janowsky, n.d., Janowsky MSS.
87 Monty Noam Penkower, *The Holocaust and Israel Reborn: From Catastrophe to Sovereignty* (Urbana: University of Illinois Press, 1994), 3–16; Sherman, *Island Refuge*, 112–222; Fink, *Defending the Rights of Others*, chap. 11; McDonald memorandum, August 25, 1939, Myron Taylor MSS, Franklin D. Roosevelt Library, Hyde Park, New York. The World Jewish Congress failed in its appeal to the League to effect a generalization of minorities rights, which Waldman dismissed as "a futile gesture" and Fagen rejected as a danger, "based upon the nationalist principle that Jews in all countries are members of a minority and need international protection." See Waldman memorandum (Fagen analysis attached), January 15, 1937, microfilm 1938, Warburg MSS. Hearing that McDonald would participate in the Evian Conference, Roger Makins of the British Foreign Office judged that the reappearance on the refugee scene of this "very tiresome individual," whose Letter of Resignation he termed "a very ill-advised document," was "unlikely to help the work of the committee." Sherman, *Island Refuge*, 100.
88 *Refugees and Rescue*, 77; Cecil remarks, February 6, 1935, *Parliamentary Debates*, House of Lords, vol. 95, 827–835; Bentwich-Cecil interview, May 19, 1936, A255/398, CZA; July 3, 1938 resolution; November 18, 1938 resolution; both in A306/47, CZA. On the evening of November 9–10, 1938, a savage Nazi pogrom destroyed synagogues and Jewish shops throughout the Third Reich, and sent 30,000 Jews to concentration camps. The shattered glass in streets led to the name *Kristallnacht*.
89 Immanuel Kant, *Perpetual Peace* (1795); Cohen preface in Oscar I. Janowsky, *People al Bay, The Jewish Problem in East Central Europe* (London: Victor Gollancz, 1938), 5–10; Janowsky and Fagen, *International Aspects of German Racial Policies*, 259. An early, critical analysis of McDonald is Haim Genizi, "James G. McDonald: High Commissioner for Refugees, 1933–1935," *Wiener Library Bulletin*, 30:43–44 (1977): 40–52. Both Cecil and the definitive history of the League acknowledged that organization's basic failure. See *A Great Experiment, An Autobiography by Viscount Cecil* (London: J. Cape, 1941), 252–253; Francis Paul Walters, *A History of the League of Nations*, vol. 1 (London: Oxford University Press, 1952), 400. A Universal Declaration of Human Rights was unanimously adopted and proclaimed by the United Nations General Assembly on December 10, 1948, with eight abstentions (all the Soviet bloc states—Byelorussia, Czechoslovakia, Poland, Ukraine, and the USSR, as well as Yugoslavia, South Africa, and Saudi Arabia). This represents the first global expression of rights to which all human beings are entitled, to quote from the preamble, as "the foundation of freedom, justice and peace in the world."

Notes to Chapter 3

1 In 1933, the Jews of Poland numbered about 3,000,000 (9.5 percent of the total population), the European part of the Soviet Union, 2,525,000 (3.4 percent). Romania had 756,000 Jews (4.2 percent), Lithuania, 155,000 (7.6 percent). In prewar Central Europe, the largest Jewish community was in Germany, with about 500,000 members (0.75 percent).This was followed by Hungary with 445,000 (5.1 percent), Czechoslovakia with 357,000 (2.4 percent), and Austria with 191,000, most of whom resided in the capital city of Vienna (2.8 percent). In Western Europe, the largest Jewish communities were to be found in Great Britain, with 300,000 Jews (0.65 percent); France, with 250,000 (0.6 percent); and the Netherlands, with 156,000 (1.8 percent). "The Holocaust," *Holocaust Encyclopedia*, United States Holocaust Memorial Museum, accessed on January 6, 2011, http://www.ushmm.org/wlc/en/?ModuleId=10005143.
2 Monty Noam Penkower, *The Jews Were Expendable: Free World Diplomacy and the Holocaust* (Urbana: Illinois University Press, 1983); Monty Noam Penkower, *The Holocaust and Israel Reborn: From Catastrophe to Sovereignty* (Urbana: Illinois University Press, 1994); Monty Noam Penkower, *Decision on Palestine Deferred: America, Britain and Wartime Diplomacy* (London: Frank Cass, 2002).
3 W. H. Auden, "Refugee Blues," *New Yorker* 15:9 (April 15, 1939), 21; reprinted in W. H. Auden, *Collected Shorter Poems, 1927–1957* (London: Random House, 1966), 157–158; Humphrey Carpenter, *W. H. Auden, A Biography* (London: George Allen & Unwin, 1981); David Ben-Gurion, *Zikhronot*, vol. 6 (Tel Aviv: Am Oved, 1967), 293, 540.
4 Gershom Scholem, *A Life in Letters, 1914–1982*, ed. and trans. A. D. Skinner (Cambridge, MA: Harvard University Press, 2002), 301–302. Benjamin (1892–1940), a philosopher, translator, and often considered the most important literary critic in the German language between the two World Wars, had toyed for many years with the idea of going to Palestine. In 1932, he left his Berlin home for the Balearic Isles and, ultimately, Paris. At the outbreak of World War II, this "stateless" assimilated Jew was interned for two months as a German citizen. Benjamin fled to the south of France one day before the Germans entered Paris and, with a group of refugees, crossed the Spanish border. When the police chief of the border town of Port-Bou in Catalonia threatened to send him back to France, he committed suicide on the evening of September 25, 1940. The other persons in his party were allowed passage the next day, and safely reached neutral Lisbon.
5 Saul Friedländer, *Nazi Germany and the Jews*, vol. 1: *The Years of Persecution, 1933–1939* (New York: Harper Perennial, 1997), 72; Jack Ewing, "Hitler's First Anti-Semitic Writing Finds a Buyer," *New York Times*, June 7, 2011; Victor Klemperer, *I Will Bear Witness, 1942–1945, A Diary of the Nazi Years*, trans. M. Chalmers (New York: Modern Library, 2001), 353. A good summary of Hitler's constant and consistent antisemitic views is Eberhard Jäckel, *Hitler's Weltanschauung, A Blueprint for Power*, trans. H. Arnold (Middletown, CT: Wesleyan University Press, 1972), chap. 3.
6 *The Letters of Marin Buber, A Life of Dialogue*, ed. N. N. Glatzer and P. M. Flohr (New York: Schocken, 1991), 474. In October 1938, the Polish-born Heschel had been deported from Frankfurt back to Poland, where he then taught Jewish philosophy and Torah at Warsaw's Institute for Jewish Studies. Six weeks before the German invasion of Poland, Heschel left for London with the help of Julian Morgenstern, president of Hebrew Union College (HUC). His sister Esther was killed in a German bombing. Heschel's mother was murdered by the Nazis, and two other sisters, Gittel and Devorah, died in Nazi concentration camps. He never returned to Germany, Austria, or Poland. Heschel arrived in New York City in March 1940, and served on the faculty of HUC in Cincinnati for five years. In 1946, he took a position at the Jewish Theological Seminary of America, where he served as Professor of Jewish Ethics and Mysticism until his death in 1972.

7   *New York Times*, Mar. 26, 1933; Michael Wildt, *Hitler's Völksgemeinschaft and the Dynamics of Racial Exclusion, Violence against Jews in Provincial Germany*, trans. B. Heise (New York: Berghahn, 2012).
8   London *Times*, January 31, 1935, and February 1, 1935. Also see Lothian's lecture, March 5, 1935, file 8/371, Chatham House Archives, London. His view changed in 1938, and he wrote to Foreign Secretary Lord Halifax (champion of appeasement) urging him to make clear that British government would side with Czechoslovakia if Nazi Germany resorted to force. In March 1939, Lothian admitted that he now realized "that Hitler is in effect a fanatical gangster who will stop at nothing to beat down all possibility of resistance anywhere to his will," and he called for a "grand alliance" against aggression.
9   Michael Kater, "Everyday Anti-Semitism in Prewar Nazi Germany: The Popular Bases," *Yad Vashem Studies* 16 (1984): 129–159; Marion A. Kaplan, *Between Dignity and Despair* (New York: Oxford University Press, 1998). Also see Dov Kulka, "Public Opinion in Nazi Germany and the 'Jewish Question,'" *Jerusalem Quarterly* 25 (Fall 1982): 121–144.
10 Zara Steiner, *The Triumph of the Dark, European International History 1933–1939* (Oxford: Oxford University Press, 2011), 1040–1043; Michael Marrus, *The Unwanted, European Refugees in the Twentieth Century* (New York: Oxford University Press, 1985), 145; David Bankier, *The Germans and the Final Solution, Public Opinion Under Nazism* (Oxford: Oxford University Press, 1992). For some unemployment figures in Europe at the time, see Herbert A. Strauss, "Jewish Emigration from Germany: Nazi Policies and Jewish Responses (I)," *Leo Baeck Institute Yearbook* 25 (1980): 356.
11 Vicki Caron, *Uneasy Asylum: France and the Jewish Refugee Crisis, 1933–1942* (Stanford, CA: Stanford University Press, 1999), 202. Although finding a destination proved difficult, about 36,000 Jews left Germany and Austria in 1938 and 77,000 in 1939. 1939 also marked the first time the United States filled its combined German-Austrian quota (which now included annexed Czechoslovakia). However, this limit did not come close to meeting the demand; by the end of June 1939, 309,000 German, Austrian, and Czech Jews had applied for the 27,000 places available under the quota. "German Jewish Refugees 1933–1939," *Holocaust Encyclopedia*, United States Holocaust Memorial Museum, www.ushmm.org/wlc/en/article.php?ModuleId=1000548.
12 JTA, January 9, 12, 16, 18, 20, 22, 24–26, 30, and 31, 1933. For the Minority Treaties, which were meant to protect Jews, see Oscar I. Janowsky, *The Jews and Minority Rights (1898–1919)* (New York: Columbia University Press, 1933); Carole Fink, *Defending the Rights of Others, The Jews and International Minority Protection (1878–1938)* (Cambridge: Cambridge University Press, 2004). The Legion of the Archangel Michael, known in the foreign press as the Iron Guard, was the principal fascist movement in Romania during the interwar period. Led by the charismatic Corneliu Zelea Codreanu until his death in 1938, the religiously oriented Iron Guard would reach the height of its power under Horia Sima and Ion Antonescu during World War II. For its beginnings, see Nicholas M. Nagy-Talavera, *The Green Shirts and the Others, A History of Fascism in Hungary and Rumania* (Stanford, CA: Stanford University Press, 1970), chaps. 9–10.
13 *New York Times*, October 20, 1934; McDonald to Warburg, September 18, 1934; microfilm #1923, Warburg MSS, American Jewish Archives, Cincinnati, OH; McDonald to Fuld, September 15, 1934, box 1, AR 7162, Leo Baeck Archives, New York City; Laski memorandum, September 1934, file 76, David Mowshowitz MSS, YIVO Archives, New York City; Pawal Korzec, "Antisemitism in Poland as an Intellectual, Social and Political Movement," in *Studies on Polish Jewry 1919–1939*, ed. J. A. Fishman (New York: YIVO Institute, 1974), 83.
14 Laski to Adler, October 2, 1934, Adler-Laski, Joint Foreign Committee (JFC) files, American Jewish Committee Archives (AJCA), New York City; JTA, October 8, 1934; September 1934–August 1935 "Strictly Confidential Report," file 215A, World Jewish Congress Archives (WJC), American Jewish Archives, Cincinnati, OH; Schmolke to American Joint Distribution Committee, October 13, 1934, file C1610/67; McDonald

to d'Avigdor-Goldsmid, November 17, 1944, file C1609/62; both in League of Nations Archives (LNA), Geneva.

15 JTA, February 15 and 19, 1935; Mr. X (Desider Friedman) and JFC member interview, January 10, 1935, file 77, Mowshowitz MSS; JTA, February 13, 15, 17, 20, 24, 26, and 27, 1935. Manifestations of "quiet" antisemitism in Austria were common in this decade; denunciations of "Jewish predominance" in the economic and social arenas had been nourished by the dominant Catholic clergy since the Middle Ages. Bruce F. Pauley, *From Prejudice to Persecution* (Chapel Hill: University of North Carolina Press, 1992), 268–273.

16 JTA, August 8, 1935; Friedländer, *Nazi Germany and the Jews*, 141–165; A. J. Sherman, *Island Refuge, Britain and Refugees from the Third Reich, 1933–1939* (London: Paul Elek, 1973), 58–61; JTA, September 20, 1935; *Palestine Post*, November 15, 1935; *New York Times*, December 30, 1935.

17 JTA, January 3, 7, 13, and 19, 1936.

18 JTA, February 2, 5, 12, 14, 19, and 21, 1936; Moskowitz to Waldman, December 27, 1937, Foreign Countries/Poland, AJCA; Celia S. Heller, *On the Edge of Destruction, Jews of Poland Between the Two World Wars* (New York: Columbia University Press, 1977), 113. Also see Anna Landau-Czajka, "The Image of the Jew in the Catholic Press during the Second Republic," *Polin* 8 (1994): 146–175. For the Polish opponents of antisemitism, see Ronald Modras, *The Catholic Church and Antisemitism: Poland, 1933–1939* (Chur: Harwood Academic Publishers, 1994), chap. 14.

19 JTA, March 11, 1936; Joshua Rothenberg, "The Przytyk Pogrom," *Soviet Jewish Affairs* 16:2 (1986): 29–46; "Report on the Situation of the Jews in Poland," JTA, January 1, 1936, file 122, Mowshowitz MSS; Va'ad HaLe'umi, February 16, 1936, J1/7236, Central Zionist Archives, Jerusalem; Laski-Goodman-Brotman memorandum and interview with Beck, March 26, 1936, Foreign Countries/Poland, AJCA; JFC minutes, April 22, 1936, Board of Deputies of British Jews Archives (BDA), Public Record Office (PRO), Kew, Great Britain; Daniel Blatman, "The Bund in Poland, 1935–1939," *Polin* 9 (1996): 58–82. In the aftermath of the Przytyk pogrom, many people were arrested. The trial started on June 2 and involved forty-three Polish and fourteen Jewish defendants, the latter charged with aggressive behavior towards Polish peasants. The verdict was pronounced on June 26, with eleven of the Jews sentenced to prison terms of six months to eight years, while thirty-nine Poles received sentences from six months to one year. The accused Jews claimed that they were acting in self-defense, but the court rejected those arguments. The verdict outraged the Jewish community in Poland, leading to a number of large, nationwide strikes. News of this pogrom horrified the Polish Jewish population, as well as Jews around the world, and contributed to a significant emigration of Jews from Poland. For Jewish resistance to these attacks, see Heller, *On the Edge of Destruction*, 285–291.

20 JTA, September 16, 1936, November 1 and 27, 1936, December 16, 1936.

21 JFC Report, November 11, 1936, Minutes, BDA; Bela Vago, *The Shadow of the Swastika, The Rise of Fascism and Anti-Semitism in the Danube Basin, 1936–1939* (Westmead: Saxon House for the Institute of Jewish Affairs, 1975), 191, 202.

22 JTA, February 8–10, 1937. Tolischus would receive the Pulitzer Prize for Journalism in 1940 for his writing in Berlin during World War II.

23 JTA, February 8, 10, 12, 14, 17, 17, 18, 25, and 26, 1937; Heller, *On the Edge of Destruction*, 118. In June 1936 Sławoj-Składkowski had endorsed the anti-Jewish economic boycott with a qualification: "yes, but without violence." Korzec, "Antisemitism in Poland," 90.

24 JTA, March 1, 2, 3, 12, 16, 18, 24, 29, and 30, 1937; Vago, *The Shadow of the Swastika*, 216.

25 JTA, August 6, 8, 18, 19, 20, 24, 25, 27, and 29–31, 1937; Szold to sisters, August 27, 1937, Henrietta Szold MSS, Hadassah Archives (HA), New York City; Klemperer, *I Will Bear Witness*, 231; Friedländer, *Nazi Germany and the Jews*, 184–185.

26 JTA, September 1, 3, 5, 9, 10, 13, 15, 19, 21, 26, and 28, 1937.

27 JTA, September 2, 9, 12, 13, 14, 22, and 24, 1937.

28 JTA, September 2, 3, and 5, 1937; Kennard to Foreign Office, October 6, 1937, FO 371/20816, PRO; Rendel-Michaelowski interview, October 1, 1937, FO 317/20815, PRO (copy in S25/22745, CZA); Rendel minute, October 15, 1937; Rendel memorandum, October 25, 1937; both in FO 371/20816; Rendel memorandum, October 27, 1937, FO 371/20818; Rendel note, October 28, 1937, FO 371/20819; all in PRO. The Colonial Office's Middle East expert, Harold F. Downie, observed to Rendel that if the British commission investigating the practicality of partitioning Palestine heard the Polish government, it could not well refuse to hear others, "and this opens up the prospect of grave embarrassments." Downie to Rendel, October 23, 1937, S25/22745, CZA.

29 JTA, November 3, 4, 5, 8, 9, 11, 14, 16, 18, 24, and 26, 1937; Klemperer, *I Will Bear Witness*, 241; William Shirer, *The Rise and Fall of the Third Reich* (New York: Simon & Schuster, 1959), 418–422.

30 JTA, December 9, 14, 15, and 29–31, 1937; Mihail Sebastian, *Journal 1935–1944*, trans. P. Camiller (Chicago, IL: University of Chicago Press, 2000), 133, 128, 119, 238; Vago, *The Shadow of the Swastika*, 249; Nagey-Talavera, *The Green Shirts and the Others*, 294; Frederick B. Chary, *The Bulgarian Jews and the Final Solution, 1940–1944* (Pittsburgh, PA: Pittsburgh University Press, 1972), chap. 1.

31 JTA, January 4, 6, 9, 10, 11, 12, 14, 19, 24, and 30, 1938; Klemperer, *I Will Bear Witness*, 249; Meir Michaelis, *Mussolini and the Jews, German-Italian Relations and the Jewish Question in Italy, 1922–1945* (Oxford: Clarendon Press, 1978). chap. 5; JTA, March 13–18, 1938.

32 JTA, March 3, 9, 11, 13, 16, 17, 21, 25, and 30, 1938; April 1, 1938.

33 *Proceedings of the Intergovernmental Committee*, Evian, July 6 to 15, 1938, Verbatim Record of the Meetings of the Committee, Resolutions, and Reports (London, 1938), *passim*; Warren to Chamberlain, July 9, 1938, box 77, Hamilton Fish Armstrong MSS, Department of Rare Books and Special Collections, Princeton University Library, Princeton, New Jersey; Vincent Sheean, *Not Peace but a Sword* (New York: Doubleday, 1939), 89–94. In 1940 the Dominican Republic dictator Rafael Trujillo donated 26,000 acres of his property for settlements. The first settlers arrived in May 1940; only about 800 refugees came to Sosúa, and most moved on to the United States.

34 S. Adler-Rudel, "The Evian Conference on the Refugee Question," *Leo Baeck Institute Year Book* 12 (1968): 251–265; Arthur Ruppin diary, July 18, 1938, Arthur Ruppin, *Pirkei Hayai, b'Inyan ha'Aretz v'ha'Am* (Tel Aviv: Am Oved, 1968), 302–303; Goldmann and Ruppin to Landauer, July 12, 1938, S25/9778, CZA; Brotman memorandum, July 1938, Refugees 1938, Evian Conference, AJCA; Sherman, *Island Refuge*, 120–121; Jewish Agency Executive Jerusalem, August 21, 1938, CZA; Golda Meir, *My Life* (New York: Penguin, 1975), 159; Meyerson remarks at Histadrut Va'ad HaPo'el, July 21, 1938, file P-810/6, Israel State Archives, Jerusalem. A summary after the Evian Conference by a League of Nations official concluded that the number of Jewish refugees would reach 500,000. Erim memorandum, July 21, 1938, file R5800/50/34521/34225, LNA.

35 Ezra Mendelsohn, *The Jews of East Central Europe between the World Wars* (Bloomington: Indiana University Press, 1983), 116–119; JTA, June 1, 2, 5, 1938; July 3, 7, 12, 1938; September 2, 1938.

36 Karl Schleunes, *The Twisted Road to Auschwitz: Nazi Policy Toward German Jews, 1933–1939* (Urbana: Illinois University Press, 1970), chap. 7.

37 JTA, December 6, 14, 15, 21, 23, and 27, 1938; Jerzy Tomaszewski, "The Polish Right-Wing Press, the Expulsion of Polish Jews from Germany, and the Deportees in Zbąszyn," *Gal-Ed* 18 (2002): 89–100; Joseph Tenenbaum, "The Crucial Year 1938," *Yad Vashem Studies* 2 (1958): 66; Nagy-Talavera, *The Green Shirts and Others*, 147–148; Vago, *The Shadow of the Swastika*, 361;

38 Hitler speech, January 30, 1939, in *The Speeches of Adolf Hitler*, ed. N. H. Baynes, vol. 1 (London: Oxford University Press, 1942), 737–741; JTA, February 2, 1939. Even Mussolini was "very well satisfied" with Hitler's address, and he had his foreign minister get word to

the *Führer* "that the words uttered last night have given a great deal of joy and satisfaction to all the Italian people." *The Ciano Diaries, 1939–1945*, ed. H. Gibson (Garden City, NY: Doubleday, 1947), 19.

39 JTA, February 5, 12, and 16, 1939; Mendelsohn, *The Jews of East Central Europe between the World Wars*, 120; JTA, March 3, 6, 7, 12, 1938.

40 JTA, March 16, 17, 20, and 22, 1939; *Documents on British Foreign Policy, Third Series*, vol. 4, ed. E. L. Woodward, R. Butler, and M. Lambert (London: HMSO, 1951), 562, 566; JTA, March 27, 1939.

41 JTA, May 1, 2, 3, 5, 9, 10, and 19, 1939; *Foreign Relations of the United States, 1939*, vol. 4 (Washington, D.C.: Government Printing Office, 1955), 757–758; Murray to Hull, May 15, 1939, 867N.01/1599, State Department Archives, Suitland, MD; David Wyman, *Paper Walls, Paper Walls, America and the Refugee Crisis, 1938–1941* (Cambridge, MA: University of Massachusetts Press, 1968), chaps. 1, 4; Henry Feingold, *The Politics of Rescue, The Roosevelt Administration and the Holocaust, 1938–1945* (New Brunswick, NJ: Rutgers University Press, 1970), chap. 1; Gordon Thomas and Max Morgan Witts, *Voyage of the Damned* (London: Stein & Day, 1974). A strong protest against the White Paper was sent by the six major US Zionist organizations; no reply was received. Cable to Chamberlain, July 2, 1939, FO 371/23238, PRO.

42 *New York Times*, June 7, 1939; Sherman, *Island Refuge*, 253; JTA, June 4, 6, 12, 13, 14, 21, 22, 23, and 29, 1939; George Kennan, *From Prague after Munich, Diplomatic Papers, 1938–1940* (Princeton: Princeton University Press, 1968), 189.

43 Penkower, *Decision on Palestine Deferred*, 20–21; JTA, August 4, 14, 18, 20, 22, 23, and 27, 1939; Vago, *The Shadow of the Swastika*, 415; Bernard Wasserstein, *On the Eve, The Jews of Europe before the Second World War* (New York: Simon & Schuster, 2012), 407–408.

44 Andres Kasekamp, "Radical Right-Wing Movements in the North-East Baltic," *Journal of Contemporary History* 34:4 (October 1999): 587–600; Dorothy Thompson, "To a Jewish Friend," *New York Herald Tribune*, November 14, 1938; Niebuhr address; Swing address; both on October 31, 1938, HA.

45 For widespread isolationist sentiment in the United States, see Wickham Steed, "Notes on American Visit, Oct. 2–15, 1937," A159/3, CZA. As an illustration of American views, a survey by the American Institute of Public Opinion on November 22, 1938, shortly after *Kristallnacht*, found that, while 94 percent of respondents disapproved of the Nazis' treatment of Jews in Germany, 77 percent replied "No" when asked if a larger number of "Jewish exiles from Germany" should be allowed to come to the United States to live. In April 1938, the results to the question "Do you think the persecution of the Jews in Europe has been their own fault?" were as follows: "Not at all"—31 percent; "Entirely"—10 percent; "Partly"—48 percent; "No opinion and no answer"—11 percent. *Public Opinion, 1935–1946*, ed. H. Cantril, ed. (Princeton: Princeton University Press, 1951), 382, 385, 381. These sentiments persisted for some time, Philip Graham of the *Washington Post* warning Joe Rauh right after the Japanese surprise attack against the US Pacific naval base in Hawaii's Pearl Harbor on December 7, 1941, not to say "Thank God." Rauh responded thus because he was "so depressed we were not preparing for war that my reaction was 'Thank God.'" Graham realized, however, that "there could be an anti-Semitic kickback and the last thing any Jews should say is 'It's good.'" Katherine Graham, *Personal History* (New York: Knopf, 1998), 135.

46 *New York Times*, November 15, 1938. Viewing the German rulers' hatred of Jews as directed "in the higher sense" against the Christian and classical foundations of Western morality, Mann responded to the Munich agreement of September 1938 with this phrase to close friend and literary scholar Erich von Kahler: "The shame, the disgust, the shattering of all hopes." *Kristallnacht* drew a fuller reaction in a letter dispatched from Paris: "The shortsighted, feeble, and uncomprehending policy of the Western powers in Europe has conferred upon the National Socialist regime a plenitude of power, which enables these creatures to fulfill their wishes and evil instincts to the utmost, without fear or consideration for anyone."

Letters of Thomas Mann, 1889–1955, trans. R. and C. Winston (New York: Knopf, 1971), 248, 282, 288. Von Kahler, a Czech-born Jew who left Germany when Hitler came to power, reached the United States in 1938. Dropping the "von," he taught at a number of universities and became a member at Princeton University's Institute for Advanced Study. Kahler's many books included *The Tower and the Abyss* and *The Jew among the Nations*.

47 *Daily Express*, June 20, 1938; *New York Times*, July 3, 1938; Timothy S. Benson, *Strube, The World's Most Popular Cartoonist* (London: Political Cartoon Society, 2004).

48 Wise to Mack, April 15, 1933, box 115, Stephen Wise MSS, American Jewish Historical Society, New York City; David Aberbach, "Patriotism and Antisemitism: The Crisis of Polish-Jewish Identity between the Wars," *Polin* 22 (2010): 380; Antony Polonsky, "'Bal w Operze', Julian Tuwim's Jewish Apocalypse," *Gal-Ed* 18 (2002): 119–143; Einstein to Nathan, July 14, 1936, folder 1.12, Adele and Morris Bergreen Einstein papers, The Archives and Special Collections Library, Vassar College, Poughkeepsie, NY; Lauterbach memorandum, April 29, 1938, S5/653, CZA; Alexander Ringer, *Arnold Schoenberg, The Composer as Jew* (Oxford: Oxford University Press, 1990), 230–244; Wasserstein, *On the Eve*, 412.

49 Brandeis-Szold conference, August 6, 1939, file 53, Robert Szold MSS, Zionist Archives, New York (now at the CZA).

50 Avraham Barkai and Paul Mendes-Flohr, *German Jewish History in Modern Times*, ed. M. A. Meyer, vol. 4 (New York: Columbia University Press, 1998), 330; Daniel Frankel, *Al Pi Tehom, haMediniyut haTziyonit u'Sh'eilat Yehudei Germania, 1933–1938* (Jerusalem: Magnes, 1984), 286; Abraham Margaliot, "The Problem of the Rescue of German Jewry during the Years 1933–1939; the Reasons for the Delay in Their Emigration from the Third Reich," in *Rescue Attempts during the Holocaust*, ed. Y. Gutman and E. Zuroff (Jerusalem: Yad Vashem, 1977), 260–263; Ya'akov Shavit and Liat Shtayer-Livni, "Mi Kara Ze'ev? Eikh Heivin Ze'ev Jabotinsky et Tiva shel Germania haNatzit v'et Kavanoteha?," in *Ish baSa'ar*, ed. Avi Bareli and Pinhas Ginosar (Sdeh Boker: Machon Ben-Gurion l'Heker Yisrael, 2004), 345–368. Jabotinsky's metaphor about the effect of a volcano, delivered on Tish'a B'Av to a Vilna audience in 1938, is cited in Shmuel Katz, *Lone Wolf: A Biography of Vladimir (Ze'ev) Jabotinsky*, vol. 2 (New York: Barricade Books, 1996), 1,649. An early use of *Shoah*, the term later adopted in the State of Israel for the Holocaust, appeared in S. Gorelik, "Yom haShloshim b'Yanuar," *Davar*, January 30, 1934.

51 Prinz interview with the author, April 7, 1977; Joachim Prinz, *Rebellious Rabbi*, ed. M. Meyer (Bloomington: Indiana University Press, 2008), 98–179; Joachim Prinz, "Zionism under the Nazi Government," *New Palestine*, September 17, 1937; American Jewish Congress Convention, November 27, 1937, American Jewish Congress Archives, New York City; *Heinrich Heine, A Biographical Anthology*, ed. H. Bieber, trans. M. Hadas, (Philadelphia: The Jewish Publication Society of America, 1956), 331. Heine, who had reluctantly converted to Protestantism as "the ticket of admission into European culture," had already written in the play *Almansor* (1821) that "where they burn books they will eventually burn people." While this oft-quoted line referred to Christians in Spain burning a *Qur'an* while forcibly converting the Moors in the early sixteenth century, Heine also hinted thereby at Romantic nationalist student groups in Germany who burned "unpatriotic" books in October 1819. Prinz would subsequently become a leader in the US civil rights movement, besides heading prominent Jewish organizations.

52 Simon Dubnow, "An International League for Protection of the Jewish People against Aggression," file 174A/76, WJCA; Y. Meirson, "Siha im Professor Shimon Dubnow," *Davar*, July 19, 1939; Sophie Dubnov-Erlich, *The Life and Work of S. M. Dubnow*, trans. Judith Vowles, ed. Jeffrey Shandler (Bloomington: Indiana University Press, 1991), 233–236. Dubnow was shot on December 8, 1941, in Rumbula (Rumbuli), a wooded area near the railway station of that name, five miles from the Latvian capital. From November 29 to December 8, 1941, 28,000 Jews from the Riga ghetto, as well as 10,000 who had been transported by train from Germany, Austria, and the Protectorate of Bohemia and Moravia, were murdered there.

53 Natan Gross, "Mordechai Gebirtig: The Folk Song and the Cabaret Song," *Polin* 16 (2003): 107–117; *The Literature of Destruction: Jewish Responses to Catastrophe*, ed. David G. Roskies (Philadelphia: The Jewish Publication Society of America, 1988), 358–359, 371–372. "*S'brent!*" became popular among Jewish youth and resistance fighters during the Holocaust. Gebirtig was murdered on the "Bloody Thursday" of June 4, 1942, while being marched to the Kraków train station on the way to the Belzec death camp. For Bialik's "B'Ir HaHareiga," see Monty Noam Penkower, *Twentieth Century Jews: Forging Identity in the Land of Promise and in the Promised Land* (Boston: Academic Studies Press, 2010), chap. 1. For two prescient pre-World War II novellas by the American-based Yiddish poet Jacob Glatstein which focused on Poland, *Ven Yash iz Geforen* ("When Yash Set Out") and *Ven Yash iz Gekumen* ("When Yash Arrived"), see Jacob Glatstein, *The Glatstein Chronicles*, ed. R. Wisse, trans. M. Deshell and N. Guterman, (New Haven: Yale University Press, 2010).
54 Wasserstein, *On the Eve*, xix, 436; Hansson lecture, December 10, 1938, www.nobelprize.org; Weizmann-Macdonald interview, May 13, 1939, S25/7563, CZA; *The Letters of Martin Buber*, 478–486. Even after the Holocaust, which he called "the greatest crime of our time," Gandhi felt that the Jews should have practiced *Satyagraha* and "thrown themselves into the sea from cliffs . . . It would have aroused the world and the people of Germany." Louis Fischer, *The Life of Mahatma Gandhi* (New York: Harper & Brothers, 1950), 346–348.
55 Sheean, *Not Peace but a Sword*, 138–139; *Encyclopedia Judaica*, vol. 9 (Jerusalem: Keter, 1972), 532.
56 Elif Batuman, "Kafka's Last Trial," *New York Times Magazine*, September 22, 2010. The Jewish Theological Seminary defrayed most of the costs of transporting the Great Synagogue's sacred objects. The Danzig community hoped that distributing its "homeless" Torah scrolls among the most important synagogues in the United States would "draw attention to the plight of German Jewry to a much greater extent" and "arouse keener sympathy for these helpless people." With no claim having been made for the return of the collection after fifteen years, as stipulated in the community's original agreement with the JDC, in April 1954 the Danzig Collection became a permanent part of the Jewish Museum in New York City. In March 1980, 150 of these objects were exhibited at the Jewish Museum. Troper to Baerwald, Mar. 9, 1939, Danzig Museum Collection, 1933–1944, American Jewish Joint Distribution Committee Archives, New York City; *Danzig, 1939: Treasures of a Destroyed Community*, ed. V. B. Mann and J. Gutmann (New York: Wayne State University Press for the Jewish Museum of New York, 1980). The Danzig community archives (about 2000 files), reflecting its history from 1765 to 1938, were shipped to the Jewish Agency in Jerusalem, which turned them over to the newly founded Jewish Historical General Archives. This was the first major community collection to be deposited in the Archives, now called the Central Archives for the History of the Jewish People. Many of the remaining Danzig Jews were aboard the ill-fated *Patria*, which exploded in Haifa Bay on November 25, 1940. See Penkower, *The Jews Were Expendable*, chap. 2.

Notes to Chapter 4

1 Yosef Heller, "'HaMonism shel haMatara o haMonism shel haEmtsa'im'?: HaMakhloket haRa'ayonit v'haPolitit bein Ze'ev Jabotinsky l'vein Abba Ahimeir, 1928–1933," *Zion* 52 (1987): 318–324; Abba Ahimeir, "MiPinkaso shel Fashishtan," *Do'ar haYom*, October 28, 1928; Abba Ahimeir, "HaDiktatura haLe'umit baOlam haGadol," *Do'ar haYom*, January 29, 1929; Uri Zvi Greenberg, "HaTziyonut haArtila'it v'haMekonenim b'Shuleha," *HaOlam*, July 27, 1923; Uri Zvi Greenberg, *Hazon Ehad haLigyonot* (Tel Aviv: Saden, 1929); Yehoshua Yeivin's articles, *Do'ar haYom*, January 20 and 27, 1929; Abba Ahimeir, *Brit haBiryonim* (Tel Aviv: HaVa'ad le'Hotza'at Kitvei Ahimeir, 1972); Joseph Schechtman, *Fighter*

and *Prophet: The Vladimir Jabotinsky Story, The Last Years* (New York: Thomas Yoseloff, 1961), 160–162; Josiah Wedgwood, *The Seventh Dominion* (London: Labour, 1928).

2   Yosef Heller, *Lehi, Ideologia u'Politika, 1940–1949*, vol. 1 (Jerusalem: Merkaz Zalman Shazar, 1989), 25, 231 notes 60 and 61; Louis Rapoport, *Shake Heaven and Earth, Peter Bergson and the Struggle to Rescue the Jews of Europe* (Jerusalem: Gefen, 1999), 21; Aryeh Naor, *David Raziel, Parashat Hayav shel Mefaked haRashi shel haEtzel* (Tel Aviv: Misrad haBitahon, 1990), 45, and chaps. 5–6. For the most recent article on the debate as to the formation of the Irgun Tzva'i Le'umi, see Efraim Even, "'Hukam, Hukam, Hukam'. Al Reishito shel haEtzel," *Makor Rishon*, Shabbat, July 22, 2011, 14–15.

3   *HaMetzuda*, ed. H. S. HaLevi (Tel Aviv: Machon Jabotinsky, 1978), 19, 24, 55, note 51; Rapoport, *Shake Heaven and Earth*, 21; Naor, *David Raziel*, 69, 77.

4   Schechtman, *Fighter and Prophet*, 251–252; Jewish Telegraphic Agency (JTA), December 16, 1934; *HaYarden*, January 15, 1935. Ahimeir would serve a prison sentence of eighteen months for leading *Brit HaBiryonim*, and be released in August 1935. For Arlosoroff's murder and its lasting effect on Israel's political divide, see Monty Noam Penkower, *Twentieth Century Jews: Forging Identity in the Land of Promise and in the Promised Land* (Boston: Academic Studies Press, 2010), chap. 8.

5   Schechtman, *Fighter and Prophet*, chap. 14; National Board, January 30, 1935, Hadassah Archives, New York City; US Zionist-Revisionists meeting, February 7, 1935, HaTzahar-US files, box 2, Jabotinsky Archives (hereafter JA), Tel Aviv; Hanokh Rosenblum, "Artzot-haBrit v'Yehudeha b'Hashkafato shel Ze'ev Jabotinsky," in *Ish baSa'ar*, ed. Avi Bareli and Pinhas Ginosar (Sdeh Boker: Machon Ben-Gurion l'Heker Yisrael, 2004), 427–432. For Jabotinsky's address to the American Economic Committee on Palestine, see Minutes, February 6, 1935, microfilm #24, Brandeis MSS, University of Louisville, Louisville, KY. Jabotinsky's response to American Zionist leader Stephen Wise, where he emphatically championed "old-fashioned parliamentarism" over any "totalitarian State" and repeated the Revisionist contention that "in Palestine there is room for all the Jews who will ever need it and for all the Arabs with their progeny," is in JTA, March 17, 1935.

6   Schechtman, *Fighter and Prophet*, 276–278, 296–298.

7   Ibid., 282–290; JTA, September 9 and 12, 1935.

8   Schechtman, *Fighter and Prophet*, 300–304, 346; JTA, April 29, 1936; May 13, 1936; Jabotinsky press conference, May 21, 1936, A330/779, Central Zionist Archives (hereafter CZA), Jerusalem; Abba Ahimeir, "Giborim v'Lo K'doshim!," in Abba Ahimeir, *HaTziyonut haMahapkhanit* (Tel Aviv: HaVa'ad le'Hotza'at Kitvei Ahimeir, 1966), 98–100.

9   Schechtman, *Fighter and Prophet*, 448–454, 457–458; Rafaeli interview with the author. In stressing the common links between Kook and Jabotinsky, Evan Kaplan overlooks their differences. See Evan Kaplan, "A Rebel with a Cause: Hillel Kook, Begin, and Jabotinsky's Ideological Legacy," *Israel Studies* 10:3 (Fall 2005): 87–103.

10 Penkower, *Twentieth Century Jews*, chap. 9; Betar's Third World Conference, Warsaw, September 11–16, 1938, *A Report* (Bucharest: n.p., 1940); transcript of conference; both in Menahem Begin Heritage Center archives (hereafter MBHCA), Jerusalem; Yosef Heller, "Ze'ev Jabotinsky u'Sh'eilat 'haHavlaga', 1926–1939: Hashkafat Olam b'Mivhan haMetziut," in *Temurot baHistoria haYehudit haHadasha*, ed. Shmuel Almog et al. (Jerusalem: Merkaz Zalman Shazar, 1988), 300–305; Yisrael Eldad, *Ma'aser Rishon* (Tel Aviv: Hadar, 1975), 19–25. Jabotinsky also altered his 1937 poem "Kula Sheli" ("It is All Mine") to call twice for revolt and highlight the gallows, as well as to claim that Betar was "divinely chosen to rule." Halpern had called for this platform between July and December 1937 in a three-part series published by *Hayarden*. He later broke with Stern and began the "Cana'anite" movement. See Yonatan Ratosh, *Raishit haYamim, Petihuyot Ivriyot* (Tel Aviv: Hadar, 1962). His platform for the Betar conference is in file 2/32-2B, JA.

11 Haim Lazar-Litai, *Af-Al-Pi, Sefer Aliya Bet* (Tel Aviv: Machon Jabotinsky, 1957), chap. 16; Schechtman, *Fighter and Prophet*, 458–460, 463–464, 477–480. For Katzenelson, see

Y. Ahimeir, ed., *HaNasikh haShahor, Yosef Katzenelson v'haTenu'a haLe'umit b'Shnot haShloshim* (Tel Aviv: Machon Jabotinsky, 1983).

12 JTA, January. 5 and 18, 1939; February 14, 1939; Lubinski to Ziff, May 29, 1939, and June 30, 1939; box 1/1, Palestine Statehood Committee Papers (hereafter PSC), Sterling Library, Yale University, New Haven, CT; Chaim Lubinski interview with the author, January 19, 1987; William Ziff, *The Rape of Palestine* (New York: Longmans, Green, 1938); Ziff to Germain, August 23, 1939, Box 1/2, PSC; Yitshaq Ben-Ami, *Years of Wrath, Days of Glory* (New York: Robert Speller, 1982), 213–224.

13 Ben-Ami, *Years of Wrath, Days of Glory*, 220; Lubinski to Mack, March 25, 1939; Lubinski to Brodie, April 2, 1939; Mack to Brandeis, April 24, 1939; Mack to Wise-Szold-Brodie, April 27, 1938; all in A251/10, CZA; Szold-Brandeis conference, August 6, 1939; Goldmann to Brandeis, September 5, 1939; all in file 59, Robert Szold MSS, Zionist Archives (hereafter ZA), New York (transferred to the CZA); Alexander Rafaeli, *Dream and Action* (Jerusalem: n.p., 1993), 80–83.

14 Schechtman, *Fighter and Prophet*, 481–482; Hecht interview with the author; *La Suisse*, August 21, 1939, 1, in Foreign Office papers (hereafter FO) 371/23239, Public Record Office (hereafter PRO), Kew; Herzl Rosenblum, "Peter Bergson," *Haboker*, October 20, 1944.

15 Ya'akov Shavit and Liat Shtayer-Livni, "Mi Kara Ze'ev? Eikh Heivin Ze'ev Jabotinsky et Tiva shel Germania haNazit v'et Kavanoteha?," in *Ish baSa'ar*, ed. Avi Bareli and Pinhas Ginosar (Sdeh Boker: Machon Ben-Gurion l'Heker Yisrael, 2004), 345–368; Schechtman, *Fighter and Prophet*, 482–484; Naor, *David Raziel*, chap. 19; Ya'akov Eliav, *Mevukash* (Jerusalem: BaMahteret, 1983), 132–141; Lubinski interview with the author.

16 Schechtman, *Fighter and Prophet*, 368–374; Ya'akov Vinshal, *Yerma, Pirkei Hayav shel "Poresh" Gadol* (Tel Aviv: Ahiasaf, 1968), 121; Jabotinsky to Chamberlain, September 4, 1939, FO 371/23250, PRO; Vladimir Jabotinsky, *The Jewish War Front* (London: Allen & Unwin, 1940). The book, which saw print in June 1940, was republished in New York City in 1943 by the Jabotinsky Foundation under the title *The War and the Jew*. Curiously, Jabotinsky minimized German antisemitism in this volume, arguing that the Polish hatred of Jews on economic grounds was more worrying in the long run.

17 Schechtman, *Fighter and Prophet*, 375, 429–433; Ben-Ami interview with the author; JTA, January 18, 1940; March 11, 1940; July 26, 1940; Schwamm et al. memo, January 27, 1940, Box 4/2, PSC; William Perl, *The Four-Front War: From the Holocaust to the Promised Land* (New York: Crown, 1979), chap. 6; Eri Jabotinsky, *Avi, Ze'ev Jabotinsky* (Tel Aviv: Stimatzky, 1980), 168–208.

18 Kook interviews nos. 2 (1988) and 3 (July 3, 1988) with Manor, file P2-10, MBHCA.

19 JTA, March 14, 20, and 26, 1940; Lothian to Foreign Office, June 8, 1940, and reply June 14, 1940, FO 371/24566, PRO; Breslau to Wise, June 10, 1940, box 107, Stephen Wise MSS, American Jewish Historical Society, Center for Jewish History, New York City; Memorandum of ECZA delegation visit to Washington, June 17, 1940, given the author by the late Isidor Breslau; *New York Times*, June 13, 1940; JTA, June 20, 1940. Two days before Jabotinsky's arrival, Wise declared at his Free Synagogue services in Carnegie Hall that he would not support Jabotinsky and the Revisionist movement, claiming that Revisionism was "a species of Fascism in Yiddish or Hebrew," running counter to the Jewish tradition and "the social and democratic ideals of our day and age." JTA, March 12, 1940.

20 Ze'ev Jabotinsky, *Mikhtavim* (Tel Aviv: Machon Jabotinsky, n.d.), 213–215, 219–230; May 28, 1940, meeting ECZA files, ZA; Schechtman, *Fighter and Prophet*, 394–395; Jabotinsky to Landau, July 4, 1940, FO 371/24566, PRO; Jabotinsky to Rafaeli, June 12, 1940, file P2-9, MBHCA.

21 Jabotinsky to Czech foreign affairs minister, August 1, 1940, NZO files, box 2, JA; Kook interview with Manor, July 3, 1988, P2-10, MBHCA; Schechtman, *Fighter and Prophet*, 396–398, 489–490.

22 ECZA minutes, August 6, 1940, ZA; Klinger to NZO London, August 12 and 14, 1940, box 5, NZO US files, JA; Kook interview with Manor, July 3, 1988, P2-10, MBHCA; JTA, August 7, 1940.
23 Benjamin Akzin interview with the author, August 19, 1976; Heller, *Lehi*, chap. 3; Kook interview no. 2 with Manor, 1988, P2-10, JA; Merlin to Stern, December 29, 1940, quoted in *HaIrgun haTzva'i haLe'umi b'Eretz-Yisrael, Osef Mekorot u'Mismakhim*, ed. Yitzhak Alfasi, vol. 1 (Tel Aviv: Machon Jabotinsky, 1990), 389–390. Merlin's reference to the Red Sea was based on Exodus 14–15.
24 Kook interview with Manor, July 3, 1988, file P2-10; Kook to Altman, May 7, 1941, file P2-5; both in MBHCA; Kook to Silver, April 10, 1941, Hebrew Committee of National Liberation MSS, JA.
25 JTA, January 2, 1941; February 28, 1941; April 1 and 20, 1941. For the *Patria*, see Monty Noam Penkower, *The Jews Were Expendable* (Urbana: University of Illinois Press, 1983), chap. 2. Nothing came of the NZO-Mapai tentative agreement.
26 JTA, August 11 and 22, 1940; May 5, 1941; June 3, 1941.
27 Kook interview with the author; Pierre van Paassen, *Days of Our Years* (New York: Hillman-Curl, 1939); JTA, June 16 and 27, 1941. For Helpern, see Vinshal, *Yerma*, passim.
28 JTA, September 9, 1941; November 21, 1941.
29 Penkower, *The Jews Were Expendable*, 4–11. Rather than endorse what he considered "most alarming talk" from Ben-Gurion and Weizmann of securing 3,000,000 Jews and sovereignty in Palestine, Moyne told a parliamentary delegation led by Wedgwood and Percival Harris that the "best course was to keep things as steady as possible for the present." Equipment scarcity and the new factor of the Soviet Union's entry on the Allied side, he advised Weizmann, precluded a favorable decision at this time. Moyne to Weizmann, August 28, 1941, Chaim Weizmann Archives, Rehovot, Israel; Moyne memo, September 30, 1941, PREM 4, 52/5, I–II; Moyne's talk with a parliamentary delegation, October 17, 1941, War Office 32/9502; both in PRO.
30 Kook interview with the author; Ben Hecht, *A Child of the Century* (New York: Simon & Schuster, 1954), 517; Ben Hecht, *A Book of Miracles* (New York: The Viking Press, 1939), 23–53, 112–201.
31 Kook interview with the author; Hecht, *A Child of the Century*, 516–517, 536.
32 Kook interview with Manor, July 25, 1988, file P2-10, MBHCA; *Washington Times Herald*, December 5, 1941; Pierre Van Paassen, "World Destiny Pivots on Palestine," *New Palestine*, December 12, 1941.
33 JTA, December 7 and 10, 1941; *The Battle for Jerusalem* (New York: The American Friends of a Jewish Palestine, 1941).
34 Kook interview with the author; *New York Times*, January 5, 1942.
35 E. Jabotinsky to Dayag, September 4, 1943, FO 371/40129, PRO; "I Bring a Sword," January 1947 report, box 6, Eri Jabotinsky MSS, JA.
36 Office Committee, December 8, 1941, ECZA minutes, ZA; Ben-Gurion to Goldmann, December 12, 1941, A296/6, CZA; Executive minutes, December 13, 1941, ZOA files, ZA; Ben-Gurion diary, December 21, 1941, David Ben-Gurion Archives (hereafter BGA), Sdeh Boker, Israel.
37 Kook interview with Manor, July 25, 1988; Kook to Helpern, April 9, 1942, file P2-5; both in MBHCA.
38 Kook interview with Manor, July 25, 1988; Rapoport, *Shake Heaven and Earth*, 47.
39 Kook interview with the author; *The Fighting Jew* (New York: Committee for a Jewish Army for Stateless and Palestinian Jews, 1942); *Memorandum on a Jewish Army of Palestinian and Stateless Jews* (New York: Committee for a Jewish Army for Stateless and Palestinian Jews, 1942); both in file P2-6, MBHCA; *New York Herald Tribune*, February 20, 1942; *Philadelphia Record*, February 10, 1942; *Jewish Daily Forward*, April 8, 1942; *Washington Post*, May 25, 1942; *New York Times*, August 18, 1942. Bar Kokhba was the primary leader

in the last Palestinian Jewish revolt for independence against the legions of imperial Rome, 132–135 CE.
40 Penkower, *Twentieth Century Jews*, 155–160; Kook interview with Manor, July 25, 1988. For an overview of Magnes's ideology and political stance, see Monty Noam Penkower, *Israel: As A Phoenix Ascending* (New York: Touro University Press, 2021), chap. 6.
41 Kook to Helpern, April 9, 1942, file P2-5, MBHCA; Vinshal, *Yerma*, 132–137; "The United Nations and the Jewish National Home in Palestine," American-Palestine Committee dinner, May 25, 1942, ZA. For the Biltmore Platform, see Monty Noam Penkower, *Decision on Palestine Deferred: America, Britain and Wartime Diplomacy, 1939–1945* (London: Frank Cass, 2002), chap. 4.
42 January 22, 1942 minutes, Colonial Office files 733/448-I/76147/1, PRO; Moyne to Churchill, September 30, 1941, PREM 4, 52/5, PRO; Wedgwood and Moyne speeches in Parliament, June 9, 1942, quoted in *New Judea* (May–June 1942): 122–127. For the *Struma*, see Penkower, *The Jews Were Expendable*, 150–151.
43 JTA, April 17, 1942; May 4, 1942.
44 JTA, June 23, 1942.
45 Michael J. Cohen, *Palestine: Retreat from the Mandate: The Making of British Policy, 1936–45* (New York: Paul Elek, 1978), 118–121; Penkower, *The Jews Were Expendable*, 14–15. For Wingate, see Monty Noam Penkower, *Palestine in Turmoil: The Struggle for Sovereignty, 1933–1939*, vol. 2, *Retreat from the Mandate, 1937–1939* (New York: Touro University Press, 2014), 478, 517, 554, 687.
46 Penkower, *The Jews Were Expendable*, 15–16. For the *Struma* tragedy, see Penkower, *Decision on Palestine Deferred*, 110–112.
47 JTA, July 5, 1942; August 3 and 10, 1942; October 14, 1942. The reference to "gas chambers" at this date is remarkable, since Allied acknowledgment of this fact came much later. In retaliation for the Czech underground's killing of SS Reinhard Heydrich, *Reichsprotektor* of the Protectorate of Bohemia and Moravia, the Czech village of Lidice was razed to the ground on June 10, 1942, and all 192 men and 71 women were killed, with the remaining 198 women imprisoned in the Ravensbrück concentration camp. Of these, 143 returned after the war. Of the 98 children who had been put in "educational institutions," only 16 survived.
48 Penkower, *The Jews Were Expendable*, 16–17.
49 *Washington Post*, November 25, 1942; Kook interview with the author; Ben-Ami interview with the author; Merlin interview with the author; Bergson to Swing, November 29, 1942, Emergency Committee to Save the Jewish People of Europe MSS, box 66–89, JA.
50 *New York Times*, December 7, 1942.
51 JTA, Dec. 18, 1942; January 27, 1943; February 26, 1943. Van Paassen informed the Committee that he objected to its use of his name in messages and letters, as well as being quoted in meetings, without his consent. This fact, together with his wish not to be in opposition to the Zionist leadership "at a time when discipline and unanimity of sentiment in Zionist ranks is more essential than ever," made his resolve to resign "final and irrevocable." Quoted in Arye Bruce Saposnik, "Advertisement or Achievement: American Jewry and the Campaign for a Jewish Army, 1939–1944: A Reassessment," *Journal of Israeli History* 17:2 (Summer 1996): 216. But also see Rapoport, *Shake Heaven and Earth*, 126–128.
52 Ben-Ami, *Years of Wrath, Days of Glory*, 284; Penkower, *The Jews Were Expendable*, 148–155; Ben Hecht, "Remember Us!," *Reader's Digest* (February 1943): 107–110; Hecht, *A Child of the Century*, 551–553.
53 Ben-Ami interview with the author; Hecht, *A Child of the Century*, 553ff.
54 Ben Hecht, "We Will Never Die," box 23–25, Emergency Committee MSS, JA; *New York Post*, March 10, 1943; *New York Times*, March 10, 1943; *New York Journal American*, March 10, 1943.
55 JTA, April 14, 1943; *Answer*, April 1943 and May 1943.
56 JTA, April 14, 1943.

57 JTA, April 13 and 18, 1943; Memorandum, April 16, 1943, FO 371/36659, PRO; Arthur Morse, *While Six Million Died: A Chronicle of American Apathy* (New York: Hart, 1967), 49. For the issuing of the UN Declaration, see Penkower, *The Jews Were Expendable*, 80–92.
58 Law, quoted in Morse, *While Six Million Died*, 57; *New York Times*, May 4, 1943. For the Bermuda Conference and its aftermath, see Penkower, *The Jews Were Expendable*, chap. 4.
59 JTA, May 7, 1943.
60 Saposnik, "Advertisement or Achievement," 215. For more on Truman in this connection, see Monty Noam Penkower, "The Venting of Presidential Spleen: Harry S Truman's Jewish Problem," *Jewish Quarterly Review* 94:4 (Fall 2004): 615–624.
61 JTA, May 11, 1943.
62 JTA, May 17, 1943; Penkower, *The Jews Were Expendable*, 107, 111. For the Evian Conference, which had equally done nothing to aid Jewish refugees, see A. J. Sherman, *Island Refuge, Britain and Refugees from the Third Reich, 1933–1939* (London: Paul Elek, 1973), chap. 5.
63 Hecht, *A Child of the Century*, 565–565; Kook interview with the author. For Sulzberger and the *New York Times*' stance during the Holocaust years, see Penkower, *Twentieth Century Jews*, 159–163.
64 E. Jabotinsky to Altman, May 3, 1943, file P2-5, MBHCA; JTA, July 15, 1943; "Memorandum on the Findings of the Emergency Conference to Save the Jewish People of Europe, July 20th to 25th," copy, box 66–89, Emergency Committee MSS, JA.
65 Merlin quoted in *Answer*, July 12, 1944, 20; *New York Times*, September 14, 1943. For the efforts of the Bergson group after this date, see in note 77 below.
66 JTA, September 20 and 22, 1944; Saposnik, "Advertisement or Achievement?," 196–212; Shertok to Silver, in AZEC executive minutes, October 12, 1944, ZA. For the WZO's efforts throughout the war towards the creation of a Jewish fighting force, see Penkower, *The Jews Were Expendable*, chap. 1.
67 JTA, September 22, 1944; Strabolgi and Croft statements, quoted in *New Judea* (June–July 1944): 157–158; JTA, August 22, 2001. The *New York Times*' obituary of August 20, 2001, did take note of the Jewish Army campaign as well.
68 Pierre Van Paassen, "Vladimir Jabotinsky: A Reminiscence," in *The Midstream Reader*, ed. Shlomo Katz (New York: Thomas Yoseloff, 1960), 278–295; Pierre Van Paassen, *The Forgotten Ally* (New York: Dial Press, 1943).
69 Ben-Ami, *Years of Wrath, Days of Glory*, 256, 267, 320.
70 Montor to Steinglas, December 29, 1963, A371/36, CZA; G. Hirschler, "Montor, Henry," in *New Encyclopedia of Zionism and Israel*, ed. G. Wigoder, vol. 2 (Madison, WI: Fairleigh Dickinson University Press, 1994), 948–949.
71 Merlin to Kook, July 13, 1984, file P2-5, MBHCA. Dov Gruner, who arrived aboard the *Sakariya* as a member of Betar from Hungary, served for two years in the British Army and two in the Jewish Brigade, and took part in the Brigade's fighting in Italy. Upon his release from service, he joined the Irgun and participated in a raid on the Ramat Gan police station. Seriously wounded and captured, he was condemned to death. Gruner refused to appeal the sentence, which could have saved his life, since that would have implied recognition of British judicial authority in Palestine. He was hanged in Acre prison on April 19, 1947, along with fellow Irgunists Yehiel Dresner, Mordechai Alkahi and Eliezer Kashani. Writing as "your faithful soldier, Dov," in a last letter to Irgun commander Menachem Begin, he swore "that if I had to begin my life anew I would have chosen the exact same path, regardless of the consequences for myself." In 1954, the plaza in front of that police station was renamed "Gruner Square." A monument commemorating Gruner and the three Irgun members killed in the attack on the station was constructed at the site. The monument features a sculpture by Chana Orloff depicting a young lion cub (the *Yishuv*) fighting a mature lion (the British Empire). The monument also bears a plaque that commemorates all of the *Olei haGardom*, the Jewish independence fighters hanged by the Ottoman and British authorities before the State of Israel's creation.

72 Smertenko to Sulzberger, May 29, 1945, Hebrew Committee of National Liberation MSS, JA.
73 Ben-Ami, *Years of Warth, Days of Glory*, 292; Wise report, August 4, 1943, Z6/18/6, CZA; Hayter minutes, November 11, 1943, FO 371/35041, PRO; Kook interview with the author.
74 Smertenko to Villard, May 27, 1943, file 3570, Oscar G. Villard MSS, Houghton Library, Harvard University, Cambridge, MA; Monty Noam Penkower, "The 1943 Joint Anglo-American Statement on Palestine," *Herzl Yearbook* 8 (1978): 212–241; Kohn to Shertok, July 29, 1943, Correspondence, BGA; Potter to E. Roosevelt, July 13, 1943, Emergency Committee to Save the Jewish People of Europe files, JA; Goldmann to Gruenbaum, April 5, 1943, Z6/18/15, CZA; Potter to E. Roosevelt, July 13, 1943, Emergency Committee to Save the Jewish People of Europe files, JA; Goldmann to Gruenbaum, April 5, 1943, Z6/18/15, CZA; Joseph talk with War Refugee Board, December 7, 1944, Z5/379, CZA. Moscow ignored the entire matter. See Dov Levin, "The Attitude of the Soviet Union to the Rescue of the Jews," in *Rescue Attempts during the Holocaust*, ed. Yisrael Gutman and Efraim Zuroff (Jerusalem: Yad Vashem, 1977), 225–236. And not long after the war, Stalin suppressed publication of *The Black Book*, a documentary collection compiled by Ilya Ehrenburg and Vasily Grossman in 1944–1946 about the Nazi murder of 1.5 million Jews on occupied Soviet territory. A Russian-language edition of the original manuscript appeared in Israel in 1980, with an English translation the following year.
75 Hayter-Montor meeting, December 5, 1941, Henry Manson files, Abba Hillel Silver MSS., The Temple, Cleveland, OH.
76 Haj Amin el-Husseini diary, November 26, 1941, Virginia Gildersleeve MS., Special Collections, Butler Library, Columbia University, New York City; *Answer*, October 15, 1943.
77 Monty Noam Penkower, "In Dramatic Dissent: The Bergson Boys," *American Jewish History* 70 (1981): 281–309, reprinted in Monty Noam Penkower, *The Holocaust and Israel Reborn: From Catastrophe to Sovereignty* (Urbana: University of Illinois Press, 1994), 61–90. Prior to then, a few pages about the effort of this small group from Palestine to alert and then to press a silent American public to respond energetically to the *Shoah* could be found in Morse, *While Six Million Died*; Judd Teller, *Strangers and Natives: The Evolution of the American Jew from 1921 to the Present* (New York: Delacorte Press, 1968); Henry Feingold, *The Politics of Rescue: The Roosevelt Administration and the Holocaust* (New Brunswick, NJ: Rutgers University Press, 1970); and Saul Friedman, *No Haven for the Oppressed, United States Policy toward Jewish Refugees* (Detroit, MI: Wayne State University Press, 1973). Samuel Halperin's *The Political World of American Zionism* (Detroit, MI: Wayne State University Press, 1961) avoided the Bergson Boys entirely. Melvin I. Urofsky's *We Are One! American Jewry and Israel* (New York: Anchor Press, 1978), in linking the group with the divisive anti-Zionist American Council for Judaism, would overlook the Palestinians' positive influence. Autobiographical accounts by some in the Kook circle appeared in Ben Hecht, *A Child of the Century*; Ben-Ami, *Years of Wrath, Days of Glory*, and Rafaeli, *Dream and Action*. Since then, a number of books have appeared by some in the Kook-Bergson group and about the untiring efforts of his band of Palestinian brothers. David S. Wyman, *The Abandonment of the Jews: America and the Holocaust, 1941–1945* (New York: Pantheon Books, 1984); Rapaport, *Shake Heaven and Earth*; David S. Wyman and Rafael Medoff, *A Race Against Death: Peter Bergson, America, and the Holocaust* (New York: The New Press, 2002); Judy Tydor Baumel, *The "Bergson Boys" and the Origins of Contemporary Zionist Militancy* (Syracuse, NY: Syracuse University Press, 2005); and Shmuel Merlin, *Millions of Jews to Rescue: A Bergson Group Leader's Account of the Campaign to Save Jews from the Holocaust*, ed. Rafael Medoff (Washington, D.C.: David S. Wyman Institute for Holocaust Studies, 2011). A few—very few—important articles have also seen print. Yonatan Kaplan, "Peilut haHatzala Shel Mishlahat haEtzel b'Artzot-haBrit b'Tkufat haShoah," *Yalkut Moreshet* 30 (1981): 115–138, and *Yalkut Moreshet* 31 (1981): 75–96; Gad Nahshon, "'The Answer'—HaIton sheNashal l'Atzmo et Zekhut haZe'aka," *Kesher* 15 (1994): 78–84; Saposnik, "Advertisement

or Achievement?"; Rafael Medoff, "When the U.S. Government Spied on American Jews," *Midstream* 52 (2006): 8–12; and Evan Kaplan, "A Rebel With a Cause: Hillel Kook, Begin, and Jabotinsky's Ideological Legacy," *Israel Studies* 10:3 (2007): 87–103, The last-named is a translation from that author's "Bein America l'Eretz Yisrael: Hillel Kook, Begin, u'Mishnat Jabotinsky," *HaUma* 156 (2004): 70–80. As the historian who wrote the text for the first New York City public memorial to the Holocaust, located in Sheepshead Bay, I later approved with minor corrections the text for a marker commemorating the work of the Bergson Boys during the *Shoah*. This marker was unveiled three years alter by Kook's widow, Nili, and his daughter Rebecca. Jason Maoz, "Bergson Group Honored at NYC's First Memorial Site," *Jewish Press*, October 1, 2008.
78 *Notes from the Warsaw Ghetto: The Journal of Emmanuel Ringelblum*, ed. J. Sloan (New York: McGraw-Hill, 1974), 125.

Notes to Chapter 5

1 *New York Times*, March 21, 1950.
2 Monty Noam Penkower, *Decision on Palestine Deferred: America, Britain and Wartime Diplomacy, 1939–1945* (London: Frank Cass, 2002), 115, 173, 253; P-369, Series V, Milton Steinberg MSS., American Jewish Historical Society, Center for Jewish History, New York City.
3 Penkower, *Decision on Palestine Deferred*, 46; Monty Noam Penkower, "The Genesis of the American Council for Judaism: A Quest for Identity in World War II," *American Jewish History* 86 (June 1998): 167–194. An earlier version of this article appeared in *Proceedings of the Twelfth World Congress of Jewish Studies—1997* (2001): division E, 63–71. Reprinted in Monty Noam Penkower, *Twentieth Century Jews: Forging Identity in the Land of Promise and in the Promised Land* (Boston: Academic Studies Press, 2010), chap. 4. A far more favorable view of the Council is Thomas Kolsky, *Jews against Zionism: The American Council for Judaism, 1942–1948* (Philadelphia, PA: Temple University Press, 1990).
4 Morris S. Lazaron, "Palestine: The Dream and the Reality—A Survey of Jewish Nationalism," *Atlantic Monthly* (November 1944): 85–90.
5 Milton Steinberg, "The Credo of an American Zionist," *Atlantic Monthly* (February 1945): 101–106. For the American Jewish Conference, see Penkower, *Decision on Palestine Deferred*, 199–210, 232–235.
6 Jerome Frank, "Red, White and Blue Herring," *Saturday Evening Post*, December 6, 1941, 10, 86. A story written by Mark Twain in 1882, "The Stolen White Elephant," recounts the inept, far-ranging activities of detectives trying to find an elephant that was right on the spot after all. This tale, combined with Fyodor Dostoevsky's reference in the novel *Demons* that "Belinsky was just like Krylov's Inquisitive Man, who didn't notice the elephant in the museum," may have been on Judge Frank's mind when he wrote in his dissent in *United States v. Antonelli Fireworks* (1946) and again in dissent in *United States v. Leviton* (1951) of "the Mark Twain story of the little boy who was told to stand in a corner and not to think of a white elephant."
7 Jewish Telegraphic Agency (JTA), December 5, 1941. Among the passages which Steinberg wished to cite from Frank's article were these: The practices of the Jewish tradition are "as outmoded, as much out of place in America in the twentieth century A.D., as a bow and arrow or a powderhorn, as functionless as a horsewhip in an airplane." And this: When the "old Jewish code" has been broken, "what remains of the historic Jewish religion consists principally of some noble ethical principle and spiritual values. . . . But these principles and values—typified in the Ten Commandments—are no more Jewish than Christian; they have become part of modern Christian civilization, part of the social heritage of all Americans;

to call them 'Jewish' is to be a pedantic antiquarian." And this: "Reform Jews seem to be persons who 'Unwilling to join a Christian Church have adopted what is known as reformed Judaism,'" a religious communion "actually closer to liberal Protestantism than to Jewish orthodoxy." Steinberg to Frank, April 29, 1945, Jerome Frank papers, MS 222, box 70, Sterling Library, Yale University, New Haven, CT.
8   Penkower, *Decision on Palestine Deferred*, 95. For the response of Arthur Hays Sulzberger to the Holocaust and to Zionism, see Penkower, *Twentieth Century Jews*, chap. 5. Lewis Straus was an executive board member of the American Jewish Committee. Samuel Rosenman was a speech writer for President Franklin D. Roosevelt and the first White House Counsel.
9   Frank to Steinberg, May 4, 1945, box 70, Frank MSS; copy in box 15, Steinberg papers. For Lindbergh, see Wayne Cole, *Charles A. Lindbergh and the Battle against American Intervention in World War II* (New York: Harcourt Brace Jovanovich, 1974).
10 Steinberg to Frank, May 9, 1945, box 70, Frank MSS.
11 Frank to Steinberg, May 15, 1945, box 70, Frank MSS; copy in box 15, Steinberg MSS. Joseph Proskauer was president of the American Jewish Committee; James Rosenberg was chairman of the Executive Board of the American Jewish Joint Distribution Committee and chairman of its Board of Directors.
12 Steinberg to Frank, May 17, 1945, box 70, Frank MSS; copy in box 15, Steinberg MSS.
13 Lazaron to Victor, May 31, 1945; Lazaron draft memorandum (attached), collection 71, Morris Lazaron MSS, box 3044, American Jewish Archives, Cincinnati, OH.
14 Milton Steinberg, *A Partisan Guide to the Jewish Problem* (Indianapolis, IN: Charter Books, 1945), chaps. 15–16.
15 Memo, October 1, 1945, box 14, Steinberg MSS; Holmes review, *Saturday Review of Literature* 28:43 (October 27, 1945): 38. A review by Barnard College Professor of Religion Theodor H. Gaster, very critical of Steinberg's embrace in this book of Reconstructionist Judaism, did not touch on the author's advocacy of the Zionist cause. "Books in Review," *Commentary* 2:5 (November 1946): 490–491.
16 Lazaron letter to the editor, *New York Times*, September 30, 1945.
17 Steinberg letter to the editor, *New York Times*, October 7, 1945. For the Earl Harrison report, see Monty Noam Penkower, *After the Holocaust* (New York: Touro University Press, 2021), chaps. 1–2. For the King-Crane report, see *Palestine: A Study of Jewish, Arab, and British Policies*, vol. 1 (New Haven, CT: Yale University Press, 1947), 145, 216–218, 221–222.
18 Milton Steinberg, "When I Think of Seraye," *The Reconstructionist*, March 7, 1946, 10–17.
19 Simon Noveck, *Milton Steinberg, Portrait of a Rabbi* (New York: Ktav, 1978), 195–196. For the Anglo-American Committee of Inquiry on Palestine, see Monty Noam Penkower, *Palestine to Israel, Mandate to State*, vol. 1, *Rebellion Launched, 1945–1946* (New York: Touro University Press, 2019), chap. 3. For Eleanor Roosevelt's shift to firm support of the Zionist standard, see Monty Noam Penkower, *The Holocaust and Israel Reborn: From Catastrophe to Sovereignty* (Urbana: University of Illinois Press, 1994), chap. 11.
20 Noveck, *Milton Steinberg*, 193.
21 Sumner Welles, "New Hope for the Jewish People," *Nation*, May 5, 1945, 511–512; *New York Times*, August 20, 1946; *New York World-Telegram*, June 22, 1946; Roper poll, January 1946, Shulman-Palestine Resolution 1944–1946 file, Hadassah Archives, New York City.
22 Frank to Rosenwald, April 26, 1946, box 67, Frank MSS.
23 Frank draft letter, c. December 1946, box 59, Frank MSS.
24 Frank to Rifkind, August 28, 1947, box 67, Frank MSS.
25 For *The Basic Equities of the Palestine Problem*, see chap. 6.
26 For Truman's decision, running counter to the US State and War Departments, to recognize the State of Israel *de facto* almost immediately after its official declaration of independence, see Penkower, *Palestine to Israel: Mandate to State, 1945–1948*, vol. 2, *Into the International Arena, 1947–1948* (New York: Touro University Press, 2019), 723–725.

27 JTA, July 6, 1949. For the American Association for the United Nations, see Monty Noam Penkower, *Israel: As a Phoenix Ascending* (New York: Touro University Press, 2021), chap. 4. Historians Robert M. Miller and Hugh Wilford have charged that, from its founding in 1951, the American Friends of the Middle East was part of an Arabist propaganda effort within the United States, "secretly funded and to some extent managed by the C.I.A.," with further funding from the oil consortium Aramco. It was often critical of US support for the State of Israel. See Robert M. Miller, *Harry Emerson Fosdick: Preacher, Pastor, Prophet* (Oxford: Oxford University Press, 1985); Hugh Wilford, *America's Great Game: The CIA's Secret Arabists and the Shaping of the Modern Middle East* (New York: Basic Books, 2013).
28 Morris Lazaron, *In the Shadow of Catastrophe* (Baltimore: American Council for Judaism, 1956).
29 Lazaron to Goldman, January 3, 1939, RG 31, American Jewish Archives; Penkower, *Israel: As A Phoenix Ascending*, 138; Robert Goldman interview with the author, October 30, 1975.
30 Einstein to Lazaron, April 14, 1944, file SC-3/24, American Jewish Archives.
31 Novek, *Milton Steinberg*, 195; Jonathan Steinberg, "Milton Steinberg, American Rabbi—Thoughts on his Centenary," *The Jewish Quarterly Review* 95:3 (Summer 2005): 579–600.
32 Frank to Kallen, September 2, 1949; Kallen to Frank, September 19, 1949; Frank to Kallen, July 19, 1951; Kallen to Frank, July 26, 1951; all in Horace Kallen MSS., RG 317, folder 923, YIVO Archives, Center for Jewish History, New York City; Frank to Steinberg, May 15, 1945, box 15, Steinberg MSS. Also see Horace Kallen, "Whither Israel," *Menorah Journal* 39:2 (Autumn 1951): 109–143; Sarah Schmidt, "The Zionist Conversion of Louis D. Brandeis," *Jewish Social Studies* 37:1 (Winter 1975): 18–34; Imanuel Clemens Schmidt, "A Secular Tradition: Horace Kallen on American Democracy in the United States and Israel," in *Foreign Entanglements: Transnational American Jewish Studies*, ed. Hasia Diner, Markus Krah, Björn Siegel (Potsdam: Universitätsverlag Potsdam, 2021), 85–100.
33 For the mounting support of Christians in the United States during World War II alone, see Penkower, *The Holocaust and Israel Reborn*, chap. 6.

Notes to Chapter 6

1 *Parliamentary Debates*, House of Commons, 433, col. 985; Harry S. Truman, *Years of Trial and Hope*, vol. 2 (New York: New American Library, 1965), 183. For the Anglo-American Committee of Inquiry on Palestine, the Morrison-Grady Plan, and the Bevin Plan, see Monty Noam Penkower, *Palestine to Israel: Mandate to State, 1945–1948*, vol. 1: *Rebellion Launched* (New York: Touro University Press, 2019), chap. 3, and 249, 275, 282; Monty Noam Penkower, *Palestine to Israel: Mandate to State, 1945–1948*, vol. 2: *Into the International Arena* (New York: Touro University Press, 2019), 343–362.
2 Penkower, *Palestine to Israel*, vol. 1, 33, 37, 292–293. For the 1939 White Paper, see Monty Noam Penkower, *Palestine in Turmoil: The Struggle for Sovereignty, 1933–1939*, vol. 2: *Retreat from the Mandate, 1937–1939* (New York: Touro University Press, 2014), chap. 10. For the genesis and significance of the Harrison mission, see Monty Noam Penkower, *After the Holocaust* (New York: Touro University Press, 2021), chaps. 1–2.
3 867N.01/10-1546; 867N.01/1-1747; both in State Department files, National Archives, Suitland, MD.
4 *Parliamentary Debates*, House of Commons, 433, col. 989; David Ben-Gurion, *Jewish Observer and Middle East Review*, February 5, 1965, 17; *Foreign Relations of the United States, 1947*, vol. 5, (Washington, D.C.: Government Printing Office, 1971), 1055; Meeting, February 19, 1947, Z4/10381; Shertok-Creech Jones interview, February 20, 1947, S25/7568; both in Central Zionist Archives, Jerusalem.
5 Weizmann to Epstein, February 21, 1945, Chaim Weizmann Archives, Rehovot.

6   *New York Times*, January 24, 1973; *Maintenance of Peace in Armenia, Hearings before a Subcommittee of the Committee on Foreign Relations United States Senate, 66th Congress, First Session on S.J.R. 106* (Washington, D.C.: Government Printing Office, 1919), 45–54. See also the Abraham Tulin file, Box 160, Archives, Herbert C. Hoover Presidential Library and Museum, West Branch, IA.

7   Jewish Telegraphic Agency (JTA), January 25, 1973; Gilpin to Miller, December 15, 1941, Abraham Tulin file, Box 160, Archives, Hoover Presidential Library and Museum, West Branch, IA; Abraham Tulin, *Analysis of British Policy in Palestine* (New York: The Political and Education Committees of Hadassah, the Women's Zionist Organization of America, 1943); Milton Handler interview with the author, May 16, 1976. For the Dreyfus trial, see Monty Noam Penkower, "The Dreyfus Affair and its Echoes," in The Highest Form of Wisdom: A Memorial Book in Honor of Saul S. Friedman, ed. Jonathan C. Friedman and Robert D. Miller II (New York: Ktav, 2016), 177–211.

8   Tulin to Silver, January 28, 1946, file 4, folder 3, Abba Hillel Silver MSS, The Temple, Cleveland, OH; Penkower, *Palestine to Israel*, vol. 1, 263–264. "Do you think for a moment we're going to war with England over what they've done or that protests will be of any value?" Acheson asked Handler, continuing thus: "Why don't you deal with the real situation—what are we going to do in Palestine?" Handler interview with the author.

9   Simon Rifkind interview with the author, July 25, 1974; Simon Rifkind et al., *The Basic Equities of the Palestine Problem* (New York: Arno Press, 1977), preface.

10 Rifkind interview with the author; Rifkind interview, October 1978, Kibbutz Lohamei HaGetaot archives, Israel; Penkower, *Palestine to Israel*, vol. 1, 113, 143, 160, 197. The Intergovernmental Committee on Refugees, created after the 1938 Evian Conference on Refugees and charged with approaching "the governments of the countries of refuge with a view to developing opportunities for permanent settlement" and seeking to persuade Germany to cooperate in establishing "conditions of orderly emigration," did little to save Europe's Jews during the Holocaust.

11 Rifkind interview with the author.

12 *New York Times*, November 12, 1988; Handler interview with the author, May 26, 1976; Lourie to Gurfein, May 12, 1947, file chet-tzadi 93/10, Israel State Archives (ISA), Jerusalem. Gurfein would receive additional funds to employ Lawrence Eno and Saul Padover, former assistant secretary of the interior, OSS member, and currently teaching American political history at the New School for Social Research, along with a few stenographers. For the US War Refugee board's creation, see Monty Noam Penkower, *The Jews Were Expendable: Free World Diplomacy and the Holocaust* (Urbana: University of Illinois Press, 1983), chap. 5. One evaluation of its work, estimating that the Board had saved 200,000 Jews, is in David S. Wyman, *The Abandonment of the Jews, America and the Holocaust, 1941–1945*, part 4 (New York: Pantheon Books, 1984). In an afterword to Rafael Medoff's *Too Little and Almost Too Late: The War Refugee Board and America's Response to the Holocaust* (Washington, D.C.: David S. Wyman Institute for Holocaust Studies, 2017), 249–254, I summarized the latest research.

13 Murray I. Gurfein interview with the author, June 7, 1979; Gurfein memorandum for the Harry S. Truman Research Center, April 18, 1978 (courtesy of Judge Gurfein). In January 1944, Gurfein had suggested that vessels be obtained from the Anglo-American shipping pool to rescue Jews in the Balkans via the Black Sea to Turkey and then Palestine, but his OSS superiors deemed this "impolitic" in view of the Palestine issue. Gurfein interview with the author. Having been in the 1930s one of the key assistants to District Attorney Thomas E. Dewey, where he helped smash labor racketeering, exposed waterfront gangsterism, and subsequently revealed how a federal judge had been bribed, Gurfein also advised Dewey, then Governor of New York State, about a public statement on Palestine in early October 1946. KPG to Lockwood, October 4, 1946, file 4:249/19, Thomas Dewey MSS, University of Rochester Library, Rochester, NY.

14 JTA, May 14 and 16, 1947.
15 Handler interview with the author. Earlier in May, Tulin had compiled and annotated the 318-page *Book of Documents*, a revised edition of his earlier volume for the Anglo-American Committee of Inquiry on Palestine, submitted by the Jewish Agency's New York headquarters to the General Assembly, *Relating to the Establishment of the National Home for the Jewish People*. A copy is in the Simon H. Rifkind papers, box 46, folder 7, American Jewish Historical Society, Center for Jewish History, New York City.
16 Abba Eban, *An Autobiography* (New York: Random House, 1977), 73–77.
17 Handler interview with the author.
18 Handler interview with the author; Jerome N. Frank, "Red, White and Blue Herring," *Saturday Evening Post*, December 6, 1941, 10, 86; JTA, December 5, 1947. For the genesis of the American Council for Judaism, see Monty Noam Penkower, *Twentieth Century Jews: Forging Identity in the Land of Promise and in the Promised Land* (Boston: Academic Studies Press, 2010), 115–142.
19 Hander interview with the author.
20 Penkower, *Palestine to Israel*, vol. 2, 434, 445.
21 Gurfein memorandum, April 18, 1978.
22 Meeting, August 31, 1947, DAG-13/3.0.0, Box 2, UN Archives, New York City; *Official Records of the Second Session of the General Assembly, Supplement no. 11, UNSCOP, Report to the General Assembly*, vol. 1 (New York: UN, 1947); Elad Ben-Dror, *UNSCOP and the Arab-Israeli Conflict: The Road to Partition*, trans. H. Watzman (Abingdon: Routledge, 2022). For the broader contemporary context, see Penkower, *Palestine to Israel*, vol. 2, chap. 7.
23 Kenan to Lourie, September 9, 1947, file chet-tzadi, 2267/16, ISA; JTA, September 14, 1947.
24 *The Basic Equities of the Palestine Problem*, preface.
25 Ibid., 1.
26 Ibid., 2–4. Turkey officially yielded its jurisdiction over Palestine in the 1923 Treaty of Lausanne. Ibid., 27.
27 Ibid., 4–6.
28 Ibid., 6–7. Roosevelt, in whom the Jews had placed their greatest hopes in their most anguished hour, had actually temporized on Palestine. His public pledges in 1944 and early 1945 to support Zionist objectives were balanced with secret pledges via the State Department to Muslim rulers. Twice in 1944, his private intervention helped kill strong pro-Zionist resolutions in Congress. A liberal who sought to eschew solutions by force, and thus would be shocked by Ibn Saud's unyielding stance during their only encounter on February 14, 1945, he focused on some form of international Palestine trusteeship and thinly dispersed settlements of Jews the world over as a way of avoiding antisemitism. See Monty Noam Penkower, *Decision on Palestine Deferred: America, Britain and Wartime Diplomacy, 1939–1945* (London: Frank Cass, 2002), *passim*.
29 Ibid., 9–10. The last reference was to the voyagers aboard the *Exodus 1947*. See Aviva Halmish, *Exodus, HaSippur haAmiti* (Tel Aviv: Ha'Amuta l'Heker Ma'archot haHa'apala al Shem Shaul Avigur, 1990).
30 *The Basic Equities of the Palestine Problem*, 10–17.
31 Ibid., 18–26. The Peel Commission allotted to the proposed Jewish State less than one-fifth of Western Palestine and less than one-twentieth of the original mandate. See Monty Noam Penkower, *Palestine in Turmoil*, vol. 2, chap. 6.
32 *The Basic Equities of the Palestine Problem*, 29–30.
33 Ibid., 30–33.
34 Ibid., 34–40.
35 Ibid., 41.
36 Ibid., 41–43. Estoppel is a legal principle that prevents someone from arguing something or asserting a right that contradicts what they previously said or agreed to by law.
37 Ibid., 41–53.

38 Ibid., 53–62. For the February 1939 London Conference at St. James Palace, see Penkower, *Palestine in Turmoil*, vol. 2, 624–649,
39 *The Basic Equities of the Palestine Problem*, 62–69. For the *Patria*, see Monty Noam Penkower, *The Jews Were Expendable*, chap. 2. For the *Struma*, see Penkower, *Decision on Palestine Deferred*, 92, 110–112.
40 *The Basic Equities of the Palestine Problem*, 70–77. The authors claimed (ibid., 77) that "tens of millions of dollars" were paid to Arabs by the purchase of lands, "at tenfold and a hundred fold." For Lowdermilk, Nathan, and the TVA experts, see Penkower, *Decision on Palestine Deferred, passim*.
41 *The Basic Equities of the Palestine Problem*, 77–79.
42 Ibid., 81–83.
43 Ibid. 83–85. The massacre of Assyrians was covered by Western media sources, and it inspired the intellectual development of Raphael Lemkin, the Polish-Jewish jurist who would go on to coin the word "genocide." The British, although represented by a powerful military presence as provided by the Anglo-Iraqi Treaty of 1930, failed to intervene or allow the well-disciplined Assyrian Levies under their command to do so, and helped whitewash the event at the League of Nations.
44 Ibid., 85–89.
45 Ibid., 89.
46 Ibid., 90–93,
47 Ibid., 94–95.
48 Ibid., 96–99.
49 Ibid., 99–102.
50 Ibid., 103–105.
51 Ibid., 105–106.
52 Ibid., 106–107.
53 Handler interview with the author; *New York Times*, January 24, 1973; Silver to Gurfein, December 18, 1947, file 93/03, ISA. Burnet Hershey, head of the American War Correspondents Association, thought the legal brief "perhaps the most important modern document and clarification of the Palestine problem—succinct, juridical, without being dull and above all unhysterical. I am sure it contributed largely to the decisions of the U.S. delegation and must have had some influence on the Russians as well." Hershey to Rifkind, November 12, 1947, box 66, Jerome Frank MSS, Sterling Library, Yale University, New Haven, CT.
54 Silver to Tulin, December 17, 1947; Lourie to Tulin, May 3, 1947; both in file chet-tzadi 2274/38, ISA.
55 Handler to Shertok, December 1, 1947; Shertok to Handler, December 11, 1947; both in file chet-tzadi 2273/53, ISA.
56 *New York Times*, January 24, 1973; American Technion Society tape of the award ceremony. The Hebrew inscription *ish hayil v'rov poalim* is derived from Chronicles.
57 *New York Times*, January 15, 1995, November 12, 1998, and December 18, 1997.
58 *New York Times*, May 16, 1997, January 14, 1957, July 25, 2003, and April 7, 1982. American "legal realism," a controversial philosophical movement, was concerned with directing attention from the "law in the books," the doctrinal law of the appellate courts, to "the law in action," the patterns of usage and practice that prevail in daily life, in the lower courts, and in business.
59 *The Basic Equities of the Palestine Problem*, n.p.; Penkower, *Palestine to Israel*, vol. 2, 711. The Rifkind obituary carried this paragraph: "In 1945 and 1946, as an adviser on Jewish affairs for the Army in Europe, Mr. Rifkind championed uprooted Holocaust survivors who were then in Germany and Austria and made appeals for more aid to them. That experience helped lead him to champion the creation of the State of Israel and led President Harry S. Truman to award him the Medal of Freedom." The Medal, instituted by Truman and reestablished in

February 1963 by President John F. Kennedy as the Presidential Medal of Freedom, is the US government's highest civilian award.

Notes to Chapter 7

1. Ariella Marsden, "Poland Tries to Rewrite Country's Role in Holocaust—PM Email Leak," *Jerusalem Post*, August 15, 2022. Yad Vashem, the State of Israel's official memorial to the Holocaust, was established on August 19, 1953, and is located on the western slope of Jerusalem's Har Herzl.
2. BBC News and CNN, May 30, 2012.
3. Andrew Kornbluth, *The August Trials: The Holocaust and Postwar Justice in Poland* (Cambridge, MA: Harvard University Press, 2021).
4. Mirosław Tryczyk, *The Towns of Death: Pogroms against Jews by Their Neighbors*, trans. Frank Szmulowicz (Lanham, MD: Lexington Books, 2021); Michał Bojanowski, "Cities of Death," *Chidusz*, December 28, 2016; Mirosław Tryczyk, "Reply to Krzysztof Persak," *Studia Litteraria et Historia* (May 2016): 1–13; Jakub Muchowski, "Whose History? Encounters of Professional and Vernacular Historians over Contested Heritage of WWII," in *Actas del IV Congreso Internacional de Filosofía de la Historia. El pasado propio: historia y memoria en la formación de identidades colectivas*, ed. Daniel Brauer, Omar Acha, Adrián Ratto, and Facundo Martín (Buenos Aires: TeseoPress, 2019), 61–74.The communities that met this fate were Radziłów, Wąsosz, Jedwabne, Szczuczyn, Bzury, Skaje, Goniądz, Rajgród, Jasionówka, Kolno, Suchowola, Brańsk, Lipník, Danowo, and Dzięgiele.
5. Tryczyk to Penkower, September 1, 2022. Trycyzk's most recent volume, *Drzazga: Kłamstwa silniejsze niż śmierć* (*Splinter, Lies Stronger than Death*), published by the Kraków press Znak in 2020, begins with his grandfather's participation in the 1941 pogrom in the village of Wólka Dobryńska. See Agnieszka Wądołowska, "Splintered Histories: Confronting the Legacy of Wartime Pogroms in Rural Poland," *Notes from Poland*, June 1, 2020, https://notesfrompoland.com/2020/06/01/splintered-histories-confronting-the-legacy-of-wartime-pogroms-in-rural-poland/.
6. Sylwia A. Karowicz-Bienias, "Henryk Mania—Polak skazany za zbrodnie nazistowskie," Przystanek Historia, February 3, 2022.
7. Monty Noam Penkower, *After the Holocaust* (New York: Touro University Press, 2021), 157–170.
8. Jewish Telegraphic Agency (JTA), April 20, 1983.
9. JTA, April 18 and 20, 1983; John Kitner, "Polish Police Ban March on Uprising," *New York Times*, April 18, 1983.
10. JTA, April 18, 1983. For the antisemitic campaign under Communist Party leader Władysław Gomulka, see Dariusz Stola, "Anti-Zionism as a Multipurpose Policy Instrument: The Anti-Zionist Campaign in Poland, 1967–1968," *Journal of Israeli History* 25:1 (2006): 175–201; Feliks Tych, "The March '68 Antisemitic Campaign: Onset, Development, and Consequences," in *Jewish Presence in Absence: The Aftermath of the Holocaust in Poland, 1944–2010*, ed. Feliks Tych and Monika Adamczyk-Garbowska, trans. G. Dąbowski and J. Taylor-Kucia (Jerusalem: Yad Vashem, 2014), 451–472; *Polin: Studies in Polish Jewry* 21 (November 2008): 20–379; Miri Freilich, "The Polish Exodus of 1968," *Polin: Studies in Polish Jewry* 35 (2023): 337–352.
11. JTA, April 20–21, 1983.
12. Michael T. Kaufman, "Debate over Holocaust Stirs Passions in Poland," *New York Times*, March 8, 1987; Jan Blonski, "Poor Poles Look at the Ghetto," *Yad Vashem Studies* 19 (1988): 341–356; Shmuel Krakowski, "Relations between Jews and Poles during the Holocaust—New and Old Approaches in Polish Historiography," *Yad Vashem Studies* 19

(1988): 317–340; Anthony Polonsky, "Polish-Jewish Relations During the Second World War: A Discussion," in *Polin: Studies in Polish Jewry*, ed. Anthony Polonsky, vol. 2: *Jews and the Emerging Polish State* (Liverpool: Liverpool University Press, 2008), 337–358. Also see Adam Kirsch, "Czeslaw Milosz's Battle for Truth," *New Yorker*, May 22, 2017.

13 The *Umschlagplatz*, at the edge of the Warsaw Ghetto on the corner of Zamenhof and Niska Streets, was the site from which approximately 265,000 of the city's Jews had been packed in sealed freight cars with little water and poor ventilation, and deported at SS *Reichsführer* Heinrich Himmler's order in July 1942 to their deaths sixty-two miles away in Treblinka's three gas chambers.

14 John Tagliabue, "Polish March Lauds Heroes of '43 Ghetto," *New York Times*, April 18, 1988; James Young, *The Texture of Memory, Holocaust Memorials and Meaning* (New Haven, CT: Yale University Press, 1993), 179.

15 *New York Times*, April 15, 1993; Monty Noam Penkower, *The Holocaust and Israel Reborn* (Urbana: University of Illinois Press, 1994), chap. 13. A church, topped by a large cross, that once held SS headquarters right across from Birkenau and the tall cross in Auschwitz-I remain. *Times of Israel*, January 30, 2020.

16 Sergio I. Minerbi, "Pope John Paul II and the Jews: An Evaluation," *Jewish Political Studies Review* 18:1/2 (Spring 2006): 15–36; Jules Isaac, *The Teaching of Contempt: The Christian Roots of Anti-Semitism* (New York: Holt, Rinehart and Winston, 1954). Golgotha, also called Calvary in Latin, is said to be connected to the traditional site of Jesus's crucifixion, now in the Church of the Holy Sepulcher in the Christian Quarter of Jerusalem. "For the glory of the Most Holy Name" (*"Kiddush HaShem"*) refers in this instance to martyrdom, the ultimate Jewish expression of sanctifying the name of God.

17 JTA, September 28, 1995. In 2006, a new obelisk placed at the intersection of Mila and Dubois Streets, designed by the same two artists, included fifty-one names which had been identified from the estimated one hundred fighters at the 18 Miła Street headquarters.

18 Andrzej Bryk, "Polish Society Today and the Memory of the Holocaust," in *Remembering for the Future*, ed. Yehuda Bauer et al., vol. 3 (Oxford: Pergamon, 1989), 2365–2376.

19 Jan Tomasz Gross, *Neighbors, The Destruction of the Jewish Community in Jedwabne, Poland* (Princeton, NJ: Princeton University Press, 2001); Joshua D. Zimmerman, ed., *Contested Memories: Poles and Jews during the Holocaust and Its Aftermath* (New Brunswick, NJ: Rutgers University Press, 2003); Antony Polonsky and Joanna B. Michlic, eds. *The Neighbors Respond: The Controversy over the Jedwabne Massacre in Poland* (Princeton, NJ: Princeton University Press, 2004); Marek Chodakiewicz, *The Massacre in Jedwabne, July 10, 1941: Before, During and After* (Boulder, CO: Columbia University Press, 2005); Israel Bartal, Antony Polonsky, and Scott Ury, eds., *Jews and Their Neighbors in Eastern Europe since 1740* (Oxford: Littman Library of Jewish Civilization, 2012); A. H., "A Difficult Film," *The Economist*, December 19, 2012; Darius Libionka, "The Debate Around the Jedwabne Massacre," in *Jewish Presence in Absence: The Aftermath of the Holocaust in Poland, 1944–2010*, ed. Feliks Tych and Monika Adamczyk-Garbowska, trans. G. Dąbowski and J. Taylor-Kucia (Jerusalem: Yad Vashem, 2014), 847–896. The investigation at the same time by Polish journalist for the *Gazeta Wyborcza* Anna Bikont resulted in her non-fiction book *My z Jedwabnego* (Wołowiec: Czarne, 2004), later published in French and English as *The Crime and the Silence: Confronting the Massacre of Jews in Wartime Jedwabne* (French, Paris: Denoël, 2011; English, Jerusalem: Carmel, 2015), and winner of the European Book Prize in 2011. Julian Barnes, "Even Worse than We Thought," *New York Review*, November 19, 2015. A forensic murder investigation by the Polish Institute of National Memory, following the controversy surrounding Gross's book, confirmed that the perpetrators of the Jedwabne mass murder were indeed ethnic Poles. For the play *Our Class*, inspired by Gross's book, see Jamie Betesh Carter, "When Neighbors Turn Against Neighbors," *Tablet*, January 19, 2024.

20 *Die Welt*, September 13, 2015; Ofer Aderet, "Historian May Face Charges in Poland for Writing that Poles Killed Jews in World War II," *Haaretz*, October 30, 2016; "Academic Avoids Prosecution for Holocaust Claim," Polandin.com, November 26, 2019.
21 Ruth Ellen Gruber, "An Alternative Warsaw Ghetto Uprising Memorial," *Times of Israel*, April 23, 2013; *Times of Israel*, December 22, 2018.
22 Vanessa Gera, "Museum Exhibits to Celebrate Centuries of Jewish Life Confront Poles with Their Country's Own Dark Chapters of Anti-Semitism," *Times of Israel*, April 13, 2013; Nissan Tzur, "Polish Prof. to Be Axed for Anti-Semitic Views," *Jerusalem Post*, June 2, 2013; JTA, June 20, 2013. In 2020, Jasiewicz would be employed at the Polish Academy Institute in the Department of Eastern Problems Analysis.
23 *Haaretz*, October 28, 2014.
24 Anna Bikont, "Jan Gross' Order of Merit," *Tablet*, March 16, 2016.
25 Vanessa Gera, "International Historians Defend Ottawa Scholar Who Studies Poland and Holocaust," *Associated Press*, June 20, 2017; JTA, November 18, 2018. Also see Jan Grabowski, *On Duty: The Role of the Polish Blue and Criminal Police in the Holocaust* (Jerusalem: Yad Vashem, 2024), and the dissertation by Sylvia Szymańska Smolkin, "Fateful Decisions: The Polish Policemen and the Jewish Population of Occupied Poland, 1939–1945," University of Toronto, Toronto, 2017.
26 Monika Sieradzka, "Poland: 50 Years since 1968 Anti-Semitic Purge," Deutsche Welle, March 8, 2018, https://www.dw.com/en/poland-marks-50-years-since-1968-anti-semitic-purge/a-42877652. That August, the POLIN museum would feature a month-long exhibit highlighting the Gomulka government's 1968 campaign against Jews, with the final panels examining the continued presence of Polish antisemitism, especially online and in right-wing publications, which surged after the law was passed in 2018 making it a crime to blame Poland for Holocaust atrocities. "Today, 50 years after March [1968] events, the mechanism of hunting for and stigmatizing the 'others' has been put into motion yet again," the exhibition text warned. Rob Gloster, "In Warsaw, the Chilling Tale of 1968 Anti-Semitic Purges," *Jewish News of Northern California*, August 24, 2018.
27 Monika Scislowska and Vanessa Gara, "With Daffodils, Poland Marks 75th Anniversary of Warsaw Ghetto Uprising," *Times of Israel*, April 19, 2018; BBC, "Poland Holocaust Law: Government U-Turn on Jail Threat," July 27, 2018; *Times of Israel*, July 23, 2018; Aviva Ravel, *Faithful unto Death: The Story of Arthur Zygielbaum* (Montreal: Arthur Zygielbaum Branch, Workmen's Circle, 1980). Zygelbojm's cremains were eventually brought to the United States and interred at the Mt. Carmel Cemetery in Glendale, Queens County, New York, in 1961, the monument briefly noting "chose martyr's death." In May 1996, a plaque in his memory was dedicated at the corner of London's Porchester Road and Porchester Square, near where he had died. A granite memorial to Zygelbojm was incorporated in a building at 5 S. Dubois Street in Muranów, a housing project built after World War II on the ruins of the Warsaw Ghetto. In 2008 a plaque was added to the building in Chełm, Poland, where he had lived.
28 BBC, "Poland Holocaust Law: Government U-turn on Jail Threat," July 27, 2018; *Times of Israel*, July 23, 2018.
29 *Times of Israel*, October 19, 2018.
30 Anne Applebaum, "Putin's Big Lie," *Atlantic*, January 5, 2020; *Guardian*, January 9, 2020. The Russian leader would soon express his views in a leading American bimonthly conservative international affairs magazine. See Vladimir V. Putin, "The Real Lessons of the 75th Anniversary of World War II," *National Interest*, June 18, 2020.
31 *Times of Israel*, April 19, 2020.
32 *Times of Israel*, July 13, 2020; October 10 and 24, 2020.
33 *First News*, November 15, 2020; JTA, November 13, 2020.
34 Jonathan Brent and Jan Grabowski, "When Writing History Becomes a Crime," *Tablet*, February 26, 2021; Reuters, August 16, 2021. Engelking's seminal works include, in English

translation, *Holocaust and Memory: The Experience of the Holocaust and its Consequence, an Investigation Based on Personal Narratives* (Leicester: Leicester University Press, 2001); with Jacek Leociak, *The Warsaw Ghetto: A Guide to the Perished City* (New Haven, CT: Yale University Press, 2009); and *Such a Beautiful Sunny Day: Jews Seeking Refuge in the Polish Countryside, 1942–1945* (Jerusalem: Yad Vashem, 2016).

35 Alan Charlish and Joanna Plucinska, "Polish PM Upsets Jews Calling Compensation Pay 'Victory for Hitler,'" Reuters, May 21, 2019; Amy Shapiro, "Israel Skips Poland Antisemitism Meet, but Some Still See Thaw in Ties Ahead," *Times of Israel*, November 12, 2021. With few if any Jews remaining after World War II, numerous deserted cemeteries and dilapidated synagogues becoming mute witnesses to the singular tragedy of the Holocaust, the Communist regime had declared that Jews were no longer owners of property in Poland. Yet, on the local level, mainly in provincial towns, Jewish representatives were frequently treated as "property owners" in legal, conceptual, and moral terms. Yechiel Weizman, *Unsettled Heritage: Living Next to Poland's Material Jewish Traces after the Holocaust* (Ithaca, NY: Cornell University Press, 2022). Also see Michael C. Steinlauf, *Bondage to the Dead: Poland and the Memory of the Holocaust* (Syracuse University Press, Syracuse, N.Y., 1997).

36 *Times of Israel*, April 28, 2022; *Israel National News*, September 20, 2022.

37 Lazar Berman, "After Year-Long Spat over Holocaust Law, Poland Says It's Returning Envoy to Israel," *Times of Israel*, July 4, 2022; *Times of Israel*, October 18, 2022.

38 *Times of Israel*, September 1, 2022. A German foreign ministry spokesman quickly rejected the claim, declaring that the Polish government in 1953 had waived further reparations from East Germany and thus "the issue is closed from the point of view of the Federal Government." *ITV News*, September 2, 2022. After coming under fire for the demand, the report's author Arkadiusz Mularczyk, vice-chairman of the Parliamentary Assembly of the Council of Europe, defended its inclusion by saying that "international conventions state that occupiers are responsible for the population's safety." *Times of Israel*, September 23, 2022.

39 Ofer Aderet, "Poland's Demand for German Damages Includes Crimes Committed against Jews by Poles," *Haaretz*, September 6, 2022; Marc Santora and Joanna Berendt, "Mixing Politics and Piety: A Conservative Priest Seeks to Shape Poland's Future," *New York Times*, September 21, 2019.

40 Michael Fleming, "Confronting the Holocaust: Documents on the Polish Government-in-Exile's Policy Concerning Jews 1939–1945," *Israel Journal of Foreign Affairs*, December 5, 2022, https://dol.org/10.1080/23739770.2022.2143921. Also see Michael Fleming, *In the Shadow of the Holocaust: Poland, the United Nations War Crimes Commission and the Search for Justice* (Cambridge: Cambridge University Press, 2022).

41 Tovah Lazaroff, "Israel Seeks to Repair Poland Ties, Resume Holocaust Education Trips," *Jerusalem Post*, February 8, 2023.

42 *Jerusalem Post*, February 14, 2023.

43 Jan Grabowski and Shira Klein, "Wikipedia's Intentional Distortion of the History of the Holocaust," *Journal of Holocaust Research*, February 9, 2023, 1–58. Wikipedia's weakness had already been picked up by the Polish government, as shown by a leaked email exchange between Prime Minister Morawiecki's advisors concerning the Hebrew-language Wikipedia (ibid., 57). On March 6, 2018, at the height of the diplomatic crisis between Israel and Poland over the Holocaust Law, Morawiecki's advisor wrote to the chief of staff that he had asked Warsaw's former ambassador in Helsinki to "correct" the Hebrew entries in Wikipedia. A "large budget" to do so can be arranged "if the Foreign Office allocates more money." By a vote of nine to one on February 13, the committee decided to open the case. The proceedings, which start with an evidence-gathering phase, are expected to last up to six weeks, after which they can decide to ban and restrict offending editors.

At the end of February 2023, it was reported that, by a vote of nine to one, Wikipedia's Arbitration Committee will tackle this issue. No one could recall the committee taking such a step in its nearly two decades of existence. Beyond that, an unorthodox last resort option is

also available. Wikipedia's so-called Supreme Court could ask for help from an even higher authority: the Wikimedia Foundation, a nonprofit that owns the encyclopedia. The foundation intervened in 2021 in what some see as a similar scenario of a far-right takeover on the Croatian-language Wikipedia, hiring an outside expert to disentangle the web of obfuscation and banning a set of editors. JTA, February 28, 2023.
44 *Jerusalem Post*, March 7, 2023; *Times of Israel*, March 8, 2023.
45 *Jewish News Syndicate*, March 27, 2023.
46 *Israel National News*, March 30, 2023.
47 Ofer Aderet, "Scandalous, Disturbing and Unbelievable," *Haaretz*, April 10, 2023; *Forward*, April 10, 2023.
48 Iwona Irwin-Zarecka, *Neutralizing Memory: The Jew in Contemporary Poland* (New Brunswick, NJ: Rutgers University Press, 1989); Yisrael Gutman and Shmuel Krakowski, *Unequal Victims: Poles and Jews during World War II* (New York: Holocaust Library, 1986); James M. Markham, "Facing Up to Germany's Past," *New York Times Magazine*, June 23, 1985. Joining the Nazi Party in 1938 and receiving the honorary rank of *SS Oberführer* that same year, Ernst von Weizsäcker served as state secretary of Nazi Germany's Foreign Office in 1938–1943, and as the Third Reich's ambassador to the Holy See in the war's last two years. In 1947, he was arrested and placed on trial in the Nuremberg Military Tribunals. He was sentenced on April 2, 1949, to seven-year imprisonment (later reduced to five years) based on replies that he had signed stating that the Foreign Office did not raise any objection to the deportation of Jews. Eighteen months later, he was released after a new examination of his case by the Legislative Affairs Office of US High Commissioner for Germany John J. McCloy as part of a general amnesty. He died on August 4, 1951, of a stroke at the age of sixty-nine, and was buried in his Nazi diplomatic corps uniform, complete with swastika armband. Robert Wistrich, *Who's Who in Nazi Germany* (New York: Macmillan, 1982), 335–336.

Notes to Chapter 8

1 Monty Noam Penkower, *The Federal Writers' Project: A Study in Government Patronage of the Arts* (Urbana: University of Illinois Press, 1977); Monty Noam Penkower, "The 1943 Joint Anglo-American Statement on Palestine," *Herzl Yearbook* 8 (1978): 212–241.
2 Christopher Hawtree, "Gerald Green," *Guardian*, September 22, 2006; Gerald Green, *Holocaust* (New York: Corgi Books, 1978); Elie Wiesel, "Trivializing the Holocaust: Semi-Fact and Semi-Fiction," *New York Times*, April 16, 1978.
3 Alf Lüdtke, "'Coming to Terms with the Past': Illusions of Remembering, Ways of Forgetting Nazism in West Germany," *Journal of Modern History* 65 (1993): 544–546; *Ein Jahr, ein (Un-)Wort!*, Spiegel Online, 1979; Gerald Green, *The Artists of Terezin* (New York: Schocken, 1979).
4 *The Black Book* (New York: Yiddish Scientific Institute, 1946); Ben Hecht, *A Child of the Century* (New York: Simon & Schuster, 1954); Arthur Morse, *While Six Million Died: A Study in American Apathy* (New York: Hart, 1967); Raul Hilberg, *The Destruction of the European Jews* (New York: Franklin Watts, 1973); Lucy Dawidowicz, *The War against the Jews* (New York: Holt, Rinehart and Winston, 1975); David Wyman, *Paper Walls, America and the Refugee Crisis 1938–1941* (Amherst: University of Massachusetts Press, 1968); Henry Feingold, *The Politics of Rescue: The Roosevelt Administration and the Holocaust, 1938–1945* (New Brunswick, NJ: Rutgers University Press, 1970); Saul L. Friedman, *No Haven for the Oppressed: Official American Policy Toward European Jewish Refugees, 1938–1945* (Detroit, MI: Wayne State University Press, 1973); Bernard Wasserstein, *Britain and the Jews of Europe, 1939–1945* (Oxford: Oxford University Press, 1979).

5   Penkower, "The 1943 Joint Anglo-American Statement on Palestine," 234–235.
6   The French Jewish historian Marc Bloch quoted from Coulanges' introduction to *La Gaule romaine* (1875). Carlo Ginzberg, "Our Words, and Theirs, A Reflection on the Historian's Craft, Today," *Cromohs* 18 (2013): 108.
7   A comprehensive study about Schulte subsequently appeared in Walter Laqueur and Richard Breitman, *Breaking the Silence* (New York: Simon and Schuster, 1986).
8   Richard J. Evans, "Why Are We Obsessed with the Nazis?," *Guardian*, February 6, 2015.
9   David Wyman, *The Abandonment of the Jews: America and the Holocaust, 1941–1945* (New York: Pantheon Books, 1984).
10 James H. Kitchens III, "The Bombing of Auschwitz Reexamined," *The Journal of Military History* 58:2 (April 1994): 233–266; Richard H. Levy, "The Bombing of Auschwitz Revisited: A Critical Analysis," *Holocaust and Genocide Studies* 10:3 (Winter 1996): 267–298; Martin Gilbert, *Auschwitz and the Allies* (New York: Michael Joseph, 1981); Stuart G. Erdheim, "Could the Allies Have Bombed Auschwitz-Birkenau?," *Holocaust and Genocide Studies* 11:2 (Fall 1997): 129–170; Dino Brugioni, "Auschwitz and Birkenau: Why the World War II Photo Interpreters Failed to Identify the Extermination Complex," *Military Intelligence* 9:1 (January-March 1983): 50–55; Richard Breitman, "Allied Knowledge of Auschwitz-Birkenau in 1943–1944," in *FDR and the Holocaust*, ed. Verne W. Newton (New York: St. Martin's Press, 1996), 175–182; Michael Fleming, *Auschwitz, the Allies and Censorship of the Holocaust* (Cambridge: Cambridge University Press, 2014).
11 Penkower, *The Jews Were Expendable*, chaps. 5–7; David Kranzler, *The Man Who Stopped the Trains to Auschwitz: George Mantello, El Salvador, and Switzerland's Finest Hour* (Syracuse, NY: Syracuse University Press, 2001); David Kranzler and Joseph Friedenson, *Heroine of Rescue: The Incredible Story of Recha Sternbuch Who Saved Thousands from the Holocaust* (New York: Mesorah, 1984); Sharon R. Lowenstein, *Token Refuge: The Story of the Jewish Refugee Shelter at Oswego, 1944–1946* (Bloomington: Indiana University Press, 1986); Raul Hilberg, *Perpetrators, Victims, Bystanders, The Jewish Catastrophe, 1933–1945* (New York: Aaron Asher Books, 1992), 255.
12 William D. Rubinstein, *The Myth of Rescue* (London: Routledge, 1997); David Cesarani, review of The Myth of Rescue, by William D. Rubinstein, *English Historical Review* 113:454 (November 1998): 1258–1260; Walter Laqueur, "No Exit?," *Commentary* 104:4 (October 1997): 59–62; Robert Edwin Herzstein, "Is It Time to Stop Asking Why the West Failed to Save More Jews?," *Holocaust and Genocide Studies* 12:2 (Fall 1998): 326–338.
13 Yehuda Bauer, *American Jewry and the Holocaust: The American Jewish Joint Distribution Committee, 1939–1945* (Detroit, MI: Wayne State University Press, 1981); Yehuda Bauer, *Jews for Sale?* (New Haven, CT: Yale University Press, 1994); Dina Porat, *Hanhaga b'Malkod* (Tel Aviv: Am Oved, 1986), translated as *The Blue and the Yellow Stars of David: The Zionist Leadership in Palestine and the Holocaust, 1939–1945* (Cambridge, MA: Harvard University Press, 1990); Dalia Ofer, *Escaping the Holocaust : Illegal Immigration to the Land of Israel, 1939–1944* (Oxford: Oxford University Press, 1991); Hava Eshkoli, *Elem: Mapai l'Nokhah haShoa, 1939–1942* (Jerusalem: Yad Yitzhak Ben-Zvi, 1994); Yechiam Weitz, *Muda'ut v'Hoser Onim, Mapai l'Nokhah haShoa, 1943–1945* (Jerusalem: Yad Yitzhak Ben-Zvi, 1994); Hava Eshkoli Wagman, *Bein Hatzala l'Geula* (Jerusalem: Yad Vashem, 2004); Tuvia Friling, *Hetz baArafel* (Jerusalem: Merkaz l'Moreshet Ben-Gurion, 1998), translated as *Arrows in the Dark: David Ben-Gurion, the Yishuv Leadership and Rescue Attempts during the Holocaust* (Madison: University of Wisconsin Press, 2005); Efraim Zuroff, *The Response of Orthodox Jewry in the United States to the Holocaust: The Activities of the Va'ad Ha-Hatzala Rescue Committee, 1939–1945* (New York: Ktav, 2000); Zohar Segev, *The World Jewish Congress during the Holocaust: Between Activism and Restraint* (Berlin: Walter De Gruyter, 2014); Shlomo Aronson, *Hitler, the Allies, and the Jews* (Cambridge: Cambridge University Press, 2004); Judy Tydor Baumel-Schwartz, *The Bergson Boys and the Origins of Zionist Militancy* (Syracuse, NY: Syracuse University Press, 2005); Judy Tydor Baumel-Schwartz, *Perfect*

Heroes: The World War II Parachutists and the Making of Israeli Collective Memory (Madison: University of Wisconsin Press, 2010).

14. Richard Breitman and Alan M. Kraut, *American Refugee Policy and European Jewry, 1933–1945* (Bloomington: Indiana University Press, 1987); Richard Breitman, *Official Secrets, What the Nazis Planned, What the British and Americans Knew* (London: Penguin, 1998); Richard Breitman and Alan Lichtman, *FDR and the Jews* (Cambridge, MA: Belknap Press, 2013); Jerold Auerbach, "FDR and the Jews," *Society* 53:1 (June 2014), 298–301; Robert N. Rosen, *Saving the Jews, Franklin D. Roosevelt and the Holocaust* (New York: Thunder's Mouth Press, 2006). Breitman also defends FDR when writing a conclusion to *Refugees and Rescue: The Diaries and Papers of James G. McDonald, 1935–1945*, ed. R. Breitman, B. M. Stewart, and S. Hochberg (Bloomington: Indiana University Press, 2009), 329–338.

15. William vanden Heuvel, "America, Franklin D. Roosevelt and the Holocaust," lecture at the US Holocaust Memorial Museum, October 24, 1996, 13–14; "Guilt in America," *Forward*, January 27, 1995, 15; "The Holocaust Was No Secret," *New York Times Magazine*, December 22, 1996, 31; "America and the Holocaust," *American Heritage* 50:4 (July-August 1999): 38–52; Arthur Schlesinger, Jr., "Did FDR Betray the Jews?," *Newsweek*, April 18, 1994, 14; William vanden Heuvel, "FDR Did Not Abandon European Jewry," *Washington Jewish Week*, February 27, 1997, 21; Arthur Schlesinger, Jr., *Journals, 1952–2000* (New York: Penguin, 2007), 789; David Woolner, review of *FDR and the Jews*, by Richard Breitman and Alan Lichtman, *Journal of American History* 101:1 (June 2014): 300–301.

16. David Wyman and Rafael Medoff, *A Race Against Death: Peter Bergson, America, and the Holocaust* (New York: The New Press, 2002); David S. Wyman Institute for Holocaust Studies, newsletters; Laurel Leff, *Buried by the Times: The Holocaust and America's Most Important Newspaper* (New York: Cambridge University Press, 2005); Haskel Lookstein, *Were We Our Brothers' Keepers?: The Public Response of American Jews to the Holocaust, 1938–1944* (New York: Hartmoer, 1985); Deborah E. Lipstadt, *Beyond Belief, The American Press and the Coming of the Holocaust, 1933–1945* (New York: The Free Press, 1986); Robert W. Ross, *So It Was True, The American Protestant Press and the Nazi Persecution of the Jews* (Minneapolis: University of Minnesota Press, 1980).

17. Rafael Medoff, The Deafening Silence: *American Jewish Leaders and the Holocaust* (New York: Shapolsky/Carol Pub Group, 1986); Rafael Medoff, *Blowing the Whistle on Genocide: Josiah E. DuBois, Jr. and the Struggle for a U.S. Response to the Holocaust* (West Lafayette, IN: Purdue University Press, 2008); Rafael Medoff and David Golinkin, *The Student Struggle Against the Holocaust* (Jerusalem: Gefen, 2010); Samuel Merlin, R. Medoff, ed. *Millions of Jews to Rescue: A Bergson Group Leader's Account of the Campaign to Save Jews* (Washington, D.C.: David S. Wyman Institute for Holocaust Studies, 2011); Rafael Medoff and Sonja S. Wentling, *Herbert Hoover and the Jews: The Origins of the "Jewish Vote" and Bipartisan Support for Israel* (New York, 2012); Rafael Medoff and Craig Yoe, *Cartoonists against the Holocaust* (n.p.: Gussoni-Yoe Studio, 2013).

18. Rafael Medoff, *FDR and the Holocaust: A Breach of Faith* (Washington, D.C.: David S. Wyman Institute for Holocaust Studies, 2013). In 2015, Medoff, Zucker, Laurel Leff, Stephen Norwood, Judity Baumel-Schwartz, and myself, with David S. Wyman as the editor-in-chief, completed an *Encyclopedia of the American Response to the Holocaust*. This was launched on *Yom HaShoah* that same year and located on the website of the David S. Wyman Institute for Holocaust Studies (Washington, D.C.). *Yom HaShoah*, commemorated in Israel on the 27th day of the Hebrew month of Nisan, was first held in 1949. Sirens blare at 10:00 a.m. as motorists exit their cars and stand in silence throughout Israel.

19. Lucy Dawidowicz, "American Jews and the Holocaust," *New York Times Magazine*, April 18, 1982, 46ff; Monty Noam Penkower, "In Dramatic Dissent: The Bergson Boys," *American Jewish History* 70 (March 1981): 281–309; Lucy Dawidowicz, "Could the United States have Rescued the European Jews from Hitler?," *This World* 12 (Fall 1985): 27; Seymour

M. Finger, ed., *American Jewry and the Holocaust* (New York: Holmes and Meier, 1984); Henry Feingold, *Bearing Witness: How America and the Jews Responded to the Holocaust* (Syracuse, NY: Syracuse University Press, 1995); Leon Wieseltier, "Obama, the Shoah, and Syria, The President's Hypocrisy about Genocide," *New Republic*, May 21, 2014.

20 David Wyman, *America and the Holocaust*, 13 vols. (New York: Garland, 1993); Robert Abzug, *Into the Vicious Heart: Americans and the Liberation of Nazi Concentration Camps* (New York: Oxford University Press, 1987); Robert Abzug, *America Views the Holocaust, 1933–45: A Brief Documentary History* (New York: St. Martin's Press, 1999); Dina Porat and Yechiam Weitz, *Bein Magen David l'Telai Tzahov: HaYishuv haYehudi b'Eretz Yisrael v'Sho'at Yehudei Eiropa, 1939–1945, Kovetz Teudot* (Jerusalem: Yad Vashem, 2002); John F. Morley, *Vatican Diplomacy and the Jews during the Holocaust, 1939–1943* (New York: Ktav, 1980); John Cornwell, *Hitler's Pope, The Secret History of Pius XII* (New York: Viking, 1999); Pierre Blet et al., *Actes et Documents du Saint-Siege relatifs à la Second Guerre Mondiale*, 10 vols. (Vatican: Libreria Editrice Vaticana, 1974–1981); Henry Friedlander and Sybil Milton, eds., *Archives of the Holocaust* (New York: Garland, 1989–1995); Michael Marrus, ed. *The Nazi Holocaust*, part 8: *Bystanders to the Holocaust*, 3 vols. (Westport, CT: Wesleyan University Press. 1989).

21 Meir Dworzecki, "The International Red Cross and Its Policy vis-à-vis the Jews in the Ghettos and Concentration Camps in Nazi-Occupied Europe," in *Rescue Attempts during the Holocaust; Proceedings of the Second Yad Vashem International Historical Conference*, ed. Yisrael Gutman and Efraim Zuroff (Jerusalem: Yad Vashem, 1977), 71–110; Irvin Molotsky, "Red Cross Admits Knowing of the Holocaust during the War," *New York Times*, December 19, 1996; Jean-Claude Favez, *The Red Cross and the Holocaust*, trans. J. and B. Fletcher (Cambridge: Cambridge University Press, 1999); Sébastien Farré, "The ICRC and the Detainees in Nazi Concentration Camps," *International Review of the Red Cross* 94:888 (Winter 2012): 1381–1408.

22 Dov Levin, "The Attitude of the Soviet Union to the Rescue of Jews," in *Rescue Attempts during the Holocaust; Proceedings of the Second Yad Vashem International Historical Conference*, ed. Yisrael Gutman and Efraim Zuroff (Jerusalem: Yad Vashem, 1977), 225–236; Joseph Kermish, "The Activities of the Council for Aid to Jews ('Żegota') in Occupied Poland," ibid., 367–398; Yisrael Gutman, "The Attitude of the Poles to the Mass Deportations of Jews from the Warsaw Ghetto in the Summer of 1942," ibid., 399–422; Haim Avni, "The Zionist Underground in Holland and France and the Escape to Spain," ibid., 555–602; Haim Avni, *Spain, the Jews and Franco* (Philadelphia: Jewish Publication Society of America, 1982), based on his book in Hebrew (Jerusalem: Hebrew University Press, 1975); David Engel, *In the Shadow of Auschwitz: The Polish Government-in-Exile and the Jews, 1939–1942* (Chapel Hill: University of North Carolina Press, 1987); David Engel, *Facing a Holocaust: The Polish Government-in-Exile and the Jews, 1943–1945* (Chapel Hill: University of North Carolina Press, 1993); José-Alain Fralon, *A Good Man in Evil Times: The Heroic Story of the Man who Saved the Lives of Countless Refugees in World War II* (New York: Carroll & Graf, 2001); Avraham Milgram, *Portugal, Salazar, and the Jews* (Jerusalem: Gefen, 2012); Carl Ludwig, *Die Flüchtlingspolitik der Schweiz in den Jahren 1933 bis 1945* (Bern: Herbert Lang, 1957); Alfred A. Hasler, *The Lifeboat Is Full* (New York: Funk & Wagnalls, 1969); Jacques Picard, *Die Schweiz und die Juden, 1933–1945* (Zurich: Chronos, 1997); *Jewish Daily Forward*, February 14, 2013; Corry Guttstadt, *Turkey, the Jews, and the Holocaust* (Cambridge: Cambridge University Press, 2013); W. M. Calgren, *Swedish Foreign Policy during the Second World War* (London: Benn, 1977); Per Anger, *With Raoul Wallenberg in Budapest: Memories of the War Years in Hungary* (New York: Holocaust Library, 1981); Frederick E. Werbell and Thurston Clarke, *Lost Hero: The Mystery of Raoul Wallenberg* (New York: McGraw-Hill, 1982). Two informative accounts by some Jewish activists in Switzerland during the war are Heini Borenstein, *Ha'i Shveitz, Peulot*

Ezra v'Hatzala baShanim 1939–1946 (Tel Aviv: Moreshet, 1996), and Ra'aya Cohen, *Bein "Sham" l'"Khan", Sipuram shel Eidim l'Hurban, 1939–1942* (Tel Aviv: Am Oved, 1999).

23 Irving Abella and Harold Troper, *None is Too Many: Canada and the Jews of Europe, 1933–1945* (Toronto: University of Toronto Press, 1982); Michael Blakeney, *Australia and the Jewish Refugees, 1933–1948* (Sydney: Croom Helm, 1985); Jeffrey Lesser, *Welcoming the Undesirables: Brazil and the Jewish Question* (Berkeley: University of California Press, 1995); Marion A. Kaplan, *Dominican Haven: The Jewish Refugee Settlement at Sosua, 1940–1945* (New York: Museum of Jewish Heritage, 2008); Allen Wells, *Tropical Zone: General Trujillo, FDR, and the Jews of Sosua* (Durham, 2009); David Kranzler, *Japanese, Nazis, and Jews: The Jewish Refugee Community of Shanghai, 1938–1945* (New York, 1976).

24 Richard Bolover, *British Jewry and the Holocaust* (Cambridge: Cambridge University Press, 1993); Ariel Hurwitz, *Jews without Power, American Jewry during the Holocaust* (New Rochelle, NY: MultiEducator, 2011).

25 David Bankier, ed. *Secret Intelligence and the Holocaust* (New York: Enigma Books, 2006). An early study was Walter Laqueur, *The Terrible Secret: Suppression of the Truth About Hitler's "Final Solution"* (Boston: Brown and Company, 1980). In July 2005, the US government quietly released a 167-page report, based on British and American archives, entitled "Eavesdropping on Hell" by Robert Hanyok, a historian with the US National Security Agency's Center for Cryptologic History in Maryland. It suggests that, while the evidence was incomplete, details from coded Nazi messages that Britain intercepted beginning in 1941 could have confirmed and exposed the scope of the Holocaust well before the Auschwitz Protocols reached the West in the summer of 1944 and Red Army troops arrived at the Majdanek death camp. Hanyok's lengthy analysis notes that British and US efforts to sort evidence were hampered by large case backlogs and a shortage of translators. Efforts were further slowed by the two allies' reluctance to share intelligence about decoded German communications and, more generally, by military priorities assigned to intelligence sifting. The report also suggests that antisemitism may have helped create an atmosphere which affected how communications intelligence was handled. An observation from Nigel De Grey, deputy director of the Government code and Cipher School at Bletchley Park, on September 11, 1941, taking account of German massacres in the Soviet Union, also reflects an inability to appreciate the implications of that information: "The fact that the police are killing all Jews that fall into their hands should now be sufficiently well appreciated. It is not therefore proposed to continue reporting these butcheries unless so requested." Sam Roberts, "Allied Intelligence Had Early Hints of Holocaust, Analysis Finds," *New York Times*, August 1, 2005. Three years later, Stephen Tyas disclosed that British intelligence agencies began early in World War II to record conversations between German prisoners of war, providing evidence at the time of individual German officers' participation and knowledge of war crimes. Stephen Tyas, "Allied Intelligence Agencies and the Holocaust: Information Acquired from German Prisoners of War," *Holocaust and Genocide Studies* 22:1 (2008): 1–24.

26 Monty Noam Penkower, *The Holocaust and Israel Reborn, From Catastrophe to Sovereignty* (Urbana: University of Illinois Press, 1994).

27 Monty Noam Penkower, *Decision on Palestine Deferred: America, Britain and Wartime Diplomacy, 1939–1945* (London: Frank Cass, 2002).

28 Monty Noam Penkower, *Twentieth-Century Jews: Forging Identity in the Land of Promise and in the Promised Land* (Boston: Academic Studies Press, 2010).

29 Bat-Ami Zucker, *In Search of Refuge: Jews and US Consuls in Nazi Germany, 1933–1941* (London: Vallentine Mitchell, 2001); Stephen H. Norwood, *The Third Reich in the Ivory Tower: Complicity and Conflict on American Campuses* (Cambridge: Cambridge University Press, 2009).

30 Monty Noam Penkower, *The Swastika's Darkening Shadow: Voices before the Holocaust* (New York: Touro University Press, 2013).

31 Monty Noam Penkower, *Palestine in Turmoil: The Struggle for Sovereignty, 1933–1939*, 2 vols. (Boston: Academic Studies Press, 2014).
32 Penkower, *Decision on Palestine Deferred*, 97–98.
33 Raymond Ibrahim, "Christmas Slaughter, Muslim Persecution of Christians—Christmas 2014," Gatestone Institute, February 1, 2015; Nicholas Kristof, "Heroes and Bystanders," *Jerusalem Post*, February 3, 2015, 21.
34 Penkower, *The Jews Were Expendable*, 301–302.
35 Laurel Leff, *Well Worth Saving, American Universities' Life-and-Death Decisions on Refugees from Nazi Europe* (New Haven, CT: Yale University Press, 2019); Thorsten Noack, "William L. Shirer and International Awareness of the Nazi Euthanasia Program," *Holocaust and Genocide Studies* 30:3 (Winter 2016): 433–457; Paul R. Bartrop, *The Evian Conference of 1938 and the Jewish Refugee Crisis* (New York: Palgrave Macmillan, 2018); Stephen H. Norwood, *Prologue to Annihilation: Ordinary American and British Jews Challenge the Third Reich* (Bloomington: Indiana University Press, 2021); Stephen H. Norwood, "The Quakers' 'Dark Side': Appeasement, Ambivalence, and Antisemitism, 1933–1939," *National Resistance, Politics and Society* 4:1/2 (2002): 11–49.
36 Peter Duffy, *The Agitator, William Bailey and the First American Uprising Against Nazism* (New York: PublicAffairs, 2019); Steven Pressman, *50 Children: One Ordinary American Couple's Extraordinary Rescue Mission into the Heart of Nazi Germany* (New York: Harper Perennial, 2014); Julien Gorbach, *The Notorious Ben Hecht: Iconoclastic Writer and Militant Zionist* (West Lafayette, IN: Purdue University Press, 2019); Adina Hoffman, *Ben Hecht: Fighting Words and Moving Pictures* (New Haven, CT: Yale University Press, 2019); Jonathan Freeland, *The Escape Artist: The Man Who Broke Out of Auschwitz to Warn the World* (New York: Harper, 2022); Sara Kadosh, *We Think of You as an Angel: Shaul Weingort and the Rescue of Jews during the Holocaust* (Jerusalem: Yad Vashem, 2019).
37 Rafael Medoff et al., *Too Little and Almost Too Late: The War Refugee Board and America's Response to the Holocaust* (Washington, D.C., 2017); Rafael Medoff, *The Jews Should Keep Quiet: Franklin D. Roosevelt, Rabbi Stephen S. Wise, and the Holocaust* (Lincoln: University of Nebraska Press, 2019); Rafael Medoff, "Reflections on American Jewish Political Power in the 1940s: What New Research Reveals about Saul Friedman's Thesis," in *The Highest Form of Wisdom: A Memorial Book in Honor of Saul S. Friedman*, ed. Jonathan C. Friedman and Robert D. Miller II (New York: Ktav, 2016), 45–53; Rafael Medoff, "The 1943 Jewish March on Washington, Through the Eyes of its Critics," *AJS Perspectives* (Spring 2021): 36–38; Rafael Medoff, "Antisemitism in the White House," in *From Anti-Zionism to Anti-Semitism: The Past & Present of a Lethal Ideology*, ed. Eunice G. Pollack (Boston: Academic Studies Press, 2017), 70–112; Rafael Medoff et al., *Distorting America's Response to the Holocaust: An Analysis of the "Americans and the Holocaust" Exhibit at the United States Holocaust Memorial Museum* (Washington, D.C.: David S. Wyman Institute for Holocaust Studies, 2018); Rafael Medoff, *America and the Holocaust: A Documentary History* (Lincoln: University of Nebraska Press, 2022).
38 Monty Noam Penkower, "FDR Had an Option to Save More Jews," letter to the editor, *The Forward*, September 12, 2022; Monty Noam Penkower and Rafael Medoff, "Ken Burns Has a Palestine Problem," *Jerusalem Post*, September 13, 2022; Monty Noam Penkower and Rafael Medoff, "A Holocaust Mystery: Ken Burns Gets Lost in a Bermuda Triangle," *History News Network*, October 2, 2022.
39 Dan Stone, *The Liberation of the Camps: The End of the Holocaust and Its Aftermath* (New Haven, CT: Yale University Press, 2015); Andrew Kornbluth, *The August Trials: The Holocaust and Postwar Justice in Poland* (Cambridge, MA: Harvard University Press, 2021); Jan T. Gross, *Neighbors: The Destruction of the Jewish Community in Jedwabne, Poland* (Princeton, NJ: Princeton University Press, 2001); Jan T. Gross, *Fear: Anti-Semitism in Poland after Auschwitz* (Princeton, NJ: Princeton University Press, 2006); Monty Noam Penkower, *After the Holocaust* (New York: Touro University Press, 2021).

40 Jan T. Gross and Irina G. Gross, *Golden Harvest: Events at the Periphery of the Holocaust* (Oxford: Oxford University Press, 2012); Jan Grabowski, *Hunt for the Jews: Betrayal and Murder in German-Occupied Poland* (Bloomington: Indiana University Press, 2016); Jan Grabowski, *The Polish Police: Collaboration in the Holocaust* (Washington, D.C.: US Holocaust Memorial Museum, 2016); Barbara Engelking, *Such a Beautiful Day: Jews Seeking Refuge in the Polish Countryside, 1942–1945* (Jerusalem: Yad Vashem, 2016); Mirosław Tryczyk, *The Towns of Death: Pogroms against Their Neighbors* (Lanham, MD: Lexington Books, 2021).

41 Richard Breitman, *The Berlin Mission: The American Who Resisted Nazi Germany from Within* (New York: PublicAffairs, 2019); Rebecca Erbelding, *Rescue Board: The Untold Story of America's Efforts to Save the Jews of Europe* (New York: Anchor Books, 2018).

42 Laurel Leff, "Seeking the Middle, Creating a Muddle: The Failed Efforts of State Department Historians to Reinterpret the Role of US Consuls in the Nazi-Era Refugee Crisis," *Israel Journal of Foreign Afffairs* 16:2 (2002): 229–249; Zucker, *In Search of Refuge*.

43 Daniel Kertzer, *The Pope at War: The Secret History of Pius XII, Mussolini, and Hitler* (New York: Random House, 2022). Following eleven years' work, a high-level Vatican commission instituted by Pope John Paul II offered on March 16, 1998, what has become the official position of the Roman Catholic Church denying any responsibility for fomenting the kind of demonization of the Jews that made the Holocaust possible. Yet, as Kurtzer showed in *The Popes Against the Jews* (2001), the distinction made in the report between "anti-Judaism"—of which some unnamed and misinformed Christians were unfortunately guilty in the past—and "anti-Semitism," which led to the horrors of the Holocaust, will simply not survive historical scrutiny. In fact, he details how the church played a major role in leading Catholics throughout Europe to view Jews as an existential threat.

44 Hirschmann interview with Laurence Jarvik, January 20, 1979, David S. Wyman Institute for Holocaust Studies, Washington, D.C. For Hirschmann's efforts vis-à-vis Romania and Bulgaria, aided by young Palestinian Jewish emissaries stationed in Istanbul, see Penkower, *The Jews Were Expendable*, 164–175.

Index

A

Abandonment of the Jews, The, 213, 251, 255, 263
Abdul Hamid II, 13, 16
Abella, Irving, 220, 266
Abyssinia, 43, 98
Abzug, Robert H., 219, 265
Acheson, Dean, 156, 255
Action Française, 77
Address to the Rothschilds, An, 5
Adler, Cyrus, 33, 37–40, 64, 231–34, 237, 240
Adler, Hermann, 7
After the Holocaust, 228, 253–54, 258, 267
Aftermath (Pokłosie), 189
Agar, Herbert, 108
Ahad Ha'am, 10, 12, 16, 23, 25
Ahimeir, Abba, 95, 245–46
Aktion T-4. *See* euthanasia program
Akzin, Benjamin, 105, 248
Alexander II, 19
Alkalai, Judah, 9
aliya bet (unauthorized immigration), 101
Alliance Israélite Universelle, 62
Alteneuland (Old-New Land), 12, 17
Alter, Wiktor, 187
Alter, Yehuda Leib Aryeh, 16
America-Holy Land Project, 179
American Association for the United Nations, 148, 254
American Council for Judaism (ACJ), xii, 130, 138–39, 144, 150, 160, 222, 251–52, 254, 256
American Emergency Committee for Zionist Affairs, 129
American Friends of a Jewish Palestine, 100, 102
American Friends of the Middle East, 148, 254
American Jewish Committee, 27, 90, 113, 122, 130, 157, 185, 236–37, 253
American Jewish Conference, 132, 149, 252
American Jewish Congress, 31, 42, 57, 60–62, 92, 135, 160, 234, 244
American Jewish Joint Distribution Committee, 27, 75, 215, 253

American Mercury, 118
American Palestine Committee, 114
American Reform movement, 16
American Relief Administration, 155
American Zionist Emergency Council, 156, 158
Amery, Leopold, 88, 98
Amiens, 211
Analysis of British Policy in Palestine, 156, 255
Anatomy of Faith, 150
Andrzejczak, Rajmund, 198
Anglo-American Committee of Inquiry on Palestine, 143, 153, 156, 159, 165, 168, 233, 253–54, 256
Anglo-American Mandate Convention, 163
Anglo-Jewish Association, 52, 231
Anglo-Palestine Club, 107
Anielewicz, Mordechai, 191
Anschluss, 84, 101
antisemitism, 27, 29, 31, 35–36, 38–46, 49–52, 60, 66, 68, 103, 105–7, 111, 118, 121, 123, 136, 163–64, 167–71, 177, 197, 215, 218, 220, 225, 233–35, 241, 253, 255–60
Antonescu, Ion, 212, 240
appeasement of Nazi Germany, 223
Arab League, 142, 154
Arab Revolt, 96, 98, 223
Arab states, 130, 149, 156, 161, 164, 172, 224
Aranha, Oswaldo, 159
Archbishop of Canterbury, 88, 168
Arendt, Hannah, XV
Argentina, 4, 8, 33, 36
Arlosoroff, Chaim, 97, 246
Armenia, 28, 155, 255
Arno Press, 179
Aronson, Shlomo, 215, 263
Arrow Cross, 80, 83, 86–87
Artists of Terezin, The, 207, 262
Aryanization, 87
As a Driven Leaf, 129, 150
Asch, Shalom, 117
Assyrian refugees, 43
Assyrians, 171, 257
Atlantic Charter, 116, 131, 139

Atlantic Monthly, 130, 252
Attlee, Clement, 153, 155
Auchinleck, Claude, 115
Auden, W. H., 70, 94, 239
Auerbach, Jerold, 215, 264
August Trials: The Holocaust and Postwar Justice in Poland, The, 182, 258, 267
Auschwitz Protocol, 214
Auschwitz-Birkenau, 71, 188, 195, 197, 211, 213, 227, 230, 263
Auschwitz-I, 187, 259
Auschwitz-II, 188
Austria, 11, 13, 18–19, 25, 30, 44, 66, 69, 72–73, 75–77, 84, 87, 90–91, 101, 218, 239–41, 244, 257
Austrian Reichstag, 2
Auto-Emancipation, 7
Avenol, Joseph, 31, 58
Avni, Haim, 220, 265

B

B'Ir HaHareiga, 92, 245
B'nai Brith, 31, 42, 61, 122, 212, 237–38
Babi Yar, 224
Bacau, 80
Bacher, Eduard, 2, 6–7
Baeck, Leo, 91, 233–35, 240, 242
Baerwald, Paul, 31, 34, 57, 245
Bailey, William, 226, 267
Balfour Declaration, 19, 119, 138–39, 155, 161, 163–64, 166, 168–71, 175
Ball at the Opera, The, 90
"Ballad of the Doomed Jews of Europe," 122
Baltimore's Hebrew Congregation, 130
Bankier, David, 74, 240, 266
Baranowski, Władysław, 184
Bar Kokhba, 112, 248
Bard College, 205
Barkai, Avraham, 91, 244
Baron, Salo W., 37–38
Bartoszewski, Władysław, 189
Bartrop, Paul R., 226, 267
Baruch, Bernard, 112, 125–26
Basic Equities of the Palestine Problem, The, xii, 147–48, 162–63, 167, 171, 176, 179, 253, 255–57, 269
Basic Judaism, 145, 150
Basle Program, 14, 20, 156
Battle for Jerusalem, The, 110, 248
Bauer, Yehuda, 206, 215, 259, 263
Baumel-Schwartz, Judy Tydor, 215, 263–64
BBC, xiv, 114, 258, 260
Beck, Józef, 75, 78, 82, 241
Beer-Hoffman, Richard, 11
Begin, Menachem, 99

Bein, Alex, 3, 24, 245, 263, 265–266
Bejski, Moshe, 187
Belarus, 77, 81, 155
Believing Jew: The Selected Writings of Milton Steinberg, 150
Ben-Ami, Yitzhak, 100, 104–5, 118, 247, 249–51
Ben-Eliezer, Aryeh, 105
Ben-Gurion, David, 15, 20, 70, 89, 91, 97–98, 100–101, 105, 111, 113, 124, 215, 223, 239, 248, 254, 263
Ben-Horin, Eliyahu, 105
Ben-Yosef, Shlomo, 99
Ben-Zvi, Yitshak, 97, 215, 263
Benedikt, Moritz, 2, 6–7
Benjamin, Walter, 70, 239
Bentwich, Norman, 29–30, 33, 41, 44–45, 47–48, 51–53, 55, 58, 60–61, 96, 231–36, 238
Berchin, Michael, 107
Bergson Boys, 119, 123, 126, 128, 214, 216, 251–52, 264
Bergson, Peter, xii, 110, 120–23, 125–126, 128, 213, 215, 217, 246–47, 249–52, 263–64
Bergsonites, 217–18
Bérenger, Henri, 33, 43, 84
Bergen-Belsen, xiv
Berkowicz,, Michael, 13
Berle, Adolf Jr., 116
Berlin, 7, 29, 31–32, 44, 54, 56–58, 62–63, 70, 72, 76, 87, 91–92, 127, 199, 217, 226, 228, 239, 241, 263, 268
Bermuda Conference on Refugees, 119, 211, 227
Berne, 83
Bernheim, Franz, 29, 231
Bersohn and Bauman Children's Hospital, 195
Bernstein, Philip, 129–30
Bessarabia, 76–77, 80, 85
Betar, 95–97, 99–101, 104, 106–7, 246, 250
Bevin, Ernest, 153, 156, 173, 254
Bevin Plan 153, 254
Bey, Mardem, 154
Biała, 81
Bialik, Hayim Nahman, 92, 231, 245
Białystok, 49, 78, 80, 183
Bielsko, 81
Biltmore Platform, 113, 249
binationalism, 128, 145, 175, 185
Bingham IV, Hiram, 229
Bingham, Harry, 217
Birnbaum, Nathan, 10
Bishop of Łukom, 183
Bishop Tit, 82

Black Book, The Nazi Crime against the Jewish People, The, 207
Blakeney, Michael, 220, 266
Board of Deputies of British Jews, 30, 56, 85, 231, 236, 241
Bollag, Uri, 25
Bolover, Richard, 266
Borysław, ix
Bosnia, 225
Boston Globe, 56
Botein, Bernard, 137
Branczyce, 81
Bratislava, 86, 88
Breitenstein, Max, 1
Breitman, Richard, 213, 215, 228, 231, 234, 263–64, 268
Brenner, Michael, 24
Bridges, Styles, 109
Briscoe, Robert, 100, 102
Brit HaBiryonim, 95, 245–46
British Eighth Army, 115
British Foreign Office, 30, 56, 62, 64, 82, 238
British government, 17, 61, 123, 142, 156, 158, 206, 214, 226, 240
British Guyana, 71
British Royal Commission on Palestine, 93
British War Cabinet, 166
Brno (Brünn), 86
Brod, Max, 93
Bru, Frederico Laredo, 87
Brugioni, Dino, 213, 263
Buber, Martin, 15, 23, 71, 93, 239, 245
Bucharest, 74, 79–80, 246
Buchenwald, xiv
Budapest, 1, 15, 80, 83, 214, 265
Buhuși, 81
Bukovina, 76, 80, 82–83
Bulgaria, 80, 84, 211, 268
Bullard, Robert Lee, 155
Bund, 11, 78, 81, 185, 187, 194, 241
Bundestag, 203
Burns, Ken, 227, 267
Bydgoszcz, 81
Bzury, 199, 258

C

Caldwell, Taylor, 117
Calgren, W. M., 220, 265
Cambodia, 225
Camelots du Roi, 77
Camp of National Unity, 81
cantonization, 205
Cantors Association of America, 118
Carmeli, Peretz, 96
Carmelite nuns, 187–88

Carol II, King, 83
Castille Hotel, 4
Cecil, Robert, 29, 88
Central Conference of American Rabbis (CCAR), 130
Cernauti, 74, 82
Cesarani, David, 214, 263
Chamberlain, Joseph, 17
Chamberlain, Neville, 72, 102, 153
Chandler, Albert B., 120–21
Chełmno death camp, 184, 225
Chetwode, Philip, 119
Child of the Century, A, 207, 248–51, 262
Christian Century, 56, 145
Christian Council on Palestine, 130
Christian Social Party, 3–4
Church, Samuel Harden, 109
Churchill, Winston, 88, 108, 154
Clemenceau, Claud, 21
Codreanu, Zelea Cornelieu, 82, 240
Cohen, Arthur A., 150
Cohen, Benjamin V., 158
Cohen, Eli, 200, 202
Cohen, Lionel, 48
Cohen, Moris R, 28, 37–39, 45, 51, 59–60, 62–63, 65, 232, 234–38
Cohn, Ernst, 51, 235
Comité des Delegations Juives, 29, 38
Commentary, 145, 213, 253, 263
Committee for a Jewish Army of Stateless and Palestinian Jews, 109–11, 114–19, 123–24, 126
Common Sense of Religious Faith, The, 145
Concordat, 31, 232
Conference on Jewish Relations, 37–38, 237
Confronting the Holocaust, 199
Congo, 225
Congregation Beth-El Zedeck, 129
Congregation Rodeph Shalom, 100
Copeland, Aaron, 117
Cornwell, John, 219, 265
Creed of an American Zionist, The, 132
Cristea, Miron, 80
Cronbach, Siegfried, 7
Cuza, Alexander, 74
Cuzist Party, 74
Cyprus, 17, 144, 165
Cyrankiewicz, Josef, 184
Czaplińska, Agata, 202
Czechoslovakia, 35, 56, 60, 66, 69, 76–77, 84, 101, 107, 162, 238–40
Czeladź, 81
Czernek, Przemysław, 196
Czernowitz (Cernauti), 74
Częstochowa, 78, 81, 188

Czwórka, 81
Czyżew, 78

D
D'Avigdor-Goldsmid, Osmond, 36, 233, 241
D'Avigdor, Sylvie, 13
Dąbrówka Kościelna, 77
Dachau, xiv, 85, 158
Daladier, Edouard, 223
Dalton, Hugh, 164
Daniel Deronda, 4
Dante Alighieri, 213
Danzig, 76, 79, 82, 84, 88, 94, 245
Davar, 92, 244
David, 118, 135–36, 215.
David, Anthony, 24
Davidson, Joe, 112
Davis, James S. J., 121, 123
Dawidowicz, Lucy, 207, 218, 262, 264
De Coulanges, Fustel, 208, 263
De Graeff, Jonkheer, 32
De Haas, Jacob, 13
de Hirsch, Maurice, 4
de Madariaga, Salvador, 60, 236
de Rothschild, Edmond, 13
de Rothschild, Robert , 34
De Sousa Mendes, Aristides, 220
Debrezin (Debrecen), 80
Decision on Palestine Deferred, 69, 221, 239, 243, 249, 252–53, 256, 257, 266–67
Democratic Fraction, 16
Der Angriff, 79, 89
Der Judenstaat, 1, 7, 9–21, 23–24
Dessauer, Adolf, 7
Destruction of the European Jews, The, 207, 262
Dewey, Thomas E., 118, 255
Die Fackel, 12
Die Judenfrage als Rassen-, Sitten- und Kultur-Frage, 1
Die Menorah, (The Menorah), 14
Die Traumdeutung, 11
Die Welt, 14, 22, 190, 260
Dill, John, 112
Dingell, John D., 107
Displaced Persons (DPs), 142–43, 154, 158, 163, 170, 228
Divine Comedy, 213
Długołęcki, Piotr, 200
Długosiodło, 81
Döbling Cemetery, 20
Dodd, William, 142
Dodds, William, 120
Dominican Republic, 84, 220, 242, 266
Douglas, Melvyn, 117
DPs. *See* Displaced Persons

Dreifuss, Havi, 203
Dreyfus trial, 3, 155, 255
Dreyfus, Alfred, 3
Drohobycz, 81
Drumont, Edouard-Adolphe, 2
Dubnow, Simon, 92, 244
DuBois, Jr., Josiah, 217, 259–60, 264
Duda, Andrzej, x, 192
Dühring, Eugen, 1
Duffy, Peter, 226, 267
Dumas Fils, Alexandre, 2
Dworzecki, Meir, 219, 265

E
East Galicia, 75
Eban, Aubrey (Abba), 159–61, 256
École Militaire, 3
Edelman, Marek, 185, 190–91
Eden, Anthony, 82, 108, 200
Edlach, 18
Eichmann, Adolf, 72, 211
Eine Krone für Zion, 12
Einstein, Albert, 57, 87, 125, 149, 156, 177
Eisenhower, Dwight D., 145, 157, 161
El Alamein, 115–16
El-Al fraternity, 96
el-Husseini, Haj Amin, 116, 127, 251
El-Sadat, Anwar, 108
Elath, Eliyahu. *See* Epstein, Eliyahu
Eldad, *See* Sheib, Israel
Eliot, George, 4
Elisha ben Abuyah, 129
Elkes, Elchanan, xiv
Elon, Amos, 24
Emergency Committee for Zionist Affairs, 104, 111, 129
Emergency Conference to Save the Jews of Europe, 123, 128
Emerson, Ralph Waldo, 130
Emir Feisal, 170
Endecja, 183
Endek Perty, 77–78, 80–81, 83, 85
Engel, David, 265
Engelking, Barbara, 181, 196, 228, 268
Eno, Lawrence R., 157, 178–79, 255
Epstein, Eliyahu, 155
Erbelding, Rebecca, 228–29, 268
Erdheim, Stuart, 213
Erlich, Henryk, 187
Eshkoli Wagman, Hava, 263
Eternal Jew, The, 83
Ethiopia, 43, 98
ethnic cleansing, 183
European Jewish Association, 202
European Union, 197, 199, 202

Evans, Richard J., 212, 263
Evian Conference on Refugees, xii, 66, 84, 90, 122, 133, 220, 226, 233, 255
euthanasia program (Aktion T-4), 226

F
Fagen, Melvin M., 28, 39–54, 48–50, 59–60, 62–65, 233–38
Fahy, Charles, 156
Fatah, xvi
Favez, Jean-Claude, 265
Fear: Anti-Semitism in Poland after Auschwitz, 189
Federal Writers' Project: A Study in Government Patronage of the Arts, The, 205, 262
Feilchenfeld, Ernst H., 30, 231–32
Feinberg, Nathan, 29
Feingold, Henry, 207, 218, 243, 251, 262, 265
Ferdinand I, 21
Fight for Freedom, 108
Final Solution of the Jewish Question, 69, 73, 169, 188, 209, 230
Finger, Seymour M., 218
First Zionist Congress, 14, 20–21
Fleming, Michael, 213, 261, 263
Flexner, Bernard, 38
Foreign Policy Association , 27
Forgotten Ally, The, 125, 250
Fortas, Abraham, 157, 178–79
Fosdick, Raymond, 33
Four Freedoms , 116
Fourth Zionist Congress, 21
France, 2, 6, 29, 32–33, 41, 60, 62–63, 69, 72, 84, 88, 104, 155, 211, 217, 220, 237–40, 265
Frank, Jerome, xii, 134, 252–53, 257
Frankfurter, Felix, 155, 222, 232
Franz Joseph I, Emperor, 4
Frederick of Baden, 13
Freedland, Jonathan, 227
Freud, Sigmund, 11
Frick, Walter, 72
Friedlander, Henry, 219, 265
Friedman, Saul, 207, 251
Friling, Tuvia, 263
Fry, Vivian, 217
Ft. Oswego camp, 214, 218
Fuld, Stanley H., 160, 178, 233, 240

G
Gądecki, Bishop Stanisław, 189
Galician Jewry, 17
Galilee, 109, 163, 175

Gandhi, Mohandas, 93
gas chambers, 115, 165, 216, 249, 259
Gebirtig, Mordecai, 92, 245
Gemlich, Adolf, 71
General Assembly, xii, 79, 147, 149, 153, 158–59, 161–62, 177, 195, 238, 256
Geneva Convention, 29
genocide, 31, 156, 216, 257, 262
George VI, 93
Ger, 16
German Jews, 30–31, 39–40, 53, 231, 234, 237, 242
German Kaiser, 4, 13
Germany, xi, xiv, 3, 9, 11, 13, 25, 27, 29–37, 39–49, 51–53, 55–65, 67, 69–80, 82, 84–85, 89, 91–93, 100–102, 111, 119–20, 123, 128, 142–43, 145, 157, 165, 171, 179, 193, 195, 197, 199, 202, 206, 218–19, 223, 226, 228–29, 231–33, 236–37, 239–45, 255, 257, 261–62, 266–68
Geschlecht und Charakter, 12
Gfollner, Johannes A., 74
ghetto benches, 78, 83
GI Bill of Rights, 178
Gilbert, Martin, 213, 227, 263
Gillette, Guy, 112
Ginzberg, Asher, 10
Goebbels, Joseph, 72, 122
Goga, Octavian, 79
Golden Harvest, 190, 228, 268
Goldman, Robert, 149, 254
Goldmann, Nahum, 60–61, 75
Golinkin, David, 217, 264
Golomb, Eliyahu, 97
Gomulka, Władysław, 185, 258
Gorbach, Julien, 227, 267
Gordon, A.D., 23, 243
Göring, Hermann, 72, 74, 85
Grabowski, Jan, 181, 192, 196, 228, 260–61, 268
Grand Mufti, 116, 127
Green Shirts, 74, 79, 240, 242
Green, Gerald, 206, 262
Greenbaum, Edward, 113
Greenberg, Chaim, 118
Greenberg, Uri Zvi, 95, 245
Grigg, Edward, 106, 115
Grodno, 77
Gross, Jan Tomasz, 259
Gross, Irina, 268
Gruner, Dov, 126, 250
Güdemann, Moritz, 6–7, 10
Gunther, Frances, 100
Gunther, John, 100, 103, 105

Gurfein, Murray I. 158–61, 176, 178, 255–57
Gutman, Yisrael, 220, 251, 262, 265
Güttland, 88
Guttstadt, Corry, 220, 265

H

Habima Theatre, 168
Habsburg government, 6
Hácha, Emil, 88
Hadassah, 88, 97, 156, 241, 246, 253, 255
Hadera, 170
HaEkdach, 96
Hagana, 95–96, 99–100, 209
Hague, 44, 235
Haj Amin al-Husseini, 169, 171
Haley, Alex, 206
Halpern, Ben, 24
Halpern, Uriel, 100, 246
Hamas, xvi
HaMetzuda, 96, 246
Handler, Milton, 156, 158, 178, 255
Hansson, Michael, 93
Har Herzl, x, 258
Harrison, Earl, 142, 144, 154, 165, 228, 253
Hart, Moss, 118, 233, 250, 262
Hasler, Alfred, 220, 265
HaTikva, xiv, 105, 149, 185
Havas news Agency, 87
havlaga, 98–99, 101
Hayalim Almonim (Anonymous Soldiers), 96
Hayes, Carlton, 38, 233
Hebrew, ix–xxiv, 8, 12–14, 22, 70–71, 96, 113, 124, 126, 130, 133, 149, 151, 168, 179, 189, 191, 213, 220, 239, 247–48, 251, 257, 261, 264–65
Hebrew Committee of National Liberation, 124, 248, 251
Hebrew University, ix, 70–71, 96, 113, 168, 265
Hechler, William Henry, 13, 18
Hecht, Ben, xii, 108–13, 117–18, 122–23, 126, 227, 247–51, 262, 267
Hecht, Reuven, 101
Heine, Heinrich, 5, 21, 92, 244
Heinlein, Herbert, 87
Helpern, Jeremiah (Yerma), 102, 105, 107–8, 112–114, 119, 248–49
Henderson, Loy, 161
Hertzberg, Arthur, 9, 24
Herzl, Theodor, xi, 1, 3, 5, 7, 9, 11, 13, 15, 17, 19, 21, 23–25, 132
Herzog, Yitzhak, 198
Heschel, Abraham J., 71, 239
Hess, Moses, 10

Hess, Rudolf, 72
Heydrich, Reinhard, 72–73, 249
Hezbollah, xvi
HIAS, 178
Hibbat Zion, 9, 13
Hibben, John, 72
HICEM, 75
High Commissioner for Refugees, xi, 27–28, 30–32, 55, 66, 76, 238
Hilberg, Raul, 214, 262–63
Hilfsverein, 82
Himmler, Heinrich, 72, 209
Hirschmann, Ira, 214, 230, 268
Histadrut, 242
Hitler, Adolf, 71, 120, 128, 208, 242
Hlond, August Cardinal, 77, 188
Hoffman, Adina, 227, 267
Holmes, John Haynes, 140, 253, 265
Holocaust, ix–xviii, 2, 4, 6, 8, 10, passim
Holocaust and Israel Reborn, The, 221, 238–39, 251, 253–54, 259, 266
Holocaust survivors, xiii–xiv, 145–46, 161, 164–65, 178, 257
Holy Temple, x
Hongkew district, 88
Hood, John, 162
Hoover, Herbert, 117, 155, 217, 255, 264
Höre Israel, 11
Horowitz, David, 160
Horthy, Miklós, 212, 214
Hotin, 82
House of Commons, 84, 106, 124, 153, 166, 254
Hovevei Zion, 10, 16
Hugo, Victor, 21
Huleh, 170
Hull, Cordell, 38, 84, 122, 218, 237, 243
Hungary, 1, 22, 40, 69, 74, 79, 80, 84, 86–87, 211, 239–40, 250, 265
Hunt for the Jews, 192, 268
Hurwitz, Ariel, 221, 266
Hussein bin Ali al-Hashimi, 170
Hyman, Joseph, 75, 232

I

Ibn Saud, 154, 164, 256
ICA, 36
Idelson, Vladimir R., 48–50, 52
IDF, ix
illegal immigrants, 99, 169
illegal immigration, 100–101, 103, 126, 208, 215
Imrédy, Bela, 86
In re Gault, 178
In the Shadow of Catastrophe, 148, 254

Index | 275

India, 142, 149, 162
Institut de Droit International, 65
Intergovernmental Committee on Refugees, 157, 211, 233, 255
International Aspects of German Racial Policies, 65, 238
International Federation of League of Nations Societies, 29, 66
International Holocaust Remembrance Day, 195
International Red Cross, 123, 127, 209, 211, 265
Iran, xvi, 112, 162, 225
Iraq, 108, 171, 225
Irgun Tzva'i Leumi, xii, 96, 99–105, 109, 111, 123, 125, 246, 250
Iron Wall, The, 95
Isaac, Jules, 188, 259
Israel, Wilfrid, 91
Italy, 21, 29, 83–84, 107, 127, 242, 250

J

Jabotinsky, Eri, 100, 106–8, 111, 123, 247–48, 250
Jabotinsky, Vladimir (Ze'ev), xii, 21, 91, 93, 95–111, 124, 126, 244–48, 250, 252
Jackson, Robert, 158
Jagiellonian University, 186
James, William, 150
Janowsky, Oscar I, 28, 37–55, 59–60, 62–65, 232–34, 238, 240
Japan, 236
Jaruzelski, Wojciech, 186–87
Jasiewicz, Krzysztof, 191, 260
Jassy, 74
JDC, 27, 31, 33–34, 47, 57, 75, 82, 88, 232, 236, 245
Jedwabne, x, 80, 189–90, 192, 199, 258–59, 267
Jefferson, Thomas, 135–136
Jerusalem, ix–xvi, xvi, 9, 14, 16–17, 20, 23, 25, 57, 70, 95–96, 99, 101, 105, 109–110, 115–16, 124, 127, 132, 141, 157, 162–63, 175, 226, 231, 236, 240–42, 244–48, 251, 254–55, 258–65, 267–68
Jew in Love, A, 108
Jewish-Ottoman Company, 16
Jewish Agency for Palestine, 91, 97, 154
Jewish Army, xii, 95, 102–124, 126, 130, 248–50
Jewish Aviation League of America, 107
Jewish battalion, 127, 211
Jewish Brigade, 123–24, 126, 250
Jewish Central Committee of Poland, 184
Jewish Chronicle, 7, 15, 108, 113

Jewish Colonial Trust, 10, 19
Jewish Colonization Association, 36, 47
Jewish Combat Organization (ŻOB), 185
Jewish commonwealth, xvi, 6, 10, 20, 96, 111, 130–33, 139–40, 149–50, 157, 162, 167–68, 172, 224
Jewish Daily Forward, 113, 248, 265
Jewish division, 104, 107–8, 114, 124
Jewish emigration, 4, 18, 73, 81, 87, 94
Jewish Frontier, 118
Jewish Labor Bund, 78
Jewish Labor Committee, 42
Jewish Legion, 95–99, 112, 119, 125
Jewish National Fund, 14, 19, 57
Jewish National Home, 119, 127, 154, 158, 163–71, 249
Jewish Question, the, 3–8, 20, 32, 39, 69, 73, 104, 135, 169, 188, 209, 230
Jewish Refugee Committee, 56
Jewish Social Studies, 38, 238, 254
Jewish Socialist Bund, 11
Jewish Telegraphic Agency, 71, 105, 222, 246, 252, 255, 258
Jewish Theological Seminary, 94, 129, 239, 245
Jewish War Front, The, 102–3, 247
"Jews Fight for the Right to Fight," 110
Jews' State, The, 7
Jezre'el Valley, 170
Johnson, Edwin, 112
Johnson, Lyndon B., 178
Joint Anglo-American Statement on Palestine, 205, 251, 262
Joint Foreign Committee, 29, 78, 90, 231, 236–37, 240
Joskowicz, Menahem, 189
Journal of Holocaust Research, 201, 261
Judenjagd, 192
Jüdische Akademische Lesehall, 7

K

Kabara, 170
Kaczyński, Jarosław, 196, 199
Kadimah Society, 10
Kadosh, Sara, 227, 267
Kafka, Franz, 93
Kahn, Zadoc, 6, 233
Kakowski, Aleksander Cardinal, 75
Kalb, Marvin, 217
Kalischer, Zvi Hirsch, 9
Kallen, Horace, 61, 150, 234, 254
Kalwary, Marian, 193
Kant, Immanuel, 67, 238
Kaplan, Marion, 73, 220
Kaplan, Mordecai, 129

Karlsbad, 77
Karski, Jan, 182
Kater, Michael, 73, 240
Katowice, 77
Katzenelson, Yosef, 100, 247
Kennedy, Joseph, 72, 178, 258
Kermish, Joseph, 220, 265
Kerr, Philip Henry, 73
Kertzer, Daniel, 229–30, 268
Kielce, 81, 188, 190
Kielce pogrom, 188, 190
King-Crane Commission, 141–42, 253
Kishinev Pogrom, 14, 18, 92
Kitchens III, James H., 213, 263
Klarsfeld, Serge, 220
Klausner, Joseph, 15
Klein, Shira, 201, 261
Klemperer, Victor, 71, 239
Knesset, ix–x, 194, 197
Knox, Frank, 112
Koc, Adam, 81
Kochavi, Aviv, 198
Kohler, Max J., 30–31, 40, 232
Kolno, 80, 258
Komorowski, Bronisław, 189–92
Kook, Avraham Yitzhak, 22
Kook, Hillel, xii, 22–23, 96, 99–101, 103–113, 116–18, 124–27, 213, 246–52. *See also* Bergson, Peter
Kopacz, Ewa, 191
Kornberg, Jacques, 9, 24
Kornbluth, Andrew, 182–84, 258, 267
Kosovo, 225
Kovner, Abba, 226
Kovno, xiv, 84
Kraków, 77, 80, 83, 92, 245, 258
Krakowski, Shmuel, 186, 258, 262
Kranzler, David, 214, 220, 263, 266
Kraus, Gilbert and Eleanor, 227
Kraut, Alan, 215–26, 264
Kristallnacht, 66, 71, 73, 85, 87, 89, 91, 93, 223, 238, 243
Kristof, Nicholas, 225, 267
Krosna, 77
Kubowitzki, Leon, 209
Kuchmann, Otto, 91
Kurds, 171
Kurdistan, 225
Kwaśniewski, Aleksander, x, 189

L
L'Osservatore Romano, 83, 230
La Femme de Claude, 2
La France Juive, 2
La Libre Parole, 2
Labour Party, 164
Lamas, Carlos de Saaved, 65
Lambert, Raymond-Raoul, 64, 243
Landau, Moshe, 177, 247
Langer, William, 112, 121–23
Lanzmann, Claude, 189
Lapid, Yair, 197–98
Laski, Neville, 30, 32, 44, 48–52, 53–54, 60–61, 75, 78, 231–37, 240
Last Angry Man, The, 206
Latvia, 74–75, 79
Lauterbach, Leo, 90
Lauterpacht, Hersh, 30, 44, 53, 235
Law and Justice Party, 193, 196, 199
Law, Richard, 120
Lawrence, T. E., 157, 171, 178, 255
Lawyer's Club, 41–41, 157, 163
Lazare, Bernard, 10
Lazaron, Morris S., xii, 130–32, 135, 138–42, 148–49, 252–54
Le Temps, 74
League of National Christian Defense, 74
League of Nations, xi, xiii, xvi, 27, 29, 37, 39, 49, 57, 65–66, 72, 76, 133, 145, 153, 163, 169, 171, 175, 231–32, 235–36, 238, 241–42, 257
legal realism, 151, 178, 257
Legion of the Archangel Michael, 74, 240
LEHI (*Lohamei Herut* Yisrael), 105, 246, 248, 255
Lehman, Herbert, 101, 125, 233
Lemann, Nicholas, 217
Lesser, Jeffrey, 220, 266
Letter of Resignation (1935), xi, 45, 48, 50–58, 62, 65–66, 77
Leuchtenburg, William E., 205
Levin, Dov, 220, 251, 265
Lewisohn, Ludwig, 24
Libya, 114
Lichtman, Allan, 215–16, 215
Lidice, 116, 249
Lie, Trygve, 162
Liebman, Charles, 34, 233
Lincoln, Abraham, 25, 135–36, 267
Lindbergh, Charles, 136, 253
Lipsky, Louis, 62, 64, 237
Lipstadt, Deborah E., 217, 264
Lithuania, 69, 74–75, 77–80, 86, 239
Littauer, Lucius, 38
Livne, Yaakov, 197–98
Lloyd George, David, 119, 166
Lodz (Łódź), 78, 81, 185, 190, 225
Łomża, 81

London Daily Herald, 83
London Jewish Chronicle, 7, 108, 113
London *Times*, 54–55, 73, 76, 79, 237, 240
Longfellow, Henry Wadsworth, 130
Lookstein, Haskel, 217, 264
Lord Croft, 124
Lord Lothian, 73, 103
Lord Moyne, 108, 114
Lord Peel, 166
Lord Strabolgi, 113–16, 119, 124, 250
Lord Wedgewood, 113
Lourie, Arthur, 158
Lowdermilk, Walter Clay, 133, 143, 169, 257
Lowenstein, Sharon, 214, 263
Lowenthal, Marvin, 6, 24
Lubavitch, 16
Lubinski, Chaim, 100–101, 247
Lucas, Scott, 112, 119–21
Luce, Clare Booth, 117
Lüdtke, Alf, 206, 262
Ludwig, Carl, 24, 265
Lueger, Karl, 3–4
Łukom, 183
Lux Veritatis Foundation, 199
Lviv (Lwów), 77–78

M
MacArthur, Charles, 108
Maccabeans, 9
Maccabeans, The, 7
MacDonald, Malcolm, 54, 93, 245
Mack, Julian, 37–39, 59, 90, 101, 232–34, 236, 244, 247
Mackenzie, William I., 58
Maglione, Luigi Cardinal, 230
Making of the Modern Jew, The, 129
Malcolm, Neill, 58, 93
Malinowo, 196
Małkinia, 81
Maloney, Francis, 120
Manchester Guardian, 30, 231
Manchuria, 29, 56, 236
Mania, Henryk, 184
Mann, Thomas, 223, 243–44
Mantello, George, 214, 263
Mapai, 97, 106, 215, 263
March of Remembrance, 194
March of the Living, 197
Markowa Ulma-Family Museum, 203
Marrus, Michael, 219, 240, 265
Marshal Piłsudski, 79
Mashiach ben David, 22
Mashiach ben Yosef, 22
Mataroa, xiv

May, Herbert L., 31, 41
Maybank, Burnet R., 121
Mazowiecki, Tadeusz, 187
McConnell, Bishop Francis, 129
McDonald, James G., xi, xiii, 27–28, 31–36, 39–60, 62–67, 76–77, 88, 176, 231–38, 240, 264
McGovern, George, 218
McMahon, Henry, 171
McNair, Arnold D., 49–52, 235
McNarney, Joseph T., 157
Mead, James M, 114
Medem, Vladimir, 11
Medicare, 178
Medinat Yisrael, xvi, 20
Medoff, Rafael, 216–18, 227, 251–52, 255, 264, 267
Mein Kampf, 72
Memel, 80, 83, 86
Memorandum on a Jewish Army of Palestinian and Stateless Jews, 39, 112
Menachem Begin Center, 226
Mendelson, Morris, 107
Merlin, Shmuel, 99, 105, 116, 118, 123, 126, 248–51, 264
Meyerson, Goldie, 85, 242
Michalowski, 82
Miła Street 18 headquaters, 185, 191, 259
Milgram, Avraham, 220, 265
Miłosz, Czesław, 186, 259
Milton, Sybil, xii, 129, 150, 156, 158, 178, 219, 252–55, 265
Minority Treaties, 28, 38, 60, 75, 240
Mit Brennender Sorge, 89
Mizrachi, 23, 215
Moderau, Marek, 189
Moffat, J. P., 32, 34, 232
Montefiore, Leonard, 52, 235
Montgomery, Bernard L., 115–16
Montor, Henry, 125, 224
Moore, E. H., 120
Morawiecki, Mateusz, 181–82, 193–95, 197, 261
Morgenthau, Jr., Henry, 214
Morley, John, 219, 265
Morse, Arthur, 233, 250–51, 262
Moscow Conference (1943), 210
Moses, 15, 135–36
Moska, 77
Mossinsohn, Ben-Zion, 30, 231
Mosul, 112
Mota, Jon, 81
Motza, 96
Motzkin, Leo, 30, 39, 231–32

"Mr. Churchill, Drop the Mandate!," 126
Mundelein, Cardinal George William, 88
Muni, Paul, 118
Munkács, 86
Murray, James, 112, 114, 122–23, 243
Murray, Wallace, 130
Muslim Brotherhood, 108
Mussolini, Benito, 85, 95, 98, 109, 229, 242, 268
"My Tribe is Called Israel," 109

N
Nachtasyl (an asylum for the night), 18
Nansen, Fridtjof, 28, 43, 93
Nansen International Office for Refugees, 28, 43, 93
Nara Party, 81
Naschauer, Julia, 2
Nasser, Gamal Abdul, 108
Nathan, Otto, 90
Nathan, Robert, 112, 169, 244
National Christian Party, 79
National Conference of Catholics and Jews, 148
National Democracy Party, 183
National Radical Camp, 81
National Soldiers' Front, 82
National Judentum, 10
Nazi ideology, 89
Nazi-Soviet Non-Aggression Pact, 195
Nelson, Donald, 112
Netanyahu, Ben-Zion, 104
Netanyahu, Benjamin, 194
Netherlands, 32, 69, 85, 162, 239
Neue Freie Presse, 1–2, 6–7, 10
New Deal, 96, 216
New Ghetto, The, 3, 9, 11
New Palestine, 91, 104, 244, 248
New Statesman and Nation, 115
New York Herald Tribune, 113, 144, 243, 248
New York Times, passim
New Zionist Organization, 98, 108
Newman, Louis, 100
Newton, Verne, 216, 263
Nicolae Domnesc Church, 74
Niebuhr, Reinhold, 88, 129–30, 243
Niemirower, Jacob, 77
Nieznalska, Dorota, 196
Nigeria, 225
Night without End, 196
Nineteenth Century, 7
Nixon, Richard, 178
Noack, Thorsten, 226, 267
Nobel Peace Prize, 93, 186

Nordau, Max, 6, 12, 14, 105
Norwood, Stephen H., 222, 226, 264
Nowa Wilejka, 78
Nuremberg Laws, 43, 47, 76, 87, 234

O
O'Neill, Eugene, 117
Obama, Barack, 182
Ofer, Dalia, 215, 263
Old-New Land,
Olive Trees in a Storm, 148
Olomouc (Olmütz), 86
Olympic Games (Olympics), 63, 78, 217
Onassis (Kennedy), Jacqueline, 178
Only Human—The Eternal Alibi, 150
Open Republic (Otwarta Rzeczpospolita), 193, 201
Operation Jericho, 211
Orăștie, 81
Order of Polonia Restituta, 184
Ormsby-Gore, William, 171
Orts, Pierre, 171
OSS, 158, 255
Ostrów Mazowiecka, 80
Oświęcim, 196
Otwarta Rzeczpospolita, 201
Ozick, Cynthia, xv

P
Pacelli, Eugenio, Cardinal (Pius XII), 31, 232
Palacios, M., 166
Palais des Nations, 65, 162
Palestine, ix, xii, xiv, xvi, 4, 8, 10–20, 25, 29–30, 33–34, 38, 42–43, 45, 62, 69–71, 74, 77–78, 82, 87–91, 93, 95–116, 119–21, 123, 125–27, 130–35, 138–49, 153–77, 179, 185, 205–11, 214–15, 218, 221–24, 227, 229, 231, 233, 237, 239, 241–44, 246–57, 262–63, 266–67
Palestine Electric Company, 106
Palestine in Turmoil, 223, 249, 254, 256–57, 267
Palestine League of Nations Union, 29
Palestine Liberation Organization (PLO), 185–86
Palestine Mandate, ix, 33, 97, 145, 163, 166–67, 170
Palestine Regiment, 115–16
Palestine Symphony Orchestra, 168
Palestine: The Dream and the Reality, 130, 252
Palestinian Arabs, 24, 133, 171, 174
Palestinian Authority, xvi
Palestinian Jews, 109–110, 117, 120, 140, 142, 248

Palestinians, 108, 126, 251
Palmach, 116
Panama Scandal, 2
Paris formula, 100, 104
Partisan Guide to the Jewish Problem, A, xii, 139–40, 253
partition, xii, 99, 149. 156, 162, 166, 173, 175–77, 256
Patria, 106, 169, 209, 245, 248, 257
Patterson, John Henry, 98–103, 105, 107, 109–110, 119
Patton, George, 218
Pawel, Ernst, 21, 24, 194
pay for slay bounties, xvi
Pearl Harbor, 109, 134, 136, 160, 243
Pearson, Lester, 158
Pécs, 80
Pejovic, Bernhardine, 231
Penkower, Monty, 24, 238–39, 243, 245–46, 248–59, 262–64, 266–68
Pennzoil, 178
Penslar, Derek J., 24
Pentagon Papers, 178
Pepper, Claude, 109, 112
Peres, Shimon, x
Peretz, Martin, 96, 217
Perlmutter, M. A., 96
Permanent Mandates Commission, 133, 164, 166–67, 169, 171
Pershing, John H., 155
Pest, 86
Petition to the League, xi, 29–30, 59, 63
Philadelphia Record, 113, 248
Phillips, William, 58, 234
Picard, Jacques, 220, 265
Pinsker, Leo, 7, 9–10, 18–19, 21
Piotrków Trybunalski, 81
Piron, Shai, 190
PiS Party, 182, 197
Pittsburg Platform, 16
Plonsk, 15
PM, 108, 261
Podlasie, 183
Pokłosie, 189
Poland, ix–xiii, xiii, 15, 40, 44–45, 60, 69, 71, 74–76, 78–79, 81–82, 84–85, 88, 90, 97, 100, 102, 181–203, 220, 223, 228–29, 238–41, 245, 258–62, 265, 267–68
Polenberg, Richard, 211
POLIN museum, 181, 191, 193, 195, 198, 260
Polish Academy of Sciences, 181, 191
Polish blackmailers, 196
Polish Blue Police, 183
Polish Catholic Church, 183

Polish Center for Holocaust Research, 181
Polish Government-in-Exile, 107, 189, 200, 261
Polish Institute of National Remembrance, 183
Polish League against Defamation, 192
Polish National Council, 194
Polish National Foundation, 182
Polish Order of Merit, 192
Polish Police: Collaboration in the Holocaust, The, 192, 268
Polish trials, 182–83, 228
Polish Workers' United Party, 187
Political Zionism, xi, 10–12, 23, 113, 130
"Poor Poles Look at the Ghetto," 186, 258
Pope Francis I, 229
Pope John Paul II, 187–88, 268
Pope Pius X, 18
Pope Pius XI, 88, 223
Pope Pius XII, 229–30
Porat, Dina, 219, 263, 265
Poręba, 81
Postwar Jewish settlement, 114
Potok, Chaim, 150
Poznań, 78, 81, 83, 85, 184, 200
Prager Presse, 56
Prague, 75, 86, 93, 101, 156, 243
President's Advisory Committee on Political Refugees, 66
Prinz, Joachim, 91, 244
Prinzen aus Genieland, 12
problem of Judaism, the, 12, 23
Proclamation on the Moral Rights of the Stateless and Palestinian Jews, 117
Prophet's Wife, The, 150
Promised Land, xiv, 5, 9–10, 12, 18, 20, 22, 70, 143, 222
Proskauer, Joseph, 122, 137, 157, 253
Protectorate, 86–88, 156, 244, 249
Protestrabbiner, 14
Protocols of the Elders of Zion, 61, 82, 237
Przydacz, Marcin, 198
Przytyk Pogrom, 78, 92, 241
Psalms, 14
Psikowski, Władysław, 189
Pulzer, Peter, 25
Putin, Vladimir, 195, 260

Q
Quai d'Orsay, 62

R
Rabbi Akiva, 129
Rabbis march on Washington, D.C., 123, 126
Rabin, Yitzhak, ix–x

Rabinowitz, Baruch, 112, 125
Radziłów, 199, 258
Radziwiłł, Janusz, 78
Rafaeli, Alexander, 99, 101, 103–105, 246–47
Ramnic, Bishop Vartolomei, 82
Rape of Palestine, The, 100, 247
Rapoport, Nathan, 184, 190, 198, 246, 248–49
Rassvet, 107
Rathenau, Walter, 11
Ratosh, Yonatan. See Halpern, Uriel
Rau, Zbigniew, 200
Raziel, David, 96, 100, 103–4, 246–47
Reader's Digest, 118, 249
Reconstructionist, 129, 143, 145, 253
Red Army, 195, 225, 266
"Red, White and Blue Herring," 134, 252, 256
Reform Judaism, 10
Reines, Yitshak Ya'akov, 23
Rendel, George, 82, 242
Report to the Secretary on the Acquiescence of this Government in the Murder of the Jews, A, 229, 289
Rhineland, 72
Riegner, Gerhart, 212, 219
Rifkind, Simon H., 38, 145, 147, 157–61, 176, 178, 253, 255–57
Riga, 92, 244
Righteous Among the Nations of the World, 187, 189, 191, 196
Ringelblum, Emanuel, 128, 252
Risorgimento, 15
Rivlin, Reuven, 191–92, 194
Robinson, Edward G., 118
Robinson, Jacob, 29, 231
Rockefeller Foundation, 33–34
Rogers Jr, Will, 128
Rohl, John C.G., 25
Rolland, Romain, 88
Roman legions, x
Romania, 69, 71, 74–77, 79, 81, 83, 85, 211, 239–40, 268
Rome and Jerusalem, 9
Rommel, Erwin, 115
Roosevelt, Eleanor, 42, 119, 143, 216, 234
Roosevelt Presidential Library, 205, 216
Roosevelt, Franklin D., xiii, 29, 32, 34, 36–37, 47, 57, 72, 74, 87, 89, 100, 110, 116, 123, 126, 128, 143–44, 148, 164, 210–16, 218, 222–24, 227–28, 233–34, 238, 243, 251, 253, 256, 262, 264, 267
Roots, 206
Roper poll, 144, 253
Rose, Billy, 118
Rosen, Robert, 215

Rosenberg, Alfred, 27–28, 30–31, 33–35, 37–41, 43, 45–46, 51–54, 57, 59–60, 62, 65–66, 72, 118, 227, 231–37
Rosenberg, James N., 137, 231, 253
Rosenberg, Walter. *See* Vrba, Rudolf
Rosenman, Samuel, 126, 136, 253
Rosenwald, Lessing, 144, 178, 253
Roskies, David, 92, 245
Ross, Robert, 217
Rotem, Sima, 190
Royal Commission on Palestine, 93, 99, 166, 168, 170, 173
Rozenbit, Marsha L.
Rubinstein, William, 214, 263
Rue de La Victoire, 3
Rumania, xi, 40, 44, 60, 82–83, 100, 223, 240
Rumbold, Horace, 72
Ruppin, Arthur, 91, 233, 242
Russian Jews, 17
Rutenberg, Pinhas, 106
Rutka, Marek, 197
Rwanda, 225
Rydzyk, Rev. Tadeusz, 199

S

"S'brent!," 92–93, 245
Saar Basin, 35
Sakariya, 103, 125, 250
Samuel, Jacob, 3–4, 24, 30, 36, 109, 118, 126, 136, 217, 251, 253, 264
San Remo Conference, xvi, 163
Sarraut, Albert, 74
Sąsiedzi, 189
Satan in Goray, 90
Saturday Evening Post, 134, 160, 252, 256
Saturday Review of Literature, 140, 253
Scarface, 108
Schacht, Hjalmar, 34
Schiff, Friedrich, 5, 232
Schlesinger, Jr., Arthur, 216, 264
Schleunes, Karl, 85, 242
Schmolke, Marie, 75, 233, 240
Schneersohn, Shalom Dov Ber, 16
Schneiderman, Harry, 39, 234
Schocken, Salman, 11–12, 24, 239, 262
Schoenberg, Arnold, 90, 244
Scholem, Gershom, 70–71, 239
Schorske, Carl L., 9, 25
Schudrich, Michael, 195, 201
Schulte, Eduard, 209, 263
Schuschnigg, Kurt, 75
Schwamm, Harvey, 100
Schwartz, Maurice, 105
Schwartzort, 80
Scott, James Brown, 65, 112, 119, 259

Scythia, 103
Second Zionist Congress, 14
Segev, Zohar, 215, 263
Seirijai, 143
Selbst-Emancipation!, 10
Sh'eirit HaPleita, xiv
Shabbatai Zvi, 5
SHAEF, 157–58, 211
Shanghai, 88, 220, 266
Sharett, Moshe. *See* Shertok, Moshe
Shavli, Eliade Mircea, 83
Sheean, Vincent, 93, 242, 245
Sheib, Israel, 99
Shertok, Moshe, 90, 115, 154, 159, 161, 177, 209, 223, 250–51, 257
Shimoni, Gideon, 25
Shirer, William L., 226, 242, 267
Shoah, x, 24, 71, 91, 151, 188–89, 195, 203, 206–7, 209, 214, 219–22, 227–29, 244, 251–52, 265
Sierra Leone, 225
Sikorski, Radosław, 182
Sikorski, Władysław, 200
Silver, Abba Hillel, 106, 123, 156, 161, 176–77, 248, 250–51, 255, 257
Simele, 171
Simpson, John Hope, 73
Sinai Peninsula, 17
Singapore, 110, 113, 116
Singer, Isaac Bashevis, 90
Singer, Simon, 7
Sixth Zionist Congress, 14, 18
Sławoj-Składkowski, Felicjan, 80, 241
Slovakia, 74, 87
Smuts, Jan, 119, 166
Śniadowo, 78
Snyder, Timothy, 192
Social and Cultural Association of Jews in Poland, 202
Society for Defense against Antisemitism, 3
Sofia, 13, 80, 83
Solidarity movement, 185
Soloveitchik, Haim, 16
Somers, Andrew, 114
Sommerstein, Emil, 80, 90
Song for Peace, x
Soroca, 75
South America, 27, 36, 82, 114
Soviet Union, 35, 69, 156, 221, 239, 251, 265–66
St. Louis, SS, 87
St. Ottilien, xiv
Stadtcasino, 14
Stalin, Joseph, 187, 210, 251
Stankowski, Albert, 195

Stanton, William, 105
Star of David, 118, 191
Stars and Stripes, 206
State of Israel, xi, xiii, xvi, 15, 20, 23, 125, 148–49, 151, 176, 179, 221–22, 225, 233, 244, 253–54, 257
State of Israel Bonds, 125
Stein, Edith, 188, 243
Steinberg, Milton, xii, 129–30, 132–45, 148, 150–51, 252–54
Steiner, George, xv
Steiner, Zara, 73, 240
Steinglas, Meyer, 125, 250
Stępiński, Zygmunt, 195
Stern, Avraham, 96, 99–100, 102, 104–5, 119, 246, 248
Sternbuch, Recha, 209, 214, 263
Stevenson, Adlai, 112
Stimson, Henry, 109, 112–13, 218
Stola, Dariusz, 193, 258
Stone, Dan, 228, 267
Storch, Hilel, 209
Stowe, Harriet Beecher, 130
Strauss, Lewis, 136, 232–33, 240
Streicher, Julius, 72
Strelsin, Alfred, 112
Stroock, Sol, 59, 61, 235, 237
Strube, Sidney, 89, 244
Struck, Hermann, 22
Struma, 114, 169, 249, 257
Sudan, 225
Sudeten German Party, 87
Suez Canal, 114–15
Sultanik, Kalman, 187
Sulzberger, Arthur Hays, 37, 41, 113, 136, 222, 250–51, 253
Suvalkija, 143
Swastika's Darkening Shadow: Voices before the Holocaust, 70, 223, 266
Swiatkowski, Henryk, 184
Świdnik, 78
Swing, Raymond, 88, 117
Switzerland, 14, 84, 101, 214, 220, 227, 265
Swope, Gerard, 177
Syria, 16–17, 108, 225, 265
Syrkin, Nachman, 10
Szamlenberg, Hanna, 189
Szczuczyn, 184, 199, 258
Szold, Robert, 91, 241, 244, 247
Szyk, Arthur, 117

T

Tannhäuser, 6
Taylor, Melissa Jane, 229
Taylor, Myron, 84, 122, 238

teaching of contempt, 188
Technion, 168, 177, 257
Teleki, Pál, 86
Tell, William, 101
Temple B'rith Kodesh, 129
Temple in Jerusalem, x, 17
Tennessee Valley Authority, 169
"the exiled Jew", xv
The Fighting Jew, 112, 248
The Jews Were Expendable: Free World Diplomacy and the Holocaust, xiii, 69, 205, 239, 255
The U.S. and the Holocaust, 227
Theresienstadt, 219
Times of Israel, 197
Third Reich, xi, 27, 29, 55–57, 59, 66–67, 69, 73–74, 78, 85, 89, 97–98, 102, 111, 116, 203, 209–10, 220, 222, 224, 226–27, 235, 238, 241–42, 244, 250, 266–67
Third Republic, 2
Thomas, Elbert, 112
Thomas, Norman, 59
Tobruk, 115
Tolischus, Otto D., 79–80, 241
Tomki, 81
Towns of Death, The, 183, 228, 258, 268
Transjordan, 34, 97–98, 156, 164
Transnistria, 211, 214, 230
Transylvania, 80
Treblinka death camp revolt, 195, 209, 224, 228
Troper, Harold, 220, 245, 266
Trotsky, Leon, 11
Troy, Gil, 25
Trujillo, Rafael, 242, 266
Truman, Harry S, 112, 117, 120–21, 143–44, 148, 153–54, 157, 164–65, 205, 250, 254–55, 257
Trybuna Ludu, 187
Tryczyk, Mirosław, 184, 258, 268
Trzaskowski, Rafał, 195–96
TSAZ, 202
Tulin, Abraham, 155–62, 176–77, 179, 255–57
Turkish empire, 164, 170
Tusk, Donald, 182, 190
Tuwim, Julian, 90, 244
Twain, Mark, 135, 252
Twentieth Century Jews, 222, 245–46, 249–50, 252–53, 256, 266
Tygodnik Powszechny, 186

U
Uganda, 14, 18
Ukraine, ix, 74, 77, 81–82, 86, 96, 197, 202, 238

Umschlagplatz, 187, 194, 259
UN. *See* United Nations
Union of American Hebrew Congregations, 149
United Jewish Appeal (UJA), 143
United Nations (UN), xii–xiii, 20, 33, 114, 120, 131, 141, 143, 145, 147–49, 153–60, 162–64, 170, 172, 176–77, 195, 238, 249–50, 254, 256, 261–62
United Nations Special Committee on Palestine, 20, 147, 158–59
United Palestine Appeal, 102, 106, 125, 224
universalism, xv, 133
University of Vienna, 1
UNSCOP. *See* United Nations Special Committee on Palestine
UNSCOP majority recommendations, 175–76
Untermyer, Samuel, 30
Updike, John, xiv
Upper Silesia, 29–30, 76, 231
US Congress, 220
US consuls, 229, 266, 268
US Holocaust Memorial Museum, 192, 217, 219, 227–28, 235, 264, 268
US Refugee Economic Corporation, 36, 42
US State Department, 32, 111, 130, 135, 149, 226
US War Refugee Board, xii, 131, 158, 209, 228, 230
Ussishkin, Menachem, 10, 18
USSR, 220, 238. *See also* Soviet Union

V
Va'ad HaHatzala, 207, 213, 215, 241–42, 263
Vale of Esdraelon, 170
Vámbéry Arminius, 16
van Asbeck, Baron, 167
Van Paassen, Pierre
van den Heuvel, William, 216, 264
Varniai, 77
Vatican, 31, 83, 122–23, 188, 211, 219, 229–30, 265, 268
Versailles Peace Conference, 28–29, 37, 75
Vervier, Cardinal, 88
Vichy France, 217
Vichy Syria, 108
Victor Emmanuel III, 21, 229
Vienna, 1, 3–5, 10–11, 22, 24–25, 77, 84–85, 87, 90, 98, 105, 227, 229, 239
Vietor, Tommy, 182
Vilna, 11, 226, 244
Visegrád Group, 197
Vrba, Rudolf, 227

Vital, David, 17
Völkischer Beobachter, 56–57
von Bismarck, Otto, 5
von Hessen, Philipp, 229
von Keller, Friedrich, 29, 32
von Mackensen, August, 16
von Neurath, Konstantin, 87
von Plehve, Vyacheslav, 18
von Weizsäcker, Ernst, 203, 230, 262
von Weizsäcker, Richard, 203

W
Wagner-Rogers bill, 87
Wagner, Richard, 6
Wagner, Robert F., 38
Walaszczyk, Józef, 196
Wald, Lillian D., 59
Waldman, Morris D., 30, 38–39, 41, 43, 45–46, 48, 52, 54, 60–64, 231–32, 234–38, 241
Wałęsa, Lech, 186–87
Wallenberg, Raoul, 214, 220, 265
Wallenberg: A Hero's Story, 207
Walter, Bruno, 11, 70, 72, 117, 133, 169, 215, 227, 263, 266
War against the Jews, The, 207, 262
Warburg, Felix, 31, 33–36, 41, 43, 47, 52, 57–58, 61, 232–238, 240
Warsaw, 13, 71, 75, 77–81, 103, 128, 181, 184–98, 200, 202, 246, 252, 259–61, 265
Warsaw Ghetto revolt, 184–87, 190–91, 193, 202
Warsaw Jewish cemetery, 198
Warsaw Uprising, 186, 192
Washington Post, 113, 116, 243, 248–49
Wasserstein, Bernard, 93, 207, 243–45, 262
Wauchope, Arthur, 90, 98, 223
"We Remember: A Reflection on the Shoah," 188
We Will Never Die, 118, 249
Wedgwood, Josiah C., 88, 96, 99, 106–7, 110, 113, 246, 248–49
Weingort, Shaul, 216, 227, 267
Weininger, Otto, 12
Weisgal, Meyer, 25
Weiss, Shevah, ix, 178, 206
Weitz, Yechiam, 215, 219, 263, 265
Weizmann, Chaim, 19, 22, 33–34, 93, 98, 102, 104, 108, 115, 124, 144, 155, 168, 170, 211, 224, 232, 248, 254
Welles, Sumner, 135, 144, 148, 253
Wells, Allen, 220, 266
Wentling, Sonja S., 217, 264
Wentworth, Richard L., 207
West Germany, 206, 262

Wetzler, Fred, 227
Wetzler-Vrba Report, 214
While Six Million Died: A Chronicle of American Apathy, 207, 250
White Paper (1939), 74, 87, 89, 100–101, 103, 109, 113–14, 127, 130, 133, 153, 164, 166–69, 173, 176, 210, 222, 224, 243, 254
White Russian émigrés, 43
White, Thomas W., 84
Whitehall, 47, 115–16, 122, 124, 135. *See also* British Foreign Office
Why Poland is Trying to Control Holocaust Memory, 196
Wieliczka, 81
Wiesel, Elie, 206, 262
Wieseltier, Leon, 218, 265
Wikipedia, 201, 261–62
Wildstein, Bronisław, 181
Wiley, Alexander, 120–21
Wilhelm II, 13, 16, 25
Wilkomir, 83
Willemin, Georges, 219
Wilno, 78, 80, 83
Wilson, Woodrow, 139, 233
Wingate, Orde, 115
Wir Juden, 91
Wischnitzer, Marc, 82
Wise, Stephen, 31, 34, 90–91, 97, 116, 135, 144, 160, 216, 227, 231–32, 244, 246–47
Wistrich, Robert, 15, 25, 262
Wola, 77
Wolf, Lucien, ix, 16, 244
Wolffsohn, David, 10, 13
Woolner, David B., 216, 264
World Court, 28, 37–38, 40, 43–44
World Jewish Committee, 104
World Jewish Congress, 61–64, 66, 90, 92, 187, 207, 209, 219, 221, 236, 238, 240, 263
World Zionist Congress, 11, 13, 20, 96, 98
World Zionist Organization, 14–15, 17, 19, 33, 90, 93, 95, 135, 144, 210
Woźnicki, Father Michał, 200–201
Wurfbain, Andre, 34, 51, 232, 236
Wuthering Heights, 108
Wyborcza, 181, 259
Wyman, David, 207, 213–18, 227, 243, 251, 255, 262–65, 267–68
Wysokie Mazovieckie, 78

Y
Yad Vashem, ix–x, 181, 191–92, 194–96, 203, 207, 209, 217, 219, 240, 242, 244, 251, 258–61, 263, 265, 267–68

Yad Vashem Studies, 207, 240, 242, 258
Yazidi, 225
Yeivin, Yehoshua, 95, 245
Yishuv, xiv, 17, 20, 70, 85, 92, 96, 106, 114, 127, 140, 161, 168, 211, 222, 250, 263
Yom Kippur statement, 154
Yoe, Craig, 217, 264
Young, James, 187, 259
Youth Aliya, ix
Yugoslavia, 84, 162, 238

Z
Zangwill, Israel, 7, 25
Żaryn, Stanisław, 196
ŻEGOTA, 188–89, 265
Ziff, William, 100, 247
Zion Mule Corps, 98
Zionism, xi–xv, xv, 3, 9–12, 14–15, 18, 21, 23–25, 30, 38, 56, 61, 91, 98–99, 106–7, 113, 129, 131–33, 135, 137, 139–43, 145, 147–51, 155, 159, 205, 233, 250–53
Zionist ideology, 95
Zionist Organization of America (ZOA), 156–57, 255
Zipperstein, Steven, 25
ŻOB, 185
Zohn, Arnold, 179
Zohn, Harry, 24–25
Zucker, Bat-Ami, 222, 229, 264, 266, 268
Zuroff, Efraim, 244, 251, 263, 265
Zweig, Stefan, 21, 25
Żydokomuna, 201
Zygelbojm, Szmul, 194, 260
Zyklon B, 188

www.ingramcontent.com/pod-product-compliance
Lightning Source LLC
Chambersburg PA
CBHW051111230426
43667CB00014B/2532